Praise for the *Lost Prince of the ANC*

'The Lost Prince of the ANC *is a tragic account of a liberation flame that was snuffed out at a very young age. When Mzala died, the illuminating flame of his incendiary mind and moral rectitude was lost to the project of emancipation. In this simple and honest narration of Mzala's life, the author has painted a remarkable portrait of this tragic loss. Wretchedly enough, this loss foreshadowed the deep political and moral quagmire his political home, the ANC, finds itself today. Mzala was not a Messiah who could have salvaged the ANC all alone. However, innocent and honest readers of this book will inescapably use the Lost Prince's life and ideas as a prism through which to decipher what could have been.*'
– Vusi Mavimbela, Former government advisor, former ambassador, author

'*If any freedom fighter was deserving of a serious biographical study, that candidate would be Jabulani 'Mzala' Nxumalo. Mandla Radebe does justice to that challenge and has struck gold. This brilliant study of the 'Lost Prince' of the liberation struggle resurrects the life of a legendary firebrand, whose revolutionary thoughts, provocative writings and courageous deeds, will enthral and engage our people for generations to come, and provide a treasure trove for academic research. Radebe is an astute devotee of the subject, and to borrow from the title of one of Mzala's most controversial essays, has 'cooked' his life story to near perfection. This work is infused with great personal insight, a product of the author's trusted access to Mzala's family, peers and sometime mentors, and from whom he has gleaned invaluable information to create a multi-dimensional portrait of the subject, firmly lodged in accurately researched historical context. It is a radical, free-flowing, thought-provoking, poignant and wry tribute to a revolutionary prince of the people, inducing laughter and tears – a manifest celebration of an extraordinary life. I predict this book will be one of the most significant of the liberation struggle genre for years to come. In evoking Mzala's passionate thoughts, it has set my brain ticking furiously about our unfinished revolution. We dare not duck Mzala's uncompromising gaze as from beyond the grave he forces us to consider our failings, reminds us of the destination we were committed to; and for which he gave his short, restless life. Bravo Mandla Radebe, for this labour of love!'*

– RONNIE KASRILS, STRUGGLE VETERAN, FORMER MINISTER, AUTHOR

'Vivid, detailed and incisive this book evokes the people, places, ideas and relationships woven into Mzala's fearlessness, intellectual insights, and humane commitment to a vision for transformed South Africa. In telling the story of a life lost too young, Radebe deftly finds ways to understand the history that brought us here.'

– ELAINE UNTERHALTER, PROFESSOR OF EDUCATION AND INTERNATIONAL DEVELOPMENT, UNIVERSITY COLLEGE LONDON

The Lost Prince of the ANC

The Life and Times of Jabulani Nobleman 'Mzala' Nxumalo 1955–1991

MANDLA J RADEBE

First published by Jacana Media (Pty) Ltd in 2022
Second impression 2023

10 Orange Street
Sunnyside
Auckland Park 2092
South Africa
+2711 628 3200
www.jacana.co.za

© Mandla J Radebe, 2022

All rights reserved.

The publisher acknowledges the generous assistance of the University of Johannesburg.

ISBN 978-1-4314-3298-1

Also available as an ebook

Cover design by publicide
Editing by Sean Fraser
Proofreading by Megan Mance
Indexing by L-P Content & Curation
Set in Ehrhardt MT Std 10.5/14pt
Printed and bound by Creda Communications
Job no. 003961

See a complete list of Jacana titles at www.jacana.co.za

Contents

Foreword: Minister Blade Nzimande		vii
Preface		xvii
Introduction: Comrade Mzala is dead		1
1	The Nxumalos and Mwandlas	15
2	Mzala skips the country for exile	43
3	The June 16 Detachment	59
4	The emergence of a revolutionary intellectual	83
5	*Habashwe!* Death to the Traitors: Swaziland and the Battle of South Africa	109
6	Cooking the Rice inside the Pot	135
7	The Freedom Charter is our lodestar	153
8	Towards people's war and insurrection	169
9	Chief with a double agenda	187
10	Aids: Misinformation, racism and the imperialist connection	219
11	Negotiations: Thank God things are moving	245
12	Dazzled by capital: The ANC and the transition to democracy	271
13	The Lost Prince of the ANC	301
Postscript: Socialism is the future		321
Notes		329
Selected bibliography		353
Index		365

Foreword

I wish to start by thanking Professor Mandla Radebe for undertaking and completing this important and long-overdue task of telling the story of Jabulani Nobleman 'Mzala' Nxumalo. Mzala was one of the most outstanding cadres and revolutionary intellectuals of the 1976 generation that became part of our movement led by the African National Congress. Initially, Prof. Radebe undertook to complete the work of the late Percy Ngonyama, who had started to write a biography of Mzala, but unfortunately passed away before he could complete the task.[1] Radebe correctly decided that, as much as Ngonyama's initial work remained important, it was exclusively focused on the intellectual work of Mzala, and he thus concluded that it was important to tell the story of Mzala's life, including his role as an intellectual. The product is this book.

The personal and the political
The reason I agreed to write the foreword to a book on Mzala's life has to do with the wish he expressed on his deathbed, communicated to me by his dear wife and comrade, Mpho Nxumalo. He asked that I facilitate the publication of his written works and write an introduction for such a publication. Mpho kindly handed over to me what I regard as two precious volumes of Mzala's works he himself had already pulled together to be published as two books. I subsequently handed these over to the Mzala Nxumalo Centre for further work to be done towards publication.

I first encountered Mzala when we were students at the University of Zululand in 1976. Though I knew of him, he did not know me at the time. He was very active in student struggles at the university that year, and was particularly vocal at student body meetings – so vocal and engaging, in fact, that I was under the impression that he was a senior (possibly a law) student, and yet we were both first-year students. He was very bold and articulate, unlike most first-year students, who are generally still battling to adjust to and understand university life and its politics. This was between February and June 1976, the only period the University of Zululand was open during the 1976 academic year. It was subsequently shut down for the rest of that academic year after student protests unfolded in the wake of the 1976 uprisings, starting in Soweto and leading to the burning down of the Administration Building. Most of the original copies of the matriculation certificates of first-year students were destroyed in that building, including my own.

Mzala 'ambushed' me when, in early 1988, I attended an education conference in London, as an invited academic from the then University of Natal. He had somehow managed to establish that the pseudonyms used in writing about Inkatha and the counter-revolutionary violence in KwaZulu-Natal (KZN)[2] from about 1986 were mine (Nkosinathi Gwala, Praisley Mdluli and Muntu Ncube).[3] I had adopted these to protect myself and my family from attacks by Inkatha, as I was staying at Umlazi, a stone's throw away from a new police station of the notoriously murderous KwaZulu Police, amaZP or oPopayi, as we used to derogatorily call them.

Mzala had wanted to meet with me, principally because we had a number of common political and research interests. These included our mutual hatred of Inkatha's promotion of tribalism and its ethnic mobilisation towards an agenda that was at variance with that of our movement and the struggle for liberation. We were particularly incensed about what we saw as Inkatha's use of 'Zulu nationalism' to pursue a reactionary agenda. As keen intellectuals inside the movement,[4] we were also both concerned about the surging counter-revolutionary violence in KZN from the 1980s.

Another common interest I shared with Mzala when we met in 1988 was that we were both PhD students in the process of conducting research, although on different topics, that formed an important part of key strategic and tactical issues and challenges facing the ANC-led liberation movement.[5] Because of the benefit I had had in debating with Mzala some of the issues I was researching for my PhD, I dedicated my thesis to his memory.[6] After that initial engagement in 1988 I became very close to Mzala; in March 1989, during my sabbatical abroad, Mzala recruited me into the underground South African Communist Party (SACP).[7]

Though Mzala's collected writings still need to be published – and I am determined that this be done – being asked to write a foreword to a book about his life is indeed a great honour and privilege. I hope this will fulfil, at least in part, his and his family's wish about writing an introduction to his works. I am particularly honoured because there are a number of other comrades who worked closely and much longer with Comrade Mzala than myself, who would deservedly write this introduction; I think specifically here of the likes of Comrade Essop Pahad (a veteran of the ANC and SACP, and former Minister in the Presidency), Ambassador Vusi Mavimbela (our ambassador to Brazil) and Dumisani Nduli (my former SRC President at the University of Zululand in 1977–1978 and former national secretary of the Umkhonto we Sizwe Military Veterans Association [MKMVA]). I am pleased that Prof. Radebe interviewed a number of these comrades, and this book has been enormously enriched by that, as those who read it will find out.

Mzala and Buthelezi

Many who have heard of Mzala beyond the ranks of the ANC and the SACP would know him more for the book he wrote on Mangosuthu 'Gatsha' Buthelezi.[8] But, as this book by Radebe convincingly shows, Mzala's role in the liberation struggle was much more than just writing a book about Buthelezi, significant as that was. Of course, Radebe – quite rightly – pays a lot of attention to Mzala's book, but, in handling this aspect his research has also unearthed new information that deals with what would have been tactical issues and debates inside our movement about how to relate to the bantustan system generally, and to Buthelezi in particular.

The publication of *Gatsha Buthelezi: Chief with a Double Agenda* generated a lot of heat and debate, not only outside the ranks of our own movement but also inside the ANC itself. Radebe does an excellent job in navigating the issues around this book and some of the debates that it elicited. Of course, even today Buthelezi strongly denounces the publication, and regards it not only as a denigration of his name and image, but part of the ANC's offensive against him. In fact, since its first appearance in the late 1980s, Buthelezi went to some lengths to prevent the book from being published or sold in South Africa, even resorting to legal action that led to the book being withdrawn from many South African libraries. To date, it has not been as widely read as it could have been.

Some, like Buthelezi, tried to dismiss Mzala's book as poorly researched. Radebe, however, demonstrates that much as people may not agree with some or all of what it contains, it was indeed very well researched. Radebe takes us through the lesser-known writings of the late Govan Mbeki about the ANC's approach to bantustans generally and to Buthelezi in particular. Govan Mbeki had, in the 1950s, served on the ANC committee looking at the question of the ANC's approach towards the planned introduction of bantustans by the apartheid regime. The observations of Govan Mbeki as contained in this book provide invaluable and little-known information about the ANC's canvassing of this matter inside its own ranks. Tempting as it may be, I will not seek to repeat or engage these insights as they are well covered here. What Radebe does so eloquently is show that Mzala was not the first of those within the ANC to raise issues about Buthelezi.

Radebe's book also covers some of the debates and tactical considerations in the ANC about Buthelezi in the wake of Mzala's publication. This remains an important part of the history of our struggle and Radebe helps clarify and answer some of the awkward questions about the (non)relationship between Buthelezi and the ANC. For instance, one of the matters covered is Buthelezi's call for the release of Nelson Mandela. While Buthelezi has reiterated over the years that he was among those who called for Mandela to be freed, and has also claimed that Mandela thanked him for this, Mzala and other ANC leaders had been sceptical about Buthelezi's sincerity when making this call. Govan Mbeki, for instance, as contained in his own book and outlined by Radebe, always insisted that Buthelezi's call was never genuine, but rather a selfish attempt to position himself in the forefront of the campaign to release Mandela. Some in the movement had argued that, although Buthelezi called for Mandela's release, he never called for the release of political prisoners generally. Others have even argued that Buthelezi's call for the release of Nelson Mandela was more closely linked to what they saw as his strategy to promote an internal settlement – similar to the Muzorewa option in Zimbabwe – the aim of which was to promote leaders associated with the bantustans in an attempt to eclipse the liberation movement. In raising these matters, Radebe lays the basis for historians and other scholars to do further work in order to understand certain aspects in the history of the national liberation struggle.

In fact, working through the material in Radebe's book that deals with the context within which Mzala's own book was published helps refresh memories about some of the heavy, and often difficult, debates we had in the early 1990s about the movement's approach to the counter-revolutionary violence of the apartheid regime and Inkatha, especially in KwaZulu-Natal, violence that later spread to the Pretoria, Witwatersrand and Vaal (PWV) region, now known as Gauteng. Some of us in the KZN leadership of the ANC at the time were very concerned about what we saw as a lack of proper understanding of the nature and gravity of the violence by some in our national leadership. Perhaps, in hindsight, this might not have been a lack of understanding but serious tactical differences in handling Buthelezi. Some of the debates canvassed by Radebe in the wake of Mzala's book are not unrelated to those we had to deal with in the early 1990s about the 'Natal violence', including the debates at the ANC's national consultative conference in 1990, as well as the ANC National Conference in Durban in 1991.

Another important issue that Radebe deals with in relation to the debate surrounding *Chief with a Double Agenda* is that of the ANC's attitude on how to work with bantustan leaders generally and the issue of the Bantu Authorities and their evolution into bantustans. Indeed, Radebe's book deals with issues in a way that encourages us to delve even further in order to understand these issues better. For instance, much has been made about the fact that the KwaZulu bantustan under Buthelezi never sought the sham of 'independence' adopted by Transkei, Bophuthatswana, Venda and Ciskei (the so-called TBVC states). But, substantively, there was no difference between conditions and lived experiences of ordinary people in the TBVC states and life in the KwaZulu bantustan and its surroundings.

For instance, the evolution of the Zululand Bantu Authority into the KwaZulu bantustan is littered with struggles and blood spilled over real and attempted acts of transferring government institutions for Africans into the KwaZulu bantustan, often forcibly. In order to get services in many parts of the KwaZulu bantustan in the 1980s, one had to have a KwaZulu identity card as well as the apartheid dompas.[9] For instance, one could not get a job in a government institution of the KwaZulu bantustan if one did not produce this card. In essence, this meant many African people in KwaZulu-Natal were citizens of a different political entity, one reserved exclusively for Zulu speakers. From the 1970s, but especially in the 1980s, there were bitter and often bloody struggles in opposition to the forced incorporation of areas from Natal into the KwaZulu bantustan. Part of the counter-revolutionary violence was waged in the context of this reality. The transfer of schools, government offices and Edendale hospital into the KwaZulu bantustan in Pietermaritzburg is but one example. Both the apartheid regime and the KwaZulu bantustan collaborated in the bantustanisation of large parts of KZN, often in the wake of serious opposition from communities in those areas. This was often done without even a modicum of consultation with communities targeted for incorporation![10]

One of the least-known aspects of the bantustanisation of the schooling system in the KwaZulu bantustan was the teaching of a subject known as 'Ubuntu-Botho'.[11] This was, in essence, Inkatha propaganda, seeking to foster the notion of Zulus as a nation separate from the broader South African nation the liberation movement sought to build. This was another area of common political and research interests between Mzala and myself.

One of the most sinister forms of collaboration between sections of the political elites of the KwaZulu bantustan and the apartheid regime was that of traditional leaders under the KwaZulu government and white farmers, especially those in the north of KZN, who mainly supported the National Party – particularly when it came to supporting and sustaining one of the most vicious labour and accumulation regimes in South Africa: labour tenancy. Although Mzala was born of schoolteacher parents, his home village Ngoje and the broader Vryheid region lay at the heart of labour tenancy. Labour tenancy was essentially 'free' (and often slave-like) labour provided by those on white farms in exchange for a small piece of land on those farms. They had no labour or land rights whatsoever, and were often prevented from – or seriously restricted in – owning livestock. In many instances, those who fled or resisted such arrangements were allowed to settle in neighbouring territories controlled by the chiefs (KwaNokhesheni). KwaNokhesheni itself also harboured a number of people who had been ejected from white farms as excess or aged labour.

It was because of some of these realities that Mzala strongly questioned the role of Buthelezi in the struggle against apartheid. In fact, one of the areas that still require further research is that of the genesis and evolution of violence in KZN, especially between 1980 and 1996. This is a very important period, not just for KZN, but for the entire history of the national liberation struggle in our country.

Mzala, the national question and the national liberation struggle in South Africa

Radebe's book emphasises the point that Mzala was more than just the author of a book on Buthelezi. Radebe's book covers Mzala's early life, including his very early involvement in a number of struggles in high school. In fact, it was precisely because of his experience of struggles at school that he was able to become so active and vocal at the student body meetings at the University of Zululand in his first year.

Soon after leaving for exile in 1976, Mzala accessed Marxist-Leninist literature in the camps in Angola and via political education provided by the movement. Ronnie Kasrils, who was interviewed for this book, offers further insights on Mzala in this regard. He was among the early recruits of the 1976 generation into the ranks of the SACP. Outlined here is how Mzala loved debate (including debating and replying to himself using different pseudonyms in the political journals of both the ANC and the SACP), and became a staunch, disciplined and well-rounded communist.

In fact, Mzala's love for reading and debate should serve as inspiration to the youth of our country, especially those active in our movement, both in the ANC and the SACP. This is even more important now, when there has been a serious decline of political education in our movement generally, as well as a fall in the number of cadres. One significant element of Radebe's book lies in that, by telling of the life, times and struggle of Mzala, it will hopefully motivate the youth in our movement. His was an exemplary life, particularly for someone who had done so much by age 35, the age at which he passed away in 1991.

Mzala was interested in almost any issue of political importance, but his most immediate interest and area of research (including for his PhD) and writing was the national question in the South African revolution. This book outlines how and why Mzala was interested in this subject. In fact, during my stay in Oxford between May and August 1989 (when we interacted most closely with Mzala), we often talked about his work. At the time of his death, he was doing a lot of research on southern and sub-Saharan Africa, focusing on the period from the eleventh century and looking particularly at the evolution of nations and ethnic groups in these regions.

Mzala was delving into such depth partly because he wanted to prove that national and ethnic identities are not a 'God-given' reality but rather are a product of history and struggle, and that these evolve. This was also aimed at addressing his own irritation at what he saw as Inkatha's manipulation of Zulu ethnic identity to achieve its own political ends.

Mzala would become animated when talking about his findings or new information he managed to gather about, for instance, the Monomotapa Kingdom, a precursor of the many ethnic and linguistic groups of southern Africa.[12] It is indeed a pity that there is such paucity of scholarship on southern Africa prior to 1652; one exception being the excellent, but modest, work done by the National Institute for the Humanities and Social Sciences (NIHSS), which will hopefully catalyse further research and studies in this area.

Mzala's work on the national question is even more relevant today than it was when he was writing. The struggle to build a single South African nation remains a very complex, but absolutely essential, task. Post-1994 there have emerged new concepts on the issue, and we have a duty to engage these on an ongoing basis, as Mzala would have done. The concepts of 'a rainbow nation', 'nation-building', 'Ubuntu' and so on require further interrogation and research as part of the work towards building a new South African nation. Of course, Mzala would have continued to examine the national question in relation to the dominant means of production and their ownership.

Today, black workers and professionals working in South Africa's private sector all complain about how racism remains embedded in South Africa's private capitalist corporations. Not only is it embedded, but it continues to be reproduced daily. This is in fact a reality in broader South African society, despite apartheid racist legislation and many racist structures and institutions in society having been done away with. It seems that racism has only been driven below the surface, and remains as strong as it was before 1994. In fact, the struggle to build a new South African nation is inseparable from the struggle against capitalism and its economic inequalities. These are some of the realities that continue to make Mzala's pioneering work important, and why it is still necessary to study and understand his life and writings, as Radebe's book helps us do.

The 2021 local government elections are a stark reminder of how far we are from being a non-racial society in South Africa. The voting patterns are both sobering and disturbing. The white, Indian and coloured voters vote largely for the Democratic Alliance (DA), while the ANC is mostly supported by African voters. But even among white voters there is a regression: Afrikaner voters are increasingly abandoning the DA to vote for the Vryheidsfront Plus (VF Plus).[13] Contrary to the DA's claims that it is evolving into a non-racial party, it is not mobilising white, Indian and coloured communities behind the banner of building a non-racial society; on the contrary, it is increasingly mobilising these voters around the notion of 'swart gevaar', which deepens racial polarisation and animosities in our country. These are issues that are of importance in relation to the national question in South Africa today and would have been of concern to Mzala as well.

Mzala and post-1994 South Africa

A number of people have asked what Mzala would have become post-1990, and especially post-1994, if he had returned home alive. Much as this is understandable in the context of human intellectual curiosity, I find such questions and some of the answers to them entirely ahistorical. Often, especially when they come from detractors of the ANC and the SACP, these questions are simply an attempt to discredit the current leadership of our movement. People often embark on this reactionary tendency of praising the dead in order to condemn the living! For instance, even those who condemned Chris Hani while he was alive, including sections of the media under apartheid, today praise him in order to condemn the current leadership of the ANC and the SACP. This is not only ahistorical, but deeply opportunistic. It is as if Mzala or Chris Hani, for instance, would not have had to deal with the numerous new challenges facing the movement post-1994, including current challenges we face today.

It is indeed important to learn from principled leaders and cadres like Mzala, because uninformed and opportunistic guesswork is not helpful. It is a fact that Mzala saw himself as a future academic in South Africa. It was largely because of this that he delayed his return home; he had been offered a fellowship at Yale, which he wanted to take up and use the opportunity to finish his PhD and write his biography of OR Tambo. That is yet another story well told in some detail in this book.

Whether indeed Mzala would have actually become an academic remains pure speculation – just as Comrade Chris Hani said he would not go into government – because that may not have corresponded with the decision of the movement. I am one of those who were determined to stay in academia and not go to Parliament in 1994, but the ANC and the SACP insisted I be on the parliamentary list.

Perhaps what is certain is that Mzala would have played a very important role in both the ANC and the SACP, both just before and after 1994.

My wish is that this book will be widely read, because it tells a heroic story of one of the sons of our country – one who raised his hand when a call was made to fight the criminal apartheid regime and its institutions. He also appreciated and understood the importance of intellectual work and the battle of ideas in the struggle for liberation. Thanks to Professor Radebe for helping to tell Mzala's story through this book.

Dr Bonginkosi 'Blade' Nzimande

Preface

I

On a hot summer afternoon in 2010 we sat in my late friend and comrade Moses Moyo's tiny new editor's office in his downtown Johannesburg newsroom. Moyo's office was home to more than one computer and a number of hard drives with a giant server that interrupted our discussion with a sound not unlike a loud vacuum cleaner. Sandwiched between a small retail wholesaler run by Pakistani migrants and a Nigerian-run computer shop in President Street, it is from here that Moyo ran his community newspaper, the *Inner City Gazette*.

His office, adjacent to the newsroom filled with young reporters, provided a view all the way to the grime of Doornfontein. It laid bare Johannesburg's dilapidated buildings and mountains of rubbish. Most of the buildings had been factories before being taken over by slumlords. Moyo had been courting me to join one of his many ventures since our days in the Johannesburg Central branch of the South African Communist Party (SACP).

When it was clear that he was up against a brick wall, he proposed an alternative: why don't you become our in-house columnist then, he cajoled me. When I resisted, citing complications related to my employment in one of the largest banks, he had yet another trick up his sleeve. We won't use your name, he retorted, as he paced between his office and the newsroom; we'll just call your column Mzala Nxumalo, he said without looking at me. The silly notion of using a pseudonym seemed to tickle him. Your column will be known as 'Mzala's Corner', he declared with his beguiling smile.

The idea was simple. Since the paper was geared towards ordinary residents of the inner city, we needed to present radical thoughts representing the aspirations of the subalternised working class. In true Mzala style, it should take no prisoners, he continued with a chuckle before adjusting his customary black cap. We had systematically been reading Mzala's writings in our weekly political discussions at the Communist University run by 'Vice-Chancellor' Dominic Tweedie. It was difficult to resist this naughty yet noble imposition. I mumbled something as I left the newsroom on the way back to my own office.

So began my flirtation with Mzala's radical thoughts. For more than two years I had fun trying, albeit with little success, to apply Mzala's ideas to the daily challenges facing the marginalised in the inner city. From evictions to the harassment of the hawkers, Mzala's Corner tried to raise working-class issues.

But it was not until 2018 when I was informed that Percy Ngonyama, a colleague who had been working on the much-anticipated Mzala biography, had passed on, that it was proposed that I consider finishing this project since it was so important for the SACP. Although I had read some of Mzala's writings, I was of the view that writing a biography was for historians. What does a media scholar like me know about history, I thought to myself. But the more I listened to the proposal and did additional reading on Mzala, the clearer it became that Mzala's was a story worth telling – more so in the context of a generation of takers that continues to demand the whole shebang, from free education to free houses to free healthcare, with no thought to giving back. This betrays the supreme sacrifices so many young people made for our freedom.

Mzala belonged to a generation that gave their all. This generation literally gave up their youth and their lives, with many paying the ultimate price, in their quest for knowledge and freedom. Like Mzala, many never lived to enjoy the fruits of freedom. What can our generation and those that come after us learn from these selfless revolutionaries who never demanded freebies but instead gave their lives? But, in all honesty, it was the fact that Mzala came from the same region of Vryheid as my ancestors – and, more importantly, that he was from the same clan as my mother Qhikiza Nxumalo – that tilted my decision. To an extent, there was some level of curiosity and emotional connection. I hope, therefore, that political, ideological and familial lineage have not unduly influenced my analysis.

Although Percy Ngonyama had done some important legwork, it was clear that his approach was diametrically different to how I thought

Mzala's story should be presented. Ngonyama's project sought to interpret the historical context under which Mzala had lived. My thoughts were more on just telling Mzala's story and letting the readers make their own analysis and decision on his character. Of course, it is impossible to write about a character like Mzala without being tempted to venture an opinion. However, where necessary, I have sought to provide context and interpretation of the events. In doing so, I hope that this does not betray my ambition and commitment to allow readers to make up their own minds about Mzala. Mzala's widow, Mpho Gwangwa-Nxumalo, agreed that she wanted someone who would tell Mzala's story. Therefore, a decision was made to start afresh – on a clean canvas, as Mpho put it.

II

Mzala's death may not have grabbed headlines and captivated the world as that of other iconic revolutionary figures, such as Chris Hani and Steve Biko, had. But the memory of Jabulani Nobleman Nxumalo remains etched in the minds of many, especially those close to the South African liberation struggle. Commonly known as Comrade Mzala in liberation circles, when death struck prematurely at the tender age of 35, he had achieved things many can only dream of. A political activist, a soldier of the people's liberation army, a writer and emerging scholar, Mzala is celebrated not only for his bravery but fundamentally for his intellectual prowess. Thus, by the time he departed this earth, he left an indelible mark and clear footprints through his intellectual interventions, including writings on the 'National Question, Buthelezi and Inkatha, class and race in South Africa, the Freedom Charter, armed struggle, history of the liberation movement and Zulu history'.[1]

After his demise in 1991, the sorrowful obituaries by organisations, friends and comrades such as Oliver Tambo, Brian Bunting, John Daniel and Essop Pahad constitute the first act of remembering Mzala.[2] Predictably, this has been followed by many other acts of remembrance. One of the most popular ways of remembering Mzala within the African National Congress (ANC), apart from lectures, has been the naming of structures after Mzala at sub-national level. There is hardly a province without a Mzala Nxumalo ANC or SACP branch.

Indeed, numerous strategies – such as 'commemorative events of a varied nature, which include grass-root and branch level initiatives, media statements, memorial lectures, colloquia and speeches' – have been employed to celebrate the sterling contribution of this intellectual icon. These admirable efforts, however, often come short in unravelling in-depth Mzala beyond serving to 'over-emphasise, in a teleological and chronological manner, the exile years (1976–1991) which amount to only fifteen years of Mzala's life'.[3]

The 1994 piece by Eddy Maloka in the *African Communist* was a welcome intervention and hence it has been relied upon for many years. As Maloka posits, not enough has been done to honour the various facets of Mzala's life. Many young comrades continue to draw inspiration from Mzala's practical life, including his intellectual interventions, so in order to rekindle a revolutionary culture, it is imperative to trace Mzala's life and to remind ourselves of the radical tradition that flourished, particularly in the underground days of the movement, through inter alia 'cadre development' programmes, which produced many cadres of Mzala's calibre. Sadly, this has been 'jettisoned in the backdrop of neo-liberalism induced corruption, nepotism, cronyism and non-ideological fights over positions of power and influence'.[4]

Thus, it has become urgent that we close this gap with a more detailed enquiry into the life of Mzala. Credit must go to the late Percy Ngonyama for championing this course before his own premature death, leaving an unfulfilled dream and an unfinished project. Ngonyama had argued that his efforts amounted 'to the first ever comprehensive research work on Mzala's life history, his radical leftist ideas, and his life and time'.[5] Certainly, this project builds on the strides that Ngonyama made towards unearthing the life story of this unforgettable struggle icon. Although this project is not a continuation of the work that Ngonyama started, it has nevertheless enjoyed privileged access to historical material unearthed during his research.

So, who exactly was Mzala and why does his legacy continue to occupy an important place in the movement and beyond? These questions are pertinent in the context of many 'forgotten' cadres who laid down their lives for our freedom. However, Mzala's legacy is among the few that have endured post-apartheid. These interrelated questions are at the centre of this book, which attempts to tell Mzala's story in the context of the environment that shaped and influenced him. Fundamentally, this project hopes to empower the younger generation that Mzala continues to inspire three decades after his passing.[6]

III

While the memory of Mzala is largely located in his time in exile, it would be naïve to ignore the sequence of events that shaped his worldview, including close comrades and the organisations with which he was associated. To decipher this aspect, it is important to trace his early childhood. How exactly did this environment, including family upbringing, impact his ideological outlook and the sharp intellect that is celebrated today? Very little is known about Mzala's early years and the circumstances that influenced him as a child and young man. To effectively honour this intellectual giant of the liberation struggle, it is prudent to trace all these aspects.

This book is largely driven by oral history as a primary research method. Narrative and biographical methods remain important in social sciences research and, in projects such as this, as tools that enable researchers to 'prise open the different dimensions of lived totality'.[7] In employing oral history, one is able to collect and 'interpret the autobiographical material provided by others' as the basis upon which to interpret critical and complex developments in the subject's life.[8]

Essentially, the oral history approach is aligned to in-depth, semi-structured interviews conducted with individuals who either knew Mzala personally or were close enough to him to recollect some of the critical developments in his life. Indeed, different people interacted with Mzala in various capacities within and outside the movement, academia, family and many more, and thus the interconnection of factors – including political, social, economic and historical experiences – must be acknowledged and recognised.[9] In-depth, semi-structured interviews have been useful in providing supplementary information,[10] and for snowball sampling in which interviewees were able to identify and recruit others they knew had further information about Mzala. Mpho, Titi Nxumalo, Vusi Mavimbela and Dumisani Nduli have been phenomenal in this regard. Finding new subjects to interview, particularly regarding Mzala's early life and that outside the liberation movement, was crucial since the information currently available tended 'to over-emphasise' his life in exile.[11]

As a secondary research method, historical archives that included Mzala's own writing, correspondence and historical documents have been utilised. Thus, this project has triangulated multiple research methods acceptable in social sciences research[12] in order to achieve an in-depth understanding of Mzala's life. By combining various methodologies, the author sought to limit potential biases inherent in such projects. Indeed, the application of multiple perspectives helps to guard against possible errors and to close research gaps.[13] By using this approach, it is hoped that this book will contribute some critical insights into South Africa's distinct history. This book, just like Mzala's work, is an attempt to correct the 'apartheid' version of our history.

Importantly, Mzala's work transcended and straddled different worlds. On one hand, some of his writings could certainly be understood as part of the political propaganda relevant to the time and stage of the revolution. On the other hand, a large part of it was grounded in revolutionary theory. However, in most instances, Mzala was able to rise above narrow propaganda and political pettiness to present cogent interventions that could stand independently as sound scholarly work. Therefore, while it is critical to concede that his writings, mainly in the organisational journals, had a tinge of bias, it would be far too simplistic to dismiss those writings in toto as propaganda. The ANC's political propaganda was crucial in the struggle against apartheid, a legitimate counter-propaganda in the context of a powerful apartheid state propaganda.[14] Nevertheless, it is important to engage with Mzala's work with this reality in mind. More crucial is his ability to transcend this world with quality articles in respected academic journals. Equally, his book on Mangosuthu Buthelezi, although disputed by some, including Buthelezi himself, straddled both worlds.

There are a number of diverse ideas that encapsulate Mzala. While Mzala is feted primarily in the ANC-headed movement, many in progressive circles in academia and beyond have interacted with his ideas. Some drew inspiration from his work.[15] It is in this context that this book hopes to interest activists and scholars concerned with South African liberation history. Readers interested in politics and history should find this book useful too. Marxist-Leninists with a keen interest in understanding the development of the country and the role of the working class must interact with Mzala's original writings beyond this book. This book is written with the general reader in mind. Readers with a specific interest in Mzala's critical intellectual and academic thoughts might not find this book as gratifying. In fact, the gap to complete Ngonyama's work remains.

IV

Lastly, I am grateful to a number of institutions and archives: the Bessie Head Library in Pietermaritzburg for preserving some of Mzala's writings; Digital Innovation South Africa (DISA) at the University of KwaZulu-

Natal (UKZN) for making accessible copies of *Sechaba*, *Dawn* and *African Communist* where most of Mzala's writings could be found; and the Historical Papers Research Archive at the William Cullen Library of the University of the Witwatersrand (Wits) for making public some of the most important aspects of our history. South African History Online (SAHO) and the Karis-Gerhart Collection of South African Political Materials, 1964–1990 have been particularly central to this project. Archival material from Julie Frederikse's book *The Unbreakable Thread: Non-racialism in South Africa* provided useful insights into Mzala's thoughts.

This project took place amid Covid-19, considered the worst pandemic in history since the 1918 Spanish Flu. As we grappled with this existential crisis, many people were gracious with their time, some were even willing to meet face to face. Moreover, in a context where many respected struggle stalwarts either flatly refused to speak to me about Mzala or simply ignored my numerous requests, I am grateful to the following individuals, in no particular order, for either granting me interviews or responding to questions: Balindelwe Nxumalo, Joel Netshitenzhe, Celeste Naidoo, Essop Pahad, Mangosuthu Buthelezi, Raynauld Russon, Sue Rabkin, Pallo Jordan, Ben Martins, Patric Mzolisi Mtshaulana, Cecyl Essau (late), John Pampallis, Lebona Mosia, Patric Tariq Mellet, Sunny Singh, Bongani Khumalo (late), Hlengiwe Mgabadeli, Vuso Shabalala, Lungile Pepani, Thandeka Gqubule-Mbeki, Titi Nxumalo, Sifiso Buthelezi, Kgalema Motlanthe, Robert Edgar, Nomavenda Mathiane, Xolo Mfeka, Vuyani Ntshangase, Mfaniseni Mthethwa, Phasha Nxumalo-Zitha, Dumisani Nxumalo, Zakes Nkosi, Patrick Msomi, Jonathan and Nonceba Levin, Tshidiso Mokhoanatse, Bhabhalazi Bulunga and Elaine Unterhalter.

In the quest to ensure that Mzala's memory is preserved, Bonginkosi 'Blade' Nzimande and Mpho Gwangwa-Nxumalo have been the champions of this project. Titi Nxumalo played a significant role in sharing insights about her brother and linking me with some of Mzala's close associates.

Vusi Mavimbela, Dumisani Nduli and Ronnie Kasrils have been extremely helpful and supportive, sharing many useful insights and referrals. They were no doubt genuine friends and comrades to Mzala. Many papers and articles about Mzala, such as the one presented by Zakes Nkosi (2016), Jeff Radebe (2021) and Eddy Maloka's in the *African Communist*, have provided useful context. Sadly, Cecyl Essau and Bongani Khumalo passed away in the middle of this project. Having attended Mzala's funeral, Essau had fallen in love with Vryheid and got involved in projects with the Institute for Justice and Reconciliation. Khumalo, Mzala's childhood friend, was excited about the possibilities of this project. May their souls rest in peace.

To Sibonelo 'Star' Radebe, who has been of great assistance, thank you, Bhungane. Lastly, I'm grateful to my family for their support and love even when I took time away from them to work on this project. To my wife, partner, friend and comrade, Sarah Mosoetsa – as always, you have been my pillar of strength. I love you!

In the final analysis, I take responsibility for any errors in this work.

Mandla J Radebe
February 2022

INTRODUCTION

Comrade Mzala is dead

I

The South African Airways flight was deep into the African skies when the crackling voice of the captain announced the plane's imminent descent. He mentioned the local time and temperature in Johannesburg and the estimated time of arrival. The glare of the rising sun was beginning to pierce the open window shades as if intent on damaging the retina. But it also served as a reminder of the beginning of a new day.

The slight bumpiness as the plane dropped in altitude went largely unnoticed as passengers continued with their small talk in anticipation of the landing. Sizwe, now nine years old, had been born in Tanzania, but had been smuggled back into the country for few years. The other kids had never been to South Africa. Zwide, now five, and whose striking resemblance to his dad was becoming noticeable, had been born in Lusaka, Zambia, and Balindelwe had been born in London just two and a half years back. Sizwe could neither recall his stay in South Africa nor fully comprehend the magnitude of this moment.

It wasn't long before the flight attendant welcomed the passengers to Jan Smuts Airport. And with that, the flight came to a standstill in a typically breezy, blue-sky Johannesburg. It was a normal Tuesday morning in Johannesburg, many simply going about their usual business.

II

Mpho Nxumalo-Gwangwa was back in the country of her birth, 15 years after she had left as a wide-eyed teenager. Although by 1991 many political prisoners had been released and exiled politicians – including Oliver Tambo, president of the African National Congress (ANC) – were gradually returning to the country, this was not the return Mpho had envisaged. Just a couple of months earlier, on 13 December 1990, Tambo, together with his wife Adelaide and a big entourage, had kneeled down to kiss the very same tarmac at Jan Smuts Airport as he returned to the country for the first time after more than 30 years in exile.

Tambo's return had been tumultuous, with a crowd estimated at some 5000 welcoming him at the airport. Allister Sparks reported for *The Washington Post*: 'It was Tambo's first appearance since a stroke last year left him partially disabled. He appeared frail, but smiled broadly as he waved to the wildly cheering crowd. He did not address the gathering. The stroke has affected his speech.'[1]

Tambo had been welcomed by ANC deputy president Nelson Mandela, Tambo's lifelong friend and former law partner. Mandela was accompanied by leaders and comrades from the ANC's structures in the Pretoria, Witwatersrand and Vaal (PWV) region, now known as the province of Gauteng. The boisterous crowd, dominated largely by the East Rand machinery (East of Johannesburg region), chanted ANC slogans and sang revolutionary songs sung for decades by comrades, many of whom had died before they were able to witness this day. The ailing Tambo was unable to address the gathering crowd and media. His comrade Mandela told them that Tambo 'wishes to say he is happy to be among you' and that the president would address a rally the following Sunday, at which time he would also say only a few words.[2]

Although not met with the same media frenzy and string of dignitaries, Mpho was back home with her new family, the family she could hardly have imagined when she skipped the country with her mother and siblings in 1976. Mpho's parents-in-law, Balindile Elsie and Justice Seth Benjamin Nxumalo, together with sisters-in-law Phasha and Titi and brother-in-law Dumisani were on the same flight. So was the love of her life, Jabulani Nobleman 'Mzala' Nxumalo – in a coffin. Comrade Mzala was dead.

III

The death of Mzala in London on the evening of 22 February 1991 'deprived the ANC and SACP of one of its most brilliant talents'.[3] He had been poised to become a leading theoretician of South Africa's national liberation struggle, but never lived to fulfil his great potential. When his life was snuffed out at the tender age of 35, he left behind many unfulfilled and shattered dreams. Although his death generated none of the headlines that followed the passing of other revolutionary figures, Mzala's death sent shockwaves across the movement. For the 15-or-so years he spent in exile, he had dedicated his young life to the finest cause on earth: liberating the oppressed people of South Africa.

Up until the time of his demise, not only was he a committed soldier of Umkhonto we Sizwe (MK) but he had immersed himself in the intellectual work of the ANC and the South African Communist Party (SACP). Having penned numerous articles for the *African Communist, Sechaba, Dawn* and many other publications under various names, at the time of his death Mzala was on the verge of completing his doctorate at the Open University in England. He had already been offered a year-long fellowship at Yale University, where he was to work on a political biography of Oliver Tambo.

When death struck, many tributes and obituaries pronounced his death a 'great loss'. The SACP described Mzala's passing as 'a tragic loss' that 'robbed the national liberation and working class movement of a powerful thinker, orator and writer'. The loss was captured in many characteristics used to define Mzala, from being 'a passionate and fiery fighter against injustice and humbug' to his 'voracious intellectual appetite, especially for the Marxist-Leninist classics'. Although his writing in various publications of the movement under various pennames had been prolific, it was through his book *Gatsha Buthelezi: Chief with a Double Agenda* that many came to know Mzala.[4]

This book was mentioned regularly in obituaries in the local media. *The Natal Witness*'s Lakela Kaunda wrote in the article 'Double Agenda Author Mzala Dies' that 'The author of the controversial book *Gatsha Buthelezi: Chief with a Double Agenda* Nobleman "Mzala" Nxumalo died in London last Friday'. Mzala was described as a 'prominent' member of the SACP and ANC and, interestingly, as 'a relative of King Zwelithini'.[5] Recollecting Mzala as a leading activist of the SACP, Wasantha Angamuthu wrote in the *Sunday Tribune*, '[As] an academic and author, he was well known for his controversial biography of Inkatha Freedom Party leader Dr Mangosuthu

'Gatsha' Buthelezi – *Chief with a Double Agenda*.[6] The *Cape Times* described him as having written 'a devastating critique of Mangosuthu Buthelezi and was invited by ANC deputy president Mr Oliver Tambo to write his biography'.[7] The *New Nation* highlighted that 'Mzala's interest in Zulu history and culture were made evident in his book entitled *Gatsha Buthelezi: Chief with a Double Agenda*'.[8]

To this day, many remember Mzala through that book. Centring Mzala's legacy on this book was perhaps due to the publicity it had generated since its release, leading to legal threats by Buthelezi himself. In fact, at the end of April 1991, Buthelezi – through his lawyers – issued a letter to university libraries across the country in which he warned that the book was defamatory, and 'if you do not remove the book from your shelf and/or if you distribute the book and/or lend it to others, you will be sued for damages'.[9] To date, Buthelezi still believes the book was a 'comprehensive propaganda tract' by the ANC and communists 'intended to defame me and draw into question my credentials, as a member of the Zulu Royal Family, as a traditional leader and as a political leader'.[10] Mzala's death coincided with these developments.

Essop Pahad, whom Mzala was earmarked to replace in Prague as the SACP's representative on the editorial council of the *World Marxist Review*, also paid a moving tribute to Mzala shortly after his death. He captured the death as having 'deprived our movement of one of its most brilliant talents'. He said, 'Perhaps the greatest loss of all is to our Party's ongoing attempts to indigenise Marxism–Leninism on South African soil.' Prior to his death, Mzala had revived his long ambition of translating Marxist literature into isiZulu. Pahad recalled Mzala's 'sharp, no-nonsense, polemical style' and 'biting and at times provocative criticisms', which did not please everyone within and outside the movement.[11] Perhaps the point that most aptly captured an important aspect of Mzala was made by Pahad when he said, 'He was also a devoted family man, and adored his wife Mpho and their two children.'[12] Everyone close to Mzala remembers him as person who, from an early age, was not into girls and 'having a nice time', but completely focused on the liberation struggle and dedicated to his family.

Mzala's death was a blow that still reverberates across the national liberation movement, one that robbed the movement of an intellectual thinker who would have played a critical role in a democratic South Africa. Pallo Jordan, who worked closely with Mzala in various capacities, remembers him as someone who was valued as a critical thinker who insisted on examining everything. Jordan first met Mzala in Luanda,

Angola, in 1977, where Jordan was tasked with re-establishing Radio Freedom. He says Mzala's 'death robbed the movement of a thinker with great potential'[13]. Joel Netshitenzhe, part of the 1976 generation along with Mzala, is also of the view that Mzala's passing in that period deprived the movement of a cadre who would have deepened our understanding of the opportunities and challenges during the transition. 'He would have helped in deepening our theorisation of the negotiations process, the strategic advances and the compromises; but also, critically, in understanding the implications and impact of the transition on the ANC and various components of the alliance.'[14]

Someone who was very fond of Mzala is Ronnie Kasrils, who thinks his untimely death was an enormous loss to the struggle and to the country's future. Kasrils also met Mzala in the camps in Angola in 1977, and believes that his passing 'robbed us of a charismatic young man's unique contribution. He had enormous qualities of leadership, was passionate about political education, was an extraordinary communicator, a fine orator and writer, constantly determined to develop his skills for the service of the struggle.'[15] Mzala was 'courageous and fearless', says Kasrils, 'devoted to the Marxian ideal of uniting theory and practice to change the world'.[16]

Lebona Mosia first met Mzala in 1979, when selected to undergo training in the German Democratic Republic (GDR). He echoes Kasrils's sentiments on Mzala's courageousness. In the camps in Angola, MK soldiers were commanded to recite the ten clauses of the Freedom Charter and, according to Mosia, this did not go down well with Mzala. Apparently, MK National Commissar Andrew Masondo had a habit of asking comrades random questions about the Freedom Charter whenever he visited the camps. 'Awunginikeze uClause 5, mfanawami' (Give me Clause number 5, my boy), he would command. While many shivered at the thought of being singled out, it encouraged many to immerse themselves in the basic study of the documents of the movement. But not Mzala. He was an avid reader and the issue should not have bothered him, but it did and, according to Mosia, he confronted the feared Masondo about it, insisting that reciting clauses was not important. What was crucial, in Mzala's view, was for 'cadres to understand the contents and meaning of the Charter' rather than regurgitate the clauses like parrots.[17]

Mzala's fearless and tireless appetite to engage in debate until the wee hours is also fondly remembered by many, including friends and comrades Phumelele and Blade Nzimande.[18] Phumelele recalls that they would spend time together in Mzala's London flat; 'they [would] be awake until 5 am in the morning debating all manner of things' relevant to the South African struggle. Mzala's tiny London apartment was, in fact, a hive of activity where numerous heated debates were held. Nzimande fondly recalls many late nights of engagement, which often meant missing the last bus to Oxford and having to stay over. Inevitably, a second dinner would have to be prepared as debates raged on for hours.[19]

IV

The journey from the aeroplane to the carousel to collect luggage usually involves a bus trip, then a brief walk past custom officials. As tension builds towards the security area to choose the right queue, one might have passed cabin crew in perfectly matching outfits, complete with silky neck scarves. But the experience is different when it involves collecting the mortal remains of a loved one.

The process of repatriating Mzala's remains had been exhausting for Mpho, taking almost 20 days to get his body to South Africa. The family was, however, determined to honour Mzala's dying wish to be buried next to his grandmother, Alzina Ndwandwe MaSimelane. This demanded a lot of logistical arrangements, such as preparing the body and booking flights. Titi says the lengthy process involved embalming Mzala's body and preparing the necessary paperwork, which included obtaining permits from relevant authorities.

Compounding matters for Mpho was the unavailability of her own family. Her mother was stuck in the United States, where she was now based with her husband Jonas Gwangwa, well-known South African jazz maestro. Although still exiled, Gwangwa had been granted permission to perform in South Africa a few weeks prior to Mzala's death. On receiving the news of his son-in-law's death, he attempted to extend his stay in the country, but sadly the repatriation process took longer than expected and, according to Mpho, the apartheid regime simply refused to extend his visa. Apart from being his son-in-law, Gwangwa had worked with Mzala in the Amandla Cultural Ensemble of the ANC, where Mzala was the political commissar and spokesperson. Gwangwa had stepped away from his own mainstream tours to focus his energies on leading Amandla in its mission to win hearts and minds for the anti-apartheid struggle.

With most of Mpho's siblings in Zambia or the Netherlands, she was all on her own when she landed in South Africa. Her family was scattered all over the world and unable to be with her. Fortuitously, her mother had arranged for Mpho's grandmother to be at the airport so that she could be at her side for the procession from the airport to Ngoje, Mzala's home village. Mpho had never been to Ngoje, a village just outside the small town of Louwsburg in the northern part of KwaZulu-Natal. Although Mpho had known some of Mzala's siblings in exile and spent time with her in-laws in Zambia after the wedding and on their intermittent visits to London, to Mzala's extended family and village she was an unknown *makoti* (daughter-in-law) from Soweto. She had not undergone the traditional marriage processes to introduce her to all and sundry that would have been followed under normal circumstances. As a non-Zulu, she was not steeped in the Zulu culture.[20]

All this weighed heavily on Mpho. Coordinating a funeral procession from London to Ngoje is not child's play. She was involved in almost every aspect, and this proved to be overwhelming, the pressure essentially depriving her of a chance to properly mourn the passing of her husband. Mpho says, 'The only time the loss really affected me was when we went back to England. That's when reality set in. I nearly lost my mind.'

As Mpho emerged in the arrivals hall at Jan Smuts Airport, a throng of ANC supporters jostled to greet her.[21] Titi recalls 'a very big welcome' arranged for Mzala by the comrades from Natal Midlands, but many comrades who had been close to Mzala were disappointed at the lack of support from the ANC head office in Shell House, Johannesburg. The office had not been involved in either the repatriation or funeral arrangements, and close friends and comrades had to reach out to the International Defence and Aid Fund (IDAF) to assist getting Mzala back to his home country. Based in London, the IDAF had built a reputation in anti-apartheid circles by raising and distributing funding to victims of apartheid, especially political prisoners and their families. Among the work for which it is famous is its involvement in the Treason Trial in 1956 and the Rivonia Trial in 1963.[22]

As the day of the funeral approached, the organisers were not even sure who from the ANC and SACP head offices would attend. Eventually, the SACP's office deployed Geraldine Fraser-Moleketi, then the personal assistant to the general secretary, Chris Hani. Celeste Naidoo – who, together with her former husband Patric Tariq 'de Goede' Mellet, had become close friends with Mzala and his family in London – says that, apart from Natal Midlands region, the ANC leadership was not present at the funeral.

V

The long journey to Mzala's final resting place continued amid negotiations towards transition in South Africa between the apartheid regime and ANC-led liberation movement. The negotiation process culminated towards the end of 1991 in a joint commitment by means of a Convention for a Democratic South Africa (CODESA), which incorporated 18 political groups eventually agreeing to the goal of an 'undivided South Africa'. At the end, these parties 'came to a mutual agreement that all citizens are able to enjoy a free and balanced democracy with a bill of rights as well as a multi-party system, separated power, civil liberties and specific freedoms'.[23] Many believe that Mzala would have played a meaningful role in that negotiation process.

With foresight, Mzala had written extensively on negotiations and the new South Africa. In his famous 1985 article 'Cooking the Rice inside the Pot', he had postulated the formation of a 'Provisional Revolutionary Government' as a basis upon which the democratic state could be built. He argued: 'Such a revolutionary government will represent the interests of the people; it will guarantee the fullest measure of political freedom to conduct an election campaign for the convening of the People's Assembly that will draft the new Constitution for South Africa.'[24] And, as it turned out, these were precisely some of the points that would be thrashed out during the negotiation process. A few months earlier, Mzala had told Blade Nzimande that the transition period required careful reading of Lenin's *Two Tactics of Social-Democracy in the Democratic Revolution* to ensure a transition from bourgeois democracy to socialism. As history has shown, the negotiations would take place against the backdrop of state-sponsored political violence, especially in Mzala's home province of KwaZulu-Natal and, ironically, Mzala had written extensively on the role of Inkatha and its collaborationist politics with the oppressive racist apartheid regime.

Mzala had anticipated the state-sponsored violence, often misleadingly characterised as 'black-on-black' violence in various quarters, including the media. Ben Martins, a member of the ANC's Provincial Executive Committee (PEC) and the SACP's Secretary in the Natal Midlands region, mentions that at the time of Mzala's death, the political situation in the Natal Midlands in particular was heightened due to politically motivated violence. Characterised by internecine violence and brutal killings between members of the Inkatha Freedom Party (IFP) and the ANC-aligned United Democratic Front (UDF), Martins suggests that the Seven Days War in the Natal Midlands was one of the bloodiest chapters of that conflict.[25]

Mzala could not see a racist regime like South Africa's reaching a genuine agreement for a democratic transition. He had further argued that 'no racist government can guarantee the holding of free and fair elections in South Africa, and therefore no peaceful negotiation can lead to the creation of a democratic State without the racists and the imperialists, and against them'. In his view, for such a condition to exist, political and military victory by the organised masses was necessary 'for the implementation of the Freedom Charter'.[26] By the time the negotiations were in full swing, the ANC had suspended the armed struggle, one of the fundamental pillars Mzala had punted in this article.

Marxist-Leninists like Joe Slovo and Chris Hani would later appreciate the ANC's decision on the armed struggle as an objective reality, a perspective informed by the reading of the concrete material conditions. Could it be that Mzala would have assumed a similar posture? In 1989, he had penned another article in *Sechaba*, 'Negotiations and People's Power', in which he articulated and, to an extent, clarified the ANC's position on negotiations. The question of negotiations for the ANC-headed movement, he argued, was not 'problematic in principle' as was 'provocatively suggested by the media'. Mzala argued that it was the ANC that had demonstrated commitment to negotiations as opposed to the Pretoria regime.[27]

VI

The convoy escorting Mzala's mortal remains departed the airport, a stone's throw from the World Trade Centre, where CODESA was to be held later in the year. The journey from Jan Smuts Airport – named after one of South Africa's most brutal Afrikaner military rulers and, ironically, named after Oliver Tambo today – to Ngoje is a stretch of just under 500 kilometres. Less than 50 kilometres on the N3 South motorway, the convoy took the Balfour off-ramp just after the small town of Heidelberg. From there, the road bustled with heavy-duty vehicles, all the way past dorps like Standerton, Volksrust and Utrecht to the historic sight of Ncome (Blood River) and Vryheid. The road is scenic, bordered with lush green and blessed with summer rains and mountains, especially on Mount Majuba.

Mpho and the children rode in the family car. Ben Martins says the steering committee had organised everything, including comrades to form the guard of honour and be part of the cortège to Ngoje. The delegation included alliance leaders such as Blade Nzimande and Sifiso Nkabinde, then regional secretary of the ANC in the Natal Midlands. 'It was a most painful moment to see the body arrive,' recalls Phumelele Nzimande; what was most touching was to hear Mzala's mother asking where they would leave Jabulani, talking as if he were still alive.[28]

With the family's luggage in the boot, the hearse with Mzala's coffin led the way. Not even the arrival of Mpho's grandmother, whom she had not seen in almost two decades, could console her or break the palpable silence. There was not much to talk about; Mpho was grief-stricken, overwhelmed by a feeling of emptiness, of numbness. 'I felt lost without Mzala,' she recalls sadly. Not even the familiar landscape of the Transvaal could lift her mood. Nevertheless, the presence of familiar faces like those of her grandmother and Phumelele, who were in the same car, made a huge difference. Mpho says the presence of her grandmother 'is the only comfort I had' on that journey.

Almost 400 kilometres further, the procession entered the town of Vryheid, the vehicles coming to a stop outside AVBOB funeral services. This was where Mzala would be kept until his funeral service on Sunday. They were still some 70 kilometres from Mzala's village of Ngoje, the place of Mzala's youth and countless mischievous antics. When the procession resumed finally without Mzala, it passed the Louwsburg Rural Magistrate's Court at the corner of King and Avenue streets, where Mzala apparently pulled off some of his stunts by posing as a lawyer. His younger brother Dumisani Nxumalo says Mzala would consult their father's legal literature in order to represent locals in court. His sister Phasha Nxumalo-Zitha remembers at least two occasions when Mzala represented two boys accused of theft – both Elfas 'Qhofa' Mhlongo and Kwetshi Nkosi escaped prison – while Zakes Nkosi recalls that in one of the cases local boys were accused of stealing chickens from the yard of a Mr Van Rooyen. Mzala's childhood friend and neighbour Mfaniseni Mthethwa laughs when he wonders how Mzala obtained the right of representation in court.

VII

On the afternoon of Saturday, 16 March, the procession returned to Vryheid to collect Mzala and then made its way to his village of Ngoje. It had been raining and overcast for the better part of the week, and Saturday was no different. On the outskirts of Louwsburg the unpaved road that curves towards the village is bumpy and slippery in wet conditions. The heavens opened as if welcoming back the village's departed son. The preparations to receive Mzala at the Nxumalo homestead were well underway. Whenever he had had money to spare, Mzala would send the little he had to help his parents make minor modifications to the house – and it is in this house that his body would lie one last time.

House number 185 in Ngoje is now a four-bedroom place with a kitchen, dining and sitting room and a bathroom. Before modification, it was a simple two-and-a-half-bedroom house. The half bedroom, which was initially meant to be a bathroom, became Mzala's bedroom. In the same yard, not far from the main house, was a shop known as 'the tearoom'; Mzala's parents had built it to augment their schoolteachers' salaries. A fading sign written by Mzala when he was a youngster – Yenyuka Sizwe Esimnyama (Rise Black Nation) – was still visible in front of the shop. This was a sign that highlighted the influence of black consciousness on Mzala's early life. Phasha is convinced that their parents were not aware where Mzala was heading with all these ideas of his.

That Mzala was brought home was, however, an aberration of the family's faith. His family was steeped in the Christian beliefs of the Seventh Day Adventists. They, for example, regarded bringing the mortal remains home the day before the funeral as something connected to ancestor worship, a practice they did not follow. But his parents agreed to the deviation in order to accommodate Mzala's comrades who were keen on a night vigil and to see him one last time. Nevertheless, it is usually at the arrival of the mortal remains of a departed family member at home that emotions and grief take over, as reality sets in, often exacerbated by fatigue and the sight of the coffin as it is carried into the house. Around 2 pm, Mzala was finally back home, some 15 years after he skipped the country with the help of his father.

VIII

Mzala's dying wish to be buried next to his grandmother was finally realised on an unpleasantly cold and rainy Sunday, 17 March 1991, when he was laid to rest at KwaGadlaza local cemetery in Ngoje. His tombstone is still engraved with fading logos of the alliance organisations with which he was associated: the ANC, SACP, Congress of South African Trade Unions (COSATU) and the South African National Civic Organisation

(SANCO).²⁹ The internal structures of the SACP were still weak at that time, but just months after the unbanning of political parties, the Party succeeded in giving Mzala a befitting send-off. Working together with other alliance organisations, a sizable crowd was mobilised to attend the funeral. Because of the unpleasant weather conditions, the funeral proceedings had to be shortened.

Until a group of comrades in taxis arrived, the mood was sombre and solemn. Celeste Naidoo reports that before the arrival of the comrades, there was little singing or celebration of Mzala's life. Because the unbanning was recent, there was also a cultural disjuncture between comrades from exile and those within the internal structures, recalls Phumelele.³⁰ 'The rowdy funerals of UDF [United Democratic Front] and the way we conducted funerals in the manner of just celebrating the life of a comrade' was strange to those who came from exile. 'I remember Mpho', continues Phumelele, saying, '"Are we going to be quiet at some point and just allow him to rest?"' Indeed, this was a typical funeral of a comrade.

The absence of senior leaders suggested to many a lack of regard for Mzala's contribution to the struggle. 'They don't think that this man is worthy of being buried in the ANC flag. They don't think he is worthy of their presence. This is how they treated Mzala,' remonstrates Naidoo.³¹ Since the Natal Midlands Alliance took charge of the funeral, many close to Mzala remember some sense of bitterness at what they considered a lack of support from Shell House. Blade Nzimande points out that while the ANC-led movement had limited resources and competing interests at the time, it 'could have done a little bit more on the emotional support side of things'.³²

The weather, however, disrupted proceedings. 'I had never seen so much rain; it poured,' recalls Blade Nzimande. The rain forced some comrades, especially those who had come from afar, to leave early. Celeste Naidoo remembers embracing Mpho before rushing to drive back to Johannesburg. 'It was a very rainy day, and because that part of Natal is very muddy, so you could slip.' 'The rain caused a lot of mud,' says John Pampallis; 'I think more than one car got stuck and had to be actually pulled out.'³³ Hlengiwe Mgabadeli says their car also got stuck in the mud and they had to push it. 'It was difficult, but we were relieved that we went to bury him.'³⁴ Even the hearse, according to Titi, got stuck in the mud and Mzala's father had to use his bakkie to pull it out.

The inclement weather failed, however, to dampen the spirit of the large crowd that gathered to pay their respects. They sang revolutionary songs.

Invoking a military adage, Martins says the attitude of the mourners was, 'There is no rain in the army, there is only an army in the rain.' Among the speakers were Billy Masetlha (representing the ANC Youth League), Nana Mnandi (regional chairperson of the ANC Women's League), Sipho Cele (of COSATU Northern Natal), Shakes Cele (of the ANC Midlands region) and Geraldine Fraser-Moleketi, who spoke on behalf of the SACP. In his message read at the funeral, ANC president Oliver Tambo said Mzala's death had 'robbed our people of a stalwart of our revolution who still had much to contribute to the freedom of our country. We have indeed lost a soldier, a scholar and an outstanding and uncompromising freedom fighter against the evil system of apartheid. We must pick up his spear and march to our long-awaited freedom'.[35]

With his debilitating motor neuron disease at an advanced stage, ANC and SACP stalwart and the first chairperson of the ANC in the Natal Midlands, Harry Gwala could not attend the funeral; his message was read by Shakes Cele.[36] Blade Nzimande and Vusi Mavimbela spoke as friends who had known Mzala at different stages of his life. Mavimbela told the mourners how he had met Mzala at Dlangezwa High School, the type of character he was and their plans for living together in a free South Africa. Tributes came from far and wide, including from parties such as the Philippines Communist Party, which described Mzala as a major 'shaper of Marxist-Leninist thought' reflecting his internationalist character.[37] When the gloomy day ended, Mzala lay peacefully at KwaGadlaza cemetery not far from his grandmother. His last dying wish had been fulfilled.

To this day, Celeste Naidoo, who had driven to the funeral with Frank Meintjies and Cecyl Esau, cannot hide her disappointment at what she regarded as a low-profile funeral not befitting someone of Mzala's stature. She laments some of the speakers, like Fraser-Moleketi, whom she thinks was unable to locate Mzala's contributions to the struggle appropriately. Apart from the weather and the long drive back to Johannesburg, 'I also wanted to leave because I was very disgusted by the organisation for which I was prepared to give my life, that they could treat such a man, that kind of a man, with such disrespect.'

Bhabhalazi Bulunga, one of Mzala's close associates, was equally bitter about the ANC's failure to provide sufficient support. He, however, felt that Fraser-Moleketi was the only speaker who managed to present a personal account of Mzala. She successfully located him accurately and 'didn't just speak about politics'. According to Bulunga, she spoke about his lively, sharp and sometimes irritating debates because Mzala did not want to lose.

To some extent, Cecyl Esau, who had just been released from Robben Island, seemed to agree with Naidoo. Although he had not met Mzala in person, he said that when he heard of his passing from Fraser-Moleketi, who he bumped into at the SACP's offices, he decided to attend. Esau had read some of Mzala's material and was happy to accompany Naidoo to the funeral of this legendary figure. The journey back to Johannesburg was, however, depressing for Esau because he couldn't fathom why someone he had regarded as a legend had been buried in such an unremarkable fashion. 'I did not see any official from the alliance nationally. I did not notice any comrades from the Island.' Notwithstanding such grumbles, which tend to be present at most funerals, Mzala was given a hero's send-off.

After the funeral, Mpho and the children spent some time with her in-laws in Ngoje. But their stay was short-lived because Mpho had unfinished business in London. Soon they were back in England, but for the first time they were on their own without Mzala.

CHAPTER 1

The Nxumalos and the Mwandlas

I

By the time Justice Seth Benjamin Nxumalo and his wife Balindile Elsie Nxumalo (née Mwandla) settled in Ngoje, a village just outside Louwsburg in the northern part of KwaZulu-Natal, South Africa was well on its way to becoming a pariah state. In 1948 the prime architect of apartheid, DF Malan, and his National Party (NP) had swept into office by way of an openly racist campaign.[1] Although apartheid essentially sought to 'ensure the survival of the white race' by keeping the different races separate in all facets of life, the oppression and marginalisation of African people in particular and blacks[2] in general have deep roots in South Africa. As early as the 1700s, the Dutch colonial settlers had already established laws to separate whites from Africans.[3]

Since then, the emasculation and dispossession of Africans had continued apace, culminating in the 1913 Natives Land Act, which stripped the African majority of the little remaining dignity they still had. Through this Act, Africans – who constituted more than 70 per cent of the population – were reserved 7.5 per cent of the land or 'scheduled areas',[4] and ultimately confined to ever more over-crowded reserves known as the 'bantustans'.[5] As Sol Plaatje, founding secretary-general of the ANC, put it in 1916, this reduced the African majority to 'pariahs in the land of their birth'.

Ngoje and the surrounding areas, currently falling under AbaQulusi local municipality, were not spared. Named after a clan fiercely loyal to the Zulu Royal House,[6] the area is rich in mineral resources. To this day, the coal-mining industry in KwaZulu-Natal is primarily located in the AbaQulisi region, in areas such as Dundee, Newcastle, Utrecht and Hlobane. Despite this mineral wealth, however, the current socio-economic status of the region is still largely characterised by impoverishment. This is deeply rooted in the country's history of dispossession.

Louwsburg is a typical rural South African town, with two main streets, a handful of shops, a filling station and a magistrate's court. Typical of such small towns, it has a Nederduitse Gereformeerde Kerk, colloquially referred to as the NG Kerk or Dutch Reformed Church, that dates back to the 1930s. The town is named after Dawid Louw, a member of Lucas Meijer's boer (farmer) commando that acceded to the plea of Zulu king Dinuzulu kaCetshwayo for help against his uncle Zibhebhu. It is reported that Zibhebhu kaMaphitha Zulu had attempted to establish his own independent kingdom. In return for overthrowing Zibhebhu, the boers were granted land in the northern part of Zululand. Louw was given a farm by the king, and he built his farmhouse near the slopes of Louw's Mountain.[7]

Equally, Ngoje is a typical South African village of sparsely populated rural homes in varying degrees of decay. A sprinkling of newly constructed modern structures is visible. Cattle, goats and sheep roam freely in the dusty roads that become even trickier to negotiate during the rainy season. Just like in other parts of the country, it appears that very little has changed in this village since the dawn of democracy, with not much infrastructure to speak of.[8]

Towards the end of the nineteenth century, things took a turn for the worse for this area, with the intensification of the 'mineral revolution' and a rapid rise in the population, resulting in a severe shortage of land. Typically, Africans were at the receiving end, as illustrated by the removal of Chief Khambi and his people from Mooiplaats and Scheppers farms in 1906. Having participated in the Bhambatha Rebellion, Chief Khambi of the 'Ngoje Division' was regarded as a 'loyal' chief in colonial terms. Despite this, the chief and his followers found themselves destitute and landless when the two farms they had occupied as rent-paying tenants were bought and the new owner made impossible demands when it came to rent and labour.

The new owner was the Dundee Coal Company Ltd., with mining

operations in Dundee and Waschbank, and the leading coal producer in the Natal Colony. With increasing mining activities in the Transvaal and Bloemfontein, the growing demand for mining-related manufacturing, the burgeoning growth in major cities and towns, and the improved transport infrastructure in Natal, there was a huge demand for coal. When Chief Khambi could not meet the demand for a staggering 800 men a year – the equivalent of about one able body per household – the tenants were evicted and lost access to the only source of arable land available to them. Khambi tried to reason with the colonial authorities, but to no avail.[9] Driven by their quest to accumulate and maximise profit, the company cared very little for the pleas of poor Africans. This is the sad reality that befell many communities across South Africa at this stage of the colonial project. This legacy haunts these communities even today, Ngoje included.

II

Mzala's great-grandfather, Matshana – a stock farmer from Mnxayibane village in Louwsburg, with many head of cattle – was popular for his commitment to feeding women and children during difficult times. Apparently, during the factional wars, he would produce milk from his cattle, which he then carried in an *igula* (calabash) and would go around feeding women and children while the men were out fighting. When men approached, he would feign mental illness that suggested an inability to participate in the war. As soon as they were gone, he would continue feeding the abandoned families.[10] This act earned him the praise name of uBunyalele igula lakwa Mnxayibane.[11]

One of Matshana's sons, Owen, followed in his footsteps and became a subsistence farmer. Owen married Alzina Simelane, a young woman from Nongoma with whom he fathered nine children. Born in 1924, Seth – known as Sethi by the people of Ngoje – was the second-born child and the oldest son. With the children still young, Owen left for Swaziland, where he settled and found another wife with whom he fathered eight more children. It was a lone struggle for Alzina, trying to fend for nine children on her own by working odd jobs as a domestic worker. As the eldest son, Sethi yearned to be close to his father and followed him to Swaziland. Although he found him and spent some time studying in Swaziland, things did not go according to plan. Sethi's father was doing well in Swaziland, having befriended King Sobhuza II, who in 1973 suspended the constitution and declared himself an absolute monarch.¹² Sobhuza's mother, Inkhosikati LomawaNdwandwe, was the daughter of Chief Ngolotjeni Nxumalo. Ngolotjeni (sometimes spelled Ngolotsheni) was a descendant of the Ndwandwe chief who sought refuge in the Shiselweni area from Somhlolo after the defeat of the Ndwandwes by King Shaka's marauding Zulu army.¹³ This is the same tribe from which Owen came.

Initially, Sethi seemed to be doing well in Swaziland. But, with his father having a new wife and other children, Sethi struggled to settle down and eventually decided to return to South Africa, but kept in touch with his many relatives and friends in Swaziland throughout the remainder of his life. During this period, Sethi was dogged by bad health, including a terrible bout of tuberculosis that saw him admitted to King George V Hospital in Durban. He eventually lost one lung due to the disease. It was here that Sethi met another Nxumalo family. Although unrelated, the father, who was a Methodist Church priest, had two daughters and decided to take in this 'stranded Nxumalo boy' because they had always wanted a boy in the house.

Now based in Durban, Sethi had a new, loving and stable family that sent him to school. When he finished school, they enrolled him at Ndaleni Teachers' Training College, a Methodist mission college near Richmond in KwaZulu-Natal. After completing his teacher's diploma in the early 1950s, Sethi started teaching, taking up positions in places such as Hlobane, Coronation and Glencoe. In the small town of Glencoe, in the Umzinyathi District in KwaZulu-Natal, Sethi was just two hours away from his home village of Ngoje. It is here that he met a beautiful young Balindile Elsie Mwandla.

Balindile was from a well-off family in Ndulinde, a village about 90 kilometres from the coastal city of Richards Bay. Born in 1928, she was the third-born child of Mr and Mrs Mwandla, who had three girls and two boys. Leonard Funizwe Mwandla, Balindile's father, was a well-to-do man who belonged to the group of Africans called *amazemtiti* (the exempt ones). Essentially, this was a group of Africans exempt by the colonial rulers from certain rules, which meant he was permitted to do certain things or own items black people generally were not allowed.¹⁴ Because he had financial muscle, Mwandla sent his three daughters to Inanda Seminary, an independent girls' school in Inanda township.

To ensure that they were comfortable, he bought a house in an exclusive neighbourhood that later became Clermont, a black middle-income township in Durban. The girls could make use of the house during breaks, such as the Easter holidays, instead of going all the way home to Ndulinde. He hired full-time housekeepers and, during short breaks, the girls would be fetched from school and then returned when school reopened. Often, they would be taken to shop in Durban. Mwandla also ran a herbalist chemist in Durban. He was thus making money, but still could not buy land in South Africa, and so he decided to buy farms in Swaziland, which is where the family eventually settled.

After high school, Balindile attended Mariannhill Teachers' Training College. In the early 1950s, she returned to Inanda Seminary, this time as a teacher, before accepting a post in Glencoe. Apart from teaching at the same school, Sethi and Balindile shared similar backgrounds, including Swaziland, which both regarded as part of their home.

III

The 1950s were as tumultuous as the previous decades, if not worse for black people in South Africa. The decade had begun with anti-pass demonstrations led by Florence Matomela. Shortly after, the NP government introduced new, repressive legislation – the Population Registration Act of 1950 and the Group Areas Act of 1959. Among the upheaval of this decade, perhaps what affected Sethi and Balindile most was the government's decision to assume control of schools for Africans by passing the Bantu Education Act; this was followed by a boycott of Bantu Education led by the ANC.[15]

The couple's first two children were born while Sethi and Balindile were living and working around Glencoe. The arrival of their first child in 1955 coincided with a rising resistance to apartheid by black people. The ANC was becoming radicalised and the country witnessed a number of anti-apartheid initiatives. The closest hospital to Glencoe is in Dundee, just over 10 kilometres away, and on 27 October 1955, soon after she was admitted, Balindile gave birth to a boy who they named Nobleman Jabulani. This was barely four months after about 3000 people had gathered in Kliptown, Soweto, on 26 June 1955 at the Congress of the People to adopt the Freedom Charter.

It was inevitable that Sethi would gravitate towards Ngoje. After all, it was his home, and his family was still there. Balindile found a post as a mathematics teacher in Ngoje, and soon after the birth of their daughter Phasha Essential, the predictable move began. Although Sethi continued to teach in Hlobane and only commuted home on weekends, they started building their home in Ngoje. In 1959, Balindile gave birth to twins, a girl and a boy, named Sitheni Talent (Titi) and Dumisani George respectively. The twins were a handful for Balindile, and this was compounded by the fact that Sethi was still working in Hlobane. He thus decided to take the two older children, Jabulani and Phasha, to stay with him so that Balindile could at least manage on her own while he was away on weekdays.

Titi recalls that their home was always full of people, particularly children. There were many cousins from both their father's and mother's side, as well as the children of acquaintances. Apart from the fact that Sethi could have been compensating for his own upbringing and the help he had received from a strange family, Titi believes that both their parents liked helping children. That also explained their chosen profession, she felt. They would take children in just because they knew their parents or because the child happened to share a surname with Sethi mother's. Hence, at some point, there was a girl they took in because her mother was also a Simelane, just like Sethi's mother. Not that they had a big house, says Titi. It was a two-bedroom place with another very small room that was initially meant to be a bathroom in which only a single bed could fit; that ended up becoming Mzala's room. But the house was always full of people. 'I don't even know how we used to sleep, actually,' says Titi.

To supplement their salaries, Sethi built a shop next to the main house that came to be known in the area as 'the tearoom'. The shop sold goods typically found in local shops that serviced the community: bread, canned food, soft drinks, tea, condensed milk and sweets. The children took turns working in the shop, a popular and busy place since most other shops were too far for the people of Ngoje. Apart from stealing sweets, Titi regards the experience of working in the shop as valuable.

Apart from being born to schoolteachers and coming from the family that owned the local shop, the Nxumalo children had a normal upbringing and did the same things as other children. Like most boys, Mzala used his hands to build stuff. He was fond of designing and building houses using boxes from the shop. Later he would join local boys in karate sessions, a passion he enjoyed. His childhood friend Mfaniseni Mthethwa admired Mzala's karate abilities, but he laughs when he thinks about his poor soccer skills. Dumisani says he was a beneficiary of the karate passion because Mzala always took him along to training sessions.

The household was, however, different to other households. During that period, simply being a teacher elevated one's social status. Vusi Mavimbela, whose mother was also a schoolteacher and worked with Mzala's father, mentions that in that era teacher families in small rural towns 'radiated knowledge and enlightenment'. To this effect, the Nxumalos 'shone the bright light and gave hope of the possibility of a better future to rural communities'.[16] Hence, Zakes Nkosi posits, 'It is safe to say that Mzala grew up in fairly privileged circumstances, more than many of his peers.' In the context of the difficulties that many African households faced, it is accurate to argue that Mzala did not come from a poor family.

Sethi and Balindile were devoted Christians who never missed church and instilled Christian values in all their children. Sethi's mother had been brought up in the same church and she, in turn, had raised all her children in that church. Balindile was, however, more religious and a stronger Christian than Sethi. She 'was the backbone', says Titi. Mzala was thus the third generation to attend the church.

Music is another aspect of Mzala's life that he developed at a young age. Mthethwa says there were two households in the village where Mzala spent time honing his musical skills. The Ntshisi and Masuku homes boasted an organ and a piano respectively. He loved playing jazz and gospel music, says Mthethwa. Phasha and Dumisani say they all loved music. They ended up forming a family quartet because 'we were two girls and two boys', says Phasha. They spent most of their time at home singing but also sang in church.

Mthethwa says that, as youngsters, they were influenced by their religious upbringing, the enjoyable and powerful sermons delivered by Sethi leaving an indelible impression on their minds. Sethi was a preacher who, according to Mthethwa, had been trained in theology. This was obvious in the way he structured and delivered his sermons. The sermons were laden with liberation theology, recalls Mthethwa, and 'what was emphasised was that we were all equal before God'. However, the biggest influence stemming from the church was the culture of reading instilled by Sethi and his close friend Professor Otty Nxumalo,[17] whom Sethi regarded as a brother, the duo both encouraging the youngsters to read. Mthethwa recalls that books such as *Let My People Go* by Chief Albert Luthuli – who, incidentally, grew up in the same church and had stayed in the Vryheid region at some point – were among the most widely read, as was Martin Luther King Jr's *Strength to Love*. With the likes of Professor Nxumalo in the church, there was enormous competition when it came to book reading, says Mthethwa.

With Sethi avidly collecting literature as he pursued his legal studies,

Mthethwa is convinced that it is this environment that instilled a culture of reading in Mzala. He says Mzala read a lot and so began to question things. As boys, they were not allowed onto the rugby fields or into stadiums, says Mthethwa, so 'we ended up hating rugby because of this separation'. He says Mzala started posing many questions. 'If we are all going to heaven, are we going to be separated there like it is happening on earth?' It is at this point that Mzala began his crusade for justice and equality.

Even though they may not have been politically involved in the way that Mzala was, it was impossible for many educated people to be oblivious to the political situation in the country. Thus, Sethi and Balindile would comment on the cruelty of apartheid and its impact on black people. Mzala would later describe his parents to Julie Frederikse as 'people of a very high moral integrity' that infected all their children, particularly himself, as the eldest child. This, according to Mzala, instilled in him a strong sense of justice. His awareness of the South African contradiction – the black and white, the rich and poor dichotomy – thus found a base.[18]

The AbaQulusi area, particularly Vryheid, notorious for its rampant racism particularly among white farmers, shaped the political ideas of many of Mzala's generation. Two of Mzala's friends, Vusi Mavimbela and Bongani Augustine Khumalo, hold vivid memories of the abuse and cruelty meted out against black people by whites in the area. Many families lived on white-owned farms and had to send their children to work on the farms for free before they could even go to school. In his memoir, Mavimbela details the forced removal of people from KwaBhanya village to Mondlo township – at gunpoint 'because the white government wanted to construct a railway line connecting the coalmines of Hlobane and Coronation with the seaport of Richards Bay'.[19]

It was not just the community of KwaBhanya that was affected by the 1963 forced removal to Mondlo township, however. Many black communities around Vryheid – Kingsley, the Khambule mission, and farms surrounding Vryheid – were affected by removals sanctioned by the Group Areas Act and other apartheid laws. They were dumped at an undeveloped site near the Mondlo mountain, situated approximately 25 kilometres southwest of Vryheid.[20] Even today, Mondlo suffers from an infrastructure backlog, with places such as Section C still using pit latrines.

It is within this context and his parents' influence that Mzala was instilled with a profound sense of human justice. His parents did not, however, want him to become involved in politics. Perhaps this explains why they sent Mzala to the Eastern Cape to secure a good education. According to Mzala, his parents' attitude was that they did not want to encourage him to be involved politically, 'despite the fact that there were occasional slips when they were talking and I would hear their viewpoint about the situation generally' and thus 'fitted the flesh to the moral skeleton'. Sometimes Balindile, recalls Phasha, was unable to conceal her hatred for oppression and aspects of it such as the imposition of Afrikaans. Because Mzala and his siblings were closer to her than to Sethi, who was strict, it was Balindile who most influenced their outlook on life. 'We all ended up hating Afrikaans' because of her, suggests Phasha.

In 1961 Mzala was back in Ngoje to start his primary-school education. The house was teeming not only with his siblings, but also cousins and other children his parents had taken in. He started his schooling at Louwsburg Combined Primary, a Christian school whose motto was *Thandaza usebenze* (pray and work) and where his mother was a maths teacher at the school under the principalship of Mr Samson Velefini 'Mkhende' Phakathi. At school, Mzala was a gifted student who was both confident and popular among fellow learners. Having been academically accelerated twice already and thus skipping grades, because he was young and of small build, he was referred to as a 'piece of a man'. Phasha recalls that whenever fellow students shouted this name in unison, he reacted in his typical dramatic fashion with his 'special walk'.

Growing up in a Christian household meant that Mzala was active in church, singing in the choir and playing the piano. His love for music and commitment to his faith never wavered, even when he became a staunch Marxist-Leninist later in life.

IV

In 1968, after completing Standard 5, Mzala's parents shipped him off to what is now the Eastern Cape. They had noticed that he was an academically gifted child and, according to Mzala, were keen for him to study in English because 'they saw no reason why I should do some science subjects – even at that early stage – in Zulu, as dictated by the Bantu Education system, so I went to study in the Cape from primary'.[21]

For Titi, Mzala was not a normal child. He had a searching mind that questioned everything. Sethi soon realised that Mzala needed more than reading and writing than that provided by Bantu Education system. He had been regarded as very strict when it came to the raising of his first two children and demanded independence from them at a very young age. When he took the decision to send Mzala to boarding school, there were murmurs and complaints that the 'child was too young', but Sethi would not be swayed. So it was that, at the age of 12, Sethi considered Mzala old enough to catch a train from Vryheid to Butterworth alone. His sister Phasha would join him later at Bethel College.

Established in 1917 as a mission school, Bethel College is situated on a farm less than 10 kilometres from Butterworth in the Eastern Cape. The school was founded by the Seventh Day Adventists as a private institute to train ministers of the church. Subsequently, a high school and teacher college were introduced.[22] Today, the school is marketed as a 'quiet, serene and safe environment' conducive to 'proper and focused education'.[23] Because this was a Seventh Day Adventist school, Mzala fitted in and adjusted easily, and continued to participate in cultural activities, particularly music.

Because the Seventh Day Adventists instilled values said to guarantee a successful life path for children, says Mthethwa, most parents aspired to send their offspring to Bethel College. 'They would not have taken them to any other schools,' he says. For religious purposes, this college was considered important in instilling Seventh Day Adventist values.

However, according to Mzala, one of the most significant factors contributing to his political consciousness was growing up in Natal, where the cruelty meted out by white farmers was palpable. 'I saw a lot of people being evicted from their farms and my father was a type of person who'd relate very closely with the people.'[24] Although born and raised in the countryside of Zululand, Mzala did have some interaction with the urban environment. 'There were regular periods when one would go to Durban and other urban areas.'[25] He added mischievously, with a laugh, that 'I basically come from the countryside of Natal, not far from where Gatsha Buthelezi stays'.[26]

So, by the time he moved to Bethel College, Mzala was already politicised, having on many occasions experienced contradictions that rendered African people landless – 'without a country' in their own country. Indeed, the move to Bethel College served to broaden Mzala's horizons and perceptions of the South African political reality. The fact that Bethel was a mission school that accommodated individuals from almost all ethnic groups provided him with a different experience of life. He no longer looked at the world through the confines of rural Zululand. 'One began to be aware that it's not just Zulus that exist; there are other people,' he reflected.

During the vernacular languages period at Bethal, the class would be divided into groups only to reconverge for sciences and other subjects taught in English. This, said Mzala, broadened his conception of the problem as he 'was able to relate with other people from different parts of South Africa'. By the look of things, Mzala adjusted well to the new surroundings and the way of life at Bethel College. He played piano and the organ in the school church, and was also a member of many groups, sometimes as the lead singer, with friends such as Xolo Mfeka.[27] Renowned South African playwright, composer, director and producer Gibson Kente, schooled at Bethel College, remembered the school for its singing. He said: 'There was so much singing there – there were trios, quartets...'[28]

As a lead singer, Mzala had a 'beautiful voice' that captured his audience, and played not only piano, but the guitar as well. Mfeka, who hailed from KwaMashu township in Durban, says it was mainly their background and that they were 'homeboys' that brought them closer when he arrived in Bethel College in 1969. Their personalities were, however, quite different. Mzala was an 'extrovert', 'talking but friendly' – unlike Mfeka, who remembers Mzala as a very bright student who should have consistently been on top of his class if he was not 'involved in everything'. Mfeka says there is nothing that Nobleman did not attempt, including soccer, which 'he was not good at', Mfeka adds laughing. 'He read books that had nothing to do with schoolwork.' It is the reading that intrigued Mfeka about Mzala. His reading abilities, says Mfeka, shone through in his essays and debates. 'He was above us.'

Mzala was also artistically gifted and from a young age displayed remarkable poetry-writing skills, a passion he carried through to Bethel. According to Mfeka, Mzala once told everyone he was going to build a gun and actually 'sculpted' one in the wood workshop that resembled an AK-47. But it was his reading and writing that set him above the rest. Mfeka can still visualise the small black hardcover notebook in which Mzala had written copious poems in 1971 and apparently submitted for publication. His dream was to have his own anthology published, and Mfeka says they were amazed at his astuteness, that he even knew where and how to submit. At the ages of 12 and 15, his poems were published in two anthologies: *Inkwanzi*, edited by Professor AC Nkabinde, and *Ugqozi*, by Professor DBZ Ntuli. Mthethwa, who was to become a secondary-school teacher, says some of Mzala's poems were taught in high schools before he even became a high-school pupil himself.

Some of Mzala's poems had a prescient feeling, particularly 'Ngikhumbul' ekhaya' (I miss my home), published in 1971 in *Inkwanzi* in which Mzala foretold his experience as an MK soldier. He wrote:

> Ngikhumbul' umama (I miss my mom)
> Ngikhumbul' ubaba (I miss my dad)
> Ngikhumbul' ugogo (I miss my granny)
>
> Mina ngisezikhotheni (I'm in the bushes)
> Bona bahlel' endlini (They are in the house)
> Mina ngihlal'ezidulini (I'm sitting on the mounds)
> Bona bahlal' ezitulweni (They are sitting on chairs)

The other poem in the same anthology, 'Gwalandini' (You coward), also demonstrates his vision as a fearless freedom fighter.[29] Some of his poems, however, reveal a romantic imagination; Dumisani recalls fondly and with a naughty smile the poem 'Esifubeni Sikamame' (On the lady's breast), published in *Ugqozi* in 1975. In the same collection were poems too, like 'Zingelosi Zezulu Ngihanqeni' (Heavenly angels guide me), 'Siyazama Siyehluleka' (We try and fail), 'Masiye Eceleni Komfula' (Let's go by the river) and 'Ubusika Wubusuku' (Winter is night).[30] These poems, some with deep and idealistic religious undertones, reveal Mzala's thought processes at this stage of his life.

For the first couple of years at Bethel, Mzala appears to have been generally well behaved. Because the students were only allowed home once a year, during the June holidays, his family would take a road trip to the Eastern Cape to visit him and, later, his sister, Phasha, when she enrolled at the school. These were memorable times for the young Titi and Dumisani, their mother preparing the best meals for their visits.

V

As we have seen, Mzala's love of books can probably be attributed to Sethi's influence. Sethi collected and kept books on a variety of subjects, including criminal law, to which the young Mzala helped himself. Mfeka says Mzala was reading stuff not prescribed at school, including his father's legal volumes, after which he would 'pretend to be a lawyer'. Titi says Mzala's bedroom was full of all manner of books, including banned literature, a memory shared by Phasha, who remembers that he was surrounded by books where he slept. Wherever he was, he was always carrying something to read, says Phasha: 'He read everything he came across.' It is unclear where and how Mzala got those books, but he would share them with his siblings and children from the neighbourhood, and thereby introduced them to politics too. He also kept company with friends interested in reading and political discussions.

One of those friends was Bongani Khumalo, whose family was originally from Ngoje before they were evicted from a white farm.[31] Whenever Mzala was in Vryheid, he would visit the Khumalo house in Bhekuzulu township, where they spent hour after hour discussing politics. Although they did not belong to any formal 'structures', Khumalo says, what brought them together was their love of reading. He particularly remembers the book by Bruno Mtolo *The Road to the Left*; Mzala used it as a basis from which to challenge the system. 'At that age, without structures, we led an active political life that challenged the system.'[32]

Mthethwa says Mzala's association with people such as Khumalo and Bamba Ndwandwe from Sihlengeni was clearly political. Whenever Khumalo came, says Mthethwa, they would open files and get into deep discussions. Phasha recalls that Ndwandwe would often arrive at night and they would switch off the lights and chat in the dark. Although Ndwandwe was rather loud, Phasha says she still could not hear what exactly they were discussing. Predictably, Ndwandwe also ended up in exile. Dumisani would later meet up with him in Tanzania, where he played an important supportive role for Dumisani when facing his own challenges in exile.

Growing up, Mzala had an inquisitive and questioning mind. This was also true of his younger siblings, to whom he was immensely influential. He was the big brother they looked up to and, true to form, he never disappointed. When he returned from Bethel, every evening after his parents went to bed, recalls Titi, Mzala would go to the children's bedroom with a radio; he and his siblings would then sit around and listen to Radio Freedom. Says Titi: 'We loved that moment. I think it was somewhere around 7:30 in the evening; we all knew that our time is up, and we have to gather and get hold of each other.' As Radio Freedom played, Mzala would animatedly explain all the terms and provide context. Phasha says that the first time they did this, they were concerned that their parents would find out, but Mzala persisted, and they ended up learning all the Radio Freedom songs, such as '*Bahleli bonke etilongweni / Bahleli bonke kwaNongqongqo*'. She says Mzala 'would almost go into a trance'.

Titi can still remember the news that the ANC offered as an alternative to what they were fed by local radio stations. She remembers 'the news and the introduction of the ANC, what was really happening in the country, and why the ANC was fighting for freedom'. Certainly, Radio Freedom performed a vital role in countering the propaganda of the apartheid regime.[33] Through this platform, the ANC was able to speak directly to South Africans and, in the process, influence many young minds, among them Mzala and his siblings. Once they had finished listening, Mzala would take over and explain the struggle, all the while encouraging them to ask questions. He insisted that they always think critically and question things before accepting them. '[We] really got politicised and he would tell us about Albert Luthuli and how he died,' says Titi.

Throughout this period, however, Mzala had a premonition that he was not going to live long. He repeated this statement to his young audience countless times. No one took him seriously, says Titi. She doubts that even Mzala himself really believed it. His siblings thought he was just being melodramatic. Now, with the benefit of hindsight, Titi concedes that 'maybe he knew what was inside him'. Perhaps, she suspects, he anticipated skipping the country and fighting in the liberation war.

VI

At Bethel College, the student population was black, but some of the teachers were white. Although the school was premised on the Christian faith, which taught equality, it practised segregation. It is here that Mzala also experienced the racial dichotomy first hand. Students were acutely aware that the teachers lived in separate bungalows, allocated according to race. The students came from Christian families where they had been given a good moral education by their parents, and yet here they were in an environment that contradicted the very foundation of that teaching.

It wasn't long, however, before the students discovered that black teachers were not getting the same salary as their white counterparts, and so they decided to strike in solidarity. In 1971, at the age of 16, Mzala was the ringleader of the strike. He was very good at mobilising, and was seen as an agitator with clear thought and language skills that allowed him to articulate the problem in a convincing way. The school's management reacted swiftly and called the police to quell the strike. Mzala and another student who helped organise the strike were summarily dismissed. That student was Vuyani Ntshangase, who was a class ahead but became close to Mzala because they shared a dormitory. Ntshangase says he was not around when the strike started, but upon his return he got 'briefed by Nobleman and I got myself entangled' in the whole saga. Just like Mzala, says Ntshangase, he was talkative and hence they 'were instrumental in putting across the complaints of the students to the management'.

School management was, however, firm. Ntshangase was given the option of either leaving voluntarily (assisted with a transfer report) or be expelled. He was in the middle of his matric and so he opted for the former. That was the last time he saw Mzala. In hindsight, Ntshangase believes they had no business poking their noses into those issues. Mzala was not only expelled but was also detained for two weeks – a record that would come back to haunt him later. Although Mfeka was not around when the strike took place, he was not surprised when he learnt that Mzala was involved. 'He was brave, but very respectful.'

Even though another student was expelled along with Mzala, he was the only one to be detained without trial and interrogated by the police's Special Branch. At the heart of the interrogation was his political affiliation. 'I was not politically affiliated at that stage,' said Mzala, 'although I had a very close friend who was slightly older than me at the time, who I guess had some influence in one's development – it was Abram Tiro.' Tiro was already wanted by the Security Branch for his involvement in the Black Consciousness Movement (BCM) via organisations such as the South African Students' Organisation (SASO), the Black People's Convention (BPC) and the South African Students' Movement (SASM). Tiro was eventually killed on 1 February 1974, when he opened a parcel bomb in Botswana.[34] It is little wonder that the line of questioning against Mzala focused primarily on Tiro.

According to Mzala, Tiro was not at school at the time, but he visited periodically and they became very close. Although Mfeka was unaware of their friendship, he remembers Tiro as a member of the Seventh Day Adventist church who frequently visited some older guys at the school. Apparently, Tiro had wanted to study theology at Bethel since the college was considered South Africa's 'Mecca of black Adventism'.[35] However, Mfeka is not surprised by the duo's association. 'Nobleman was politically aware,' he says, '[and] we were not at his level. We only picked up these things at varsity.'

When Mzala was expelled in 1971, he had just received his junior certificate (JC or Standard 8) and was in the middle of Standard 9. On his release, his father drove all the way to the Eastern Cape to collect him. Sethi had spoken to an old friend, the principal of Dlangezwa High School,

Dr Sibusiso Bhengu, and the following year Mzala's life as a student of Dlangezwa began. Bhengu immediately took a liking to the young Mzala and took him under his wing. He understood the boy and sought to channel his energies. They would maintain their friendship until the end. Years later, when Bhengu was based in Geneva and Mzala in London, they would visit each other.

VII

Founded in 1969 by Sibusiso Bhengu – who would become the Minister of Education in 1994 during Nelson Mandela's presidency[36] – Dlangezwa High seemed the perfect place to focus the troublesome young Mzala. The school is located just under 20 kilometres from Empangeni in KwaDlangezwa, not far from the University of Zululand. Importantly, it was famous for its good academic results and strict discipline and orderliness, thus attracting a number of students from well-off families.[37]

It is here that Mzala met Vusi Mavimbela. 'I became close to a student called Nobleman Jabulani Nxumalo,' says Mavimbela, who describes him as 'a short man with a square head [who] was light in complexion for someone born in the heart of KwaZulu. He also had sharp facial features that suggested Khoisan ancestry. He had an impressive athletic physique with a well-toned upper body. Nobleman boasted a brown belt in karate, one of his main hobbies.' Many others describe Mzala along similar lines, as 'an irrepressible character' who spoke non-stop and was always involved in debates. According to Mavimbela, Mzala 'had a voracious intellectual appetite'. The fact that both Mzala and Mavimbela came from the same region of AbaQulusi strengthened their bond. They were 'homeboys'.

Former schoolmate Hlengiwe Mgabadeli says many at the school were in awe of this light-skinned and intelligent guy although they were not sure which school he had come from. What was clear, however, was that this guy was way ahead of them. 'He knew things that we didn't know,' she recalls. As a member of the debating society, Mzala would unleash far-advanced content that made him stand out from the rest. But it was his character rather than his stature that made it impossible for people to miss him. In fact, he was a tiny man, but always raised his views forcefully and loudly, confined by neither his environment nor his circumstance.[38] For Mzala, recalls Mavimbela, it did not matter 'whether you are in a bus, classroom, lecture room or in a student meeting', he would always speak his mind. He was inquisitive, constantly searching for the essence of life and the meaning of truth, says Mavimbela. 'What distinguished him from the rest of us was his questioning and probing mind; he was most fearless, most constant and most robust.'[39]

Mzala was always involved in debates and discussions, especially political ones. That Dlangezwa was a conservative institution aligned to Inkatha politics mattered little to him. There were few teachers who demonstrated independent thinking; the majority, together with management, were loyal to the ideas and politics of Buthelezi. Also, the dominant thinking of the student body was informed by the fact that most of them came from prominent families aligned to the government of KwaZulu. Thus, the school was seen as a breeding ground and place of academic nurturing of African intellectuals for KwaZulu.[40]

True to his character, it did not take long for Mzala to critically analyse the political environment of Dlangezwa High. Eventually, he concluded that its 'Bantustanisation' by the headmaster, Mr Mthiyane, and his management was a problem. Mthiyane was Bhengu's deputy and had taken over the running of the school when Bhengu went abroad to pursue his doctoral studies. Typically, Mzala was not prepared to keep quiet about what he perceived as conservative politics permeating the school, and looked for opportunities to politicise fellow students. Mzala, as Mavimbela recalls, 'would talk whether we are in the shower, in the morning, he will make a lot of noise about what is happening'. One of his strategies was to dramatise the words of Julius Caesar, an act that he employed effectively to drive his message home. Mzala 'was no fool', according to Mavimbela. His recital 'was not just an innocent prank of a capricious student' but rather a political performance.

Mzala's advantage was thus his bold character, which enabled him to say the truth that many were too shy or scared to confront. Always restless, Mavimbela says there was nothing modest about him, his preferred stage for his disguised political speeches being the morning showers when most male students were present.

> He would get out of the shower, wrap a towel around his lower body and jump onto the cement table. With his right hand raised in a clenched fist, he would recite in a loud voice: 'Cowards die many times before their deaths; the valiant never taste of death but once. Of all the wonders that I yet have heard, it seems to me most strange that men should fear, seeing that death, a necessary end, will come when it will

come.' Then he would jump onto the floor and run to his dormitory. His cameo performance had a hugely dramatic effect: it left those who saw it hankering for more.[41]

There is no doubt in Mavimbela's mind that this was a deliberate political message by Mzala to challenge his fellow students to wake up and confront the Bantustanisation of the school. By this time, Mzala – already an ardent consumer of political material – was a seasoned political campaigner, having been exposed to SASO politics at Bethel College through leaders such as Tiro.

While others, especially his dormitory mates, would have experienced a radical and, to some extent, angry young man, some – like Mgabadeli – experienced the other side: a calm and quiet Mzala. 'You will never meet Mzala angry, he was always joyful. You would meet him talking to himself,' says Mgabadeli. She experienced him not as talkative but rather as a deeply religious person who played the organ and piano for the school church choir. His love of singing, instilled by his parents through church, never waned, and he quickly integrated himself into the school's music culture. Many knew him for his favourite song, 'I don't know why Jesus loves me; I don't know why he cares'.

VIII

In the late 1960s a form of radical Christianity known as liberation theology emerged in Latin America. At the heart of this movement was the belief that many social ills were due to capitalism and Latin America could thus be liberated by a socialist revolution.[42] This view emerged at the same time as the black liberation theology tradition whose roots can be traced back to the civil rights activism of the 1960s and drew inspiration from leaders such as the Reverend Martin Luther King Jr and Malcolm X. The understanding was that God was concerned with the poor and the weak. With Christianity, in particular, viewed in the context of overcoming oppression, the theology focused on the injustices perpetuated against African-Americans suffering as a result of segregation, and black South Africans under apartheid.[43]

This theology left an impression on the young Mzala, and was further enhanced by his fascination with the rich and ancient history of the Ethiopian Orthodox Church. From this perspective, he imagined that African people are likely to have played a meaningful role in the origination of Christianity. Thus, he 'derived inspiration from the thought that

Ethiopians, the adherents of this great Christian faith and tradition, had never been colonised and [had] defeated the invading Europeans powers', says Mavimbela.

Over a decade later, Mzala admitted to Julie Frederikse that his parents' Christian teachings were what opened his eyes to the social injustices in South Africa. He also pointed out that 'to a certain extent the struggle of black Americans had its own influence – there were people who identified more with fellows like Eldridge Cleaver and maybe even Malcom X'. Mzala found a 'close cultural affinity' to the struggle of black Americans whose books were freely available in South Africa at the time.[44] So it was that Mzala came into politics on the back of a strong Christian philosophy and thus, by the time he arrived at Dlangezwa, 'he was already very strong on politics and religion,' says Mavimbela. This grounding, combined with his natural ability to absorb complex concepts easily, distinguished Mzala from the rest. Although they were not in the same class, Mavimbela does not hesitate to point out that Mzala was indeed 'a very intelligent person'.

Already politically active, Mzala never compromised his strong activism in the Student Christian Movement (SCM). He was very enthusiastic about his faith and participated in every aspect of the Christian movement. Interestingly, Mzala was also passionate about infusing Africanist ideology into Christianity. Mavimbela posits that Mzala pushed the boundaries on the religious question, hinting that 'Jesus might have been black'. In fact, he went even further, suggesting that even Moses might have been black and that these biblical characters might have come from Africa. Years later, when Mavimbela was deployed to Egypt, he discovered that there was indeed a basis to Mzala's argument. To this day, this debate has not been closed; for instance, the Lemba people still claim to be the 'black Jews' of South Africa.[45]

It was thus clear to anyone who interacted with Mzala that his views on Christianity and his active participation in the SCM were the foundation that anchored his determination and involvement in the liberation struggle. For Mzala, Christianity provided a safe landing, if not an entry into politics. Even at the stage where he was consuming political material such as the SASO newsletters and many other political materials, he continued to walk around the school carrying books on black theology.

Whenever Mzala was involved in debates, they proved to be lively. He was not a banal speaker, and made debates come alive with well-thought-out, well-researched and well-argued points. During many debates in the dormitory or student hall, whether social or political, Mzala freely quoted from the Bible to back up his arguments. Even then, as far back as their student lives, Mavimebla was amazed by Mzala's ability to refer to the lives of Marcus Garvey, Malcom X and Martin Luther King Jr with ease. Uncompromising when making his point, his arguments were often marshalled 'by a good dose of biblical scriptures'.

Mzala was popular not only in the boys' dormitory for his dramatisation of Julius Caesar, but in the girls' dormitory too. Many young women admired him for his discipline. 'He was never in the group to be punished' for poor schoolwork or bad behaviour, recalls Mgabadeli. Also, he was never spotted in the smoking corner. He was polite and squeaky clean, and would 'never ever pass you without greeting'. Mavimbela says his friend was also extremely disciplined; he never consumed alcohol and did not smoke, but rather focused on his rigorous karate training regime. For a handsome and popular guy with 'well-toned and chiseled muscles', he did not have time for girls.

Mgabadeli believes there was something unique about Mzala. 'There was something inside him that was dictating to him how to behave and we did not have time to sit down and say tell us more about yourself before you came to kwaDlangezwa.' To Mavimbela, 'there was something in the way Mzala's brain was wired that made his mind run on overdrive and with the endurance of a mule'. Not that this did not bother the young man himself, however; in fact, Mzala worried about his inability to stop reading. Phasha says he once told his mother that he needed to be admitted to hospital so that he could just sleep because he could not stop reading. His mind was not only enquiring but, throughout his life, he challenged injustice wherever it reared its head.

IX

Mgabadeli believes that, prior to Bhengu's sabbatical, Mzala had a good time at Dlangezwa. He participated in all school activities, including being in the dishing team in the dining hall, and he became a prefect. 'Mzala was a colourful guy,' says Vuso Shabalala, who was a year behind him at Dlangezwa.[46] He remembers Mzala as one of the senior prefects involved in the SCM. Shabalala, who was younger than Mzala and 'a country boy going to boarding school for the first time', looked up to him as someone who played a prominent role in the student body. 'He was popular, although I did not know him personally.' Like so many others, Shabalala recalls that Mzala's singing ability and his piano skills were quite polished.

But things seemed to change when Mthiyane took over. Suddenly, 'we were punished for speaking isiZulu at school'. Mgabadeli is not surprised that there was a strike soon after Bhengu left because 'things were never the same'. She indicates that 'things that we used to tolerate at high school became intolerable'. It is apparent that Mthiyane was not only a hard taskmaster but also conservative. 'It was like the army style,' says Mgabadeli.

Mthiyane was also notorious for driving propaganda on behalf of the authorities. He would insist that students listen to the newscasts on the South African Broadcasting Corporation (SABC), particularly the 'commentary that was done by one SABC white guy', says Shabalala. For much of the time, he couched his propaganda as part of his English lessons, and would ask if there were any words that students did not understand. Typically, Mzala would retort by pointing out that 'the things that this guy is saying are not correct, black people are oppressed, we don't have a voice', Shabalala recalls. Politically, Mzala was streets ahead of his peers; 'he was already politically conscious, which I classified as matured at that stage'. Shabalala says many of his mates, himself included, were not really politicised – unlike Mzala, who was clearly 'already involved in some kind of organisational political activities'.

Mavimbela, too, remembers Mzala as a voracious reader who, as soon as he had finished a book, was 'ready for the next book he could lay his hands on'. Of course, a handful of progressive students, like Mavimbela, shared a similar political perspective with Mzala and so they were drawn to each other. Mzala became close to like-minded and progressive students like Mavimbela, who were not loud and thus would not express their views as vociferously as others. His radical views were, however, well known. Mavimbela believes Mzala 'became an undeclared leader of the student body because he'll speak where nobody else was prepared to stick out the neck'.

From early on, Mzala made his intentions clear: that Dlangezwa High needed to change. He used every opportunity to articulate this view – always, of course, in a well-calculated manner 'without saying let's go and strike', but he did not hesitate to point out what was wrong with the institution, says Mavimbela. Suddenly, everyone was talking about 'Nobleman'. By that time, Mzala was sharing the SASO newsletter with other progressive students. Against Mavimbela's advice, he audaciously decided to expand the network of the newsletter, and began sharing the newsletter with a wider group of students. Clearly, argues Mavimbela, 'His mission was to instigate a student strike that would challenge regulations that the students found oppressive.'

Once Mzala had pinpointed what was wrong with the institution, students 'began to challenge the authorities on a number of issues, including the quality of food, tough dormitory regulations and the behaviour of boarding masters and matrons'. Mzala did not even have to call for a strike; the students rose organically and challenged the institution simply because they were 'completely fed up'. Among the issues that angered students was the practice of opening their letters and the quality of the food. However, the discontent was largely about the manner in which the institute was run, which included 'very strict' rules that left little room 'for any freedom for students to do whatever they wanted to do', says Mavimbela.

The students saw the opening of letters not only as an invasion of their privacy 'but also as a mechanism to monitor our political communications on behalf of the apartheid regime', recalls Mavimbela. Mzala thus seized this opportunity to 'infuse the spontaneous strike with purpose and greater political content'. While Shabalala was not involved in organising the strike, he says students decided to 'march inside the school premises'. Shabalala concurs that they were aggrieved by 'corporal punishment and the reading of our letters before passing them on to us'.

However, meticulous planning meant that not many students were aware of the brewing strike. Even though the path to the boys' dormitory passed the girls' dormitory, they were kept largely in the dark. 'I think they didn't want to talk to us … maybe they looked down on us, I don't know,' says Mgabadeli. She is of the view that things fell apart when Bhengu, who had an uncanny knack for handling students' issues, left the school. 'We would never think of striking at the time of Professor Bhengu,' whom students held in high regard and believed that even the food was better when he had been around.

X

Mzala had apparently not bargained for a violent strike, and when things got out of hand he was genuinely frightened. When it was clear that the strike would turn ugly, he made numerous attempts to quell the situation, but to no avail. The students had reached a point of no return and were determined to address their grievances forcefully. Mavimbela says a group 'led by a student called Mqwebu' had acquired an assortment of weapons such as 'pangas, tomahawks and axes and ran amok looking for Mthiyane and Mphemba'. According to Phasha, Mzala had also taken his father's sword without his knowledge, claiming later that it was for self-protection. At that point, it had dawned on Mzala that, as a recognised leader of students, he would eventually be held liable. He made a quick calculation and decided not to participate in the protest action, and instead went back to his dormitory. 'We both feared for the lives of Mthiyane and Mphemba,' says Mavimbela.

According to Mavimbela, even before the strike took place, Mthiyane already saw Mzala as someone who was 'going to bring about instability in the institution, so when the strike happened, it was easy to isolate him'. Shabalala's recollection is that the majority of the students participated in the strike, with 'very few' choosing to remain in their dormitories. When the strike was over, a considerable amount of damage had been inflicted on the school's infrastructure.

Naturally, the police were called to disperse the students, and promptly arrived armed with guns and dogs which they let loose on the students. Those who were unlucky were at the receiving end of sjamboks. 'Others were captured, loaded into police vans and driven to nearby police stations,' says Mavimbela. Even though Mzala had taken a decision, in consultation with Mavimbela, not to take part in the strike so as to avoid being blamed, he was the first to be picked up from the dormitory where he had remained with other students who had not joined the strike. He was questioned and detained.

Other students in the dormitory who had not joined the strike were left untouched; only Mzala was arrested. Mavimbela suspects that some of the students acted 'as informants for the authorities' since 'the school administration and the police already knew the role he [Mzala] had played'. The school management considered Mzala the ringleader. According to Shabalala, when the police came the second time, they interviewed a number of people and it was clear that they had gathered more information from the school authorities on who could have been involved. Several students were thus taken away, including Mzala.

The school was subsequently shut down for two weeks and when it reopened a number of students were summoned to the principal's office. Among them was Mzala, his friend Manqoba Nyembezi, Shabalala and, not unsurprisingly, Mqwebu. They were summarily expelled for their involvement. Shabalala says, 'It was put to me that I played an active role in the strike. Yes, I admit and that I did not cut my hair and then I was expelled.' Mzala had thus managed to influence the first violent strike in the history of Dlangezwa High School. He later, almost nonchalantly, told Frederikse that he was also expelled from Dlangezwa, although for different reasons as Bethel College, but they 'also move from the same basis'. He hastened to add that he was charged and put on trial with 40 other students for public violence.

Apart from the backward practices by the school's authorities – opening students' letters and forcing them to listen to SABC radio propaganda – Mzala had managed to use these issues to politicise the student body. Mavimbela says Mzala was instrumental in infusing into their demands a more cogent political argument about the institution. 'It was no accident that the authorities later identified him as the dangerous mastermind behind the strike.'

Again, through this ordeal, Mzala's father remained extremely supportive. When the students were arrested, the parents got together and requested Manqoba's dad, Aubrey Nyembezi, a respected lawyer, to represent their kids.[47] Titi was too young to fully comprehend the essence of the developments, but recalls Nyembezi coming home and having serious discussions with her parents about the case. Although they had been expelled from school, they escaped with less harsh sanctions from the court and were given a suspended sentence. While he was the youngest of the lot, Phasha says that again Mzala requested to represent himself in court.

XI

The students' strike in Dlangezwa coincided with the 1973 Durban workers' strikes, which attracted close to 100 000 African workers. The apartheid regime and its capitalist class, notorious for discrimination, subjected African workers to low wages, humiliating pass laws, migrant labour, forced removals, and a general denial of basic human rights for black people. The Durban strikes also saw the re-emergence of non-racial trade unions, with African, coloured and Indian workers joining forces. There were, however, various political currents during the strikes, which included the emergence of the Black Consciousness and Africanist movements, demanding African leadership within the unions.[48]

Mzala linked their strike in Dlangezwa to not only the workers' strike, but also the general mood of the country. 'I think to a certain extent we were broadly a manifestation of that rebellion which we were very much acquainted with, although we had our own local grievances,' he said. According to Mzala, they went to trial and were eventually sentenced to six months suspended for three years. Once more, his parents' attempts to get him back on the straight and narrow in order to finish school had come to naught. Instead, he was back home again, having been expelled from yet another school. But that never stopped his father from believing in him. Instead, he was very supportive and patient with what many would have regarded as a wayward child. In fact, he would drive around, talking to friends and looking for schools for Mzala even when his mother was beginning to raise concerns.

Because Mavimbela's mother and Mzala's father were close and worked at the same school, he soon found out that Mzala's parents were arranging for him to write his examinations at another institution. Mavimbela was devastated and felt very bad that his close friend had been expelled, but derived some comfort from the knowledge that he was fine and was going to be able to complete his schooling. Mavimbela kept in contact with Mzala throughout and they would meet during school holidays.

So it was that, that same year, Mzala wrote matric as a 'private candidate', adding three more subjects (Mercantile Law, Criminal Procedure and Evidence, and Introduction to the Theory of Law) to the usual six he was expected to write. He passed all his subjects. Mzala's ability to finish school was never in question. He had breezed through the grades, and while at Bethel College had scooped top honours and distinctions. His parents had instilled in him a disciplined approach to studying from an early age and this was reflected in his outstanding record.

By the time he wrote matric, Mzala was already a member of SASO, having joined in 1973. It was around the same time that he was asked to be involved in the formation of the National Youth Organisation (NAYO) and so participated in the preliminary discussions. Mzala was in the Natal region of the organisation 'with people like Themba Kubheka [and] Mandla Langa'. His location in the northern part of Zululand was a challenge because he could only meet his comrades when he travelled to Durban. He already had close links with SASO in Durban and worked closely with individuals such as Terence Tyrone, Strini Moodley, Saths Cooper, Ralph Mgijima and Nkosazana Dlamini.

In 1974, having passed matric with flying colours, Mzala registered with the famous University of Fort Hare in the Eastern Cape.[49] However, within a week of registration, an incident occurred that he described as 'one of the most interesting things'. He was summoned to the registrar's office where he was made aware that he had been barred from attending a public school. He thus left Fort Hare without ever having been given an opportunity to settle in. He subsequently tried to ascertain the reason behind being barred. It took him a while to finally realise that, after his trial for public violence, the Special Branch police must have submitted his name. The record of his arrest for a strike at Bethel College must also have played a role.

Because he felt he had to do something with his life, Mzala registered as a part-time law student with the University of South Africa (Unisa). The following year he tried to register with the University of Zululand (Ngoye), but was again informed that he had been blocked. 'I was told about the suspended sentence, which was a bit strange because there was no link-up between the suspension to that sentence and my entering a university.' As a result, Mzala had to wait until 1976 before he could be admitted as a full-time student at a public university. 'I kept on applying until I was admitted again at the University of Zululand finally.'

XII

The period Mzala spent at home studying part-time through Unisa gave him ample opportunity to pursue his convictions to challenge apartheid and, in his quest for knowledge, he embarked on a weekly pilgrimage to Vryheid to buy newspapers not available in Louwsburg. That the only bus to Vryheid left Louwsburg in the wee hours and returned in the evening was never a deterrent for Mzala.[50] He also took this opportunity to visit his siblings, Titi and Dumisani, then in a boarding school in Vryheid, to bring them 'goodies'.

But his trips to places like Vryheid were no longer innocent. Mzala had become a political activist and was a man on a mission. He had friends and comrades in Vryheid, and Khumalo says that Mzala's genius in using his love for martial arts and his ability to dance to get closer to people was already beginning to emerge. 'Unlike me,' Khumalo recollected with a laugh, 'Mzala was a good dancer.' He would walk around to meet people and of course talk politics, says Khumalo. He was already an astute operator with a rare ability to immerse himself in the community, taking every opportunity to engage in political debates. Says Nkosi, 'He would become a boxer among the boxers, a karateka among other karateka, a tennis player among tennis players, a soccer player among the soccer players.' His intention was to gain the trust of the people and to politicise them.

He was also spending more and more time reading, writing and talking to people about the oppressive regime. Working with the likes of Khumalo and others in his networks, he arranged for Gibson Kente's musical drama *How Long?* to be staged in Vryheid. Written in Kente's famous township theatre style, this show was overtly political – a response to pressure from BCM structures that all cultural work needed to reflect the material conditions of black people in South Africa.[51] Kente responded positively to Mzala's overtures, bringing his cast to Vryheid while Mzala and his friends went around inviting people and engaging schoolteachers to bring their students. Kente said his performances in Natal townships such as Estcourt, Wembezi, Ladysmith, Dundee, Newcastle and Vryheid were staged in township halls because 'we were not allowed in the cities – we were too "dark" to get into theatres.'[52] Many believe Kente would have never have brought his show to a small town like Vryheid on his own, and are convinced that he was pleasantly surprised by the turnout and the overt nature of political mobilisation. This is the type of work that preoccupied Mzala while he was in Ngoje before he was eventually admitted to the University of Zululand.

Khumalo says that while boys his age were into girls and having fun, Mzala had little time for such mundane issues. He 'was not a womaniser, he was so focused on politics' and the greater ideal of liberating the oppressed majority.

It is apparent that after his Eastern Cape sojourn the Security Branch identified him as a potential troublemaker. One day during his usual trip to Vryheid, two black police officers followed him all the way to Khumalo's house. 'They found us seated and pulled out a book from my bookshelf at home, asked me a few questions and walked out,' says Khumalo. It was not clear what exactly they were after.

It was Bethel College that politicised Mzala. Until he went there, he did not belong to any political organisation or know anything about the ANC. He said, 'I did not know about the ANC in my young days, until I was at the school in the Cape … when I was doing … Standard 7.' But even then, this exposure was broad and related mostly to historical facts about the leaders of the ANC, such as Albert Luthuli, Nelson Mandela, Walter Sisulu, Duma Nokwe and others. The ANC did not register in the life of young Mzala until he began to participate in political debates and discussion, particularly when he joined SASO. It was when Mzala began to participate actively in political debates that 'the ANC began to feature prominently in one's mind as a factor that has to be reckoned with in terms its approach, its ideology and so on,' he said.

This was a period of rapid growth for Mzala. His voracious appetite for books made him stand out from his peers. 'But something that stood out about him is that he was full of knowledge; he gathered knowledge, had a discerning mind and he hated the system,' says Khumalo. Interestingly, Khumalo recalls that at this early stage Mzala was clear that he did not hate white people but rather the system. He 'detested the system' and hence they would find themselves getting involved whenever they experienced a situation where black people were not being treated properly. 'Even on issues of employment, if it involved a domestic worker or a worker in a café,' Khumalo says, they found themselves in the middle of a dispute. Mzala was prepared to take on the system; Khumalo says he was brave enough to confront and rebuke whites and the police for racism. He dazzled them with knowledge and they were often perplexed. Many whites and policemen regarded them as cheeky. Khumalo says that although they were respectful towards people like Mangosuthu Buthelezi whenever they saw them, Mzala was already adamant that Buthelezi's politics were dangerous.

CHAPTER 2

Mzala skips the country for exile

I

In 1976, after two years of being barred from formal education, Mzala was finally admitted to study law at the University of Zululand (Ngoye) where he rekindled his friendship with Vusi Mavimbela. By then, the winds of change were already blowing across southern Africa. The previous year, the Portuguese had been dislodged from Angola and Mozambique. The Soviet-armed People's Movement for the Liberation of Angola (MPLA), ably supported by Cuban troops, had consolidated its hold in the country after repelling rival nationalist organisations and resisting an invasion by the powerful South African Defence Force (SADF), which colluded with the United States of America (USA).[1]

Angolan independence, led by the Marxist MPLA, was to prove important for the South African liberation struggle. The apartheid regime and its backers understood this and so they exploited the divisions within the formerly oppressed groups in Angola through Jonas Savimbi's Union for the Total Independence of Angola (UNITA). In the context of the ongoing Cold War, they played the 'anti-communist' card, with the US funding UNITA against the progressive forces.

The support that UNITA received from the US was premised on its efforts to 'contain the spread of communism in Africa' by countering the support that Angola was getting from the Cuban state and its armed forces.

The imperialists were determined to overthrow the MPLA government because 'it was openly led by a Marxist-Leninist party and was fully supported by the former Soviet Union and its allies within the world socialist system'.[2] This conflict continued well into the 1980s, culminating in the battle of Cuito Cuanavale, whose victory is widely celebrated in the liberation movement. In the final analysis, Angola's revolutionary support for South West Africa People's Organisation (SWAPO) and the ANC was bound to place it in perpetual military conflict with the racist apartheid government and the US.

On the east coast of the southern Africa subcontinent, the Front for the Liberation of Mozambique (Frelimo) had led the people of Mozambique to victory against the Portuguese colonial power. Of concern for the regime in Pretoria was not only the proximity of these developments to South Africa, but that these organisations were the close allies of the ANC. While the Soviet Union provided material support to the ANC, including arms for its military wing whose members were already infiltrating the country, Angola had become a battleground for the ANC's armed wing, Umkhonto we Sizwe (MK) and the apartheid government.[3]

These developments in the region were a setback for the apartheid regime desperate to rein in the internal revolt on the home front, and so the Minister of Education declared any inter-university or student organisation 'undesirable' if its activities were deemed to be political. This was primarily targeted at organisations such as National Union of South African Students (NUSAS). Founded in 1924 with the aim of representing and promoting the interests of university and college students, NUSAS had morphed into a non-racial organisation and vocal critic of apartheid. Although Steve Biko's South African Students' Organisation (SASO) had broken away from NUSAS in 1970, citing 'white domination', NUSAS remained a force. In the mid-1970s, SASO was also being suppressed by the regime, its leaders charged under the Terrorism Act following the 'Viva Frelimo' rallies organised by the Black People's Convention (BPC) after Mozambique obtained independence.[4] NUSAS, however, endured, and in the 1980s it not only forged alliances with the United Democratic Front (UDF) and the Congress of South African Students (COSAS), but also arranged meetings with the banned ANC.[5]

The emergence of the Black Consciousness Movement (BCM) as a political force had neverthless reinvigorated South African liberation politics in the 1970s. This revival, a push of national liberation, came in the context of a lull after the ANC suffered a number of setbacks in the preceding decade. Following its banning in 1960 and the Rivonia Trial in 1963–64, which ended with the incarceration of most of its top leaders on Robben Island, and some leaders already having fled the country, the ANC had been decimated internally. 'Naturally,' as ANC President Oliver Tambo would later posit, 'the ANC had to define its attitude towards this force.' Indeed, the ANC took a positive attitude towards BCM and embraced its emergence.

In its 1973 statement, the ANC noted the emergence of 'a number of black organisations whose programmes, by espousing the democratic, anti-racist positions that the ANC fights for, identify them as part of the genuine forces of the revolution'. It went further to emphasise its ideological posture, however, by highlighting that this political formation needed to consider that:

> The assertion of the national identity of the oppressed black peoples is not the end in itself. It can be a vital force of the revolutionary action involving the masses of the people. For it is in the struggle, in the actual physical confrontation with the enemy, that the people gain a lasting confidence in their own strength and in the inevitability of final victory – it is through action that the people acquire true psychological emancipation.[6]

By 1976, the vast number of anti-apartheid activities taking place in the country intersected with the BCM ideology. Students' political activists particularly were steeped in this ideological current. Black Consciousness was thus the dominant ideological current of the day.

II

Located in the heartland of Zululand, a stone's throw from Dlangezwa High School, Ngoye – in terms of its cultural outlook – was no different to Dlangezwa. Although the students, including the *skomvans*[7] from Transvaal, came from all walks of life, most of the student body was conservative. According to Mavimbela, there was a growing Inkatha influence on campus, which included aspects of vigilantism that started to isolate students from outside KwaZulu, accusing them of anti-Inkatha, anti-Zulu and anti-Buthelezi propaganda.[8]

Of course, this was an era of rampant narrow ethnic nationalism driven largely by the apartheid regime and its bantustan policy. The Bantu

Authorities Act of 1951 had been rejected by most progressive African leaders, with Chief Albert Luthuli, then Natal Provincial President of the ANC, saying: 'It does not seem that the government has any intention of leading the African people along the road of intelligent democracy.'[9] Essentially, the bantustan model entrenched ethnic nationalism that divided the African people, and led to many seeing 'themselves primarily as members of an ethnic group rather than as South Africans'.[10]

In this context, the rising tide of the trade union movement in Natal in the early 1970s and black students' involvement in SASO represented the re-emergence of progressive politics in the province. Mzala would later write that this left Buthelezi in an invidious position. 'He found himself under serious political attack from many quarters', and 'in order to bolster his increasingly challenged national political role, he decided to create an organisational power base, outside of the legal framework of the bantustans, with which to confront critics of his political positions'.[11]

To this end, Buthelezi 'formally launched the Inkatha Cultural Liberation Movement to fan Zulu nationalism and pledge allegiance to him',[12] and this inevitably clashed with progressive anti-apartheid forces. The violence in KwaZulu-Natal from this period, which extended well into the 1990s, cannot be understood outside of this context. It is unsurprising, therefore, that within the first decade of its existence, Inkatha was linked to a number of violent events, including some inside Ngoye. In 1983, for instance, five students aligned to the UDF were killed at the University of Zululand by Inkatha members.[13]

The attacks linked to Inkatha are reminiscent of the scenes of the Matebele tribe in Sol Plaatje's book *Mhudi*. 'In all the tales of battle I have ever read, or heard of, the cause of the war is invariably ascribed to the other side,' writes Plaatje. 'Similarly,' he continues, 'we have been taught almost from childhood to fear the Matebela – a fierce nation – so unreasoning in its ferocity that it will attack any individual or tribe at sight, without the slightest provocation.'[14]

In 1983 – and without the slightest provocation, reported the media – 'Zulu warriors' pounced on unsuspecting students. The *Sunday Tribune* of 30 October 1983 reported that the students were 'eating [a] leisurely Saturday breakfast' when 'Zulu warriors armed with spears, cowhide shields, kierries and battle-axes slipped on to the campus chanting and singing'. Most students, as the *Sunday Times* of 6 November 1983 reported, 'ran into the closest hostels and barricaded themselves in bedrooms' but the unrelenting Zulu warriors stormed inside and attacked them.[15]

III

Mzala and his old friend Mavimbela had maintained communication throughout the time Mzala was outside formal educational institutions. They were by now seasoned SASO activists, and quite logically they gravitated towards the students from the Transvaal. 'Nobleman and I made friends with them, so we also had to be isolated and possibly beaten up as well,' recalls Mavimbela. Typical of Mzala, he started pointing out what was wrong with the university and with some of the students, especially those aligned to bantustan politics. True to his character, Mzala made many friends at Ngoye.

Ngoye boasted a number of political societies and an active SASO branch, which suited 'political animals' like Mzala, but a large part of the student body was not active. Mavimbela says that only 'a small section of the university' was into politics. In fact, many were from KwaZulu-Natal and were quite conservative. So, unlike at Dlangezwa, where Mzala had managed to mobilise students against the authorities, Ngoye proved a different kettle of fish. This was an institution of higher learning with senior students at postgraduate level, some completing their doctorates. These students, according to Mavimbela, assumed they knew better than 'this newcomer trying to mobilise them'. This is often the case in institutions where senior students believe they have superior knowledge and are better educated than newcomers.

But Mzala was still the same 'Nobleman' of Dlangezwa High – 'vocal and active at pointing out all the things that were wrong with the institution,' says Mavimbela. Although the majority of Ngoye's student body was conservative, this did not deter Mzala from moving full steam ahead in challenging the status quo even when it was against the advice of his friend. Mavimbela tried to reason that this was a different institution, with people going to the library all the time, and that he needed to be cautious. 'You can see they don't like what you are saying,' urged Mavimbela, 'and you are not going to start a strike here when you have just arrived and you are a first-year student.'

Mzala paid no attention. He went ahead anyway, trying to mobilise students. Vuso Shabalala, who had been a year behind Mzala at Dlangezwa High, now found himself in the same class as Mzala, both enrolled for constitutional law. 'This time we ended up talking,' says Shabalala and so Mzala 'was aware of my existence'. They were now both active in SASO and, Shabalala believes, Mzala had been informed about the role that he had played in the strike at Dlangezwa High, and so 'he regarded me as a comrade'.

But similar challenges as at Dlangezwa existed at Ngoye, if not worse. Shabalala recalls an Afrikaner lecturer 'who was quite provocative'. Apparently, right at the beginning of the year he gleefully told the class that only about 10 per cent of them would pass. He was also forceful in the manner he presented and defended the apartheid constitution. 'I remember one of the debates he started was on the separate but equal debate,' and these views, says Shabalala, left many students hot under the collar. The class also included a couple of senior students who were already doing third-year modules and, together with Mzala, they would challenge him.

To many newcomers, such as Blade Nzimande, Mzala was to be admired and, because of the way he asserted himself, they thought he was an old student. 'Mzala was very vocal and, as a result, I thought he was a third- or fourth-year student, only to find out that he was a first-year student,' says Nzimande. They were left bemused as to how a first-year student could be so vocal, 'because to me that is where I got my first political baptism'.

With Mzala, what you saw is what you got. His aggressive and uncompromising style of debating won him friends and foes in equal measure. It was only a matter of time, as Mavimbela puts it, before his 'uncompromising and outspoken personality began to attract good and bad attention'. An incident Mavimbela thought hilarious occurred when a much bigger student than Mzala decided to take matters into his own hands – literally. Mzala, who may have gone overboard in driving his point home, was badly beaten. During a debate, says Mavimbela, Mzala 'stuck to his arguments with the ferocity and tenacity of a bull terrier and often left injured souls on the debating floor'. However, the beating proved to be just a temporary setback for Mzala, and it wasn't long before he was back agitating.

Mzala had also not abandoned his activism in the Christian movement. While his friends busied themselves with soccer and jazz sessions, Mzala would spend his weekends at church gatherings. He remained active and never missed church activities. As Mavimbela puts it, '[for] Nobleman politics was infused with Christianity. When you talk politics, he would quote the Bible from time to time to support his argument.' Mzala was also a teetotaller who 'frowned at smoking and drinking'; he could not stand the jazz sessions where alcohol flowed freely. Occasionally, he tried to join but that would never last long.

IV

When he came to Ngoye, Mzala was already a member of SASO. He had also been involved in the formation of the National Youth Organisation, where he had close links with senior SASO activists. In his first year at university, he told Frederikse, he 'was an office-bearer in SASO'. This took his campus activism further afield. As an office-bearer, he attended seminars that involved students from other institutions.

Not only did these events leave an impression on him, but they further shaped his ideological perspective and growth. For example, he cited an event held at Ngoye where well-known poet and writer Mafika Pascal Gwala addressed students. They were in the habit of dressing in black when attending these meetings, but Gwala challenged them, emphasising that 'we are sufficiently black to add black clothes and other things'. Essentially, the point was that the struggle was not about 'black power but power to the people'. This left an impression on Mzala because it demonstrated the diversity of views within the BCM. 'There was no homogeneous or monolithic approach ideologically,' he said.

Mzala was one of two delegates representing the university's SASO branch, along with his local president Jerry Shongwe, at a seminar at the University of Natal to discuss the Freedom Charter. The seminar was organised by Terence 'Trixie' Tyrone at Wentworth campus and was attended by delegates from all the black campuses, including Turfloop campus of the University of the North and Fort Hare. While there were divergent views, 'particularly on the clause that South Africa belongs to all who live in it', Mzala said the meeting concluded by affirming the SASO policy that 'SASO is not anti-white but pro-black'.

It is not an exaggeration to say that Mzala spent most of his short stint at Ngoye debating politics rather than in the lecture halls. It is on this terrain that his ideological development was taking place, and it was at these meetings that he and his comrades grappled with the South African national question. At the Wentworth seminar, he said, they eventually came to the conclusion that they were striving for an inclusive South Africa 'where black and white will be able to be equals and where we'd have a fair share in the processes of political administration and the wealth of the country'. 'In other words,' he continued, 'we're striving for a non-racial society.'

It did not escape him that they, as black students, had organised themselves, and that this 'had a certain tactical relevance which had its own background'. For Mzala, it was important that black students go through this process themselves, alone, so that they could emerge as a coherent political constituency and organisation. Just like everything Mzala did, his political development was rapid in the context of the political upheavals of 1976. In hindsight, he indicated that when looking at society, his premise was 'initially humanist' and 'hence the strong moral factor'.

The political and ideological development of Mzala's generation was strongly influenced by the need to contend with the racial paradox. While having to respond to contemporary challenges as an oppressed black nation subjugated to white domination, they had to contend with the question of the involvement of white people in the struggle. 'How do we relate to the white person who is in jail, who died in jail – and, by the way, Bram Fischer died during our time of struggle,' reflected Mzala. During this time they had to respond to the question of people like Denis Goldberg and Raymond Suttner. Goldberg had been one of the Rivonia Trialists following their arrest at Liliesleaf Farm in 1963,[16] while Suttner was a political prisoner sentenced for ANC underground activities between 1975 and 1983.[17]

To emphasise this point on how they came to perceive non-racism, Mzala juxtaposed Bram Fischer, a revered Afrikaner revolutionary and freedom fighter, with Kaiser Matanzima and Mangosuthu Buthelezi, two traditional and bantustan leaders largely regarded as collaborators with the apartheid regime. Mzala and others of the 1976 generation, as well as those who came before and after, had to grapple with the fundamental question of race. Even before Mzala could skip the country, where he officially joined the ANC and the SACP, he was already clear on the national question and the non-racial character of the struggle.

V

When Mavimbela and Mzala eventually reunited in 1976, their resolve to skip the country became stronger. Though they differed on the timing, both had made up their minds. It was only a matter of time. By 1976 not only had Mzala been involved in the struggle for a while, in a sense, he said, 'we were already trying to find ways out', and 'by that time I had been detained three different times at three different places'. For Mzala and his generation, it was simply not enough to 'burn tables in meetings'; they were now looking for a way to make a more meaningful contribution. So leaving was by now an inevitability. Mzala's political activities were partly a preparation for him to achieve this objective, but he still had a burning desire to lead a strike at Ngoye, a satisfaction he had not fulfilled at Dlangezwa High. Mavimbele says, 'Nobleman still wanted to achieve what he had not managed to do at Dlangezwa High – initiate and lead a big student strike. He wanted to leave the university at the head of such mass action.'

Although he had been influential in building the momentum that had led to the Dlangezwa High strike in 1973, he had not directly initiated or led it. The strike had developed a life of its own. When it gathered momentum, Mzala had no ability to steer it and, therefore, according to Mavimbela, 'He could not, in earnest, put it in his political resumé as the product of his political activism.' At Ngoye, the plan was to skip the country once this objective was attained. The ground was fertile for that. True to his character, he was not just going to leave silently without shaking up the establishment. Just like his friend Tiro, 'He felt Ongoye needed to be shaken up,' recalls Mavimbela; 'he wanted to leave a legacy in the same way that Abram Tiro had done at Turfloop a few years earlier'. That the apartheid regime had successfully assassinated Tiro two years prior was not something that deterred Mzala.

Mzala thus persuaded his friend to stay until his plan was carried out and they would then leave the country together. Although they shared similar objectives, Mavimbela was sceptical about the feasibility of this plan. He says he did not believe that Mzala had sufficient influence to initiate such an action, especially considering the context of Ngoye 'which was far more complex and varied than Dlangezwa High'. The students were conservative, with many proudly focusing on their academics. Mavimbela thus told Mzala that he was not going to hang around for his 'Big Bang plan' and, eventually, Mzala accepted this reality.

During this period, Mzala belonged to what he called 'an underground political unit' which he headed. Because it was not guided by an ANC member, Mzala never regarded it as an ANC underground unit; it was their own initiative. With the formation of the unit – which included people such as Penuell Maduna, Wiseman Khuzwayo and Nhlanhla Ngidi – numerous questions were posed about how it related to the ANC. It had now become apparent that SASO could only take the struggle up to a particular point and, in order to take the struggle to its logical conclusion, they needed to establish contact with the national liberation movement.

Desperate to link up with the ANC, someone in the unit finally said he knew an ANC person in Hammersdale township who had been incarcerated at Robben Island. It was agreed that they needed to make contact with this person 'because we are in a cul-de-sac', Mzala recollected. They wanted to link up 'with the historical forces that are definitely going to shape the future of this country in a fundamentally different direction'. According to Mzala, even though the Freedom Charter was still a banned document, it is what drew them closer to the ANC. 'The Freedom Charter actually had its own political momentum in South Africa in a sense of guiding, of being what I would refer to as a lode star which we looked forward to.'

Mzala conceded that at this stage of their political development they were still naïve about the national liberation movement. They could not tell, in a real sense, the difference between the ANC and the Pan Africanist Congress (PAC). It was not until they actually joined the ANC that many of them eventually came to fully comprehend the essence of the difference between the two organisations.

VI

Mzala and his friend Mavimbela came up with many audacious plans to skip the country, plans that gave away their youthful exuberance. Because Mzala had been to Swaziland, he had an idea of the possibilities of crossing between the two countries illegally. Another plan they concocted was to approach Diliza Mji for guidance. Mji was a senior member of SASO and the BCM who had shared the stage with them at an event at Ngoye. Mavimbela says they also thought that if he invoked his cousin Musa's name, whom Mji knew well from varsity, he would agree. Obviously, they had not considered the risks of approaching someone in that fashion, given the prevalence of Special Branch spies. The plan, however, failed spectacularly when Mji loudly and emphatically expressed ignorance about such matters. Says Mavimbela, 'It was as if he wanted to make sure if I were wearing a wire, the Special Branch would pick up his emphatic disavowal.'

Still, this setback did not deter them from devising another plan. Mavimbela says there were several incidents around the same time that convinced him once and for all that he needed to leave. On a typical autumn day, Mzala and Mavimbela were on their way to a meeting in Durban when they decided to step out onto the platform after the train had stopped at one of the small stations on the way.

> When we came back to the compartment we found a man fiddling with our bags. Nobleman, the karateka, kicked him in the chest and the man stumbled. I kicked him in the ankles and he stumbled further

down the aisle. He jumped out of the train. Initially, we thought he was just a petty thief, but on second thoughts, we were more inclined to believe that he might have followed us from Mthunzini Station. We began to worry that we could have interfered with the Special Branch at work. When the train approached Durban, we decided to alight at one of the small stations before the main one. In case a network had been alerted to follow or arrest us at the main station, we had to throw them off the scent.[18]

Soon thereafter, as Mavimbela prepared to leave, he said his goodbyes to his friend Mzala. 'I shook hands and hugged Nobleman in a momentary bond of unbreakable solidarity.' Mavimbela then skipped the country through Swaziland before ending up in Mozambique.

VII

On 16 June 1976, hundreds of Soweto students embarked on a peaceful march protesting the use of Afrikaans as a medium of instruction. Estimated to number between 3 000 and 10 000, the students were mobilised by the Action Committee of the South African Students' Movement (SASM) with the support of the BCM. The anger of young people across the country was fast reaching a boiling point. Since Afrikaans had been made compulsory (alongside English) by the racist apartheid regime in 1974, the BCM had been gradually gaining a foothold in black townships.[19]

Black students, largely influenced by the BCM and SASO – dominant in black universities, had begun to mobilise against the language policy. On the fateful day of 16 June, the students' march was meant to culminate in a rally at Orlando Stadium. Students came from different schools in various parts of Soweto, the majority marching towards the southeastern parts of the township. On their way they were met by a large contingent of aggressive South African Police (SAP), heavily armed and clearly intent on unleashing brutal force. The SAP was notorious for being trigger-happy and for their aggressive, no-nonsense approach to black people. Whenever a chance presented itself, they shot to kill. The black townships were their killing fields.

Without any provocation, the police fired teargas at the students and, in some instances, let their dogs loose on the marchers. It was only a matter of time before the situation got entirely out of hand. And this, apparently, was what the racist apartheid police had bargained on. They immediately opened fire on unarmed children with live ammunition. Hector Pieterson, a 12-year-old student, was among the first victims. The iconic image captured by photographer Sam Nzima, showing the dying Hector being carried by a fellow student, 18-year-old Mbuyisa Makhubu, was published around the globe,[20] exposing to the whole world the brutalities of the apartheid system. For following generations, the image also served as inspiration to challenge the injustices of the system. When the dust settled, the official figures claimed that only 23 people had been killed. However, some reports estimated that about 200 people lost their lives – the latter figures most likely to be more accurate, or at least more believable. Of course, the number of casualties rose daily post 16 June, as the uprising spread throughout the country.

The events of June 1976 were to shake the foundation of apartheid. Within days, the wave of student protests spread like wildfire. 'By 18 June 1976, powder kegs filled over generations of white minority rule on Gauteng's East Rand and on campuses at the universities of Zululand and the North – two institutions designated for black Africans during apartheid – had been lit.'[21] The aftermath was devastating for the apartheid regime, triggering wave after wave of demonstrations and protests across the country. As tragic as all of this was, the situation did present Mzala with the perfect 'Big Bang' moment he had been looking for. A few months back, Mzala had thought the environment was fertile for a strike that would send a message to authorities, and the unprecedented brutality of the apartheid police and the accompanying anger of students presented an opportune moment. Mzala was ready to seize the moment and pounce.

Shabalala says that Ngoye was blessed with wonderful leaders from SASO and the Students' Representative Council (SRC), many of whom had been radicalised by the environment of the day. The SRC Chairman at the Ngoye campus was 'a colourful philosophy student who was quite militant'. Students called him 'Panel-beater' and 'his surname was Mkhonza', recalls Shabalala. The events of 16 June called for militancy. The following day, on a sombre Thursday evening, students congregated in the hall at Ngoye to decide on the way forward. As expected, Mzala was vocal on what needed to happen. 'I can still hear Mzala's voice [in that meeting],' says Blade Nzimande. During the day, students had pasted the picture of Hector Pieterson all over the university, and the SRC negotiated with university management to call for a prayer meeting. Nzimande says this 'was a smart move on the side of the SRC because what they wanted was for everybody to come to the prayer meeting'. But once the 'prayer meeting' was over, the real meeting began.

As was the norm at those meetings, says Shabalala, someone presented a motion to be debated. The meeting went on until the early hours of the morning, with Mzala among the students debating the most appropriate response. Most students were still in shock, angry at what had happened in Soweto. Many of the white lecturers at the university had 'run away', and options on whether to burn the university or 'kill the Boers' were being debated. 'I still hear Mzala's voice that we must inflict the maximum possible damage on the regime,' says Nzimande. Shabalala says a decision was eventually taken to march the following day.

On 18 June, the university decided to shut down, but still the students went ahead, marching to the police station. 'In the evening some of us were involved in disorderly activities,' says Shabalala. According to Nzimande, the students burned down the records and administration building. 'That's where my matric certificate was burned because we had submitted our original copies for photocopying.' The certificates of all first-year students in 1976 were destroyed in that fire, and the university closed its doors for the rest of the year.

But Ngoye was not the only black university that was up in arms. The damage caused by students was captured in local and international media. *Drum* magazine, for example, carried four photographs under the caption, 'Professor John Mare, Rector of the University of Zululand, gazes at the damage done to his university during the riots. The students were ordered off the campus by the police after their demonstrations.'[22] Reporting for *The New York Times* on 19 July, John F Burns observed a tense situation across South Africa's three black universities. Some demonstrating students were reported to have thrown a petrol bomb into one of the main campus buildings at one of the universities. 'The decision meant that all three black universities are now shut, since the other two – the University of the North at Turfloop in the Northern Transvaal, and the University of Zululand at Empangeni in Natal Province – were closed after disturbances that broke out during the rioting last month.'[23]

The spread of the uprising from urban centres to rural areas, homelands and black universities, in solidarity with the Soweto students, left the apartheid government scrambling for answers. The then Minister of Police, Jimmy Kruger, was reported to 'have announced in the House of Assembly on 22 June 1976 that the pattern of the riots that spread to the East Rand, the West Rand, the University of the North, University of Zululand and Alexandra Township, north of Johannesburg, had followed that of Soweto'.²⁴ He was reported in the *Cape Times* of 22 June 1976 and *The World* of 17 June 1976 to have said the pattern was to 'destroy buildings by ire, to plunder, to throw stones and objects, to set vehicles alight and attack their own people'.²⁵

Indeed, students deliberately targeted the infrastructure of black campuses such as the universities of Zululand and the Western Cape.²⁶ Shabalala says that rumours were rife that those suspected to have been involved in burning the buildings were wanted by the Special Branch, so they took a decision not to return. After the strike students never returned to campus. Says Nzimande: 'We lost that year.'

VIII

When Mzala and Mavimbela had parted a few months earlier, the plan had been simple. They were going to meet soon. 'Definitely,' says Mavimbela, 'the agreement was that he was going to join me, he was going to come. In fact, we had agreed to leave together when we started getting frustrated with the institutions, but, you know, he still had this idea that he wanted to initiate a strike at Ngoye and then leave when the strike had happened.' While the strike did happen, it was unrelated to the grievances Mzala had against the institution.

A few weeks before the strike, Mzala had visited his friend Bongani Khumalo, who was based in Durban at the time. Khumalo was surprised by this unexpected visit, but when they spoke, he says, 'I got a sense that he was skipping the country.' Mzala had commented about Khumalo's briefcase and Khumalo decided to gift it to him as a token of friendship. He recalled walking Mzala out carrying the briefcase – 'he loved being dramatic' – and when they parted, Khumalo watched Mzala cross a park and disappear into the streets of Durban.

Immediately after the strike, the Special Branch started hunting down the instigators. Mzala was one of them. They started harassing Mzala's family and searching his home for leads. In one of the visits, Mzala's grandmother had to hide his political books under her mattress. One of Mzala's uncles, Kenneth Khulekani Mwandla, stayed in Dlangezwa. One evening, with the police hot on Mzala's heels, he ran into his uncle yard's and hid at the top of a tree the entire night. His family had no idea of his whereabouts, and when his uncle discovered him in the morning, he immediately alerted his parents that Mzala was safe and with him. But it was still, however, difficult for them to go to him because the Special

Branch continued to monitor their movements.

Being an early-morning person, Sethi woke in the wee hours, and took his van as if he was going about his usual errands for the shop. Instead, however, he drove to Dlangezwa where, together with Kenneth, they orchestrated a plan to help Mzala skip the country. They decided to wait until darkness; then they put Mzala on the back of the bakkie, wrapped him in a tonneau cover, leaving only enough space for him to breathe, and his uncle placed a mattress on top to hide him. That evening Sethi drove non-stop all the way to the Mozambican border. Late at night, Sethi watched his oldest son jump the fence into Mozambique. Sethi kept the secret between himself, Balindile and Kenneth. To everyone else, including Mzala's siblings, he feigned ignorance about Mzala's whereabouts.

Titi describes this as a terribly painful and stressful period for them as siblings. Her mother did not help matters by constantly saying, 'I don't know where my child is,' especially at dinner time. Of course, technically, Balindile did not know Mzala's exact whereabouts. Accordingly, the whole family all told the same story when interrogated. Phasha says that, as siblings, they cried until their grandmother finally went to a local traditional healer, Mr Mbokazi. Upon her return, she told the children that Mbokazi told her that Mzala was alive and had gone with his uncle. However, Titi says, the way Mzala skipped the country would haunt him in exile. Some people 'started questioning him' because most generally left the country through a contact within the ANC and often in groups. But Mzala crossed the border alone, with only his father's help.

The police's Special Branch never stopped harassing the family, and it only became worse when Titi and later Dumisani also skipped the country. They would arrive at awkward hours to raid the house. The Special Branch, says Mthethwa, even arrived during Phasha's wedding after an informer mistook someone there for Titi. Phasha says being followed and harassed became a norm to them and they even developed a code language to communicate among themselves. Mzala was a wanted man and it was easy to isolate his family since they were the only one in the village where the kids had left the country to joined the liberation struggle. It was not a surprise when the SADF deployed hundreds of heavily armed soldiers to Mzala's funeral. To Balindile's chagrin, even in death the security forces haunted her son.

IX

By July 1976, Mzala had made his way to Mozambique, albeit via a different route to his comrades from Ngoye. Both Mavimbela and Shabalala, who left before and after Mzala respectively, had travelled via Swaziland. Shabalala left in around October, after the Ngoye strike, and ended up in a safe house in Swaziland before they were taken to Mozambique. 'Then we were received in Mozambique by Jacob Zuma, who I think none of us knew,' says Shabalala. Mavimbela's escape was similar to Mzala's in that he too was alone. His route to Mozambique also went through Swaziland, albeit in more dramatic fashion, which involved getting help from three unknown women. Mavimbela says Mzala was 'the one who gave me the idea that I can actually cross into Swaziland very easily because he had been to Swaziland several times'.

The first thing Mzala did when he arrived in Mozambique was to look for his friend Mavimbela. While waiting at a safe house in Maputo, Lennox Lagu, an MK veteran, told Mavimbela that 'somebody by the name of Nobleman Nxumalo ... was in Maputo and had asked about my whereabouts'. Before the end of the day, a car had dropped Mzala at the gate of the underground hideaway Mavimbela shared with the likes of Solomon Mahlangu. 'Nobleman got out and jogged towards the house. We hugged in great excitement,' recalls Mavimbela. He adds that Mzala 'lifted his clenched fist and shouted "Amandla, Comrade Vusi!"' Mzala had never addressed Mavimbela as 'comrade' before, and it finally dawned on them that they were now in the thick of things. In the real struggle.

The first thing Mzala did was to tell Mavimbela first-hand the tales around the solidarity strike. This would be their last lengthy proper conversation, because Mavimbela left for Angola soon thereafter. But they were never far away, and occasionally they did bump into each other. 'The next time I saw him was in Lusaka and then after that it was at the Kabwe Conference [in 1985].' On all those occasions, says Mavimbela, 'we didn't have time to talk'. When they met in Lusaka, Mzala was 'busy with some people', so their chat was brief, and in Kabwe 'we were all busy again; we didn't have time to talk'.

CHAPTER 3

The June 16 Detachment

I

After the 1976 Soweto uprising, a steady stream of young South Africans arrived at MK camps in Angola. This was the same year the ANC started moving its cadres there following successful engagements with the MPLA. At the heart of this move were political developments in regional and global politics.[1] Until then, ANC cadres had been largely based in Tanzania and Zambia, but ideological tensions were emerging between the ANC and presidents Julius Nyerere and Kenneth Kaunda – 'most notably Kaunda with his firm entrenchment of a "third way" solution, namely, negotiation with Rhodesia and South Africa', which the ANC opposed.[2] In the wake of the 16 June uprising, thousands of angry young men and women had fled the country to join the armed struggle.[3] They were to become known as 'the June 16 Detachment'.[4]

The ANC had appointed Cassius Make as its Chief Representative in Angola, and he and Max Moabi thus began establishing the necessary infrastructure. 'The first group of MK soldiers in Angola was sent to a camp in the south of Luanda called Gabella, in the province of Kwanza Sul. Gabella was a small town near Porto Amboim and Gambalu'.[5] Subsequently, on 7 September 1976, the first batch of 21 new recruits joined this group of MK soldiers. During this time, a group of 40 MK soldiers was receiving military training from the People's Armed Forces for the Liberation of Angola (FAPLA) and Cuban instructors.⁶ Vuso Shabalala, who arrived as one of the new recruits before the end of 1976, found about 40 MK people already undergoing training. This camp was closed in 1977 when ANC cadres were moved, first to Novo Catengue camp and later to Funda, Quibaxe, Fazenda and elsewhere.⁷

The arrival in the camps of these groups of young fighters was a welcome relief for the ANC, which to date had tried without much success to infiltrate 'combatants into South Africa or [to recruit] local people into underground units'.⁸

In the early 1970s, the ANC had tried its utmost to establish an underground presence inside the country, thus contributing to the 1973 Durban strikes. However, very little traction emanated from the armed struggle, the workers' strikes representing 'the first mass action to occur since the ANC had been declared illegal in 1960'.⁹ Like a ticking time bomb, the explosion that was the 1976 uprising had been imminent. Yet, the ANC was still caught flatfooted both by the uprising and the subsequent influx of young fighters into its camps.¹⁰ Many argue that even as the BCM was rising in the country, there was little coming from the armed struggle to complement the rising tide. Thus, when the 1976 riots erupted, 'the ANC and MK were caught by surprise' and they were not ready to exploit the situation, except for 'limited acts of sabotage' where 'railway lines were targeted, primarily in support of calls for stay-aways by students'.¹¹

To be fair, though, the ANC had not been idle, even though the period both before and after the ANC's Morogoro Conference was characterised by internal squabbles. The Morogoro Consultative Conference, held in 1969 in Morogoro, Tanzania, was 'a watershed' in the history of the ANC and its alliance partners. The conference had, as Joe Slovo described it, 'the potential of disintegrating' with criticism levelled against the leadership so acute that 'Tambo even threatened to resign' as he regarded some of the criticism as baseless. According to Slovo, had it not been for 'the brilliance of JB Marks', then national chairperson of the South African Communist Party (SACP), who 'held everyone together', the movement could have easily descended into chaos.¹²

This was also a period when the ANC's presence in Tanzania and Zambia was becoming complicated, and the organisation lived under the constant threat of expulsion. Amid all these challenges, the ANC had initiated efforts prior to 1976 when it deployed Chris Hani to Lesotho in 1973 'to start a forward front from there'.¹³ While 'the relationship between the ANC and the little kingdom would not make possible a large scale insurrection', there was some reprieve when a new generation of fighters trickled into the MK training camps between 1973 and 1974. And, as numbers grew, new safe havens became even more necessary to habour its fighters.[14]

Accordingly, after the Soweto uprising and notwithstanding the 'political, organisational and military weaknesses and problems of the ANC and its armed wing MK', the ANC represented 'the only viable "home" for the young guerrillas-in-waiting and it was to the ANC/MK that they turned'.[15] Hence, the 1976 generation continued to flock into MK camps with one idea in mind; as Vusi Mavimbela puts it, 'we were all pumped up and ready to go and take the AK-47 and go back and fight and liberate the country'.

II

The arrival of the June 16 Detachment in Angola coincided with the fifteenth anniversary of the launch of MK on 16 December 1976. It was this moment that was to be the catalyst for South Africa's liberation. Most cadres from the Natal Midlands region, such as Mavimbela and Shabalala, came via Swaziland before moving to Mozambique, Tanzania and then Angola. Mzala's younger sister, Titi, who escaped the country the following year, also came via the same channel.

As they moved from country to country, it was a steep learning curve for most of these youngsters. Many had not been out of their home regions before, let alone out of the country. When they were transferred to Matola in Mozambique, where they were received by Jacob Zuma, they usually waited until their number increased to about 30. In Mozambique, the young and curious Shabalala could already see the close cooperation between the ANC and Frelimo. Shabalala, in something of a culture shock, was also fascinated to meet peers from other provinces who spoke languages other than Zulu, which is what he was accustomed to in his home province of Natal. Together with his fellow Natal comrades, they were amazed at the ease with which the Soweto comrades switched between languages. They also found their version of Zulu curious.

Once they were briefed and all the necessary protocol completed, including the capturing of their biographies, Shabalala and his group were off to Angola. 'We flew first to Tanzania,' says Shabalala, where they spent a month. From there, they eventually flew to Angola. Mavimbela recalls travelling with Thomas Masuku, Solomon Mahlangu and Stephen Nkosi, whom he had met for the first time in Mozambique. 'For the four of us, the flight to Angola was a maiden experience as none of us had been in a plane before.' On flight they declined the offer of food, thinking they would be required to pay. Upon landing in Luanda, they were whisked to a house in the city centre. Mzala took a slightly different path on his way to receive military training in Angola, where he subsequently 'distinguished himself as a fearless soldier of Umkhonto we Sizwe'.[16]

But before Mzala had even set foot in MK training camps, he had already embarked on his first protest action: challenging the leadership of the ANC. Patric Mzolisi Mtshaulana (MK name Richard Sethunya) says he first heard of Mzala in 1976 in Tanzania while en route to Angola. 'When I arrived there,' he recalls, 'there was talk that there was a man who had organised a hunger strike because he had been in Tanzania without training for a very long time. He had been taken to Angola, I was told. Nobody told me who he was, but he was the talk of most people who secretly agreed with his views, but they did not think he went about it the right way.'[17] However, according to Patrick Msomi (MK name Moses Swanepoel), this was a spontaneous strike by all comrades at the residence. Mzala, he says, was not the cause of the strike, which came about mainly due to the lack of military training and about 30 of them decided to embark on a hunger strike. The strike was a success because the leadership came and spoke to them. Immediately, comrades were sent to train in places such as Union of Soviet Socialist Republics (USSR), German Democratic Republic (GDR) and Angola.

It is from there that Mzala was sent to the USSR for military training. He was in a small unit of five commanded by Joy Rathebe (MK name Andre Gindi), with Mzala its commissar. Msomi, a member of this unit, says they spent 11 months in intensive training specialising in military communication. In the USSR, they were given altenative names and so it was that Mzala became known as Marks Black. Although the training was intense, with classes starting promptly at 8 am, Monday to Saturday, Msomi says they had spare time and subsequently went on excursions and to classical music concerts in Moscow. Having met Mzala at the University of Zululand, where they were both students, Msomi says they became closer – both as a unit, and as friends. From their student days, he remembers Mzala as an avid reader with a brown belt in karate, also as a disciplinarian who believed in physical fitness. Mzala would, for instance, be reading a book while on a sightseeing excursion in the USSR. As a commissar, says Msomi, Mzala would admonish them if they fell asleep during classical concerts, which most South Africans found boring.

Mzala's unit was among the many in the first half of the 1970s to receive advanced military training from the Soviet Union. Charles Sitsubi was the commander of the unit that went to Moscow in 1975 to receive combat training, which he defined as 'the art of creation of the revolutionary army'.[18]

III

The gruelling and demanding physical exercises, coupled with the difficult Angolan climate, made life in the camps extremely challenging. Sometimes, the stressful conditions resulted in outright confrontations between rank-and-file comrades and the leadership.[19] Clad in camouflage uniforms supplied by the Organisation of African Unity (OAU), the training of new recruits usually began with a physical exercise routine coupled with introductory classes on military science. This would be followed by an introduction to various other subjects, including 'orientation in the terrain, topography, the theory of firearms, and military engineering'.[20]

There were numerous camps in Angola, among them Engineering, Novo Catengue and Benguela. Benguela was a dry and desolate place, the only one used by Cuban forces guarding the area.

> It was a double-storey building, while a caretaker's quarters and an unroofed building were the only other structures [in] the camp. There was no accommodation for the recruits, and no water and sanitation facilities. The 11 women in the first group to be housed at Benguela camp were given a room to share in the house and the 500 men were accommodated in tents. Malaria was a very serious problem in this camp.[21]

At the Engineering camp, cadres slept on the veranda, with the lights on, hoping that that would repel mosquitoes, but with little success. James Ngculu, a member of the June 16 Detachment, recalls that 'in this camp it became normal to find dozens of comrades lying down or walking slowly because of malaria'.[22] Stanley Manong, another member of the June 16 Detachment, remembers how they all laughed when Comrade Mzwandile 'Mzwai' Piliso, a prominent member of the ANC leadership in exile, said, 'Welcome to our new camp in Benguela.' They thought he was teasing them.[23] 'Not a single one of us believed that this was our final destination.

The place did not resemble a facility that could produce fighters capable of overthrowing the apartheid regime.'[24] Apart from the atrocious living conditions, the training was intense.

Life in the camps of Angola had many challenges. Sometimes, commanders and commissars had their hands full trying to reinforce the importance of maintaining high morale and discipline. The soldiers largely kept themselves busy with sporting and cultural activities such as soccer and choral music. There were, however, instances of ill discipline. For example, in Novo Catengue, cadres would 'cross the mountains to visit villages for liquor' and perhaps women too.[25] At times, the 'increasing problems with food and other supplies resulted in the cadres' involvement in theft from stores and dealing in the black market. Black market trade would sometimes be seen as breach of conduct.'[26]

As in any institution, there were miscreants who broke the rules. For instance, since Funda camp was somewhat integrated with the local community, cadres would exchange their tinned food for fruits and vegetables. Manong writes that 'a group of comrades led by Thabo Mavuyo used to sneak out in the evenings and procure liquor and return to the camp in a drunken state'. This group also included 'people like Jacob who were chain dagga smokers'; therefore, for Manong, it was 'no coincidence when both Thabo Mavuyo and Jacob later became *askari*'[27].[28]

The semitropical climate in Novo Catengue also proved difficult to manage because many South Africans 'were unprepared for the humidity, malaria, and a host of other minor and major diseases that plagued the area'.[29] The summer rains worsened the conditions, with leaking roofs and makeshift tents. As Jack Simons reflected in his diaries, the heavy rains often brought 'to the surface [a] multitude of flying objects! Mosquitoes ... flying ants, moths, hornets – plus crawlers: the lizards, cockroaches, beetles that invade the room in a flash if the door or window is ajar'.[30] Even Funda had challenges; it had an 'infestation of mosquitoes' and so the beds 'were fitted with mosquito nets' to protect people against malaria.[31]

It is not surprising then that some recruits could not handle the situation. Charles Sitsubi, who was among the cadres deployed to Benguela camp when it was opened, recalled that they had their first case of suicide in 1976. 'So his grave lies there near the sea ... It was simple frustrations and tensions. You know, to be in the bush was stressful to others.'[32] Titi Nxumalo says that, in Novo Catengue, many people committed suicide because theirs was a very abnormal life and many did not have the fortitude to survive. 'In the middle of the night you will just hear [a] gunshot.

Someone who was supposed to be on guard duty would see an opportunity and say, I can't take this.' James Ngculu experienced the conditions in all the camps to be very tough, 'and all experienced repeated shortages'.

While life in the camps was not smooth sailing and had its ups and downs, there were several events that comrades looked forward to. One of those was the January 8 anniversary celebration of the ANC addressed by President Oliver Tambo. Such festivities would often be followed by graduates taking the oath and swearing allegiance to MK, often presided over by Tambo himself. An avid chorister, Tambo not only participated in singing with the choir but also conducted 'songs with great verve and energy'.[33] It is under these conditions that the June 16 Detachment received military training.

IV

In 1977, Mzala returned from his training in the USSR and was based at Funda camp. Opened in 1976, Funda was central to the activities of MK. Located some 20 kilometres outside Luanda, it 'was used as a preparation camp for cadres who were being sent inside the country [South Africa]'. Previously a game reserve, it 'abounded with wild game such as warthog, buffalo, pythons and antelope'. Aboobaker Ismail (MK name Rashid), an instructor at Funda in 1976, described the camp as comprising old buildings, including a storage structure and a farm that the Portuguese had destroyed by pouring cement into the pipes when they left.[34]

There were still some peasant villages in the area, with another camp in the vicinity housing SWAPO fighters.[35] Funda, according to Johnny Sexwale, hosted cadres 'who were already selected to go home'. The idea, he pointed out, was 'to demilitarise them, in Funda, so that they must not walk like they are marching' when they were eventually infiltrated back into South Africa. Obviously, as underground operatives, their identities had to be concealed. 'But we did some training there as well, especially lots of shooting.' Continued Sexwale, 'It was final training now. They were shooting like nobody's business.'[36]

Manong remembers that Funda's features were similar to those of Benguela camp, but much smaller. 'There was a main house which was used to house female comrades and the camp administration.'[37] He reiterates Sexwale's assertions that cadres based at the camp were being prepared to infiltrate South Africa. 'On arrival we were briefed that we were to undergo a six-week course on Urban Guerrilla Warfare, after which we were to be infiltrated inside the country.'[38] The recruits were given training on an assortment of weapons, including 'the Scorpion, a Czech sub-machine gun or machine pistol that was used in South Africa by the unit of Solomon Mahlangu, George Mahlangu (MK name George Mazibuko) and Mandy Motlaung', who all received training at Funda before they were infiltrated into the country.[39] Manong recalls training by Peter Stewart, who was in charge of pistol shooting lessons. 'At times he went berserk, destroying all "targets" with his favourite weapon, which was the revolver.'[40]

V

With so much shooting going on, accidents were bound to occur. Perhaps it is this 'lots of shooting' taking place in Funda that led to Mzala's near-fatal shooting when he was mistakenly shot in the face by Stewart. 'He dropped down and comrades were at first convinced he was dead,' writes Eddy Maloka. 'He was rushed unconscious to hospital and later recovered.'[41] It was through his spirit and determination, according to Jeff Radebe, that 'when everyone thought the shot was fatal, he nonetheless reawakened after admission at the hospital. He completely recovered from those near-fatal facial gunshot wounds and was not deterred from spearheading the struggle for liberation afterwards.'[42]

While many would expect a military camp to be a place of discipline, accidents were not a rare occurrence in the camps. In an environment with so many cadres and a proliferation of weaponry, this had to be expected. For example, in the US between 2006 and 2018, 31.9 per cent of active-duty military deaths were the result of accidents, compared to 16.3 per cent of service members who died in action.[43] 'The sheer numbers of cadres in Angola, most of who were armed, did allow for accidents to happen.'[44] Describing life at Caculama camp in the town of Malanje, Kenny Leleki said, 'Comrades passed away in Angola in a number of ways. Some would be involved in a car accident, accidental shootings, tractor accidents, sacrifices, starvation and the bad conditions they were living under, ambushes and so on.'[45] Although Mzala was lucky to survive, the incident left him with a permanent scar.

Pallo Jordan says the injury damaged one of Mzala's ears, which in turn lead to hearing difficulties. When Ronnie Kasrils met Mzala in 1977, he noticed the scar immediately. 'I encountered him in Luanda in 1977.

I learnt that this injury was caused when a rifle accidently discharged, wounding him in the face.' Mzala was recently out of hospital at that time, still recovering from the injury, but 'behaving as though nothing untoward had occurred'. He had been treated by Cuban doctors at the Military Hospital in Luanda, and Kasrils believes 'the devotion of the doctors gave him a lasting regard for their skills in saving his life'.

Vusi Mavimbela only found out about the accident when he met Mzala in Lusaka. He immediately noticed that his face had changed. It was now 'slightly contorted and there was a mark under his nose which was a bullet mark where the bullet had gone in and came out at the back of his neck'. Certainly, the accident slightly altered Mzala's rather handsome face. 'You know, his face looked like somebody who had had a severe stroke,' says Mavimbela. However, the bullet had not penetrated deep enough to reach Mzala's spirit and determination. Neither did it succeed in altering his character. He remained brave and dedicated to the cause of liberation.

When Lungile Chris Pepani (MK name S'bali) met Mzala in the late 1970s, Mzala would talk about being given a second chance. Although he would not provide many details about the accident, the scar was clearly visible and 'this made his mouth to be slightly twisted'. The only bit Mzala was prepared to share with Pepani was that the accident occurred in 'a special camp' but 'he was not prepared to tell me what happened'. Some speculate that, in a special camp like Funda, many cadres already knew the basics of handling weapons, so there may have been more to the 'accident' than meets the eye. Msomi is one of those who were sceptical and believes that the way he was 'sniped' was questionable. The conspiracy theory reached comrades in other camps too. Patric Mtshaulana, who was still in military training in Benguela, 'learnt that the same man had been accidentally shot in Funda camp' as the person who had gone on a hunger strike in Tanzania; speculation was rife, he said. 'Some people had a conspiracy theory that this was not a mistake, but the ANC wanted to get rid of him because they feared him. However, after some time it became clear that the shooting was a pure accident and had nothing to do with Mzala's previous challenge of the leadership [about] training.' Titi Nxumalo does not buy into the conspiracy. She says Mzala was very close not only to Stewart but his mother Violet too.

There was, however, a lighter side to the accident. Joel Netshitenzhe recalls that 'the abiding impression of Mzala is that he liked debates – mainly as a process of searching for solutions, but also at times for its own sake'. This led to one of the urban legends regarding his love for debates 'on which he was teased ... after he had had an accident with a rifle and a bullet went through his cheek: cadres would joke that he was having a debate with friends about whether indeed a bullet comes out of the muzzle of a gun rotating; and so he put his face in front of the barrel and pulled the trigger to ascertain this'.

VI

It was not all smooth sailing when the influx into Angola began following the Soweto uprising. Even though the ANC had always been committed to the political education of its cadres, the sheer volume of numbers towards the end of 1976 and beyond required a change in strategy.[46] The influx of new recruits, many steeped in the political outlook of Black Consciousness (BC), triggered a discussion in the ANC's National Executive Committee (NEC) and prompted the leadership to bring in political education instructors.[47] Before the arrival of Jack Simons, Mark Shope and Ronnie Kasrils, political education in camps like Novo Catengue had been conducted mainly by the Cubans with the help of senior comrades.

In his July 1977 report to the NEC, Secretary-General Alfred Nzo announced that a group of suitably qualified and experienced comrades had been appointed to conduct political lectures aimed at the political development of the young comrades who had joined the ANC since the beginning of the political upsurge in the country.[48] The new arrivals were radical and pushed boundaries, and sometimes this led to clashes with the old guard. The youngsters were impatient with what they perceived to be dated ideas of the older generation.[49]

Towards the end of 1977, while still convalescing, Mzala was already up and running, beginning to cement his reputation not only as a fearless soldier but as an emerging intellectual. Observing the work of Simons in the camps, Kasrils posits, 'Perhaps the most impressive aspect of Jack's work at Novo Catengue was the dynamic group of instructors he had produced.' Mzwai had persuaded Simons to return to Zambia and, after nearly a year in the camp, where he suffered several bouts of malaria, Kasrils was called to take over. He regarded himself fortunate to have found and worked with Simons's products. 'Among them were Jabu Nxumalo (Mzala), [Lungile] Chris Pepani (S'bali) and Edwin Mabitsela, all destined to play an important role in the ANC in later years. Another product was a young man with an engaging smile whose *nom de guerre* was Che O'Gara (January Masilela).'[50]

VII

As the year drew to a close, Mzala was pleasantly surprised when his youngest sister arrived. Titi and her twin brother Dumisani had been enrolled at a new school, Menzi High in Umlazi, Durban, after having been expelled from Vryheid High as ringleaders of a strike. Clearly, they had learnt from their older brother! Dumisani was in jail, accused of torching the school with his comrades, so Titi left one morning as usual wearing her uniform as if she was heading off to school. Instead, she and four other recruits caught a train to Golela, some 350 kilometres from Durban. From there, they jumped the fence into Swaziland. Her life in exile had begun.

In Luanda, the ANC had three houses, and Titi and her group were sent to Residence Two. They arrived after midnight at an otherwise ordinary double-storey house. The women slept in the bedrooms upstairs, while downstairs was a dining room that has been converted into a makeshift dormitory for male cadres at night. Because they arrived so late, they were advised not to switch on the lights, but should just go up the stairs and someone would show them around. As Titi carefully began to climb the stairs, she heard a voice calling, 'Titi, Titi.' She was in utter shock because she was convinced no one at this place knew her by that name. Before she knew it, Mzala was pulling her and, in a hushed tone, asked, 'How are you?' She wanted to scream with excitement, but he put his hand on her mouth and said, 'Shhh!' Although it was dark, the streetlights were bright enough for her to see her elder brother.

'I was crying, and he said no, go and sleep – we will meet tomorrow morning.' Titi did not sleep that night. The thought of seeing her brother and knowing that he was alive were too much for her to contain. 'I was so tempted to just go back down the stairs, but I couldn't because … I was not aware which side he even came from.' The first thing they did the following morning was look for each other; they sat down and, out of excitement, never touched their breakfast. Of course, the first thing Titi noticed was Mzala's injury, and he explained that he had been accidentally shot by Stewart. At that time, Titi had no clue who 'Stewart' was, but she would later come to know his mother. That Mzala had survived was 'a miracle'. As a result of the injury, Mzala's eye was constantly twitching and teary.

Mzala also assured Titi that their parents knew his whereabouts, but hadn't shared the knowledge because of security concerns. He admired his father's bravery for escorting him out of the country even though he did not know where or what he was handing him over to. The thought of having a big brother around must have been a huge relief for Titi as she entered unknown territory. When they were about to depart, Mzala reached into his pocket and took out a wristwatch; he said, 'This is for you.' Titi was surprised, but Mzala said, 'I bought this for you when I was in the Soviet Union.' He told her that of all his siblings, she was the one he expected to follow in his footsteps. Mzala would continue spoiling his little sister, just as he had done when he visited them at Vryheid High. Pepani recalls that Mzala had a 'young and good-looking sister' and that Mzala would buy her things when they were in training abroad.

VIII

It was months before Mzala's first writing emerged. But the fire in Mzala's belly to confront injustices as manifested at Bethel College, Dlangezwa High and the University of Zululand had not died. Not even the freak accident could slow him down. He continued to immerse himself in the revolutionary work of the movement. The encounter with senior comrades and intellectuals such as Shope, Simons and Kasrils served as an engine that propelled his burning desire for freedom. Kasrils describes his first encounter with Mzala:

> [It was] at a neighbouring MK residence where he stayed and I had dropped in to participate in a political discussion which he was chairing. I immediately took to this fine young man, who was full of passion and most articulate. I believe he took a liking to me, too, and was most interested in discussing politics. In fact, I would say he lived and breathed the politics of liberation, and how the struggle should be waged to achieve freedom.

The arrival at the scene of someone like Kasrils must have excited Mzala, for his mind was always searching for answers. Mzala entered every debate with passion and a 'sense of humour', which livened up the discussion and which Kasrils found most engaging.

It is in the camps that Mzala interacted with Marxism-Leninism. The camps – among them, Novo Catengue – were known as 'the University of the South' because of the high quality of the political education. In his diary, Simons reflected on the 'instructors' class' and 'preparatory class' for cadres to go abroad to the GDR and the Soviet Union.[51] Patric Mtshaulana is unsurprised that Mzala ended up being a communist because he avidly read Marxist books. 'When we came to the ANC the only books that were available to us were Marxist-Leninist books. We read them. Mzala was an ardent reader. He was also very analytical and read and analysed the books he read.' Because of this, Mzala was identified by the SACP and 'sent for further training', says Mtshaulana.

However, it is the political classes given in the camps that had a lasting impact, and perhaps transformative effect on Mzala. Lebona Mosia, part of the June 16 Detachment, reserved his highest praise for Simons. 'The teachings of Prof Jack Simons were to me the most effective and transformative,' he says, 'because he applied historical and dialectical materialism to teach us how to understand our history and challenges facing us in the liberation struggle.' Mosia found that Shope was obsessed with the history of the British working class and the emergence of the trade union movement in the United Kingdom. Ronnie Kasrils, on the other hand, he says, 'was a typical rhetoric propagandist of the Communist Party of the Soviet Union'. Kasrils concurs that Simons was 'a maestro' in introducing students to Marxism. 'Shope focused more on trade unionism and working-class struggles' while he himself focused on the history of MK and international guerrilla struggles, including the theory and practice of guerrilla warfare.

These classes imbued in the recruits the revolutionary theory that would have a lasting impact on many of them. Joel Netshitenzhe found the classes by Shope and Simons to be important in introducing the new recruits to a systematic theorisation of the struggle, and a methodology that helped clarify historical and contemporary events. 'All of these classes were premised on the Marxist methodology.' However, Kasrils hastens to attribute Mzala's development to his familial upbringing beyond just these classes. He regards Mzala as fortunate for having been raised by parents who were teachers. Kasrils thinks that it was his disciplined upbringing that gave Mzala an affinity for the idea of study and debate and a thirst for information in the quest of the truth, 'more especially for a young African with a passion to right the wrongs of racism and colonialism'.

Because most of the 1976 recruits were politically inducted in the BC school of thought, Kasrils argues that 'the ANC patiently introduced them to its policy and strategy'. Many recruits proved thirsty for such knowledge. Notwithstanding their amazement 'at the presence of the few whites they encountered in the struggle, such as Joe Slovo, Wolfie Kodesh, Ruth First and Jack Simons', says Kasrils, they quickly became more politically aware. Primarily, Kasrils recalls, these young comrades displayed a great interest in

Marxism-Leninism and would often pressurise the ANC to introduce this type of education to their training and preparation. So it was that Tambo and Mzwai Piliso acquiesced to the proposal and introduced Marxism into the training, bringing people like Simons, Shope, Kasrils and Francis Meli into the training programme. In this regard, they found that Marxism was not just the preserve of white comrades. Says Kasrils: 'Mzala was one of the first such converts, and quickly grasped the essentials of political theory and the strategy that went with this.'

Pallo Jordan agrees with the impact of Simons's work in the camps. Simons helped in training a number of future political instructors but 'embarrassingly, a number of them had not been properly vetted, and were uncovered as apartheid security agents in 1981'. The objective of political education conducted in the camps and beyond, according to Jordan, was intended, in the first instance, to ground the cadres in the history of the national liberation struggle. This was to train them on how the ANC and the other liberation forces in the region understood the world and its evolution. Thus, Jordan perceives political economy as having been an important aspect of that training, based on the South African and continental historical experience. He posits:

> Many in the 1976 intake were senior high school students or freshmen and sophomores at universities. The political education they received [took place at] a profoundly formative timeframe and assisted them in connecting the dots with respect to the brutal exploitation of their parents, the control of the economy in white and foreign hands, Bantu Education, and the imposition of Afrikaans. The uncompromisingly brutal suppression of their protests also could only be explained in terms of the South African political economy.

Armed with this knowledge, Jordan believes the Commissariat of MK, led by senior cadres, became largely staffed by that generation as early as 1978. They produced the MK journal, *Dawn*, a task they continued until 1989. As Deputy National Commissar, Ronnie Kasrils had initiated the journal in 1978. The impact of the political instruction received by the new recruits could be partially appreciated through the quantity and quality of articles published in *Dawn*. It is this political education process that produced many of the ANC's public intellectuals, including Mzala. He, along with many others, contributed to 'the political doctrines of the ANC or [enriched] it from their experiences of other traditions like Black Consciousness'.[52]

IX

Although Mzala became one of the earliest and most ardent Marxist-Leninists, many argue that he never relinquished his BC roots. Mosia says he does not remember Mzala ever becoming critical of the BCM. 'He was very passionate about his BCM roots. I know this quite well, because we had extensive discussions on this matter and we shared similar roots and experiences of BCM politics.'

Pallo Jordan concurs that Mzala was very proud of his track record in the BCM and South African Students' Organisation (SASO). He believes that although he never subscribed to the Pan Africanist Congress's (PAC) variant, Mzala never abandoned pan-Africanism. Throughout this time, Mzala also vehemently denied that BCM or SASO was anti-white, and would often tell newcomers that they were anti-white-domination, anti-white-rule but not anti-white. Political education had nevertheless exposed him to the limitations of the BCM and, says Jordan, with his keen mind, Mzala quickly recognised the limitations of a purely nationalist critique of white domination and Western imperialism. This ideological current could not explain racist oppression except as a sort of malevolence. It was also unable to unpack the operations of Western imperialism and was deficient in identifying the agents of change and revolution. According to Jordan,

> He found these in the Marxist classics and in the Programme of the SACP. His shift was confirmed when he encountered old comrades from BCM days who seemed to have no clue how to take their movement forward, but were quick with catchy slogans with an emotional appeal, but incapable of galvanising masses into action.

The BCM proved to be useful only in mobilising black youths during the leadership vacuum created by the heavy-handed nature of the regime in dealing with the liberation movement. Beyond this, as an ideology, it was found wanting as a way to understand the implications of imperialism and fashioning cogent responses. These 'variants of purely nationalist ideology', as Slovo put it, failed to grasp the basic fact that the national domination of the majority black people was linked to the capitalist exploitation of black people both as a race and a class.[53] Bernard Magubane also situated the plight of black people and social inequality in the context of the capitalism practised by the white colonial settlers. Hence, 'the South African social formation itself' represented a stage in the evolution of the world capitalist system.[54]

Kasrils says most young people, like Mzala, who flocked to join the ANC and MK in the immediate aftermath of the 1976 Soweto uprising owed their political awakening to the BCM. 'Initially there was the simple clamour for weapons so that they could go back home to shoot the Boers.' However, with further military and political training in the Soviet Union and the GDR, Mzala's understanding of the problem, using a Marxism-Leninism prism, was cemented. Because of his attitude towards reading and engaging with ideas, Mzala proved to be an outstanding cadre who studiously followed the lectures and devoured the literature.

Mzala was courageous in interrogating his lecturers on key topics such as the Marxist approach to the national question, which he thought had not – despite claims by the socialist countries to the contrary – been resolved. Sometimes, he was confrontational in his quest for answers to the challenges of the South African revolution. Kasrils says he was not one to simply swallow the slogans, but strove instead to raise critical questions. Just as he had done at school, during the political education sessions he shone and was an exemplary student.

From early on in exile, Mzala agitated for the armed struggle inside the country. Kasrils says he was particularly interested in 'consistently developing critical ideas about the advancement of the armed struggle in South Africa'. This would be Mzala's obsession until the end. Certainly, Mzala was impatient with what appeared to be a long-winded and protracted struggle towards liberating the country. He was in a hurry. Apart from writing provocative pieces about the need to go inside the country and wage the struggle against the enemy there, later, when he was deployed at the front, he experimented with his own ideas.

X

Mzala's courage and conviction when it came to his ideals were confirmed in his article 'The Compromising Role of Inkatha' published in 1978 in the *African Communist*. He argued that Buthelezi was being groomed for an 'internal settlement' along the lines of similar attempts in Zimbabwe and Namibia. Writing as Ngacambaza Khumalo, Mzala advanced the notion that Inkatha was founded to safeguard and perpetuate the bantustan policy and to entrench Buthelezi's position in KwaZulu. He argued that apartheid and white supremacy could only be eliminated if 'reactionary tendencies' were consciously combated. Mzala was adamant that the re-emergence of Inkatha along a 'narrow, chauvinist and ethnocentric position' was dangerous and sought to undermine the essence of national unity.[55]

During this period the ANC still harboured hope that it could work with Buthelezi, as reflected by the meeting on 5 November 1979 between Tambo and Buthelezi in London. While it is not clear how the leadership received Mzala's harsh assessment of Buthelezi's role, according to Mtshaulana, there were rumours that Tambo was furious, not at Mzala, but at the *African Communist* for publishing the article. Kasrils considers Mzala 'the first member of the ANC to publicly raise huge doubts about Buthelezi's true intentions'. He says Mzala came under some fire over the matter, 'but, as they say, history vindicated the young man'. However, Mtshaulana believes Mzala was simply articulating the views of many of the youth at the time. Perhaps it was the same militant youth that ejected Buthelezi from Robert Sobukwe's funeral in 1978.[56]

Mzala had no qualms about testing uncharted waters. As one of the early converts to Marxism-Leninism, he was not shy in expressing his views about the importance of the race question. He thought BC was very relevant in this regard. In 1980, he again went against the grain in his letter to the editor in the *African Communist* under the heading 'Black Consciousness and the South African Revolution'. This was a rebuttal to an article by 'Toussaint' (Rusty Bernstein) titled 'Fallen Among Liberals', which essentially criticised the BCM. Having been in exile for about four years, Mzala leapt to the defence of the BCM as a legitimate movement and ideology that was likely to remain for as long as racial inequalities existed. This is how he opened the article:

> The chief defect in most hitherto written articles and adopted statements on Black Consciousness and its role in the South African revolution is that it is analysed as a phenomenon that is now obsolete and belonging to the past – i.e. it has served its role as a militant mobilising factor in the pre-Soweto era, and consequently has no longer any relevance in the present and future of our revolution. Furthermore, some analysts have dismissed it as a sheer student affair while others have despised it as mere black liberalism.[57]

As far as Mzala was concerned, 'Black Consciousness' was not a 'False Consciousness', and the polemics against Steve Biko demonstrated a failure to understand that BC was a relevant stage in the development of Black Nationalism under the particular conditions of the South African revolution. However, Mzala was clear that BC itself must also appreciate the importance of class consciousness because 'complete national liberation is impossible without economic emancipation'. Therefore, if the class bias of racism were ignored, the revolution would advance the interests of 'black quislings who are aspiring to get into the racists' shoes, singing the Muzorewa anti-revolutionary but pro-imperialist church hymn'.

Mzala was thus not defending BC blindly, but essentially expanding it by infusing a class perspective. In essence, his perspectives were not too dissimilar to Frantz Fanon's postulation that Marxist analysis 'should always be slightly stretched' when dealing with the colonial question because 'the cause is the consequence; you are rich because you are white, you are white because you are rich'.[58] Nevertheless, the emerging tension would have been even more difficult to manage without political education. Thus, in emphasising political education, Shope would tell the new recruits that 'a soldier without politics is a mercenary'.[59]

Almost a decade later, in 1990, Mzala would refer to this piece at a conference in New York on the future of socialism. He was demonstrating what the SACP in 2018 termed 'strategic consistency, analytical alertness and tactical flexibility'. Mzala still maintained that Marxism failed to deal adequately with the subject of nationalism by merely dismissing it as a false consciousness. He insisted that this was not the case. Conceding that 'there is no textbook for this problem or how to solve it', he nevertheless still considered nationalism as a natural 'reflex' in the context of the oppressed in the country of their birth.

Mzala was convinced that there was a reality that Marxist theory did not accommodate, and he felt the ANC had shied away from this problem since its inception. He perceived nationalism as containing some emotional strength pertinent to mobilising the South African people. This is what the PAC and BC had realised and sought to utilise. Their limitation, though, he argued, was their inability to articulate the phenomenon of black nationalism beyond liberation. He felt that their views of a post-revolutionary society were opaque. Although he regarded Sobukwe's articulation that everyone will be an 'African' as not too different from the ANC's conception of a post-apartheid society, he did not think that this was a common doctrine within the PAC. South Africa's liberation challenge, he continued, was different from other colonial nationalist movements in that it was not dealing with a foreign element but rather the need to reorder society.[60] Here, he was enunciating the SACP's thesis of colonialism of a special type.

XI

During this period, while Mzala was making an impression as a commissar, he was also writing for the liberation movement journals and was part of Radio Freedom. His skills were being recognised and put to good use by the movement. For example, in 1978 he was part of the ANC delegation to the International Youth Festival in Cuba.[61] Organised since 1947 by the World Federation of Democratic Youth and the International Union of Students, the World Festival of Youth and Students was regarded by the West as a propaganda platform of the Soviet Union during the Cold War era.

Reporting for *The New York Times* on 6 August 1978, Alan Riding wrote that 'most of the delegates to the 11th International Youth Festival were caught off guard. Almost 20,000 young leftists came from 195 countries expecting to participate only in solemn ceremonies condemning imperialism. But the Cuban people had carnival in mind.' The festival had a typical Cuban ambiance. Although characterised by festivities, it was not short of political engagements. 'The Africans', continued Riding, 'were the stars of the festival, reflecting Cuba's deep involvement in the continent. They received the largest applause during the inaugural parade on July 28 and their problems – Angola, Ethiopia, Rhodesia, South Africa and South West Africa – dominated both public debate and private conversation.' He continued,

> Many Africans, visiting Cuba for the first time, were deeply impressed by the multiracial society. 'I think anyone walking the streets of Havana in the evening and seeing the hundreds of Cubans milling around in all shades of skin color would be horrified at the thought of what happens in South Africa,' said Oliver Tambo, president of the African National Congress, a leading opposition group in South Africa. 'South Africa is such a sharp contrast that Cuba is the kind of world that a normal human being would aspire to.'[62]

Mzala was, however, not just a delegate to this conference; he delivered a speech that touched on both the bantustans and sanctions. Upon his return, 'he toured all the camps to make a report back'.[63]

XII

What's in a name? When American journalist and author Julie Frederikse asked Mzala, 'Do you have a first name or surname?', Mzala's response was, 'No, I just have Mzala.' It is not clear when exactly Mzala acquired this name. Upon joining MK, many cadres were given a *nom de guerre* for security reasons. However, with Mzala there is often confusion. This stems particularly from the many pen names he used in various publications. In the event held to commemorate the thirtieth anniversary of Mzala's death, Jeff Radebe said that, just like many cadres, Mzala had to live in disguise. 'That is why many cadres were known only through their *noms de guerre*. Comrade Mzala used various such *noms de guerre*, both as a military combatant and as a prolific writer. Some of these names were Khumalo Migwe, Jabulani Khumalo, Alex Mashinini, Jabulani Dlamini and Jabulani Mkhatshwa, the latter being *isithakazelo* [clan name] for Nxumalo.'[64] Awarding Mzala the Order of Luthuli: Silver in 2010, the South African Presidency stated:

> One of his most important and polemical contributions to the armed struggle was entitled *Cooking the Rice inside the Pot*, and it was signed Mzala. When no one responded in *Dawn*, he published a polemical rejoinder to his own article; it was titled: *Preparing the Fire before Cooking the Rice inside the Pot*, and it was signed Alex Mashinini.[65]

This, however, is not accurate. Alex Mashinini was, in fact, Tshidiso Mokhoanatse's MK name. Mokhoanatse says he has observed that his '*nom de guerre* has been wrongly attributed as one of the pennames of Mzala'. Mokhoanatse penned numerous articles under Alex Mashinini, including his response to Mzala, 'Preparing the Fire before Cooking the Rice inside the Pot', which has been mistakenly attributed to Mzala. Mokhoanatse's other pen name was Quadro Cabesa, under which he was published in the *African Communist*. Mokhoanatse says he did not know Mzala very well, 'except during our encounter in Angola where we were undergoing our military training and later in London while I was on a visit from the Netherlands where I was supposed to be deployed'.[66]

Perhaps it is because this confusion between Mokhoanatse and Mzala has been repeated so often that it has come to be seen as the truth. Kasrils is one who bought into this legend. Speaking about Mzala's enthusiasm and stamina for the topic, Kasrils believes he 'was disappointed that, despite the interest the article generated, there was no written response'. Kasrils believes that this may have inspired Mzala to follow up the debate by responding to his own article, but using another name. He argues that

Mzala's thesis on people's war was developed well before the SACP's insurrectionary thesis was adopted at its Cuba Conference in April 1989. Kasrils's belief that Alex Mashinini was Mzala is based on the 'similarities' in style of the two articles.

It is not clear where this mistake emanates, but it may well be linked to Mzala's penchant to debate with himself. He had a reputation for writing articles, and if no one responded, he would pen a rejoinder simply to spark a debate. Joel Netshitenzhe indicates that 'at one time – he himself confessed – when he placed a provocative article in one of the journals (most likely *Sechaba*) and no one responded, he then personally wrote a critique of that article and had it published under a pseudonym'. Mzala's propensity to debate with himself can also be seen in the article 'Further Contribution on the Arming of the Masses' in the 1982 second-quarter edition of the *African Communist* where, writing as Khumalo Migwe, he argued: 'The article "Has the Time come for the Arming of the Masses?" by Mzala ... raises one of the real fundamental strategic questions of our revolution.' He further went on to accuse Mzala of only treating the question from the strategic level and ignoring the tactical aspects.[67]

However, the confusion around the name 'Alex Mashinini' could also have been sparked when Eddy Maloka indicated that Mzala's first contributions to the *African Communist* in 1980 and 1981 under the name 'Mzala' were on armed struggle and the question of arming the masses. 'As nobody responded to him, he responded to himself in 1982 in the *African Communist* as "Khumalo Migwe".'[68] Maloka also indicated that 'he was to later try again to spark a debate around this issue in 1985 in *Sechaba*, writing as "Mzala", a debate in which "Alex Mashinini" also participated'.[69] It is easy to see how confusion could have arisen.

Nevertheless, in his 1989 discussion article in *Sechaba*, 'Omelettes cannot be made without breaking eggs', it is Mzala himself who dispels the notion that he was Alex Mashinini. In discussing the options for the movement, he draws on Mashinini's 1988 article in *Sechaba*, 'People's War and Negotiations'. Mzala characterises Mashinini as one of the theorists who advances 'a compromising and capitulationist tendency'. Mzala questioned Mashinini's 'solution' of negotiations and asked, 'Why now? What happened to all the talk about the people's war and the need to "prepare the fire before cooking the rice inside the pot"? (See my debate with Alex Mashinini before the ANC Kabwe Conference in *Sechaba* January 1985 and April 1985).' He continues:

> Comrade Mashinini did not intend this conclusion to his theoretical propositions since … he was merely attempting, although with much error, to interpret a situation that has become very sophisticated and complex. Errors in themselves do not make people less revolutionary, particularly comrades who have been in the struggle through thick and thin. The problem only arises if theoretical positions do not get constant repair and safe handling.[70]

In this article, Mzala was scathing of Mashinini's posture towards negotiated settlement. Even if Mzala was still keen to spark a discussion by debating with himself, at this stage of his life he had more on his plate than to debate with himself. He was working hard on his PhD thesis while also working and writing for *Sechaba* and the *African Communist*. Also, during this period, Mzala was beginning to write for the mainstream media, as well as working for Research on Education in South Africa (RESA). His health was beginning to deteriorate, and he was also firmly focused on a fellowship in the United States where he was to work on OR Tambo's biography. In addition, he had begun to work on Harry Gwala's biography.

It is incredulous to imagine that he would be obsessed with writing articles in debate with himself. Furthermore, on 3 March 1991, after visiting Mzala's apartment, John Daniel recorded in his notes: 'Mpho, his wife, said the following were among his pseudonyms: Khumalo Migwe, Jabulani Mkhatshwa, and Sisa Majola.'[71] Granted, there are other pseudonyms not listed by Mpho, but equally important is that she did not mention Alex Mashinini – and for obvious reasons: it was not one of Mzala's pseudonyms.

Nonetheless, during this period, Mzala was becoming synonymous with ideas and debates. For Netshitenzhe:

> Mzala had a sharp mind and the capacity to view an issue from various angles. He liked debating, and his inquisitive mind helped identify approaches on theoretical as well as practical matters that might otherwise have eluded the movement. He was systematic in his analysis and based his approaches on theoretical precepts and empirical evidence. He was a systematic researcher and a prolific writer.

Titi says Mzala's official MK name in Angola was Khumalo Migwe. Stanley Manong, who met Mzala at the Kabwe conference in 1985, writes that 'it was during that time I met Jabulani Nxumalo (MK Khumalo 'Mzala' Migwe), a comrade who was known for his prolific writing'. Mzala used this name mainly when writing for *Dawn,* the journal of Umkhonto we Sizwe, and about MK-related issues. Netshitenzhe thinks 'the name, Mzala, evolved later – which, in my recollection, was how he addressed peers, especially during debate: each interlocutor was to him an Mzala'. Sifiso Buthelezi, who was part of the Northern Natal Rural Machinery with Mzala, says he used the term 'Mzala' more than once in one sentence. That is how he addressed people.

According to Kasrils, 'few knew his real name at that time as it was customary and necessary to hide actual identities for security reasons'. Jordan asserts, 'The name Mzala was originally a nick name, for a comrade who liked to refer to others as Mzala – cousin in the Nguni dialects. As often happens in such circumstances the name is inverted to refer back to its author.' In his initial writings for *Dawn*, Mzala often used his MK name and, according to Maloka, 'hence he was called "Khumalo". But because he used to call everyone "Mzala, Mzala", the name later stuck to him'.[72] Among the first things Titi noticed when she met her brother in Angola was the way he addressed everyone as 'mzala', and they in turn called him 'mzala'. She was curious and asked: 'Yini lento yolokhu nibizana mzala, mzala?' (Why do you keep calling each other mzala, mzala?). He told her that he preferred addressing people as mzala rather than comrades. He was thinking ahead. When I'm deployed back in the country, he said, I don't want to make the mistake and end up calling people comrades in the wrong places.

CHAPTER 4

The emergence of a revolutionary intellectual

I

As 1978 drew to a close, Mzala was emerging as part of the leadership group in the camps. Patric Mtshaulana, now a political instructor at MK's Fazenda camp, was faced with a crisis when some trainees revolted. Having completed their military training, they decided that enough was enough with the unending wait and demanded to be sent back into South Africa to fight. James Ngculu, who was deployed to Fazenda in May 1978, writes that the waiting was one of the most difficult aspects of being in the camps. After waiting for over nine months, coupled with the serious shortages they faced, a rumour began doing the rounds that 'they had been dumped at Fazenda'. Discipline waned and 'eventually, in the middle of 1979, it completely broke down and Fazenda became ungovernable'. At the heart of the problem was a group from Natal that was particularly frustrated by lack of deployment to forward areas; they resorted to accusing people who were in command of the Natal Machinery of not being from Natal and that they were 'unfamiliar' with the region.

The matter escalated and leaders from Luanda were deployed to the camp to persuade these comrades to calm down. According to Mtshaulana, Mzala was part of that delegation. This is when Mtshaulana met Mzala for the first time. Initially, according to Ngculu, it was Mzwai Piliso who had been deployed to quell the situation; he 'tried his best to explain … but he failed to convince them'. Eventually, leaders with Natal origins, such as Moses Mabhida and Edwin Dlamini, had to be called in. In the end, using his natural ability as 'a good speaker, a good motivator and a very simple and humble person with strong powers of persuasion', writes Ngcula, 'Mabhida managed to placate the Natal comrades and stabilised the situation'. However, this practice of naked regionalism was not without its problems and inescapably 'created its own tension, and some viewed this as tribalism'.[1]

Mzala's presence confirms the tribal and regional card played to handle a potentially explosive situation. Mtshaulana was immediately impressed by his charisma, bravery and unorthodox approach to the revolution.

> While other members of the delegation were trying to persuade the cadres to obey orders, Mzala, when his turn came, agreed with them that we could not stay in exile forever. He therefore agreed that people should be allowed to express the view [that] they want to go home. They must be allowed to express criticisms against the forms of training they are being given. They should sooner or later be allowed to go home.

This was not just a matter of posturing to suit the needs of the moment. Mzala consistently advanced and developed this argument on numerous occasions. The emergence of the Mass Democratic Movement (MDM) in the form of the UDF and COSATU shifted things favourably for the liberation movement. Ronnie Kasrils recalls that the 'externally based ANC, SACP and MK grappled with the problem of connecting the mass political, underground and armed activity – three of the four pillars of struggle', the fourth being international solidarity. Mzala refreshed his debate through the 'Cooking the Rice inside the Pot' article, 'implying the requirement of establishing guerrilla bases at home'. To Kasrils, this introduced 'fresh thinking into the debate' and reflected Mzala's 'wonderful ability to coin catchy, relevant phrases which caught people's attention'. It is unsurprising that 'his thesis was hotly debated'.[2]

II

By now Mzala was involved in all manner of activities. His versatility and aptitude were shining through. Not only was he now a trained soldier and political instructor, but he was also reactivating the artistic abilities he had displayed while growing up, performing drama and playing piano in church. His participation in Radio Freedom and the Amandla Cultural Ensemble was thus inevitable.

Pallo Jordan's deployment to Angola in 1977 was aimed at reviving Radio Freedom, first launched in 1963. This project was essential in countering apartheid propaganda – which had, to some extent, succeeded in portraying the ANC as a terrorist organisation – and Radio Freedom became a key tool for the ANC-headed liberation movement to articulate its alternative perspectives. Although it was illegal to tune in – the apartheid regime tried to block transmission from reaching South Africa, but to no avail – many in South Africa found and listened to it. 'Through Radio Freedom, the ANC could directly connect with its supporters inside the country and influence political mobilisation, particularly during the 1970s and 1980s.'[3]

As head of Radio Freedom, Jordan was responsible for identifying and training potential broadcasters from among the ranks of the movement and, with the MK camps now based in Angola, it made sense for the station to be based there too. Jordan's method 'was to expand on the initial training the comrades had received by practical experience in radio. As we broadcast, so the comrades learnt on the job'. Through these efforts, Radio Freedom was transformed into 'a more directly agitational tool of the ANC'. Jordan and his team regarded their broadcasts 'as virtual public meetings, where effective agitators and propagandists would address thousands ... sitting in their homes'.

Jordan's team also employed 'agitprop' theatre and poetry readings which 'had become a feature of the Black Consciousness Movement [BCM] and many of the younger comrades who had come through its ranks wanted to be, aspired to be poets or to express themselves poetically'. The purpose of the agitprop technique – developed after the establishment of the Department of Agitation and Propaganda in 1920 by the Communist Party of the Soviet Union (CPSU) – was to reach the working class directly, which until then had had no access to theatres. It quickly proved to be an effective strategy in the Soviet Union; 'from art galleries to movies to street corners, Russian culture was flooded with pro-Bolshevik sentiments'.[4]

Ultimately, the work of Radio Freedom had a serious political objective, but was at the same time enjoyable for many young comrades. 'Mzala was not only steeped in Zulu Orature and Bardic Poetry, but was a creative poet in his own right, especially in Zulu. He was one of our regulars on Radio, especially when we did radio plays, documentaries or commentaries,' says

Jordan. Of course, by now Mzala was a published poet and performing artist, having performed with his Bethel College music group. He had also organised performances of Gibson Kente's *How Long?* Mzala's artistic ability is one aspect of his life that has been downplayed at the expense of his intellectual prowess. Granted, by this time he was part of the editorial team of *Dawn* magazine, and had proceeded to establish himself as one of the foremost organic intellectuals produced by the movement.

Cadres at Radio Freedom developed very strong bonds with Mzala. Jordan observed that Mzala spent a lot of his spare time in discussion with them. 'As one of the editors of *Dawn*,' says Jordan, 'he also wrote prolifically and engaged energetically in the ongoing political debates – which were the daily diet of MK cadres.' But because Radio Freedom was a propaganda arm of the movement, it received telexed coverage of international news from Associated Press, Reuters, Tass, Xinhua and the Angola Press Agency (Angop) daily, Jordan believes that 'this was among the reasons Mzala spent so much time' there. Later, when the ANC declared 1979 'The Year of the Spear' – marking the centenary of the Battle of Isandlwana, where in January 1879 Zulu warriors under the leadership of King Cetshwayo kaMpande annihilated the British army – Mzala was in the leadership mix in Angola. When Jordan was deployed to head the ANC's internal propaganda campaign, Mzala accompanied him 'on a tour of all the MK training camps in Angola'.

In 1977, when Kasrils arrived in Angola, he roped in Mzala when he 'established the commissariat for the various camps in Angola'. The group consisted of Edwin Mabitsela, January Masilela (Che O'Gara), Vumile Ngculu (James), and Lungile Chris Pepani (S'bali). Mzala became Kasrils's assistant in Luanda, and the group of commissars was 'moulded into a dynamic collective, very bright and capable, and they stimulated one another's development'. Kasrils remembers this group with nostalgia:

> They were all brave and dedicated, and I would say that they raised political understanding in the camps to a very high level indeed. They were also fun and engaging to be with, loved sport, concerts and organising cultural programmes in the camps. Had they been around in the difficult 1983-84 period when MK was mobilised to counter UNITA [Union for the Total Independence of Angola] banditry, the confusion that led to a mutiny would not have occurred. By then these comrades had been deployed to serve in the underground structures in the forward areas [of] neighbouring South Africa. The absence of

developed cadres such as them left an unfortunate vacuum of political leadership in Angola despite the outstanding calibre of those such as the MK commander Timothy Mokoena.

The ANC attributed the 1983–84 mutiny in the Angolan camps, labelled Mkatashinga,[5] to apartheid agents and agents provocateurs. While others have perceived the ANC's crushing of the mutiny as undemocratic and unjust, an alternative narrative emerging from 'memoirs and biographies of former soldiers paints a more nuanced picture that reveals the situation to be more complex than the ANC's official view and those of its distractors [*sic*]'.[6] Nonetheless, no revolutionary organisation has ever dealt gently with a mutiny. Because they are considered dangerous, they are dealt with decisively, whether rightly or wrongly.

III

Mzala's first signs as a prolific writer emerged in 1978 in the article 'The Compromising Role of Inkatha'. These initial thoughts would eventually lead to his book *Chief with a Double Agenda*. Later, as a scholar, Mzala's work can be understood as that of a historian who closely studied Zulu nationalism and the national question. However, indicative of the impatience of the 1976 generation, he consistently advanced the notion of waging the war inside the country. In this debut article in the *African Communist*, Mzala presented a coherent Marxist perspective as a context in which to examine the origins and role of Inkatha. Writing as Ngacambaza Khumalo, he argued:

> A scientific revolutionary strategy demands a correct appreciation of the political character of the forces which are ranged against one another in the South African struggle for liberation. We can only eliminate apartheid and white supremacy, establishing a national democracy and prepare the road for the advance to socialism if reactionary tendencies in all their forms and all levels are consciously combated.[7]

Less than two years since he had skipped the country, it is evident in this article that Mzala had immersed himself in Marxist literature as the basis for his political principles. His thoughtful analysis on the reactionary role of Inkatha and the need to address the national question were clearly analysed from a Marxist standpoint. He further argued that although there were emerging talks of Inkatha as 'a national organisation geared for the total emancipation of the South African black community as a whole', this new image of Inkatha posed a danger 'to the national unity of the oppressed because of its tribal orientation and origin. It gives the notion that the Zulus are more important ethnic groups around which national unity should be fostered.'[8]

Reviewing the book *How Long Will South Africa Survive?* by RW Johnson in the August 1979 edition of *Dawn*, and writing as Khumalo Migwe, Mzala was already displaying his robust and ruthless style of polemics. In his opening salvo he posited, 'This book has a very attractive title, particularly for us South Africans actively involved in a protracted struggle to overthrow the Pretoria regime. More than that, this title gives one an impression that the author is either a prophet or a profound political analyst.' He continued on the offensive: 'We are dealing here with a confused and above all a highly contemptuous bourgeois economist.'

Mzala's bone of contention was the author's reductionist approach in dealing with a complex South African problem. In his attempt to examine, among other things, the causes of the Soweto uprising in 1976, Mzala says Johnson argued that the 'revolt was caused by the United States of America manipulating the gold price, causing balance of payment problems, unemployment of blacks and therefore a fall in living standards. Had there been no fall in the price of gold, Johnson argues, the "problems" in Soweto could not have arisen.' Mzala dismissed what he perceived to be Johnson's obsession with the United State's manipulation of gold, which he [Johnson] believed would bring pressure to the 'social, political and economic structure' and lead to the eventual collapse of the apartheid regime. Mzala could not fathom Johnson's assertions that the collapse of Portuguese colonialism in Africa was not brought about by armed struggle by the people of Angola and Mozambique but rather out of choice to join the European Economic Community.[9]

In December of the same year, still writing as Khumalo Migwe, Mzala penned another piece in *Dawn* on the 'Critical Remarks of the Question of the Terror Tactic'. In this piece Mzala entered the debate by presenting three theses that demonstrated that, while his political outlook was materialist, he was still grappling with the moral questions instilled by his Christian upbringing. In responding to the question of whether terror can be a justifiable tactic, he argued that this question, although it involved a moral issue, should not be approached from 'a purely abstract moral point of view'. He wrote that 'our evaluation must be based on the objective analysis of whether such action fits into the immediate aims as well as the long-term goals of the movement; whether such action mobilises the people for the revolution or for the oppressor'.[10]

It is not clear what prompted Mzala to tackle this question. Could it be the moral dilemma he had to contend with as a trained revolutionary fighter but also a Christian who, at some point, would have to face the possibility of meting out extreme forms of terror in the course of the liberation? He argued that his article had not set out to disprove that terror tactics at certain moments of the revolution are not justified. Rather, he wanted to emphasise that 'the terror tactic in place of mobilising the masses is a manifestation of anarcho-liberalism and a nihilistic tendency born of theoretical ignorance and frustration'. For him, the armed struggle was a people's struggle since it was a struggle for national liberation. Guns, therefore, did not make a revolution, he argued; rather, it was the type of man behind the gun that determined the pace of the revolution. 'Power will always belong to the people.'

Through these articles Mzala had announced himself as a deeper thinker with a rare ability to put his ideas down on paper. In a sense, it is his writings, beyond the memories of those who knew him, that have immortalised him. Those who never had a chance to meet him at least have a chance to interact with his thoughts through his writing.

IV

In 1979, Mzala was selected as part of a group of 10 comrades to train in the GDR. This is where he met comrades like Lebona Mosia, and where he and others, such as Patric Mtshaulana, got to know each other better. From its early days in exile, the ANC selected some of its promising cadres for training abroad, in destinations such as the Soviet Union and the GDR. However, solidarity between the ANC and the Socialist bloc, the GDR in particular, can be traced back to the 1950s. The GDR trained a number of MK fighters through its solidarity-based assistance programme intended to train and educate people from developing countries. Kasrils estimates that about a thousand MK soldiers 'underwent military training in the GDR between 1976 and 1989'.[11]

The Soviet Union also contributed immensely to the ANC, its support ranging from financial assistance, medical aid, food and other civilian supplies, to academic education, military and political training.[12] With the

ANC committed to sending as many of its young cadres for further training abroad as possible, Jack Simons's work included presenting 'instructor's classes' for those comrades.

Apart from being serious and dedicated to the task at hand, there were light moments that reveal Mzala's strange sense of humour. One Saturday afternoon, says Mosia, they were relaxing in the TV room with comrades from SWAPO when one of the female cadres said to Mzala, 'You talk too much like a priest.' Mzala remained quiet for some time before responding in a cool, composed and relaxed manner: 'I think the priest was the most educated person in your village.' '[That] was classic Mzala,' said Mosia.

Pepani says that Mzala displayed the highest level of discipline among them. 'First and foremost, Mzala was a very serious person, very strict person, both in his personal and social life.' He was regarded as someone who led by example, and 'had problems with a disconnect between theory and practice'. He was unlike many leaders today who speak the revolutionary language but who don't act it. Says Pepani: 'Those people, some of them are just revolutionary when they speak on the stage but, in their normal day-to-day lives, the examples they show to themselves, to the family, to the people, they do not live like a Chris Hani, like an Mzala.' At this stage, Mzala was already displaying the characteristics of a leader who lived by his convictions. Pepani experienced him as a person 'who believed that theory without practice is like groping in the dark'. He, said Pepani, applied this principle 'even socially and personally'.

This approach to life complemented his upbringing as well as his deep religious beliefs. Even though Mtshaulana had already met Mzala, it was in the GDR that 'I met him really'. Considered a somewhat reserved person, Mtshaulana often watched his comrades getting into heated debates with Mzala on a wide range of topics. 'I was always listening, trying to understand who this man is, what does he want. And then one day we were just sitting and I asked him where he went to school.' The response was fascinating, as it revealed Mzala's deep religious roots as a person who had been to Bethel College.

It was this disclosure that revealed Mzala for Mtshaulana. 'I suddenly had an understanding of him' because in every lecture Mzala was posing the question, 'Why does it matter whether we come from the apes or the baboons or from God? Is that now the thing we must be emphasising here?' Mtshaulana initially thought this 'was a philosophical question because the whole thing of the difference between the premise of matter and ideas, idealism versus materialism, is a philosophical question'. But, for Mzala, this was beyond simply philosophy; it touched on his Christian beliefs. It was very hard for him to accept that he could not be a communist because of his religion. The question was further complicated by the fact that while in the GDR, according to Mtshaulana, the Polish Communist Party was purging Roman Catholic members as a result of pressure from the GDR that people who did not accept the basic question of philosophy could not be communists. This became an issue for Mzala for the duration of the programme. 'The communist party there was trying to get someone to convince him,' says Mtshaulana. On entering the class, 'the first question [every lecturer] asked is, who is Mzala?'

Apart from the fact that Mzala 'demonstrated an analytical capacity combined with an intellectual curiosity', Pallo Jordan emphasises that he 'was raised in the Seventh Day Adventist church and had a very religious upbringing. He brought the disciplines of latter-day Protestantism with him into the movement. He read the classics of Marxism that were available avidly! He pored over the English-language journals from Cuba, the Soviet Union and other socialist countries, while keeping abreast of developments on the home front.' Mzala was a critical thinker who did not take anything at face value. Jordan remembers that he insisted on examining everything. During this period there were comrades among the leftists who saw themselves as atheists, and Mzala was constantly engaged in dialogue on the philosophical issues.

> I remember him becoming very excited on one such occasion when I mentioned the existence of 'anti-matter'. 'What does that mean then, for materialism?' he inquired. I cleverly ducked the query saying: 'Dialectically, if there is matter in nature, there must be its opposite, "anti-matter"!' 'Then one should not be so dismissive of religion,' he concluded. To this day I have often wondered whether my response had offered him some comfort in the residual religious sentiments he still harboured, his Marxism notwithstanding.

Jordan was pressed on the topic by others who had been present during that discussion.

> I explained that I was an agnostic. Perhaps I did not have the courage to deny the existence of God; but I was sceptical enough to question the notion of an absolute, masculine monarch, to whom we attributed omniscience, omnipotence and benevolence, but who demanded regular

appeals for a nurturing attention, extravagant praises and degrading obsequiousness.

Mzala found that rather amusing, and retorted, says Jordan, 'Take refuge in the Zen-Buddhist notion that belief in God is neither here nor there. There is nothing you can do about his/her existence; and if he/she does not exist, that too is beyond your powers!'

For Lungile Pepani, it is his strict religious background that instilled in Mzala his strong principles and discipline. But once these deeply ingrained values encountered Marxism-Leninism, Pepani says, a clash was inevitable. 'He found new contradictions,' says Pepani, but still Mzala continued living like a revolutionary. Typical of critical thinkers, Pepani remembers him as 'a very curious person, who always wanted to see the truth in the course of his learning'. In a conversation he revealed to Pepani some of the readings he had been doing, including Marxist-Leninists and revolutionary movements in Latin America. He told Pepani that he saw a very close connection between religion and communism.

Just as had been the case in his school days, in the GDR Mzala was a man in a hurry to accomplish his mission. He took every opportunity to prepare himself theoretically. On one occasion Pepani bumped into him on his way to take a bath. 'He had a towel and a book,' says Pepani, and when quizzed Mzala why he was taking a book to the bath, he retorted, 'I don't have to waste time ... there is no time. We have limited time on this earth, you know. We should live productively.' He teased his comrades about wasting time by going to the bath only to sing revolutionary songs. For him, bath time was reading time. He would sit in the bath, reading a book until the water got cold and he would then top it up with hot water again. His comrades teased him that he would drown in a bath one day.

Unlike at mainstream universities, where there is competition among students for top marks, this group, according to Pepani, was special in that 'we wanted to make sure, like in the military, that we all march at the pace of the slowest. So that when we come out, we are all able to march at the pace of the fastest.' So, outside of the normal timetable, they organised themselves into study groups to look at various articles and debate among themselves. 'Mzala was very articulate,' recalls Pepani. '[He] was a very big debater and he could relate all the things we were learning to the movement, the alliance, the South Africa situation. Very amazing, right at the beginning when we came there.'

Mzala also served as motivator to his fellow comrades whenever some were feeling down. In December many would think about their families whom they had not seen in a while. When Pepani was feeling down, Mzala said he should imagine how the enemy would feel 'if they could hear that an MK commander is sad because he is thinking of his family'.

Another important aspect of Mzala was his candour, which often rubbed others the wrong way. He never minced his words when he believed in something. 'He was a very straightforward person,' says Pepani and thus he came 'through sometimes a little bit undiplomatic'.

Mzala was a sincere, honest man who had no time for mischief, like chasing after girls. Pepani recalls that when they arrived in the GDR there was a SWAPO delegation of female cadres, mostly of their own age group. 'You can imagine, we were coming from the camps,' and there was a lot of interest and excitement from both sides. Naturally, both groups spent time together, and Pepani naughtily recalls that maybe it was only Mzala who did not find a 'person'. And this was not because Mzala was incapable or unattractive – far from it. He was a man on a mission and had long concluded that such activities would only derail him from his objective of liberating South Africa. Instead, Mzala remained loyal to his family and would buy gifts for his younger sister.

V

Soon Mzala found himself in Maputo, Mozambique. This, says Vuso Shabalala, was the first time since 1976 that Mzala was in the forward areas. He was getting closer to his dream of waging a people's war on the home front. His arrival in Maputo was preceded by the finalisation of the ANC's 'Theses on our Strategic Line', also known as 'The Green Book'. In fact, it is probably this development that created opportunities for the deployment of many comrades in forward areas. In 1978, an ANC delegation led by Oliver Tambo had visited the Socialist Republic of Vietnam where one of the lessons espoused was that the revolution must 'walk on both feet' – military and political.[13] After that visit, the ANC set up the Politico-Military Strategy Commission (PMSC) led by Tambo and comprising Thabo Mbeki, Joe Modise, Moses Mabhida, Joe Gqabi and Joe Slovo.

The Commission completed its work by March 1979, and its report (The Green Book) was tabled to the NEC. The Green Book identified 13 strategic themes, the principal one for the struggle being 'the seizure of power by the people as the first step in the struggle for the victory of our national democratic revolution'.[14] At the heart of the strategy was mass political mobilisation that emphasised popular struggles inside the country such as the ones led by the youth and student organisations and trade unions, and the mass uprisings in the townships led by the civic organisations. Ultimately, the armed struggle, led by MK, was to 'serve as a secondary means to deepen mass mobilisation'.[15] In a nutshell, the focus was on 'participation from all layers of society in a revolution'.[16]

Sue Rabkin, who arrived in Maputo from London in 1979, met Mzala in 1980. A British citizen, Sue was drawn into the South African struggle when she met and married David Rabkin in the United Kingdom (UK). David's family had settled in the UK in the 1960s, but since David felt he had unfinished business there, the couple found themselves back in Cape Town in the early 1970s. They soon became involved in the underground activities of both the SACP and the ANC, and began working with comrades like Jeremy Cronin, 'producing underground propaganda for the South African Communist Party'.[17] Not long afterward, they were producing their own independent propaganda publication titled *Vukani/Awake*. Consisting of a single sheet, David wrote about current affairs on the front, while the flip side was divided into two: the top half on Marxist theory written by Jeremy Cronin and the bottom half on how to work underground by Sue.[18]

On 28 July 1976, Sue, David and Jeremy were arrested and charged with conspiring with members and supporters of the ANC and SACP.[19] Their arrest can also be understood in the context of the post-Soweto uprising crackdown. David was sentenced to 10 years and Jeremy to eight years. Possibly because she was pregnant with her second child, Sue was spared a lengthy prison term; she was sentenced to three years, which was suspended and she spent only one month in jail. Because she was a British citizen, Sue was subsequently deported.

Back in the UK, she continued her connections with the South African struggle. When Mac Maharaj was released from Robben Island, 'he smuggled out the Mandela autobiography'[20] and, on his arrival in London, needed a typist, so he approached the SACP for help. The National Chairperson, Dr Yusuf Dadoo, promptly directed him to Sue. For the next two and a half years, Sue worked on Mandela's autobiography. The Green Book had, however, changed the focus for the ANC and soon Maharaj was summoned to headquarters in Lusaka. 'He told me that he [was] now the secretary of internal political reconstruction and he must just finish up this book, and he must now set up the organisation inside the country.' When the book was done and Maharaj was saying goodbye to Sue, to his utter shock, she was quite emphatical: 'You can't be serious. You're not going to leave me here.'

Both Maharaj and Dadoo were reluctant to allow a 'young white woman with two babies' to head off to the frontline states. It was simply too dangerous. But Sue was resolute. She was confident that her underground experience in Cape Town had prepared her well for the mission. Sue still considers this episode an example of the sexism that existed in the movement. 'All those years in the women's liberation you get used to this, so I fought' – and Dadoo eventually relented. Thus, Sue was deployed to Maputo, as part of what was then called 'internal political reconstruction'. This is the environment Mzala encountered in Maputo.

VI

With Mozambique having gained independence in 1975, Frelimo was now in charge of the country. This enabled the ANC to operate freely in the country. However, due to the country's proximity to South Africa, this was not without risks. It was not very difficult for the apartheid regime to strike, as it had done in Angola in Operation Savannah, employing advanced technology to deploy its armed forces deep into the country.[21] On 14 March 1979, South African Air Force attacked Novo Catengue.

In fact, the apartheid government did not limit its activities to simple cross-border raids in Mozambique. It killed many people, including innocent civilians, and left scores injured. It also resorted to political executions by means of parcel bombs, planting bombs in offices and even poisoning activists. In 1981, it launched Operation Beanbag, one of the apartheid regime's deadliest cross-border operations in Matola, Mozambique.[22] Matola, about 15 kilometres from the capital Maputo and a typical densely populated area, harboured MK fighters located in several ANC safe houses. On the morning of 30 January 1981, a team of Special Force commandos headed by Colonel (later General) Jac Buchner and assisted by Major (later Brigadier) Callie Steijn of the SADF's Military Intelligence drove over 70 kilometres from the South African-Mozambican border and launched an attack on three houses in Matola, leaving behind a trail of destruction and devastation.[23]

The precision of the operation, however, pointed to inside information. Of course, they had pieced together information extracted from interrogated detainees such as Steven Mashamba, who later became an *askari*. By the time the raid was over, 20 lives had been lost. Among them was José Ramos, a Portuguese citizen, who apparently bore a striking resemblance to Joe Slovo. Momentarily, this led to misplaced euphoria on the side of the SADF, who thought they had struck a telling blow that had killed Slovo.[24] They were soon disappointed when news spread that the dead man was not Slovo. Three attackers (all Rhodesians) were killed, as well as 16 South Africans, including a number of senior MK operatives and 'members of the elite Special Operations unit, including the commander of the first attack on Sasol, Mr Motso Mokgabundi'.[25]

The very same SADF Special Forces commandos struck again in other cross-border operations, one in Maseru on 9 December 1982. In fact, during this period the apartheid regime launched attack after attack, including Operation Skerwe (meaning 'fragments' or 'shrapnel') in which ANC facilities in Matola again came under fire on 23 May 1983. This was followed by, among others, Operation Plecksy, which targeted ANC residences and offices in Gaborone, Botswana, on 14 June 1985, and Operation Leo, targeting ANC facilities in Botswana, Zimbabwe and Zambia, on 19 May 1986.[26]

In between, the apartheid regime carried out a number of other operations in Mozambique. On 17 August 1982, the regime struck a devastating blow. Ruth First, a long-standing ANC and SACP activist and wife of Joe Slovo, was executed by a parcel bomb at Eduardo Mondlane University. Then, on 7 December 1983, two ANC members were injured when their house in the suburb of Xipamanine was bombed. In 1988, Albie Sachs survived an explosion of a bomb placed in his car in Maputo; he lost an arm and the sight in one eye. Planted by the South African security agents, the bomb was intended for Indres Naidoo. In July 1989, Enoch Reginald Mhlongo, Themba Ngesi and Samuel Phinda died after they were poisoned by apartheid agents. It was clear that being deployed in the forward areas was not an easy task. Death angels seemed to hover all around. But still, this deployment excited Mzala because he believed that the ANC needed to take the war against the apartheid regime right into South Africa.

VII

When Sue arrived in Maputo, 'there was hardly anything'. With Thabo Mbeki and Jacob Zuma having been expelled from Swaziland where they had been based, Mbeki, says Sue, went to Lusaka and Zuma to

Mozambique. Mozambique, Swaziland, Botswana, Lesotho and London had been identified as the five forward areas, with Harare added to the list when Zimbabwe gained independence in 1980. It was these forward areas, where the internal machineries were based, that served as launching pads for internal underground structures. 'It was the closest we could get,' Sue reckons. However, long before the new strategy was given impetus by The Green Book, the Revolutionary Council (RC) had 'looked at the notion of establishing structures inside the states bordering on South Africa to facilitate the establishment of an ANC influence inside the country'.[27] When the RC became the Political Military Committee, these forward structures became political machineries responsible for building the political underground in South Africa.

Frene Ginwala, who became the first speaker in the National Assembly of democratic South Africa, had moved to Mozambique in the early 1960s on the advice of ANC Secretary-General Walter Sisulu. Ginwala joined her parents, successful merchants already living in Lourenço Marques (Maputo), and became a strategic link for the ANC. She would later play a pivotal role in facilitating the escape of many comrades from the country.[28] According to Sue, Ginwala's parents had three properties in Maputo, and when Mozambique gained independence 'Frene gave those properties to the ANC. One of them became the ANC office, which we later called Beirut.' Another was a flat used by Zuma and the third 'was called the Internal House'.

It was from here that the political machinery operated. When she arrived in Maputo, Sue found only Indres Naidoo and Sunny Singh (known as Bobby), the latter having been recently released from Robben Island. Their primary task, together with the Swaziland machinery, was to find routes into South Africa and 'to recruit and to build an organisational structure inside the country for the overthrow of the apartheid regime – not a small task,' says Sue. They were soon joined by Ronnie Kasrils, who came from Angola. Sue regarded these comrades as 'the crème de la crème of the camps, of which Mzala was one'.

After working closely with Mzala in Angola between 1977 and 1980, when Kasrils was deployed to Maputo he 'brought Mzala to join the underground structures'. Kasrils and Mzala continued to work 'closely together in the period 1980–1984 in Maputo' until subsequent deployments took them in different directions. 'I lost touch with him, as happened in the struggle. It was dangerous to keep in contact through letters, so it was difficult to keep up friendships,' says Kasrils. By then, Kasrils had strongly motivated for Mzala's recruitment into the SACP.

In 1979, after a stint inside South Africa where he was deployed to Soweto under the Transvaal urban machinery, then headed by Siphiwe Nyanda, Vuso Shabalala was deployed in Maputo. Shabalala was already in Maputo when Mzala arrived as part of a newly formed political service unit, headed by Kasrils, that was to provide support to the political community as the senior organ in Maputo.

VIII

On his arrival in Maputo, Mzala stayed at the Internal House where selected comrades were being orientated while developing plans to execute the struggle. Later, Mzala and some of his comrades would be deployed to Swaziland, where they operated underground. Due to its size, Swaziland was a very difficult and dangerous place in which to operate. When Mzala arrived at the Internal House, says Shabalala, he was to be deployed in the political machinery in Swaziland, but in the interim he had to stay in the safe house. Shabalala had been appointed chairperson of that unit, with Sue as its secretary and Sunny Singh its treasurer. Although Indres Naidoo continued to head the political machinery in Maputo, working closely with Sue and other comrades, according to Shabalala, 'the unit was being reconstituted'.

With Shabalala as commissar, other members of the unit included Rocks Mashinini (Tsietsi Mashinini's elder brother) and Florence Maseko (Phumla Williams). Shabalala says that Mzala was by then 'real top class' in the politics of both the ANC and the SACP. He had been to the Soviet Union and the GDR and had 'been deployed to the West [Angola] and that's why he was deployed this side as one of those people who were thought to be politically matured and would be able to participate in the building of the political structures inside the country in the 1980s'.

Living conditions in the military residences were, however, challenging. Although the place had a homely feel, with children running around, they had to consistently look over their shoulders. Sue had two kids and Naidoo had a little boy about the same age as Sue's children, so it was rough living in a house with no furniture and little or no money. Some comrades 'didn't have toothbrushes' and 'no one had a towel' or even spare clothes. This was the life of freedom fighters. When they left South Africa, many had just a small bag, Sue recalls that 'they didn't come out with suitcases'.

Sunny Singh, born in Cato Manor (uMkhumbane), Durban, had joined the underground MK Durban Central Unit in January 1962, and it was not long before he was carrying out 'some sabotage' missions in the Durban area.[29] 'The cell sabotaged the railway line under the Victoria Street (now known as Bertha Mkhize Street) Bridge – this was the main Durban–Johannesburg railway line.' However, a member of their cell turned out to be a police informer and betrayed them, and in August 1963 they were arrested.[30] Singh was sentenced to 10 years on Robben Island and finally released toward the end of 1974. He was immediately placed under house arrest but continued to be very active. In 1976, he skipped the country to Mozambique where he worked under Naidoo in Maputo. He says: 'Then subsequently Zuma became head of the ANC political council and Mzala was in the political and military committee in Maputo. That is where I met him.'[31]

Even though Mzala was still very young, Singh says of the time he spent with him, Sue and Naidoo in Maputo, he admired him greatly. To him, Mzala was both straightforward and brave:

> You see, I came to admire him for simple reason, he was straight, he didn't waiver, stutter. He had an independent mind and he always challenged issues. He even challenged Zuma on many occasions. He had an independence of thought and no fear. Running sometimes on critical issues, he had his own thoughts about issues.

Running the ANC safe houses remained a challenge, but it was their love of books that brought Sue and Mzala closer. Sue says running the house was a huge operation because everyone had to be fed, and the only books were 'socialist realism books from the Soviet Union that the Soviet embassy used to give us'. They were inspiring books with wonderful and 'great heroics of young people in the Red Army, fighting the Second World War and revolution'. Sue remembers the books with fondness. 'They were fantastic, and we all read all those books. That is how Mzala and I came together.'

In Maputo, Mzala worked with two ex-Robben Islanders, Riot Mkhwanazi and Shadrack Maphumulo. The latter was a senior member of MK's Natal military machinery; he was killed on 12 December 1986 in Manzini, Swaziland, shot by SADF Special Forces operatives when he resisted abduction.[32] Mzala was deployed to the Northern Natal rural machinery. Sue says this unit boasted a number of brave comrades, including Vuso Shabalala (Paul Goitsemang). In this unit, working with Riot and Shadrack and comrades from different machineries, Mzala was tasked to create some kind of base. The objective was for comrades to extend themselves 'so that they could operate in that area, and recruit and produce propaganda and create conditions for MK to come and operate there and organise workers and gather information about what the enemy is doing that you could pass on to MK'. Sue says this included all aspects of an organisation that was trying to overthrow a regime.

Sue spent time with Mzala during the preparations for this task and, she says, Mzala's impatience with the delay to execute the struggle inside the country was palpable. 'He was at his most frustrated, because he just wanted to get in and he was sick of this staying in Maputo continuously discussing.' During this time, Sue says, he would often argue, 'Could we please put the porridge in the pot and cook the porridge in the pot and not outside of the pot?' Because Mzala could not live without political engagement, Sue provided him with that, beyond just being a reading buddy. While in Maputo, 'we worked all day every day together and so the discussions got hotter and hotter and hotter'. Again, among Mzala's priorities was instigating an armed insurrection inside the country. 'We must cook the rice inside the pot'; according to Sue, hundreds of people from the forward areas will immediately remember Mzala for this. 'This was his big cry, that we are doing everything wrong. We are not moving fast enough.'

Mzala used a number of expressions to define how he felt about something. He would not use just simple words. 'He said many profound things.' However, at the heart of his arguments was always the need for the ANC to go inside the country and mobilise a revolution there. He never hesitated to express his observations of the difficulties of waging a struggle so far from home. His view was always that 'you really need to be in the middle of your country to do this', says Sue. You need to have that organic connection with what is going on politically. It was very frustrating. So, he kind of summed up what everybody felt.

Sue fondly remembers Mzala as 'incredibly forceful, very passionate, very argumentative and difficult to budge'. But, most importantly, 'he was also prolific, and that was why Slovo loved him'. Joe Slovo would often say, 'You know, this young man really has potential because of his writing.'

IX

In December 1979, three inmates escaped from Pretoria Central Prison. Tim Jenkin, Stephen Lee and Alex Moumbaris were serving different sentences for 'producing and distributing' pamphlets on behalf of 'banned organisations' – the SACP, the ANC and MK. Their escape is the stuff of legend. It was captured by *Dawn* as one of the many illustrations that 'the battle for South Africa is definitely on'. A 1979 article titled 'People's War Gaining Momentum' claimed that MK cadres were moving freely within the country's white areas. The article stated that 'three ANC militants and combatants of Umkhonto we Sizwe; Alexander Moumbaris, Stephen Lee and Timothy Jenkins [sic], all serving a long-term sentence under the Terrorism Act, escaped from the maximum security prison in Pretoria'.[33] After breaking out, they skipped the country to Mozambique.

When the news about the escape broke, Sue's hopes were raised. David (her husband) was serving a sentence in the same prison. She was sent to the border to collect him and the others 'because we thought David would escape with [them]'. Sadly for Sue, David was not with them. Sue recalls going back 'to Maputo with Tim Jenkin and Alex Moumbaris who we had collected. I went into the Internal House, and I sat at the dining-room table in the kitchen, and I just put my head in my hands, and I just couldn't stop sobbing because I couldn't understand why David hadn't escaped.'

Mzala watched as his debating and political sparring partner fell apart. Sue says, 'Mzala did not know what to do. He had never seen me like that. He just sort of kept getting up and sitting down.' Joe Slovo's entrance gave Mzala a reprieve. Because Slovo wanted to talk to Sue, Mzala left. After that incident, having been exposed to his friend's emotional side, Mzala became more sensitive towards Sue. 'Instead of battling with me all the time' about what Marx and Lenin would have said about this or that situation, he developed a soft spot for her and his other side, as a soft, caring person, was revealed to her. He was no longer the undiplomatic, candid revolutionary. Importantly, at this moment, he did not see Sue as a white woman but rather as a comrade, a fellow combatant with the same desires he had for his very own family.

While Mzala's posture on non-racism had taken shape during his student activist days in SASO, where he was one of those who argued they were 'not anti-white but pro-black', it was only after he was fully exposed to Marxism-Leninism that he began to clearly articulate the relationship between race and class. By the time he arrived in Maputo, having worked closely with white comrades like Ronnie Kasrils and Jack Simons, his views on non-racialism were solidifying. He had been to socialist countries such as the Soviet Union and the GDR, countries that opposed apartheid. In Maputo, he got closer to comrades like Sue, Ruth First and Joe Slovo.

In a solemn tribute to Ruth First in the article 'Why We are with the Communists' in the *African Communist* in 1983, Mzala not only elevated the importance of ideology in advancing the struggle but shared some personal insights about his role in Maputo. It was First's humility and commitment to the liberation of South Africa that Mzala most admired.

> Comrade Ruth, however (and this will certainly come as a shock to those enemies of the ANC and the SACP whose propaganda seeks, in vain, to show that the ANC is led by white communists), was at one time a member of an ANC unit in Mozambique of which I was chairman – it was in this unit that I first met her and worked with her, albeit for a short while.

Here, Mzala demonstrated that not only was First prepared to subject herself to the leadership of younger comrades, but that the liberation struggle was fundamentally non-racial. He went on to point out First's modesty and her dislike for 'any sort of pomposity or pretentiousness'; rather, she was a 'seasoned revolutionary activist' who educated and encouraged younger comrades in the unit through 'her example'. According to Mzala, comrades admired her for her virtues. Mzala reflected how the political principles of people like First contributed to their ideological transformation as former BCM members sceptical about the sincerity of the whites who cast their lot with the black man's struggle.

> Our experience with white liberals in South Africa, those 'beloved friends' who only paid lip-service to the struggle and joined on condition that they were guaranteed leadership positions, made some of us doubt whether there was any white person who could be trusted, who could be a sincere revolutionary and fight his 'kith and kin' because, we used to say, after all, blood is thicker than water. But our experience in the ANC, with Comrade Ruth and other white comrades (some of whom were together with us bitten by the same mosquitoes in our military camps) has proved that even if blood is thicker than water, revolutionary convictions are the thickest of all.

Mzala's experience with First in the unit had revealed that her skin colour was 'as insignificant as the kind of trousers comrade A, B or C came wearing to the meeting'.[34] This article best illustrates Mzala's nuanced perspective on non-racialism. He followed this up with a more ideological piece, 'Karl Marx and the Colonial Question', in the next edition of the *African Communist*, writing as Khumalo Migwe. Here, Mzala grappled with the question of oppression and argued that 'Karl Marx would not have been a Marxist himself if he had not resolutely supported the liberation struggle of the colonial people against the imperialist bourgeoisie oppressing them'. Mzala spent some time reflecting on the 'fundamental principle of internationalism' to locate the South African liberation struggle. In addressing the social injustices of capitalism, he posited that the present 'class unconsciousness' of the white workers should not 'blunt our reasoning'. He was advocating for a future South African nation, 'one nation that shall no longer be colour conscious'.

Of course, this is an entry point to his favourite subject – the national question. He used Marx and Engels' attention on Ireland's subjugation by the English invaders to elaborate his point. Mzala eventually arrived at an obvious conclusion, one that he built up to in the article, that socialism is 'the only way out'. He wrote: 'There can be no true national equality until class division is ended; only socialism can create the conditions in which national division and race discrimination can be abolished.'[35] This article thus demonstrated Mzala's rapid ideological growth and clarity as a Marxist-Leninist scholar.

X

The political machinery was considered especially important in the context of new arrivals in exile. After 'jumping the fence' into Mozambique, comrades were placed in ANC residences where they awaited further instruction. They were interviewed about their background and presented with options of either studying further or undergoing military training. Most of them, says Sue, would choose to join MK immediately. This was to be expected of young comrades keen to go back to the country with AK-47s to liberate the country. The commissars in the transit camps had an arrangement with the political machinery to interview all new arrivals.

One day the Internal House received a call to come see some students from Turfloop (University of the North) who were on their way to Angola. Mzala and Sue drove to the specific residence and there they met five 'cool dudes slouching on the chairs'. Typical of students from Turfloop, they were militants who had been involved in a number of activities. Although not hostile, they exuded scepticism when Mzala and a white woman walked in to interview them. They had this 'we thought we will look at the ANC here' expression, which Sue was accustomed to by now.

Mzala must also have been used to the curious stares and scepticism of new arrivals at white comrades. Noting the curious gaze, he upped the ante and confronted the situation. 'So, you want to join the ANC?' he asked, a question to which they all responded in the affirmative. 'Okay, well, let me tell you,' he said, 'Matanzima is a white man in a black man's skin and Joe Slovo is a black man in a white man's skin.' After a brief silence, one of them said, 'Yeah, but Joe Slovo doesn't know what it's like to live in a mud hut and to eat morogo.' That is when Sue spoke for the first time. 'You're absolutely right; that's why Slovo said it's going to be the African working class that leads the revolution.' At that moment they all sat up straight. Almost in unison, they said, 'We'll go with her.'

These comrades included the likes of Collins Chabane, Pitso Moloto (Ryder), Solly Molale and a comrade known simply as Themba. They were to become known as 'Sue's warriors', because 'I saw them through'. Even when they sent off for military training, Sue would still get calls if they were involved in misdemeanours like 'smoking dagga'. Sue ascribes their closeness to her to Mzala's intervention on the race question. Even when they came up with silly ideas such as blowing up a bus full of white schoolkids because 'this would make everybody sit up and take notice of the ANC', they had guidance from comrades like Mzala around them. Sue says this is one aspect of his work that Mzala not only enjoyed but in which he excelled. He was a genius in dealing with new recruits and 'was so chuffed when they said they will go with me because he took it that he had introduced the ANC correctly. This is a non-racial organisation that is fighting for a non-racial, free democratic South Africa.'

XI

Throughout his time in exile, Mzala continued to demonstrate his passion for reading and a phenomenal ability to put his ideas out there. 'Mzala read everything he could lay his hands on,' says Sue, but she is quick to point out that he was not the only one. 'Most of our machinery were students.' Having been a university student, Mzala's reading rigour was advanced and not like that of other comrades such as Riot Mkhwanazi who had received his education on Robben Island. However, even by university standards, Mzala was an exception. Apart from just writing for the liberation movement publications, he later distinguished himself as a mainstream scholar.

'He was like blotting paper; he devoured everything he could get his hands on and he wrote prolifically,' Sue remarks. She says that in Maputo, just like in the camps, his writings were warmly received, and most comrades were keenly interested in his thoughts. 'He had an audience.' He wasn't worried that his thoughts sparked debate; in fact, that was his goal. Sue says that he often conceded when someone made a good point, but that did not keep him from driving his own point vociferously. He was a ferocious debater. 'He'd follow me around sometimes in the house when I was cooking for the kids or trying to bath them or something and carry on with this point.' Sue says, as most people do, that Mzala grew tremendously from his time in Maputo. 'It was a very interesting period.'

When he arrived in Maputo, Vuso Shabalala says he was either reviewing, writing or engaging in a political discussion. At that time, he was grappling with the issue of Black Consciousness, often engaging those around him, and if you happened to be next to him, he would ask, 'What do you think about this, Mzala?' recalls Shabalala. Typical of Mzala, 'he would push you into his position'.

Another question that preoccupied Mzala was the need to find a solution on 'how to advance and intensify the struggle inside the country'. Shabalala recalls his strong views about the leadership's lack of any 'sense of urgency'. At some point, Mzala believed that if someone like Mandela 'was here he would have had a greater sense of urgency' as opposed to the one displayed by the exiled leadership. Mzala would express these ideas in a series of articles from 1980 onwards. In the article 'Armed Struggle in South Africa' in the *African Communist* of 1980, Mzala argued:

> In this period of struggle the urgent task of our movement is to inject into the masses of our people a feeling of confidence in their own potential to overthrow the racists, by means of vigorous revolutionary action, the main content of which must be effective and sustained guerrilla operations including a nation-wide sabotage campaign reminiscent of the early sixties, and thus continue from where Rivonia left off.

He was careful to ensure that he did not come across as an adventurist. Hence, he stated clearly that 'this does not mean that we must go and grab guns and start fighting tomorrow, anywhere'. Instead, citing Lenin, he posited that the Marxist theory of revolution differs from others in that 'it combines complete scientific sobriety in the analysis of the objective state of affairs and the objective course of evolution with the most emphatic recognition of the importance of revolutionary energy, revolutionary creative genius and revolutionary initiative of the masses'. He argued further that 'we must severely criticise the adventuristic theories of the Narodnik type which completely separate the subjective factor from the real objective conditions that prevail'.

The line that Mzala pushed in this article was that 'armed struggle', as the highest form of political struggle, demands 'greater sacrifices from the people'. This point is raised in the context that 'any manifestation of militarism which separates armed people's struggle from its political context can result in untold tragedy and disaster', which could be costly to the movement and set it 'decades back, if not cause its total collapse'. Hence, he argued that 'no matter how skilful or courageous our guerrilla units can be, the lack of mass support could mean their doom'.[36]

Mzala's mind was unrelenting on this question. He soon followed up this article with another in the *African Communist* of 1981, aptly titled 'Has the Time Come for Arming the Masses?' He opened this article by posing two questions: 'What are the prospects of the strategy of "Arming the Masses" in the South African revolutionary war of liberation? Has the time come?' His main thesis was that, due to disunity, fighting as a divided people, the African people had been conquered by the white invaders. Mzala argued that the 'political events of the post-Soweto era in general and the 1980 upsurge in particular throw light on the practical significance of the strategic principle of "Arming the Masses" and compel us to determine more precisely the tasks of the revolutionary vanguard in the present situation in South Africa'. In debating these issues, Mzala was clear that he was not providing 'some sort of recipe or formula' for the revolution since 'strategy and tactics of waging the struggle are determined by concrete and ever changing conditions'.[37]

Mzala had support from many comrades on the need for urgency in advancing the struggle. Shabalala is one of those sympathetic to this view. 'When we left in 1976, we were very young people and, in our minds, we were going to be trained militarily and then come back home immediately but now we had spent something like four or five years just between 1976 and 1980.' Some comrades were stuck in Angola and hadn't been sent on a single mission. It came as a no surprise when there were revolts, such as the one in Fazenda camp, and mutinies like Mkatashinga.

To some extent, Mzala's views represented those who thought the pace of the struggle was too slow. Shabalala thinks that Mzala's views were informed partly by the fact that he had come from the West (Angola), where there were many disgruntled young people itching for action. A view began to emerge among these comrades that 'something was wrong' and that something needed to be done. Mzala was not someone who would keep quiet on such issues, and it is during this period that 'he started talking about the cooking of the rice outside the pot'.[38]

Mzala took this question seriously, to the extent that he started lobbying comrades and seeking their views about a memorandum he was drafting. 'Mzala,' Shabalala says, 'was an agitator.' He went around seeking everyone's views on the need for the NEC to convene another consultative conference. 'He had drawn up a document about this,' says Shabalala, although he is unsure whether it was ever received by the NEC. Mzala, for some reason, called it 'Memorandum Three', and at the heart of it was a call for a consultative conference to discuss the burning question on 'how to intensify the struggle inside the county'.

We will see later that Mzala's wish was granted when the ANC convened a consultative conference on 16 June 1985 in Kabwe, Zambia. Attended by over 250 delegates, the conference took place against a backdrop of escalating cross-border operations by the apartheid regime, divisions within the movement culminating to mutinies in the camps and, most importantly, 'the impatience of trained guerrillas who wanted to be deployed in the country'.[39] This is exactly what Mzala had been agitating for since his early days in exile.

Maputo was thus an important part of the tapestry of Mzala's life. When he left, he was a different person to the one he had been when he arrived. While his passion and character were still the same, he was displaying signs of intellectual maturity.

CHAPTER 5

Habashwe! Death to the Traitors: Swaziland and the Battle of South Africa

I

In 1980, Mzala was deployed to Swaziland. Renamed as the Kingdom of Eswatini in 2018, this is the last country on the continent governed by an absolute monarchy.[1] Currently, the country is ruled by King Mswati III, who took over following the passing away of his father King Sobhuza II in 1982. Swaziland is a landlocked country in southern Africa and one of the smallest on the continent. It shares a border with Mozambique to its northeast and with South Africa to its north, west and south.

The underground of the ANC operated in an environment 'fraught with secrecy and dangers'.[2] The problems in Swaziland were compounded by the size of the country, which made it easier for apartheid operatives to launch numerous attacks against MK cadres. Sue described Swaziland as 'the size of a pocket handkerchief, and a very difficult place to stay underground'. This, according to Sue, made the work of comrades deployed there 'incredibly complicated'.

Prior to their expulsion from Swaziland in 1976, Thabo Mbeki, Albert Dlomo and Jacob Zuma had laid a solid network for ANC underground activities to handle 'the exodus of youths into Swaziland after the June 1976 Soweto uprising'. Up until then, Swaziland had formed part of the crucial 'Eastern Front' for the ANC struggle, but the apartheid regime had countered by means of 'an extensive network of highly placed agents in the Swazi establishment'. This was rendered ineffective to some extent, mainly due to a number of Swazis, including the absolute monarch King Sobhuza II, who were sympathetic to the ANC. In fact, King Sobhuza II considered himself a member of the ANC.³ Nevertheless, authorities in Swaziland – and the police system in particular – were 'notoriously in the control of the South African security forces'.⁴ When the 1970s drew to a close, ANC activities had taken root in Swaziland to such an extent that this unnerved the authorities, leading to the closure of the Eastern Front at the beginning of the 1980s.⁵

After working closely with Ronnie Kasrils on the political committee in Maputo, Mzala was thus deployed to Swaziland. Kasrils recalls that 'he became a key member of the MK structure responsible, with the late Shadrack Maphumulo and others, for organising the then rural Natal'. For Kasrils, 'this was a very testing period for his skills, working under dangerous and difficult conditions, with the possibility of death at any moment in a country where South Africa's death squads operated with impunity, in league with some treacherous elements of the Swazi security forces.' Indeed, the apartheid regime did not hesitate to execute those it deemed terrorists. In fact, a number of comrades, including Maphumulo, were killed in Swaziland. Because these activities were shrouded in secrecy, it is difficult to traverse the period to piece together information about specific incidents and individuals. But there is no doubt that Swaziland was under serious pressure from the apartheid regime to 'flush ANC and MK representatives' out of its territory.⁶

However, just before Mzala left Maputo on deployment in Swaziland, he took part in yet another controversial campaign. According to Vuso Shabalala, Mzala and his unit were involved in the development of a leaflet titled *Habashwe* (Let Them Die) that essentially '[called] for spies to be killed inside the country'. Shabalala says that, apart from processing reports, it was standard practice for them to receive propaganda material from headquarters in Lusaka, and sometimes from 'London via Lusaka or directly from Maputo'. These would then be transported to Swaziland or given to people who would be going directly from Mozambique to South Africa. Sometimes, according to Shabalala, they would also generate propaganda material themselves before having it cleared by the political committee and then disseminated to the machineries in Swaziland.

When he was in Maputo, Mzala 'would usually be the first to put up a draft, which would then be discussed, modified and then finalised to put to the political committee'. Shabalala recalls one in particular, because it was produced shortly after the Natal raids. They then had it cleared with the local political committee. Although the political and military machineries were under 'one senior organ' they were separate from each other, each taking its own decisions, but nevertheless collaborated. Shabalala says, this leaflet – 'of great demand from the military machineries' – was widely distributed inside the country, to an extent that 'it was picked up by the media, even internationally, and got to the attention of head office'. This led to an instruction from headquarters 'to stop every leaflet distributed because it was not ANC policy to advocate for the killing of people'.

Indeed, the leaflet made news to such an extent that parts of it were kept in the Congressional Records of the House of Representatives in the United States. In an article in the *Christian Science Monitor* of 11 March 1987 titled 'Switching Sides: Young Blacks leave ANC for Arms of Pretoria – South African Police Keep an Eye Out for Disenchanted Dissenters', Ned Temko interviewed an *askari*. The introduction reads in part:

> For safety's sake, the slight, soft-spoken black man calls himself simply 'John.' In the past decade, he recounts, he has fled his native South Africa, trained as an African National Congress activist in Angola, East Germany, and the Soviet Union – and beaten a dissident to death in what he terms an ANC 'prison' in Angola. Now, he has switched sides. He works for the South African police. Hundreds of other blacks have made the same journey – even crossed the same fences – in the intensifying battle over South Africa's future. It is a tangled struggle, fought with ideology as often as with guns or mines.

The article, couched in clearly anti-communist jargon, also quotes the pamphlet Shabalala was referring to: '"The future is within our grasp!" blared an ANC pamphlet handed to this reporter in a black township shortly before the Emergency.' The article goes on to say: '"*Habashwe Abafe!*" proclaims an ANC pamphlet distributed in South Africa: "Death to the Traitors!" It pictures seven ex-ANC men who testified against former cohorts in South African courtrooms.'[7] The ANC leadership had thus every reason to be concerned. Newspapers like the *Christian Science Monitor* used such pamphlets to portray the ANC as a dangerous terrorist organisation set to introduce a communist dictatorship in South Africa. With this, and true to his character, Mzala had left Maputo with a bang.

II

One of the first places Mzala stayed in Swaziland was at the home of Mandla 'Stokes' Sithole, which housed several ANC people. Sithole, a high-school teacher in Matsapha and originally from Mpumalanga township in Hammersdale, had opened his house to ANC activists. One of the people who stayed there was a young Bhabhalazi Bulunga from the rural northern Natal village of Hluhluwe. Bulunga had joined the ANC in 1979 and was now a student at the University of Swaziland. Although now a senior ANC operator, having received training in Angola and abroad, Mzala got along with Bulunga. Bulunga's work and his knowledge of northern Natal would be useful for Mzala.

Bulunga remembers Mzala as someone steeped in Marxism, but a type that he found to be more practical and based on history. He had the ability to simplify complex revolutionary concepts and 'with his personality you were always energised whenever he entered the room'. Bulunga admired his capacity to analyse and was awed by his energy. 'I have never met someone like that.' He was brave and pursued his objectives until he succeeded. But Bulunga laughs when he recalls that Mzala had no tact. 'It didn't matter how senior the person if he differed' and hence Bulunga believes that, to an extent, he irritated people with hierarchical orientation. However, Mzala was a free-spirited individual whom it was difficult to get angry at. 'He didn't care about material stuff,' recalls Bulunga.

Another individual who met Mzala at this time is Dumisani Nduli, who had arrived in Swaziland in 1978 and was now a part-time schoolteacher at Mbabane's St Francis High School. He was introduced to Mzala by Judson Khuzwayo in 1980. The instruction was clear: 'Give him orientation on how we work in Swaziland and assist his machinery in political development of the rural areas.'

Nduli was struck by the intelligence of this character Khuzwayo had brought to him. The first thing he noticed was that Mzala was 'steeped in Marxism-Leninism politics and did not drink or smoke, but [was] very intelligent'. Mzala rode a red motorbike with which he would circle the Anglican Mission, the church school area where Nduli worked, three times before parking it near the house of the parish priest, which had become

Nduli's home. Although circling the church school area was a necessary exercise 'that would assist to detect if you are followed or not', says Nduli, the downside was that the 'parish priest noticed that I had a regular visitor who did this strange and annoying thing before parking his bike near his house'.[8]

Mzala was an avid biker. Bulunga says he was so mad about bikes that he established a bikers' association in Swaziland. Lungile Pepani, by then also deployed in Swaziland on different missions, recalls Mzala's passion for motorbikes and that sometimes he would be clad in biking gear. Mzala also spent a lot of time with ANC activists Jonathan and Nonceba Levin, occasionally even overnight. Jonathan says Mzala owned three bikes and a car in Swaziland and had names for each of them. The 50cc bike was called Chicken, the 100cc The Stallion and the big one he called Oshkosh. He used Oshkosh for longer distances and Nonceba says he rode it at breakneck speed.

Jonathan says Mzala had an amazing energy and mixed easily with people. While walking one day, they came across a bus full of South African school kids visiting Swaziland. Mzala – not one to miss a good opportunity to politicise, says Jonathan – jumped aboard the bus and started engaging the youngsters politically. Jonathan remembers him as an unorthodox character big on arming the masses, but laughs when he thinks how mischievous Mzala could be. One day Mzala deployed Bulunga and Gavin McFadden, an activist who was a Swazi citizen, on a mission to South Africa. He told Nonceba that Jonathan had agreed that they could use the car since they were travelling locally – only for them to be arrested crossing the border into South Africa. Jonathan was forced to report the car stolen after advice from Maphumulo, lest his cover be blown.

Mzala's creativity often confused the enemy. Kasrils says that, while in Swaziland, he showed tremendous creativity and audacity, posing initially as a Swazi journalist, which helped him move relatively freely around the country. Various names and publications are bandied about in this regard. Eddy Maloka says Mzala disguised himself as a journalist for the *Swaziland Observer*, using the name Jabulani Dlamini.[9] While John Daniel, who was teaching in Swaziland at the time, says Mzala also wrote for the *Times of Swaziland* under the pseudonym James Simelane.[10] But it is the *Swaziland Observer* where Mzala had a stint as a journalist. He had approached Nonceba, who was working for the same newspaper, with what Nonceba initially thought was an audacious proposition to write stories for the paper. They thus devised a plan to convince the editor Phil Nandu, including using Mzala's uncle's name Jerry Simelane, and it worked. Soon Mzala and Nonceba were interviewing the vice chancellor of the University of Swaziland, Professor SM Guma. Mzala wrote several stories as Jerry Simelane, even covering the Hells Angels' bike rally on their Swaziland tour.

Underground operatives, according to Kasrils, needed to be able to socialise with people of every walk of life, and carry out public activities if possible. Mzala performed this task with aplomb, befriending 'students and journalists who assisted him' in his duties. Another form of disguise was a pipe between his lips, which remained forever unlit. Among the places he stayed was the University of Swaziland, where he developed close links with the students.[11]

It is here that he met Raynauld Russon, the son of South African exile Joseph 'Jabavu' Russon. Russon Senior was an activist and leader of the Coloured People's Congress in Natal, and in the 1950s participated in the Defiance Campaign and the Congress of the People in Kliptown. The young Russon, now a student at the then University of Botswana, Lesotho and Swaziland (UBLS),[12] came into contact with Mzala in around 1982.

Russon was the leader of the Politics and Sociology Student Association, which arranged regular public symposia at UBLS. Mzala happened to be in the audience at one of these events, but not just as an observer; he was hard at work. At the end of the symposium a 1.6-metre-tall, medium-built male approached the unsuspecting Russon and introduced himself as Jabu Dlamini, a freelance journalist. He asked to be a guest speaker at one of the sessions. One of the first things Russon noticed about this stranger was that his left eye twitched endlessly. Russon politely asked him to suggest a topic that he could present to his executive committee for discussion.

When time passed without a response, Mzala followed up. A few weeks later, during a tea break, Russon was approached by fellow student Nokuthula Simelane who told him that there was someone who wanted to see him in the car park. There he found the same gentleman who had approached him at the symposium. Once more, he introduced himself, and asked whether his request had been processed. The manner of his approach suggested to Russon that this question was 'obviously meant to remind me who he was'.

Suddenly, Mzala asked whether he was related to 'Oom Jabavu'. At that moment, it occurred to Russon that this stranger had done a background check on him. Still in the car park area, under the African sun, with students moving about, Russon was curious to find out how Mzala knew his dad. Then Mzala dropped Stanley Mabizela's name. 'Mabizela,' says

Russon, 'had been very close to my dad and frequented our house with Bafana Duma.' Russon thus confirmed that Jabavu was indeed his father. The statement prompted 'a firm handshake and [he] said comrade'. At that moment Russon was uneasy and sensed trouble. 'The freelance journalist had been digging information about me and I felt really uncomfortable and he sensed it.' It was now patently clear to Russon that he was talking to someone who was either 'an apartheid informer trying to trap me or an ANC activist'.

To reassure a clearly worried Russon, Mzala reached into his bag and pulled out an ANC membership form. He proceeded to explain his mission to recruit South African exiles in Swaziland into the ANC. Russon says that Mzala promised to come around the following day to collect the form. 'I spoke to a few activists and they all confirmed knowledge of this guy. His name was Comrade Mzala ... I quickly realised where the name came from because he called everybody Mzee.' The form required a brief paragraph on the history of the person joining, so Russon remained anxious. Subsequently, he did not use his own name on the form, but rather that of his father, Jabavu Russon. Although Russon trusted Mzala, he was not completely certain, especially considering the number of informers in Swaziland: 'BJ Vorster had said that out of every three people leaving South Africa to join the ANC, one was his agent.'

Mzala had been working hard to recruit members and to create political awareness in Swaziland. When he collected the form, he told Russon he was on his way to Maputo where he would submit his form 'and, if approved, I [Russon] would be given some duties to perform'. Russon did, however, warn Mzala about his fears since his family was in the process of obtaining Swaziland citizenship and he didn't want to 'jeopardise our attempt'. Mzala assured him that their work would be 'strictly underground and protected'.

III

When he first arrived in Swaziland, Mzala spent time obtaining some basic information from Dumisani Nduli about the operations of the Mbabane Special Branch police operatives. 'We started talking about rural Natal,' recalls Nduli. However, Nduli was a Durban boy with few contacts in rural Natal or even places like Ingwavuma or Phongolo, so the focus of discussion soon shifted. Mzala was developing contacts across Swaziland using various forms of disguise. He was familiar with Swaziland, since both his grandfathers had settled there in the 1940s and thus he had relatives from both his mother's and his father's side. These networks proved invaluable.

Now a step closer to achieving his dream of 'cooking the rice inside the pot', as part of the Natal rural machinery Mzala could directly influence the course of the revolution and prove his assertions about the need to stop the prevarication about the question of the armed struggle inside the country. Linked to this aspect of the struggle was the role of Inkatha, which he had been analysing for some time. Nduli says Mzala soon pointed out that 'he was interested in Gatsha Buthelezi and his speeches in [the] KwaZulu Legislature and his Inkatha rallies'. Coincidentally, there was a man who worked for the KwaZulu Legislature who was dating one of Nduli's students. A meeting was arranged for Mzala to meet this person, and it was agreed that he would smuggle all the latest speeches and archival material from Ulundi, KwaZulu's capital. This material, according to Nduli, would assist Mzala in writing his book.

In between his hectic schedule, Mzala still revelled in debates. As expected, he stayed in houses frequented by ANC underground cadres. 'Their long nights were spent in debate after debate' and Mzala used these to present and refine his 'cooking the rice inside the pot' theory. 'His argument was that one of the major problems for the ANC was that the pot was in Mozambique, the matches in Lusaka, and the stove in South Africa. What was needed was to synchronise the working of these elements in order to prepare a meal.'[13] Jonathan and Nonceba recall his animated discussions on 'cooking the rice inside the pot' with laughter. This was after the 1981 gruesome Matola raid where the SADF had massacred 15 MK members. Mzala would stand in Jonathan's house and illustrate his point. 'At some point there will be over 20 comrades,' says Nonceba and Mzala will use them to demonstrate his theory of the pot, the fire, the water and the rice, which he argued were all in different places with the leadership in Angola. In this way, he was able to simplify otherwise complex concepts.

Wherever he was, Mzala was agitating. Nduli says there is nothing under the sun they did not discuss. But Mzala was particularly keen to get insights on Buthelezi. They couldn't help but laugh at some of Buthelezi's embarrassing moments, including his 'tantrums' after being chased from Robert Sobukwe's funeral and his 'weird behaviour' during the unveiling of Chief Luthuli's tombstone. According to Nduli, while being driven with Luthuli's widow, Nokukhanya Luthuli, Buthelezi 'was wildly waving even to the bushes of Groutville'. He 'desperately' wanted to be seen with Mrs Luthuli; he even ensured he was the main speaker. Nduli is uncertain whether Mzala had made up his mind about the book at that point, but he was clearly keen on understanding Buthelezi and Inkatha, especially after Buthelezi's denunciation of the ANC shortly after he met with ANC leaders in October 1979.

Prior to this meeting, Buthelezi had expressed his opposition to economic sanctions and armed struggle. After the meeting, Buthelezi became more vocal and opposed strikes and stay-aways organised by the UDF and COSATU. Buthelezi believed that sanctions 'damaged the South African economy'. Over and above this, 'he also denounced the UDF and COSATU as surrogates for the ANC. He especially attacked prominent Indians and Xhosa-speaking blacks among the leaders of the three organizations.'[14] For Mzala, this stance justified his scepticism of Buthelezi and Inkatha in the context of the South African liberation struggle.

IV

At one point, Nduli says, Mzala suddenly disappeared without a word. This was to be one of his many disappearing acts. Then, about two months later, he resurfaced and told Nduli that he had been to South Africa. This, according to Nduli, was without the approval of the leadership. Mzala had decided to test whether entering South Africa via the Mahamba border was a viable option. He was not going to sit around without testing his ideas. He told Nduli he was familiar with the area and had gone all the way to the Zulu Royal Family to gain support for MK operations. Also, he had wanted to actually see the area rather than simply 'theorising about it'. He repeated his long-held view that the leadership seemed very comfortable in exile and 'he could not discern any sense of urgency on their part'.

There are claims that, on some of his sojourns, Mzala met Zulu King Goodwill Zwelithini kaBhekuzulu, with whom he had apparently developed a rapport. While this remains unverified, King Zwelithini's affinity for the Nxumalos is well documented. Just like King Sobhuza II, King Zwelithini's mother Queen Thomozile Jezangani kaNdwandwe came from the same clan. Some have sought to use the fact that the king's mother was an ANC activist to confirm the feasibility of any relations with Mzala.[15] Nevertheless, the Royal House has always had ANC members, among them Prince Mcwayizeni kaDinizulu, who acted as a Regent when his brother Cyprian Bhekuzulu kaSolomon passed away. He was later elected to the ANC's NEC and was a member of parliament for the ANC.[16] Mzala would later tell his sister, Phasha Nxumalo-Zitha, that King Zwelithini had shared with him insights about politics within the royal family – information that was to be crucial in the writing of his book *Gatsha Buthelezi: Chief with a Double Agenda*.

Eddy Maloka writes:

> One day Mzala took an initiative. He moved to Ingwavuma on his own, established links with contacts and then, after some days, returned to his unit in Swaziland. He was greatly moved by this experience, and came back arguing that the claim that South Africa had no conditions for the conduct of classical guerrilla warfare was a myth. He had seen and been in the bush himself![17]

Mzala was prepared to go to any lengths in pursuing his mission to initiate an armed struggle inside the country. He would repeat this assertion to Sifiso Buthelezi, one of the unit members, insisting that the theory that there were no bushes in South Africa conducive to guerrilla warfare was unfounded.

Mzala's rash approach was, however, dangerous on many levels. Not only did he risk being captured by the enemy, but some within the movement could have interpreted his actions suspiciously, either as ill-discipline or as collaboration with the enemy. Already there had been murmurs owing to the manner in which he skipped the country. This, according to Titi Nxumalo and Nduli, left Mzala with some sort of stigma. 'I was rather shocked,' says Nduli about this move. But it made sense a few years later when Mzala penned his 'Cooking the Rice inside the Pot' article. It was now nine years after the 1976 uprising that led to Mzala's generation joining the ANC in exile and 16 years after the Morogoro Conference. Many young cadres did not want to spend the rest of their lives in exile. Nduli says Mzala was in a hurry for action inside the country.

V

It was not until late in 1982 that Mzala once again made contact with Raynauld Russon. This time he presented himself as a 'full-scale businessman driving a lime green 5-series BMW. He had a full beard and had a pipe in his mouth as some form of disguise.' Noticing that his new comrade found the new look amusing, Mzala was quick to offer an explanation. 'Mzee,' he said, 'I'm a businessman and no cop can stop and search me when I'm dressed like this.' Sifiso Buthelezi remembers the green BMW and Mzala's new look as 'a good cover for him'. Mzala the 'businessman' never uttered a word about Russon's ANC membership. 'We must work, Mzee, and we will depend on you,' he told Russon. True to this statement, a trip to Maputo was soon arranged for Russon, and it is there that he met 'Job Tabane (Cassius Make) who briefed me on what needed to be done'.

This was followed by several meetings, including a significant one that took place in Maputo in December 1982. This meeting was attended by, amongst others, 'Cassius Make (Job Tabane), ANC Khumalo (Ronnie Kasrils), Barney (Richard Molokoane), Ngalitshe, Bomber, Gavin McFadden and Lesley Pupuma', and it is then, according to Russon, that the solid basis for the formation of the People's United Democratic Movement (PUDEMO) in Swaziland was laid. PUDEMO soon became critical to the support of MK operations in Swaziland during this tumultuous period. Mzala sang PUDEMO's praises in his 1990 article in the *African Communist*, 'Africa Notes and Comments'.

These were difficult times in Swaziland, recalls Russon, with the state becoming even more hostile to the liberation movement after the Pretoria Accord, negotiated between Swaziland and Pretoria. The death of King Sobhuza II in August 1982 further exacerbated matters. Russon says that this increased hostility led to over a hundred ANC operatives being arrested and deported to Mozambique. Those who were less fortunate were handed over to the South African authorities. Maloka writes that 'it was very dangerous to operate in Swaziland in those years' and the 'Accord resulted in the setting up of a secret police unit and a witch-hunt for ANC members'.

The Pretoria Accord became an Achilles heel for the ANC. Though kept under wraps, the ANC was aware of this agreement, which was only made public in 1984 by South Africa's foreign minister Roelof 'Pik' Botha.[18] By means of a statement on 15 July 1982, the ANC pleaded with the Swazi government, 'praying' that it would consider its memorandum 'in the interests of the unity of the African peoples and as a reaffirmation of our common resolve to liberate the mother continent from racist and colonial apartheid domination'. The ANC considered the agreement 'fraught with grave dangers for the brother people of Swaziland and South Africa'.[19]

With this agreement in place, it came as no surprise to Russon that Swazi forces engaged ANC combatants in 1983 and 1984, killing many cadres and handing others over to Pretoria.[20] When several MK cadres were arrested around Manzini and Matsapha in 1983, Russon says Mzala was fuming. He was adamant that they were going to liberate the arrested comrades. 'We are going to storm that police station with Akas [AK-47 rifles] and release the comrades.' At that moment, Russon was convinced he had encountered a 'true revolutionary and I imagined a Che Guevara operation with combatants storming the police station and removing the comrades by force'. Maloka confirms that Mzala suggested to his unit that they rescue the arrested comrades. 'However, the mission had to be aborted after some tactical considerations.'[21] Russon says it was impossible to doubt Mzala's commitment to the struggle, but there were times that he thought that Mzala was 'very sharp and intellectual to a point that the balance between ideal and real was rather murky'.

Mzala was arrested several times, including during the course of 1983 when he was deported to Mozambique.[22] However, soon after that 1983 deportation, Mzala – clearly a man on a mission – returned to Swaziland in around December of that year, based in the Shiselweni district as the commissar for the northern Natal rural machinery, which sought to establish a training camp in Ingwavuma.

They were always in danger in Swaziland. One night, their safe house was raided by the police. Fortunately, there was no one home at the time, but there were concerns for the weaponry and, more importantly, the documents, which could have risked their entire operation if discovered. 'The unit moved on the house at one in the morning, but they found that the police had gone. Fortunately, only the arms had been taken.'[23]

VI

As part of the northern Natal rural machinery, Mzala got involved in the Ingwavuma operation. It is the Mngomezulu family that unlocked the area for the ANC, with Mzala among the cadres at the forefront. According to Nduli, Jameson Nongolozi Mngomezulu had been cajoled by Jacob Zuma to quit his job in Swaziland and go back to Ingwavuma to set up underground MK units. To lure him back, the ANC had 'built a house for the Mngomezulu with the assistance of his sister Nokuhamba Nyawo'. Already at an advanced age, Mngomezulu's main tasks included infiltrating cadres into South Africa. He would send the guerrillas to his sister to look after, the family constantly on the lookout for police. They would make their move only when it was safe, and his sister would then help the guerrillas cross into Swaziland.[24]

The small town of Ingwavuma played a crucial role in the liberation of South Africa. Nestled in the countryside of KwaZulu-Natal, Ingwavuma lies near the border between Swaziland and South Africa. This region, says Kasrils, 'abutted on Swaziland and forms part of the Lebombo mountain range. This geographical feature is 800 kilometres long and an average of 600 metres high. It forms the border between South Africa, Swaziland and Mozambique.' Due to the strategic location, it made sense for the ANC to set up a base here for its underground work. During the 1980s, the Natal rural machinery used the area as a transit point for MK cadres infiltrating from Swaziland and Mozambique. With the help of Mngomezulu and his sister, the MK underground had established safe houses and set up base in the area.

That the ANC succeeded to get a foothold in Ingwavuma and develop networks, Shabalala says, was thanks to the 'exile community' of Ingwavuma. Chief Ntunja Mngomezulu had been banished from his area and fled to Swaziland with his followers, where they became refugees. There are various versions of how the Mngomezulu infighting came about in Ingwavuma. Some claim that Mbalekelwa Mngomezulu, the *induna* (headman) of the Lindizwe Area in Ingwavuma, is alleged to have participated in the fraudulent appointment of Ntunja Mngomezulu as the chief of the Mngomezulu community. This was followed by unrest and an inquiry, which found against Ntunja Mngomezulu. After fleeing to Swaziland, Ntunja 'continued to terrorise the community from his base in Swaziland'.[25] However, Chief Ntunja Mngomezulu remained so popular that many people of Ingwavuma continued to pay their allegiances to him even when he was exiled.

The revolutionary role of Jameson Mngomezulu was the key that unlocked Ingwavuma. Not only was he close to Ntunja, he was also a veteran of the Luthuli Detachment[26] with a long history in the ANC, a respected cadre and 'an experienced MK commander who had been trained in North Africa in the 1960s'.[27] He worked with many dedicated cadres such as Johannes 'Pass Four' Phungula, the commander of the Natal machinery. His intervention allowed the ANC to establish bases and operate from Ingwavuma, infiltrating both personnel and equipment into South Africa.

The apartheid regime was alive to Ingwavuma as a frequent entry point for ANC cadres and, after the Soweto uprising, there was a marked increase in acts of sabotage in the area. Between October 1976 and May 1981, no fewer than 112 attacks and explosions were reported. This, coupled with 'skirmishes between guerrilla fighters and members of the security forces', led to increased vigilance on the part of the army. With several MK units infiltrating the area, there were a number of shoot-outs with the army. 'Some of the operatives moved further south to Nongoma and Vryheid, where arms caches were buried.'[28] As a result, there was a visible increase of army patrols along the border, with camps mushrooming from the north to the south and along the Lebombo mountains.

The situation became precarious when Swaziland demanded Ingwavuma and KaNgwane back in what became the 'abortive' land deal.[29] KaNgwane was a bantustan reserved for Swazi-speaking South Africans in what was then known as the Eastern Transvaal, while Ingwavuma fell under KwaZulu, it was also dominated by Swazis. The Swazi government argued that the 'proposed land cession was an attempt to reunite the Swazi peoples who had been divided for the past hundred odd years by boundaries imposed by the colonial powers'.[30] While keen to develop a presence there, the ANC was not in favour of the takeover. This – along with the 1982 pact, which sought to counter the ANC's efforts to '[use] the Eastern Transvaal (including the KaNgwane Bantustan) and Northern Zululand (including the KwaZulu Bantustan) to infiltrate MK military cadres into the country'[31] made the ANC's operations in the area untenable. That the ANC was able to continue operating is largely due to the Mngomezulu community. When Mzala returned after being deported in December 1983, he spent most of his time in Ingwavuma. 'This was part of the ANC strategy to transfer command structures and political leadership into the country, and Operation Vula was the culmination of this process.'[32]

To Shabalala's dismay, Mzala was adamant about the feasibility of operating in the area, and of reaching even further inside South Africa. Mzala's restless mind was now in overdrive. Sifiso Buthelezi recalls the experiences of Ingwavuma vividly. He was deployed to Swaziland towards the end of 1983, and that is where he met Mzala, the commissar of the northern Natal rural machinery, for the first time. He says Mzala was advocating for a classic guerrilla warfare, where the movement would have 'liberated zones' in its march towards total liberation. Mzala, says Sifiso Buthelezi, had identified Ingwavuma as the ideal starting point for this scenario.

Mzala had put the Ingwavuma situation to the political committee in Maputo, which included people like Ronnie Kasrils and Riot Mkhwanazi. When the need to deploy someone to the area arose, Shabalala swiftly volunteered because, due to his position in the political service unit, he was familiar with the area and its dynamics. Shabalala says Mzala was then moved to the military machinery. They worked closely together and developed a strong relationship. With Shabalala and the political machinery having managed to penetrate the area, the next step was to 'assist Mzala's operation military project' to get ordnance in Ingwavuma while infiltrating cadres inside the country. Now living among the Mngomezulus and able to go in and out of Ingwavuma, Shabalala became an entry point for Mzala.

Kasrils says the opportunities that lay in Ingwavuma and the Lebombo mountains had not been that obvious to the ANC until Mzala pointed them out. Hence, Kasrils believes Mzala's most significant achievement during this period, 'and in MK's history', was his role in urging for the opening of a guerrilla front in the Ingwavuma region.

> The area was conducive to guerrilla infiltration and establishing of bases, which appears obvious in retrospect. It had been overlooked, however, by MK until Mzala appeared on the scene and was quick to recognise the potential. This reflected his natural bent for such openings and I was inspired to learn this from the young man who I had trained in Angola. Needless to say, I was immensely proud of him.

It was clear to Mzala, recalls Kasrils, that the terrain offered an opportunity for infiltrating MK cadres and weaponry, linking with the rural communities there, and preparing for operations.

> I remember how thrilling it was when he guided me to the border with Ingwavuma, to meet a local chief, and gaze in astonishment at the sheer cliff face stretching like a wall from the south to the north of Swaziland with Ingwavuma up on the heights of that mountain range. The opening of the area was exploited with Mzala and his commander in Swaziland, Shadrack Maphumulo beginning the project, later to be developed by Paul Goitsemang (Vuso Shabalala) after Mzala was redeployed.

Kasrils says subsequent operations within Ingwavuma, and engagement with the SADF, were later to be described by MK commander in the area, Comrade Mugabe, in *Dawn* magazine. In penetrating the area, Buthelezi says they had to carry their heavy military backpacks since they could only get to the mountains of Ingwavuma on foot. To minimise the chances of being spotted, they walked only at night, crossing crocodile-infested rivers along the way. Though there were many units using that route, including urban machineries, the mission of Mzala's unit was clear: to recruit and train people there 'in guerrilla warfare and the use of arms' so that they could be sent back into the country.

Buthelezi says that, once they had established the base in Ingwavuma, Mzala would often come back very excited in the middle of the night. 'Mzee, I have just returned from the thick bushes of South Africa ... I am coming from there and I want you to go there,' he would tell comrades. He was convinced that MK soldiers could be sent deeper into the South African bush to prepare for guerrilla warfare. Buthelezi sees similarities between Mzala and Chris Hani. 'What made Chris popular was that he wouldn't just send soldiers, but he would be involved in fighting with us.' Mzala would be there personally with comrades in Ingwavuma doing reconnaissance and demonstrating that 'a classic guerrilla warfare can be waged'. Writes Maloka, 'In line with his "pot" theory, Mzala did not believe in what he termed "remote control". He intended to move into the country and be based in Ingwavuma with his unit.' Chris Matlhako, former second deputy general secretary of the SACP, characterises this period as 'an epic story of courage, commitment similar to Fidel Castro's July 26 Sierra Maestra episodes'.[33]

Having been in Ingwavuma for a while, Shabalala thought the operations were not only risky, but reckless. He says he made that point very clear. 'Those boys were not there for more than a month or two before they were discovered by the army.' However, in the case of Buthelezi's unit, they were sold out by a comrade who deserted while en route to Swaziland with Commander Mugabe. The next time they saw him was when he emerged as a state witness against them in court.

Jameson Mngomezulu's heroics ended fatally on 1 June 1985 when, together with three members of his 'refugee community in southern Swaziland', he was abducted and forcibly taken to South Africa by apartheid operatives. They were taken to Moolman, just outside Piet Retief in KwaZulu-Natal, before being moved to Leeuwspoor, a farm close to Jozini, which was the headquarters of the northern Natal security police.[34] The police wanted information on the 'terrorist threat', including the names and the number of comrades who had been infiltrated into the country. Mngomezulu would not budge. The security agents 'believed he was involved in infiltrating MK guerrillas into South Africa. He died as a result of being severely tortured.'[35] When Mngomezulu slipped into a coma, the police lost all chance of extracting information from him and decided to blow up his body 'at a missile range near Sodwana Bay'.[36]

After Mngomezulu's assassination, his sister Nyawo courageously revived the base and continued to work with MK cadres. At an MK celebration in Ingwavuma in 2009, Jacob Zuma praised the role played by rural villagers in the struggle. He said the struggle was won through ordinary men and women in the deep rural areas such as Ingwavuma where villagers provided MK with shelter, food and reconnaissance information. He thanked the people of Ingwavuma for playing such an important role in enabling MK to establish a base and recruit in this area. Despite the risks, Nyawo – at the mature age of 63 – and her family had immersed themselves in the struggle.

VII

Although deeply involved in the revolutionary process in Swaziland and agitating for urgency in executing the struggle, Mzala went about his mission in a very logical and sensible manner. He was not reckless and adventurist in his writings. Writing as Khumalo Migwe in a series of articles that appeared in *Dawn* in 1982 titled 'Lessons of Our People's War', Mzala drew on historical experiences to demonstrate the importance of all the pillars of the struggle. In the March 1982 edition, Mzala argued:

> The preparation for armed struggle is one of the painstaking tasks a liberation movement can be faced with. Often than not the urge to take up arms and carry on military operations in desperation, hoping that the masses would join in spontaneously, has led to serious setbacks. A few people taking to arms do not equal a revolution, unless the decisive masses of the people are already in motion of struggle towards revolutionary objectives, and the armed action is related to it, as a feature of it.

He further drew on lessons from the Spanish Communist Party, demonstrating that 'it is therefore not enough to base the decision for armed struggle on the manifestations of the advanced sections of the population only; even with them, support should not be assumed but should be concretely ascertained'. It was clear to Mzala that preparation for the armed struggle meant, first and foremost, political preparation. This entailed the mobilisation of the masses around their concrete grievances while preparing and readying them to support and reinforce combatants.

He concluded by pointing out that the significance of political work among the masses was underlined by the necessity to develop political leadership at grassroots level. 'No strategy of revolution will supersede the one that transfers the liberation initiative from few leaders in exile, to the local leadership within the country.'[37] Thus, it is apparent that Mzala was not just an irrational rabble-rouser who sought to start trouble. On the contrary, he was one of the movement's fountains of wisdom in concretely analysing the prevailing conditions in order to advise and enable it in advancing the struggle.

Mzala continued with the same line of argument in the April 1982 edition of *Dawn*. Through these interventions, he demonstrated appreciation of the ANC's strategy as contained in the The Green Book enunciating the key pillars of the struggle.

> It would not be correct to mechanically say that only those who have maintained the primacy of the political to the military have necessarily succeeded, in as much as on the other hand, history yet knows not of successes of guerrilla war in those situations where the political was ignored. Striking the necessary balance, depending on the concrete situation of a given country, constitutes the art of guerrilla warfare – and art cannot be reduced to scientific formula.

Mzala further argued that the prominence of armed struggle in liberation movements across the world, including those on the African continent, should not obscure the reality that independence was gained through supplementary means 'including general strikes' and 'mass demonstrations'. He went on to highlight the aims of MK as not just about destroying the enemy's military forces, 'but also about boosting the political struggle, and in particular at helping the insurrectionary masses of South Africa break up all forms of enemy control and oppression, win sovereignty and set up revolutionary power'.[38]

However, for Mzala the strategy of people's war was not an end but a means to take the struggle to its logical conclusion, which was socialism. Paying tribute to Ruth First in the article 'Why We are with the Communists' in the *African Communist* in 1983, he articulated his views on the strategy to transition to a socialist South Africa. Moving from the premise that 'South Africa's mode of production is clearly capitalist', with highly developed industrial monopolies and 'the merging of industrial and finance capital', he indicated that the country's agricultural system was based along capitalist lines. Therefore, he argued, 'the transition to socialism is a logical continuation and development of the present revolutionary process in our country, and this proposition, in my view, should be raised to the level of debate even within the African National Congress (whose present documents, be it the Freedom Charter or Strategy and Tactics, do not anywhere mention the word "socialism")'.

For Mzala there was no wall between the national and class struggle. In this regard, for him the national democratic revolution was the terrain upon which the socialist struggle needed to be concomitantly waged. 'Essentially a social problem,' he argued, 'the national question is, in the final analysis, subordinated to the general tasks of the class struggle of the proletariat.' For Mzala, capitalism was the 'most flagrant manifestations of national oppression'; national liberation could only relax national tensions and therefore provide partial or provisional solutions. It was only socialism that guaranteed lasting and fundamental solutions to the national question.[39]

So it was that Mzala grappled with the national question, a subject that would go on to form the backbone of his scholarly work. It must be around this time that he penned another ideological missive 'A Tale of Two Nations: The Presentation of the National Question in South Africa', which appeared in the second-quarter edition of the 1984 *African Communist*. Written as Sisa Majola, Mzala took advantage of the sixtieth anniversary of Lenin's death to examine the application of the Leninist principles to the solution of the national problem in South Africa. By now, Mzala was displaying signs of advanced Marxism-Leninism analysis and its application to the South African problem. He was touching on issues such as 'historico-economic conditions of the national question', 'The special features of colonialism', 'The meaning of the right to self-determination', and 'The merging of nations into a single South African nation'.[40] In this regard, Lenin's posture on the right of the oppressed nations to self-determination provided a useful framework for Mzala in understanding the South African problem.

VIII

Mzala made effective use of his familial links in Swaziland. Bulunga recalls how Mzala's maternal aunt, who had married into the Simelanes, facilitated Mzala's and the ANC's work. Mzala was very close to his Swaziland family, his aunt and cousins – to the extent that his relaxed attitude toward them worried Bulunga as a possible weak point when it came to security. However, Nonceba – who was also acquainted with the Simelanes, among them Mzala's cousin Goodwill Simelane – says Mzala was good at concealing this relationship, and it took her a while to actually figure it out. In 1983, through his aunt, he arranged a family meeting with his parents and younger sister Titi. By then an MK soldier based in Angola, Titi had decided that she was getting married in December and Mzala, being the elder brother, thought it important for this union to receive the blessing of their parents. The meeting took place at his aunt's house.

Phasha says it was during this period that she finally had a chance to see his brother. He had sent her a letter through a man who had pretended to be old and frail, requesting her and Tom Zitha, Phasha's husband, to come over to Swaziland. Apart from the fact that he was yearning to see his sister, Mzala also wanted to meet his brother-in-law. The meeting took place in Matsapha. When the ANC tried to recruit Phasha and Tom, Mzala protested and asked that they not be involved as three of Phasha's siblings were already in exile.

Kasrils has fond memories of him and Mzala spending a week in a retreat from heavy security searches in a Swazi game park, where they pretended to be tourists. Equally, Mzala effectively exploited such strategic retreats as a reprieve from his punishing schedule.

> We enjoyed the rest, and the opportunity to assess the struggle, in the tranquillity of watching wild game and sharing braaied meat in the evenings. He was a lovely companion, full of good conversation and wit. Mature beyond his years – I was in my mid-forties and he 17 years my junior, yet we could relate as equals, not to say that he showed me no respect in terms of the age difference.

Kasrils enjoyed spending time with Mzala and uncovered a funny side of him, especially in his creative use of words and ability to capture attention by coining interesting terms that made comrades laugh. This is visible in most of his writing, even when dealing with serious subjects. The choice of titles for some of his articles, such as 'Cooking the Rice inside the Pot' and 'You cannot have an Omelette without Breaking the Eggs', reflect his sense of humour. But the story that amuses Kasrils most and reveals Mzala's passionate character occurred at a movie theatre in Mbabane, Swaziland. In the midst of a widespread crackdown against MK's underground presence, Kasrils says they decided to watch an epic film of Libya's resistance against

Italian colonialism. The theatre was packed, with half the audience being MK cadres in various disguises, who slipped in as the lights were dimmed.

> I was there with fellow commander of the region, Ebrahim Ebrahim. In the middle of a harrowing scene of torture by Italian soldiers a voice shouted out: 'Fascists! Damn fascists!' The voice was unmistakenly that of Mzala. When I met him sometime later and pretended to admonish him for putting us all at risk of exposure had there been a police agent present, he was initially perturbed but then twigged that I was pulling his leg. He saw the joke and we ended up in hysterics. He could laugh at himself. He was very endearing.

Mzala never neglected his intellectual engagements, and it was during these months that he wrote 'Latest Opportunism and the Theory of the South African Revolution', published in 1984. According to Eddy Maloka, it was a polemical response to the formation of the National Forum[41] and the adoption of its 'Azanian Manifesto' in June 1983. 'He intended to finish the pamphlet within four weeks and have it distributed inside the country in time for the second conference of this National Forum. But he was, unfortunately, arrested again, and put in prison for five months.'[42] Among the treasured possessions he managed to smuggle into prison was the manuscript, which he later completed while in prison. Says Maloka:

> He took it with him after deportation to Tanzania via Mozambique. In Tanzania he gave it to some Bulgarian comrades for publication in Sofia. The pamphlet was later despatched into South Africa from Zimbabwe. It was only intended for internal use, hence there is no mention of the publisher nor the year of publication.[43]

That this is considered a pamphlet conceals the fact that it was a substantial document of 143 pages with five chapters developed under difficult conditions. The first chapter, titled 'Opportunism and the Struggle against the Freedom Charter', has four sections that provide background to the Freedom Charter, including 'The Role of Ideology in the Struggle for Liberation'. Chapter 2, 'Critical Remarks of the Seven Resolutions of the "National" Forum Conference', critically engages with each resolution. Chapter 3, 'What can we Learn from this Manifesto', has seven sections that deal with issues such as the class alliances, while Chapter 4, titled 'The Opportunist Substance of the Slogan: "One Azania, One Nation"', deals with the complexity of the national question. In the last chapter, 'Unity and Struggle for Liberation', Mzala unpacks the nuances around the concept of the unity of the oppressed masses on the basis of the Freedom Charter 'as a historic step to a socialist and finally classless South Africa'.[44] In 1985 he broke down this rebuttal of the Azanian Manifesto in a four-part series 'The Freedom Charter is our Lodestar' published in the July-to-October editions of *Sechaba*.

IX

At the beginning of 1984, the ANC's work in the forward areas was becoming increasingly complicated by developments in the region. Although various machineries continued to operate in Swaziland – including the northern Natal rural machinery, which sought to infiltrate the rural parts of Natal – it was not easy. Tensions between Mzala and Shabalala were heightening due to their differences in approach, with Mzala remaining adamant that the time was ripe to infiltrate South Africa, while Shabalala remained sceptical.

Matters would come to a head during a strategic review meeting held in Maputo in 1984. The session involved all political machineries as well as the political leadership, including the military committee. Joe Slovo attended on behalf of the military committee, and the political committee was represented by Jacob Zuma and Ebrahim Ebrahim, its chairperson and secretary respectively. At the meeting, Ebrahim presented a political overview of the situation in South Africa 'with special emphasis on Natal', which – according to Shabalala – he used 'loosely to include both Natal and what was then KwaZulu'.

Shabalala says one of the items presented at the meeting was the 'so-called people's war document'. This, he says, was the first time that most of them in the political machinery had encountered the document, which was still being finalised, and yet they were expected to provide feedback. 'I got absolutely angry. I was shaking.' Out of rage, Shabalala stood up and fired a question: 'How can you say we must comment on this document when it has already been implemented?' To Shabalala, it was clear that Mzala was behind the document.

At the heart of Shabalala's unhappiness with the people's war strategy was what he perceived to be extremely risky proposals that bordered on craziness. For the rural areas, the strategy proposed base areas and operational areas. Shabalala's version is that the document sought to create the base areas where the units would be located.

Those would be their bases and then when they operate, they would go into their operational areas. So, in a place like Ingwavuma, for instance, it could be regarded as a base area and the units that are there would then operate much further south and they will carry out that operation whether hitting a police station or whatever, and then retreat to that base area.

Shabalala thought this was 'just absolutely crazy', especially since Ingwavuma was swarming with SADF personnel. As someone who had spent his formative years in the countryside of Natal, Shabalala felt he was familiar with the terrain under discussion and, to his mind, the area did not present itself for the opportunities being proposed in the document. But Shabalala felt misunderstood by comrades like Slovo. At one point in the meeting, says Shabalala, Slovo asked why Comrade Paul Goitsemang (Shabalala's MK name) was so angry at the proposal, especially as it was going to be implemented by comrades who trust each other and would have analysed each particular situation. But Shabalala says his concerns were that this document was 'already being implemented by the Natal machinery'.

Shabalala's belief that the strategy was already being carried out in Ingwavuma was thus essentially an accusation of Mzala, who was one of the military commanders. Shabalala, however, regarded Ingwavuma as an operational area in which he had organised underground structures for political work 'which would include preparing for men to come in'. This, in fact, was his primary concern, because he regarded it as 'reckless' to 'throw in men there, who are almost certain to be discovered'.

Because Mzala was headstrong about this strategy, having punted it on various platforms, he felt attacked and betrayed by Shabalala. Granted, due to their different personalities, they would regularly irritate each other; as Shabalala puts it, 'I am not a passionate person like him and if we are having a discussion, I wanted it to stop somewhere to give myself time to think and maybe read up on things.' Of course, Mzala – having received training abroad – was more advanced politically, and he had been a little ahead of Shabalala since their school days. Shabalala notes:

> [Mzala] had been to a political training school, he knew Marxism now. He was quoting Marx, Engels, Lenin and everybody all the time. But there was nothing wrong with our personal relationship because I respected him, too. I knew him as a good person but then

our relationship was spoiled. This was a political machinery meeting and obviously, the political machineries were not implementing this people's war document.

The heated exchanges at this meeting, says Shabalala, put a permanent dent in their friendship. After the meeting, Shabalala says, 'I think we exchanged few words. I think he felt like I betrayed him or something. There was not much that was said between us then; I was not even able to explain to him what I meant nor to anybody. The meeting ended and comrades started leaving.' This was to be the last substantial exchange between Shabalala and Mzala until their very brief encounter at the ANC's Kabwe Conference in 1985.

One individual who left a lasting impression on Mzala during this period is Jacob Zuma. In 1990 Mzala described Zuma as someone he held in high regard, one of the few ANC leaders with a real working-class background and a 'tremendous' hard worker. For Mzala, Zuma showed no interest in mere theory, but rather focused on reality. He saw him as someone who put in a genuine effort. 'He gets up very early in the morning to work,' said Mzala, 'and not just to impress anybody.'

X

On 16 March 1984, Mozambique concluded the Nkomati Accord[45] with the apartheid regime. This unexpected turn of events in regional relations and the so-called 'peace initiatives' took 'the form of a non-aggression pact between South Africa and Mozambique and an agreement on the disengagement of forces between South Africa and Angola'.[46] With the Accord coming in the footsteps of the 1982 pact between South Africa and Swaziland, suddenly the space in which to operate in the forward areas shrunk for the ANC. All along, Mozambique had been a secure base for MK, and every time they were in trouble in the Swazi Kingdom, they retreated to Mozambique. 'All that changed when Mozambique signed the Nkomati Accord with the apartheid state in 1984.'[47]

The Accord was a major offensive step for the apartheid regime against the ANC. 'Many comrades were being arrested in Swaziland,' writes Eddy Maloka, with Mzala also 'arrested again, and put in prison for five months', he 'lost contact with his unit, and he never managed to see how the base in Ingwavuma grew'.[48] When the pamphlet 'Why the Need for Anonymity?' – which referred to 'Benjamin Singaye alias Mzala Nxumalo

...' – was published by the City of London Anti-Apartheid Group in the late 1980s with some inaccurate information about Mzala, Mzala penned the following note: 'The first part of this pamphlet ... was the information I gave to the Swazi police when they detained me in 1984 – but it is all false information. The last part, also false, is the creation of the SA Embassy in London, I'm sure. This just shows how Swaziland collaborates with SA and its Embassies.'[49] Among the glaring inaccuracies was that he had attended Ohlange High School in Durban and that in 1976 he went to exile in Swaziland where he was arrested for car theft.

Sue Rabkin was still in Maputo when the Nkomati Accord came into effect. She says this was a very difficult time, both in Mozambique and Swaziland. The Accord caught everyone by surprise, as reflected in the editorial of the *African Communist* which posed the questions: 'Which analyst would have been bold enough to foretell that in April 1984, the Mozambican government, headed by the Frelimo party, would be deporting the cadres of the South African revolutionary movement from their country? Or raiding ANC homes and offices in Maputo, under the supervisory eye of a joint Mozambican–South African commission?' The editorial pointed out that the ANC's presence in Mozambique had been reduced 'from a substantial working cadre to a "diplomatic mission" only of 10 approved members, with the President and one or two others having the right of entry'.[50]

Sue says they had only two days to clear out of Mozambique, and debated whether to keep a skeleton staff to support the machineries. They had put too many people into Swaziland to suddenly recall them. 'I mean, [we'd] been sticking people over the border and jamming them into this tiny little place called Swaziland,' she says. Suddenly, comrades were staying indoors, afraid to step outside. 'It was a bit like [Covid-19] lockdown,' she says, because 'the enemy was present, they had free rein in Swaziland.' Over and above the free rein of apartheid operatives, Sue says the movement was also heavily infiltrated and Swaziland did not present the best opportunities for hiding.

Those who were lucky were deported to safer countries. Those who were not so lucky, like Maphululo and Mngomezulu, were kidnapped and killed. Mzala was among the lucky ones. Mtshaulana says Mzala's group, which was sent to Tanzania from Swaziland, arrived at the time when 'we were preparing for the ANC conference in Kabwe'. It is around this period that Mzala put the final touches to his famous missive 'Cooking the Rice inside the Pot'.

CHAPTER 6

Cooking the Rice inside the Pot

I

In 1984, Mzala was deported from Swaziland to Tanzania via Mozambique. He stayed at the Dakawa Development Centre, 55 kilometres from Mazimbu where the famous Solomon Mahlangu Freedom College (SOMAFCO) was located. Many comrades who had been deported from Mozambique and Swaziland were sent there. The camp in Mazimbu was established in 1978, after the Tanzanian government donated land to the ANC in order to start a school for young South African exiles. With the influx of so many more refugees, many of them adults, a need arose for another centre. The Dakawa Development Centre was established in 1982 to cater for this need. One of the centre's objectives was 'to cater for the educational needs of youth as well as adults, by preparing them in basic education for acceptance into SOMAFCO'.[1]

Young arrivals in Tanzania were sent to the Ruth First Student Orientation Centre at Dakawa. There, their educational level could be assessed, and they would attend classes in Mathematics, English, Political Studies, and the History of South Africa and the ANC until the next school year began at SOMAFCO. For adult arrivals, Dakawa was intended to function as a development centre where they could learn skills that would be useful for the ANC in exile as well as for a future, liberated South Africa. It was envisaged that the Dakawa centre would have several functions – educational (the Student Orientation Centre, and a vocational training centre that was to be established); agricultural (crop and animal husbandry); small-scale industrial (garment factory, art and silkscreening studio, mechanical workshop, for instance); and supportive (medical facilities, library, day-care centre and primary school, for example) – but in 1982 these were still mostly ideas on paper.[2] There was, however, a great deal of international support for the centre. Alpheus Manghezi asserts that 'it is a tribute to the Nordic states, to various other European and African countries, as well as to organs of the United Nations, especially UNESCO, for providing the funds and other assistance towards the establishment of the infrastructure in the two settlements'.

In 1989, Lionel 'Rusty' Bernstein, a stalwart of the ANC and SACP, was deployed to establish an ANC Political School in Mazimbu and Dakawa. On his return, he wrote that when he first went to Mazimbu in 1978 the place was basically a bush with no development to speak of. 'The grass was as high as an elephant's eye and small, ebony-breasted birds, capped and clothed in scarlet, flashed in and out or perched swaying on the feathery tips.' Eleven years later, the place was quite different.

> Now the grass is cut and the main road tarred, wide enough for buses, tractors and trucks. Driven from the roadside the birds congregate in the high grass and bulrushes at the river. Just beyond the bridge at the river is the barrier and checkpost that marks the entrance to Mazimbu. The checkpost is manned by Tanzanian officials. Everyone who enters or leaves needs a pass to permit them to do so. Mazimbu is a South African enclave in the heart of Tanzania, a sort of five-star camp for political exiles. There cannot be refugees anywhere living in a more pleasant and beautiful setting.[3]

The ANC had developed the camps to accommodate its cadres as well as the children born in exile. With the help of international aid, both infrastructure and personnel were developed, including teachers, medical professionals, mechanics and others.[4] These facilities, including fixed and movable assets estimated to be valued at US$600 million, were eventually handed over to the government of Tanzania by ANC President Oliver Tambo in 1992.[5] By that time, the ANC had been unbanned in South Africa.

II

It is in this community that Mzala immersed himself in 1984, getting involved in the Amandla Cultural Ensemble and rekindling his association with Radio Freedom. Although he was based at Dakawa, Mzala occasionally visited SOMAFCO.[6] Mpho (then still Gwangwa) had become active in various student activities since returning from Cuba, where she had been studying. While in Cuba, Mpho fell pregnant and had to return to Africa for the birth of her son Sizwe. The child was smuggled into South Africa to allow Mpho to continue with her studies. She became a student at SOMAFCO, playing an active part in the Young Women's Section and the students' executive. Because of her involvement, she had been identified as one of the students to be groomed for political leadership. Patric Mtshaulana was the teacher responsible for teaching Development of Societies. He had spent time with Mzala in the GDR, and on his return he was among the first teachers to be deployed to Tanzania, where he was working with students and assigning them various tasks. In his first engagement with Mpho, he appointed her newsreader, which entailed monitoring the radio and then analysing news and developments in various countries, including South Africa. 'In the evening, we would then get together [in the school hall] as students to indicate what was happening in the country,' says Mpho.

Whenever someone new arrived at the camps, Mtshaulana had a habit of organising lectures and conferences to which they would be invited as speaker. When Mzala and Mtshaulani rekindled their friendship, the next logical step was for Mzala to make a presentation on the 1976 Soweto uprising. Mtshaulana held Mzala in high esteem. 'If you want to give a picture of the man as he was, as a human being, Mzala is always smiling, always entertaining, always articulate – so articulate that even when he talks about very serious things he does it in a very common way.' He recalls how Mzala once criticised the ANC leadership:

> You know comrades, when you drive a car you have the view of where you are going through the windscreen, but the view from behind you have two ways of looking at it: you can use your mirrors and then you have three mirrors for that purpose, but you can also turn around and look back. But if you do so it's dangerous; you will end up crashing the car. And our ANC leaders are trying to tell us about the Freedom Charter; they are trying to tell us about Rivonia; they are looking back. Use your mirrors; they are the only way to look at the dangers that you have just passed.

Mtshaulana is overcome by emotion when he reflects on Mzala. He says this was his 'philosophical way of criticising the nepotism of the ANC. They are always trying to look into 1912, 100 years [back].'

John Pampallis had been a staff member at SOMAFCO since 1980; he taught History and English, and from the beginning of 1988 was also deputy vice-principal. Pampallis was immediately impressed by the new arrival:

> He was very dedicated. I mean, completely immersed in the struggle, nothing else. Every time I saw him or spoke to him, he was talking politics, about the ANC and his technical strategies. I didn't always agree with him. I mean, I was one of the people who were building the pyramids in Egypt.[7] Mazimbu was one of them.

With the consultative conference around the corner, Mzala was already in conference mode. Still impatient with the pace of the revolution, he was a man in a hurry and on a mission. He felt that the leadership was not looking through the windscreen, but turning its head to look back, including when it came to the question of race. Mzala's input for the pre-conference discussions was through his article 'Cooking the Rice inside the Pot'.

III

On the day of Mzala's lecture on the Soweto uprising, Mpho felt he presented as if he had been there in Soweto. Mzala had not bargained on meeting this feisty young lady who had been there on the march and had witnessed first-hand all the activities. As soon as the exchange began, their eyes locked for the first time and there was a spark. 'It was really love at first sight,' says Mpho. Although she realised that she had a thing for this guest, she immediately left for her dormitory after the session. Her pride would not let her show even the slightest of hints.

Weeks later, on a sunny Saturday afternoon, while waiting for transport from Dar es Salaam back to SOMAFCO, Mpho bumped into Mtshaulana and Mzala. Mtshaulana seized the opportunity and officially introduced his friend to Mpho. It was clear right away that Mzala had a crush on Mpho. But still nothing happened. Having grown up in a musical environment, Mpho had befriended another teacher, Sipho Duma (Richard Sibengile). Duma was into music and read avidly. Also a close friend of Mzala, he was planning a birthday party on 28 November 1984. Mtshaulana let Mzala know that his crush frequented Duma's place, drawn there by the books and music.

Duma had invited Mpho to act as DJ at his party, telling her that she was the only one he could entrust with his music. Unbeknown to Mpho, Duma had asked Mzala to be master of ceremonies. 'It didn't bother me,' she said. When curfew approached, Mpho whispered to Duma that her time was up, and she was off. Mzala was still busy with the programme. From the corner of his eye, he could see that his target was leaving, and so Mzala promptly cut his speech short and ran after her.

Mpho made a feeble attempt to dissuade her suitor. 'I have curfew,' she told him, but Mzala's response was simply, 'I'll walk with you to the dormitory ... I need to talk to you.' They walked all the way to Mpho's dormitory and stopped at the door. In a scene reminiscent of *Romeo and Juliet*, the prospect of love made Mzala more determined to evade all obstacles Mpho was putting in his path. He used all his charm to profess his undying love to Mpho. 'The rest is history,' says Mpho, blushing.

So it was that Mpho and Mzala found themselves in the honeymoon phase of their love. They had a lot in common. 'Our music and political analysis were our greatest interaction; cycling was another. I loved cycling. On Saturdays, I would take the bike and cycle around SOMAFCO.' Although Mzala was more into motorbikes, he would cycle along with his new love. As a new couple, they spent their time together attending mainly political functions. Mpho was president of the Young Women's Section and so had many speaking engagements, and Mzala tagged along. Mpho also sang and participated in cultural groups, another aspect of their lives that coalesced.

In December 1984, two of Mzala's friends were getting married at Dakawa camp, and Mpho and her cultural group were billed to perform at the weddings. One of the weddings coincided with Mpho's twenty-first birthday on 17 December. On a bus on their way back from the wedding, Mzala put on quite a show. Much like his cameo performances in Dlangezwa High School boys' dormitory shower, where he would stand on the cement table and recite Julius Caesar, Mzala stood up and declared his undying love for Mpho to all and sundry. Some were tempted to dismiss this as infatuation-driven euphoria, but Mzala was serious about his commitment to his new love. He told everyone who cared to listen that this was the woman of his dreams, and that he was going to marry her. Mpho recalls, 'All my comrades were there. There were so many comrades inside the bus and I remember sitting on his lap. Yes, he was that excited.' But Mzala's show was not over. He continued to tell everyone that he wanted to 'wish his woman a happy twenty-first birthday' and started singing. This is how their life together began.

Soon, Mzala had moved to Dar es Salaam, with Mpho still based in Morogoro. Their meeting point now became Dar es Salaam. During one of their rendezvous, while walking in town, Mzala spotted a motorbike with two helmets. The owner was inside the nearby pub. 'He loved motorbikes,' says Mpho. While he was animatedly describing and explaining the bike's features to Mpho, the owner emerged from the pub and Mzala said, 'I'd love to be on the motorbike with my wife.' While Mpho was still trying to contest the wife part, Mzala had managed to persuade the biker. 'I don't know how he managed to convince this guy. The next thing that guy was giving us the helmets.' They dashed around Dar es Salaam. 'I have never been on a motorbike [before] and I think thereafter. Oh, my goodness! That was such an adrenaline rush.' Mpho was having a wonderful time; 'It was exciting,' she gushes.

Daily, Mpho was discovering new aspects about Mzala. He was not just the intellectual she encountered as a guest lecturer or the brilliant public speaker who programme-directed Duma's birthday party. Neither was he limited to his involvement in cultural groups or Radio Freedom. Mpho soon discovered a free-spirited individual who did not mind standing up in a crowd to declare his undying love for her. Mpho was pleasantly surprised by his romantic side. 'He was quite romantic at heart.'

One evening, in the middle of dinner, Mzala noticed a piano. The restaurant was teeming with patrons, including ANC comrades, such as Manto Tshabalala. Both Mzala and Mpho were oblivious, however; deeply in love, Mzala requested to play a song for Mpho. 'He loved Nat King Cole,' she says, and he promptly proceeded to play the piano and belted out the song, 'Mona Lisa'. 'I ended up standing by him and singing together.' Their magic soon rubbed off on other patrons, and it wasn't long before they had the entire restaurant on its feet. 'I think we ended up having a free meal from the restaurant because of his performance,' laughs Mpho. Afterwards, they were mobbed and congratulated by patrons and comrades. 'Wow, you also sing,' said Tshabalala to Mpho. 'I just felt the moment.'

Mpho recalls the early stage of their relationship with fondness.

Yes, there was no dull moment with him. Mentally he could engage me. Socially, he was also fun. Mzala could spend time recording music for me and send it and say, you see when you are educated, this is the music that you need to listen to. Whenever I had something that I was writing, I would call him. I would make an appointment through the teachers' residence to speak to him over the phone. He used to write beautiful letters. I knew that when there was a car coming from Dakawa, I had a note from him.

IV

Despite being madly in love, Mzala remained focused on his revolutionary responsibilities. During this period, he penned what is perhaps one of his most popular intellectual interventions, 'Cooking the Rice inside the Pot'. The article was published in the January 1985 edition of *Sechaba*, and immediately became one of the main discussion documents prior to the conference planned for 16–22 June 1985.[8]

The central thesis of the article was the need to expedite the people's war inside South Africa. Mzala's point of departure was that events unfolding inside the country were indicative that the people's war was already happening and that MK needed to tap into this revolutionary process. 'Our people have long ago discovered that what is needed in South Africa is a new society, a new political and economic system, a radical change of all that is existing,' he wrote.

Mzala acknowledged that while the principal task of the struggle was to overthrow the racist minority government that oppressed the black majority, the struggle had to simultaneously deal with the class question. Thus, he perceived the apartheid regime as presiding over a capitalist state backed by the imperialist power block. He argued:

> At the moment, the state power in South Africa is in the hands of the White minority that is backed up by imperialist economic power; the so-called Republic of South Africa is a class State of the bourgeoisie that operates for the purposes of denying us our national right to the wealth of the country, the right to participate in its administration, and to enjoy all human rights that are consistent with any democratic society.

To Mzala's mind, the apartheid system was ripe for the taking and had to be destroyed through 'the revolutionary struggle of the masses in political actions and armed struggle'. Once this task was achieved, 'an assembly of people's representatives, elected on the basis of universal and equal suffrage, by secret ballot' would have to be convened.

> The People's Assembly will promulgate laws that will declare all racist laws null and void; it will pass laws that are in conformity with the Freedom Charter. No agreement can be reached with the racist regime to convene such a People's Assembly; no racist government can guarantee the holding of free and fair elections in South Africa, and therefore no peaceful negotiation can lead to the creation of a democratic State without the racists and the imperialists, and against them.

Mzala was convinced that a military victory to topple the racist government was imperative in order to implement the Freedom Charter. In the preamble of his article, Mzala asserted the importance of mass mobilisation. He was opposed to the notion of 'vanguard' control of the revolution at this stage or in a post-apartheid democracy. 'The decisive role of the masses in revolution cannot be substituted by an elite corps of professional revolutionaries. We seek to establish the power of the people and not of the vanguard movement.' Mzala regarded the working class as constituting the majority of the masses under capitalism and thus the motive force of the revolution.

> Only a mass movement that is led by the working class will have nothing to secure and to fortify in the present South Africa, since the working class has the objective mission to destroy, not just appearances, but, on the contrary, the essence of oppression; not just its form, but the thing itself, the root of the social evil. As a mass movement that is rooted among the working masses it is no longer a formal organisation but an actual material force, and no amount of banning orders can destroy it, no amount of arrests of its leading persons can weaken it. It is invincible!

Apart from his clear articulation of the role of the working class in dislodging the apartheid regime, Mzala also reaffirmed his vision concerning the role of armed forces as important but complementary. He was convinced that the popular uprising in South Africa in the mid-1980s had created fertile ground for an armed struggle inside the country to complement spontaneous actions. 'It may be said without exaggeration that we are now passing through a period of history when our people, more than ever before, prefer to die fighting in open struggle against this infamous racist system rather than perish from constant starvation, dying prematurely from diseases caused by horrible conditions of poverty.' Mzala was reading the mass actions as evidence of the people's willingness to confront the racist regime. He saw the 'desperate outbursts' of the people as a pointer ...

> ... to the imperative necessity for strong organisation and leadership in order to wage a skilled political struggle for victory. It is not enough to call ourselves the vanguard contingent; we must act in such a way that all the other contingents recognise and are obliged to admit that we are not tailing behind semi-spontaneous mass upsurges but are marching in the vanguard. The arena from which alone it is possible to organise the masses and provide real, dynamic and comprehensive leadership, is among the people themselves.

For Mzala, the motive force behind the revolution was not the exile leadership but the masses back home. He was almost annoyed with what he perceived to be 'building pyramids in Egypt'. For him, the movement needed to de-exile itself. He wrote:

> Leadership, in the final analysis, means going to the masses, merging with them into an invincible fighting force. History's great call to our movement headed by the African National Congress is to begin a process of de-exiling ourselves, of transferring the initiative of the liberation process to the actual arena of our struggle, inside South Africa.

It was inside the country that Mzala thought the struggle should be waged. When it came to this question, he was not merely theorising and speaking in abstract terms; only a few months previously, until he had been deported from Swaziland, he had been involved on the ground in setting this process in motion. Thus, Mzala was expressing his concrete political action beyond simple theorising.

> We must fight our way back into our country; we must find ways of dispatching units of our political and military leadership to the various pockets of mass resistance inside South Africa. Yes, let us always remember that while we engage ourselves in building pyramids in Egypt, the main task is still to cross the Red Sea back into our own land.

To bolster his argument, Mzala used the editorial of the *African Communist*. His was not the lone voice of a disgruntled and impatient freedom fighter calling for the 'transfer' of the liberation initiative to the 'actual arena of our struggle, inside South Africa'. Reflecting on the situation after the signing of the Nkomati Accord, the *African Communist* had argued: 'The ANC leadership outside South Africa, like the Communist Party leadership, has never seen itself as permanently in exile. It has always seen itself as a temporary caretaker for the movement which had to be rebuilt, regrouped and re-established at home ...' The editorial continued:

> If the curtailment of facilities in Mozambique is to have any long-term influence on our movement, it will be simply to lend urgency to this process of fighting our way back to the country; and thus to expedite the speed at which an internal revolutionary leadership is once again established – this time securely surrounded by an armed cadre and an aroused and supportive population. The difficulties for us arising from the Nkomati Accord are short-term; the challenges and opportunities are long-term.[9]

Mzala viewed the prevailing political situation in South Africa as presenting opportunities for the movement to establish bases inside the country in order to escalate the offensive against the apartheid regime. This is how he put this point:

> The present all-around crisis facing the ruling class in South Africa, the current revolt following the rejection of the latest racist Constitution, in which dozens of our people have been killed by the army and police, this unprecedented situation of ungovernability in South Africa, puts intense pressure on us to meet this long-term challenge and re-establish revolutionary bases and leadership centres of our liberation movement within the borders of South Africa, among our fighting masses.

He did, however, concede that the challenge facing the movement would be a formidable one, one that required 'supreme sacrifice from all of us'. But he still thought this could not be more formidable than their decision to leave the country to seek assistance from other countries. Therefore, the movement had to speed up the process of going back to South Africa and waging a people's war. 'We have no choice here,' he wrote. 'Otherwise we will be attempting to cook the rice outside the pot.'

In 1984, black townships, especially in the Transvaal (now partly Gauteng), were virtually ungovernable. This was the start of a long period of resistance against the regime. In the Vaal Triangle, the civic movement was organising school boycotts, demonstrations and stay-aways against municipal tariffs and services. Often, these led to clashes with the police and councillors. By the time 1984 drew to a close, more than 150 people in the Vaal Triangle had lost their lives, a number that increased the following year, leading to the government declaring a State of Emergency.[10]

Other townships, such as Soweto and many others across the country, were no different. By this point, the UDF was playing a more prominent role, and its leaders – among them Albertina Sisulu, Allan Boesak, Frank Chikane, Cassim Saloojee, Popo Molefe and many others – were using numerous platforms, from funerals to pulpits, to challenge the apartheid regime. Mzala used these developments at home to advance his thesis of 'cooking the rice inside the pot'. He was emboldened and believed that the regime was vulnerable and that 'the masses themselves had realised that the only way out is to wage a war'.

To bolster his argument, he found information from all manner of sources, including the media. He presented some statistics of the violent revolt taking place throughout South Africa, including official account of deaths, injuries and damage to property, to point out that ...

... [The] people's combat diary is there for everybody to inspect ... show me any army anywhere in the world which, despite such odds, and armed with old bottles and dustbin lids, caused the damage enumerated in the above-mentioned statistics! Such is the present mood of the masses. Umkhonto we Sizwe has demonstrated the way forward through an armed propaganda campaign; now, more than ever before, the time has come for both our movement and the masses in general to be placed on a war footing.

For Mzala, this situation was ripe for a people's war, and what the exile mission needed was to develop strategies to link the movement with the fighting people at home. To this end, the masses had to be armed 'for a real and decisive victory over the racists in correspondence with the development of our army inside the country; in this way, it will no longer be a war by a few scattered groups, but a planned national war'. As always, he was careful to guard against adventurism. Hence, he reverted to history to argue his point. Invoking lessons from the Spanish Civil War, he quoted General Enrique Líster:

In organising a guerrilla movement one should never confuse popular sympathy with popular support; these are two different things. In Spain the guerrillas enjoyed the sympathy of people, who regarded them as heroes. But the sympathy did not go beyond that. It never became the active and massive support for the guerrilla operations which was essential, and on which the guerrillas had counted.

To Mzala, launching a guerrilla operation inside the country was nevertheless feasible, given the fighting masses who needed training by the ANC but who could also serve as an important link for supplies. He concluded the article by looking ahead. 'Future historians,' he wrote, 'who will judge our situation with the benefit of hindsight, having the advantage of the so-called "bird's-eye view" will indeed say that we won our victory because we truly fought a people's war.'

V

Mzala's article did not go unnoticed. While some comrades welcomed his intervention as an accurate account of the state of affairs within the movement, others thought Mzala had missed the mark. The article thus sparked a lot of debate. Two comrades in particular responded to Mzala in the subsequent edition of *Sechaba*. The first was Nyawuza, who contested Mzala's formulation of the 'exile structure', the process of 'de-exiling ourselves' and the transferring of the liberation process to the 'actual arena of our struggle, inside South Africa'. Nyawuza said he was not worried by the title of Mzala's article until he came across some 'unfortunate formulations'.

The central thesis of Nyawuza's submission appeared to be that the ANC was a unitary structure and could not be demarcated by members in exile and those inside the country. A line that did not sit well with Nyawuza – and the same can be said of many comrades – was what he perceived to be an accusation that the ANC was 'building pyramids in Egypt'. It is this line that, decades later, is still engraved in the minds of many comrades. Nyawuza regarded Mzala's article as reflecting 'revolutionary impatience'. He concluded by saying, 'I only hope that by those "pyramids in Egypt" Comrade Mzala is not referring to SOMAFCO; otherwise that will be uncomradely of Comrade Mzala.'[11]

A more coherent piece, 'Preparing the Fire before Cooking the Rice inside the Pot' by Alex Mashinini (Tshidiso Mokhoanatse), appeared in the same edition of *Sechaba*. Mashinini took Mzala back to previous articles written in 1981 and 1982 by Khumalo Migwe on 'arming of the masses'.

Of course, Khumalo Migwe was Mzala's MK name. Mashinini argued that both Khumalo Migwe and Mzala deal extensively with the issue, 'but failed to emerge with a comprehensive solution to this problem because they omitted, firstly, a closely linked aspect of this question – under what conditions is the programme of arming the masses realisable in South Africa's own set of conditions?'

Mashinini wrote, 'This failure on their part' – referring to Migwe and Mzala – 'has often led to imaginations (though theoretically important) which hang on a very thin thread connecting them to reality.' Here, Mashinini was referring to the 'guerrilla warfare' and 'liberated areas' theses advanced by Mzala and Migwe. According to Mashinini, the 'arming of the masses' could not be treated in isolation from the broader military question as part of the strategy of revolution – and this was the error he accused Mzala of committing.

In his article, Mashinini articulated steps that should not be skipped in building momentum towards a people's war. Presenting what he called 'some burning military questions', he argued:

> A wrong strategy will, in the final analysis, lead to the total defeat of the army pursuing it, while wrong tactics may not necessarily lead to the failure and defeat of strategy. But when, on the other hand, the tactics are continuously wrong and not compatible with strategy, this will inevitably lead to strategic failures.

Mashinini concluded by stating:

> It is only when we've embarked on and successfully carried out the programme of 'every house a guerrilla base, everything a weapon, everyone a soldier', that we can be in a position to build up an invincible political army of the armed masses as a main force in our just war of liberation for the creation of a free, democratic and non-racial society in our country, South Africa.[12]

Mzala's generation was, however, not the first to raise such issues so sharply within the movement. As early as 1969, a document known as the 'Hani Memorandum', produced and signed by Chris Hani and six other MK cadres, had raised similar concerns. In that document – produced following the failure of the Wankie and Sipolilo campaigns – the comrades raised similar issues as those raised by Mzala. 'We, as genuine revolutionaries, are moved by the frightening depths reached by the rot in the ANC and the disintegration of MK accompanying this rot and manifesting itself in the following way,' began the memorandum.

The document went on to highlight 16 points that demonstrated the 'rot'. Similar to the 'building of pyramids in Egypt' thesis, the memorandum accused the ANC leadership in exile of having created 'a machinery which has become an end in itself'. This leadership, it argued, 'is completely divorced from the situation in South Africa. It is not in a position to give an account of the functioning branches inside the country'. The document continued: 'We are disturbed by the careerism of the ANC Leadership Abroad who have, in every sense, become professional politicians rather than professional revolutionaries.' Issues of nepotism were also raised:

> We consider the youth in MK as the most revolutionary. We strongly feel that we should be consulted on matters affecting the youth. For instance, we must be informed about the revolutionary International Youth gatherings and we should be given priority in the sending of delegates. The farce of the Bulgaria ANC Youth delegation should never be repeated and those responsible should acknowledge the mistake they made. The Youth of South Africa is not located in London or in any European capital. We therefore take particular exception to the appointment of certain students as leaders of the ANC Youth. Thabo Mbeki who went to London on a scholarship sponsored by NUSAS [National Union of South African Students] is a leader of ANC bogus Youth Organisation.

Also raised by these comrades was 'the glaring practice of nepotism where the leadership used its position to promote their kith and kin and put them in positions where they will not be in any physical confrontation with the enemy'. It was argued that leaders sent their children to universities in Europe out of harm's way; the view was that these comrades were being groomed for leadership positions to take over once MK combatants had toppled the apartheid regime. 'We have no doubt,' they argued, 'that these people will just wait in Europe and just come home when everything has been made secure and comfortable for them, playing the typical role of the Bandas and others.'[13]

Mzala's frank assessment of the situation within the movement could thus be understood as a continuation of this tradition by MK combatants to engage robustly and frankly in the interest of the liberation struggle.

VI

Although, for security reasons, the venue had not been announced, preparations for the consultative conference were well underway before June 1985. Typical of the ANC's conferences, the build-up was characterised by tensions and robust engagements. Some leaders were accused of rigging the elections of delegates to regional meetings and even the consultative conference itself. There were also squabbles about some of proposed resolutions.[14]

Stanley Manong says that, once the date of the conference was announced, there was a flurry of visits from senior leaders of the ANC to their region, with leaders such as Alfred Nzo and Joe Modise suddenly appearing in the camps. 'It is evident that from the visits made by these leaders that they interpreted Angola to be their main stronghold, especially after the conclusion of the Regional Conference.'[15] Of course, Angola was a strategic region for the conference, especially as this was where the younger, active and vocal comrades were concentrated. And, of course, some mutinies had taken place there because of cadres' unhappiness with the state of affairs.

Reflecting on this time, Vusi Mavimbela says they all knew that the debates at conference 'would be intense and heated'. The opening of the NEC to non-African comrades was one hotly debated topic as the conference approached. For Mavimbela and other younger comrades, they knew the battle was already lost for the old-timers with their anachronistic view on race. In Mzala's analogy, they were still looking over their shoulders to 1912.

The younger generation did not hold such conservative ideas. 'The majority of cadres at the conference left South Africa in the 1970s and early 1980s. They participated in [the Mass Democratic Movement] before leaving and had first-hand experience of activist participation across the colour line at all levels of their organisations.'[16] Besides, as Mavimbela posits, the younger generation held white comrades like Joe Slovo in high regard and saw them as heroes.

Mzala believed there were efforts by some ANC leaders to block a group of comrades from Tanzania from attending the conference. This group comprised about a hundred comrades – mainly deported from Swaziland, himself included – with some considered critical of the leadership. Just when the delegates to the conference were being elected, the group from Swaziland was suddenly informed that they were to move to Lusaka –

arriving just too late to attend the meetings electing the delegates there. Complaints were raised, but these were later mollified by a separate conference arranged for comrades who had been in forward areas, at which they could discuss specific issues. However, Mzala felt that even this meeting was engineered to exclude cadres such as himself by withholding information about meetings or being informed very late. Fortunately, Mzala was nominated as a delegate through the intervention of Joe Slovo and Chris Hani.[17]

Mpho recalls a number of instances where some comrades made efforts to sabotage Mzala. Because of his eloquence and knowledge, they did not want him to be present in meetings; they knew, too, that he was well read and could think on his feet. 'But where they could not do anything was in 1985 in the Kabwe Conference, when the underground machinery requested that Mzala should represent them.' Even when he moved from Tanzania for the conference, efforts were made to block him from attending.

VII

The pre-conference tension continued into plenary, with Mzala associating himself with delegates from Angola who had adopted an openly sceptical stance towards the ANC's senior leadership.[18] Apparently, a group of Angolan delegates was sitting in the corner, constantly criticising the leadership. At the heart of their disproval was the issue of the selection of delegates who obtained accreditation without being elected by their structures. Mzala said that whenever they tried to raise the matter of how delegates received accreditation, they were greeted by a choir of boos.[19] But he was never deterred; after the reports in plenary, he raised his hand and asked why MK was suffering so many casualties inside the country. He also wanted to know how much money was being directed into South Africa as opposed to being spent outside.[20]

Mavimbela reflects: 'In the plenary sessions, delegates from the camps in Angola were particularly caustic in their criticism of the leadership.' He continues:

> My friend Nobleman, now popularly known as Mzala, was not known for keeping his views in his back pocket and was very vocal. He pointed to the high rate of casualties among MK cadres on the home front. He also did not believe that the movement's allocation of resources was proportional – most resources were deployed in the rear instead of on

the front line where they were most needed, he argued. He said that that contradicted the priorities the ANC had set itself in its statements. His views were echoed by the Angolan contingent.[21]

Brian Bunting, who presided over elections with Jack Simons, also observed delegates from the regions complaining about not knowing each other and that Mzala was 'sitting in a corner with others who were openly critical of leadership'. Bunting said that even if Mzala had ambitions to be elected into the NEC, 'he would not have been elected since he sat in a corner with a group that was constantly criticising the leadership'. His combative style of engaging notwithstanding, Pallo Jordan – who chaired the commission on strategy and tactics – cannot recall Mzala playing such a role. He says:

> At Kabwe, in his contribution from the floor of the plenary session, following the Presidential address, Mzala identified himself as one among the MK cadreship who hoped that Kabwe would be a watershed conference, like the 1949 Conference that adopted the Programme of Action. They pushed for an inclusive NEC that was open to non-African members; they were the advocates of a strategy of people's war; in Commissions they called for an escalation of the armed struggle, beyond armed propaganda; they argued for an expansion of the front of democratic forces inside the country.

He does not recall Mzala and his comrades being particularly critical of the leadership:

> Far from being critics of the leadership they were bringing to the fore ideas, strategic thinking and conceptualisation that was doing the rounds among the leadership itself. They were keenly aware of the developments in other parts of the world, and the success of the Sandinistas of Nicaragua had not escaped their attention. The notion of insurrection was revived in the commissions and post-Kabwe, *Dawn* published extracts from A Neuberg's *Armed Insurrection*, and articles about insurgency in other parts of the world.

Manong paints a picture of hostility from some senior comrades during the conference:

> I would be failing in my duty not to mention that Zola Skweyiya, and to some extent Kader Asmal, were sometimes intolerant of views that

were critical about the establishment. Instead of being impartial as a Chairperson, Zola Skweyiya would abruptly interject anyone whose views were opposed to those who were supporting the status quo.

Manong met Mzala in person for the first time on the day of the election of NEC members. He was complimentary about this encounter, and says Mzala came to see him after he had spoken at the plenary the previous night. 'He offered words of encouragement by saying the majority of the delegates were disappointed with the fact that the chairperson of the plenary, Ruth Mompati, did not afford me more time to speak because most delegates wanted to hear what was happening in Angola.' Mzala assured Manong that he was not surprised by the way other delegates attacked them 'because they had been foretold that the Angolan delegation was handpicked'.

The conference concluded on 22 June, much earlier than anticipated. Among the decisions and recommendations under 'Strategy and Tactics' was to 'set up a machinery to study key nerve centres of every urban area so as to identify priority targets in cases of insurrection; provide knowledge on how and where to deploy forces; study enemy's capacity to respond speedily to a major crisis'. The ANC was thus a step closer to a people's war, thereby cooking the rice inside the pot.

CHAPTER 7

The Freedom Charter is our lodestar

I

In 1985 Mpho was planning to complete her O-Levels and thereafter register for an electronics degree in Japan. But in September she discovered that she was pregnant. With his ambitions of returning to the front scuppered, Mzala was now deployed in Zambia. He was later assigned to the Amandla Cultural Ensemble as its political head – the ensemble, coincidentally, headed by Mpho's father, Jonas Gwangwa. These developments were peculiar for Mpho. Here was the father of her soon-to-be-born child touring with Amandla, which was headed by her own dad. Gwangwa, however, remained unaware of the entire saga.

As the group was preparing to tour the Soviet Union for the 1985 youth conference, Mpho's thoughts were that this would be a perfect opportunity for Mzala to engage her father. This was going to be much easier, she thought, since her elder sister was also scheduled to attend the conference. Mpho had already levelled with her. 'Talk to her and she will then talk to my father,' she told Mzala. But her sister was not ready to have such a conversation with her father and Mzala, and so the suspense continued. While in the Soviet Union, Gwangwa was surprised that every time they went shopping Mzala would buy baby clothes. When the group returned in

May 1986, Mzala arrived 'with a trunk full of baby clothes'.

Through all of this, Mpho's mother Violet was still busily planning for Mpho to head abroad to continue her studies. Only when she had organised tickets did Mpho muster the courage to break the news, through a note, that she was highly expectant and could not fly. 'The plan was not to have this child before marriage,' but things happened so fast, she explained. 'My dad was furious,' she recalls. 'This man has been travelling with me, he has not said anything, he is quiet,' he fumed.

The night before the child was born, Mzala dreamt that they were having a baby boy and his name was to be Zwide.[1] At this stage, they did not know the gender. Finally, on 20 May 1986, Mpho went into labour and gave birth to a baby boy. Mzala duly named him Zwide. Mzala's mother would later try to give the child another name, but with little success. For a while after Zwide's birth, Mpho stayed at the Charlotte Maxeke Children's Centre in SOMAFCO, which catered for mothers with babies.

After their son's birth, Mpho found Mzala to be a rather liberated man, one who always wanted to be involved in the smallest chores involving the child. Every morning he would arrive at the centre with food for Mpho, and then 'he would wash Zwide's clothes, napkins and put them on the washing line'. Mpho watched in amazement; she says Mzala would not be bogged down by stereotypes. 'He was the only man that would come and do such things and he didn't care. He would say, this is my child also, I will do as I want.' Immediately thereafter, Mzala arranged for Mpho and Zwide to join him in Zambia.

II

Mzala was now employed in the ANC's Research Department, with special responsibilities to ANC President Tambo.[2] He had started working on his book on Gatsha Buthelezi and was hopeful it would be finalised soon. Also, Mzala had ambitions to pursue his studies abroad. He was involved in multiple ventures, and during this period he wrote to Jack Simons about a project he was working on with Francis Meli. 'You have requested me to put down my request in writing,' began the letter. He informed Simons that he and Meli were working on 'The History of the Alliance of the ANC and SACP', which they hoped to publish as a book in the coming year or two. 'Meli is handling the period before 1940, and my lot is the period between 1940–1962; we will then deal with the latter period together in London.'

In the letter, Mzala was buoyant about the feasibility of this project. On 18 September 1985, Simons responded. 'Your letter (undated) reached me about a week ago.' He continued:

> I decided that any contribution I might make would perhaps be most useful if I put down on paper my ideas about the relationship between ANC and CP at various stages. They start with contrasting origins, cultures, interests and aims, developing a similar outlook only slowly. The basis of cooperation is recognition of a common adversary, but they conceive the enemy in different terms, the ANC as an oppressive white minority, the CP as imperialist capital. The conceptual differences have persisted to the present time, but gradually the two organisations arrived at an understanding about strategies that constitutes the binding force between them.

Simons went on to highlight 'defining stages' up until 1962, Mzala's immediate cut-off. In the letter, he patiently articulated developments between 1910 and 1918, the catalyst being the formation of the Union of South Africa which 'precipitated the formation of country-wide parties, among them the ANC and NP. ANC protests against the all-white parliament and its franchise.' He paid particular attention to the African strikes of 1920, the formation of the Communist Party, the 1922 Rand Revolt and the formation of the Industrial and Commercial Workers' Union (ICU) as among the events that fell within the period 1919–1924.

Simons highlighted the ICU's rejection of the Communist Party, Gumede's light from the East, the Communist International initiation of the Black Republic thesis and the anti-pass campaigns as significant events between 1925 and 1941. From 1941 until 1955, Simons mentioned the emergence of the All African Convention, the passive resistance campaign and declaration of unity by the ANC and the Indian Congress, the ANC Youth League Programme of Action, the National Party assuming office, the Defiance Campaign and the Congress Alliance taking shape.

Lastly, Simons noted the formation of the South African Congress of Trade Unions (SACTU), the Women's March to Pretoria, the Sharpeville Massacre, the Treason Trial and the launching of the armed struggle as significant between 1955 and 1962. Simons concluded, 'I hope you find this catalogue of events useful. You may want more information. If so, perhaps you'll list your questions on paper to give me an idea of what you are looking for.'

It is not clear what eventually happened to this project, although Francis Meli's book *South Africa Belongs to Us: A History of the ANC* was released in 1989. This book did not mention anything about Mzala's involvement. However, in his paper 'The National Question in the Writing of South African History: A Critical Survey of Some Major Tendencies', published posthumously in March 1992 by The Open University's Development Policy and Practice Research Group, Mzala cited Meli's book. He also reviewed the book for the *African Communist*.

With balanced scholarly analysis, Mzala mentioned Meli's disputing of the charge that the ANC's nationalism was reformist in character. He stated, 'Not everyone would agree with Meli, either when he suggests that "deputations and appeals were part of traditional African political custom".' He continued, 'Meli's point, however, is one of partisanship. Throughout his book … his partisanship to the ANC is unquestionable. Partisanship, however, becomes a problem when it is no longer tempered with objective realism. In these days of glasnost and perestroika, blank pages in history should not be allowed.'[3] In this paper, Mzala expressed himself in a scholarly fashion, interacting with the work of a close comrade whose work, just like the comrade himself, he was familiar.

III

In 1984, Mzala had written a pamphlet titled 'Latest Opportunism and the Theory of the South African Revolution', which was his initial response to the National Forum and the adoption of its Manifesto of the Azanian people (Azanian Manifesto) at its conference held on 11–12 June 1983 in Hammanskraal, north of Pretoria. According to one of its authors, Neville Alexander, the Manifesto was adopted 'as the unifying programme of principles of what was intended to be a united front against the apartheid strategy of divide and rule as manifested in, among other things, PW Botha's tricameral constitution'.[4] At the conference, the Freedom Charter came under attack.[5]

Mzala turned his attention to this document soon after the Kabwe Conference, launching a spirited defence of the Freedom Charter, and by extension the ANC-led liberation movement, in a four-part series in *Sechaba* titled 'The Freedom Charter is our Lodestar'. The first article appeared in the July 1985 edition, where Mzala threw down the gauntlet:

Criticism of the Freedom Charter has lately been coming from a Committee calling itself the 'National Forum' and launched by certain individuals in South Africa as an organisational opposition to the United Democratic Front (UDF). At its founding conference, the National Forum adopted a number of resolutions as well as a 'Manifesto of the Azanian People', which is meant to be an alternative document to the Freedom Charter.

Before Mzala tore into the Manifesto, he showed some irritation with *The Pace* magazine's sudden interest in political issues. He described the publication as 'a magazine that does well in promoting showbiz but which dismally fails to give one good political portrait of South Africa'. He then made some effort to detail the process followed in putting together the Freedom Charter. 'If *The Pace* magazine ... imagines that the Congress of the People that adopted the Freedom Charter in 1955 was something similar to the National Forum Conference that was held in Hammanskraal ... then it needs to research the historical facts thoroughly, and correct its distorted vision of history.'

He went back to 1953 when the ANC instructed its NEC 'to make immediate preparations for the organisation of a mass assembly of delegates elected by people of all races in every town, village, farm, mine and kraal'. Therefore, he argued, the development of the Freedom Charter was not a secret event – 'the whole country was made aware of the coming Congress of the People, and various organisers were given the task to imbue the masses of the oppressed people with the feeling of tremendous importance of such a gathering'.

In this way, argued Mzala, the Freedom Charter became the charter of the people, its content sourced directly from them in their homes, workplaces or wherever they could be found. He contrasted this massive effort to the Azanian Manifesto, which 'was manufactured in Hammanskraal' by a handful of people. Mzala keenly demonstrated the inclusive nature of the development of the Freedom Charter before he began to discuss its contents. As a way of showing that this was a document developed by and for the people as a whole, he argued:

> Our people gathered together in Kliptown to speak of freedom. Of the total of 2 884 delegates, 721 were women. There were 2 186 African delegates, 320 Indians delegates, 230 Coloured delegates, as well as 112 Whites. Hundreds of delegates were prevented from coming by the action of the police.

Outside of the Congress of the People, it was the founding of the UDF in the 1980s and not the National Forum Conference that evoked a similar response with 'over 15 000 people from all over the country and all races' coming together under the UDF's banner. Unlike the Azanian Manifesto 'which pretends to be socialist', Mzala argued that the 'Freedom Charter is based on the historic realities of our country, and one of those realities is that all Black people, workers and non-workers, are nationally oppressed and are consequently involved in a national democratic revolution'.[6]

He began the second part of his analysis in the August 1985 edition of *Sechaba*. 'The real essence of the present phase of our revolution is not the winning of socialism,' he wrote, 'but, as the Freedom Charter reflects, the winning of people's democracy, a true republic with power to the people, all the people!' He accused the drafters of the Azanian Manifesto of failing to comprehend the significance of this step – that it was 'the struggle for true national independence and self-determination' that was critical.

Leaning towards Antonio Gramsci's concept of hegemony, Mzala indicated that imperialism maintained power not only through force but also by ideological manipulation. One of those ideological tactical manipulations included discrediting the Freedom Charter. Taking a dig at the National Forum leaders, he noted that it was not unusual for 'quasi-leaders' to be 'groomed like horses, miseducated and let loose to carry out these plans'. In view of this reality, he thought 'it would be ridiculous to ignore the fact that those who oppose the Freedom Charter become toys in the hands of imperialism'.

Mzala regarded the Azanian Manifesto as an ideological offensive by imperialism against the national democratic movement and urged the movement to be vigilant. 'Those of us who have experienced factionalism during the long years of our struggle against oppression have always found that the oppressors always try to foment splits in the national liberation movement on ideological and other grounds – using as their main instrument racial prejudice, chauvinism, tribalism, anti-communism or ultra-left rhetoric.' Thus, he emphasised the importance of revolutionary theory as the anchor that has kept the movement together and made it the 'vanguard organisation' against settler colonialism and imperialism. 'Without revolutionary theory there can be no revolutionary movement,' he asserted.

Mzala had observed tendencies of 'anti-communist hysteria', in which forces like 'the PAC factionalists' proclaimed that the Freedom Charter was a communist document and 'in this way virtually joining the Pretoria government in proclaiming the moral justification for the Suppression of Communism Act of 1950'. He concluded: 'The communist bogey has never deterred our people from upholding the principles of the Freedom Charter and the democratic movement led by the ANC and its allies.'[7]

The third part appeared in *Sechaba* in September 1985, where Mzala dealt with the concept of 'racial capitalism' as enunciated in the Azanian Manifesto. Noting the resolutions of the National Forum conference highlighting that 'the struggle waged by the toiling masses is nationalist in character and socialist in content', Mzala exposed the ideological shortcomings of this Forum. First, he explained the basic elementary difference between the nationalist struggle and the socialist struggle. They are not the same thing, he said, 'and they do not belong to the same historical period'. The two, according to Mzala, represent two distinct categories of the revolution. To this end, he deemed it fit to elucidate the notion of nation-formation:

> Impelled by the developing productive forces, which also engendered corresponding bourgeois relations of production, the bourgeoisie brought together different nationalities into single nations around a common life. Nationalism, strictly speaking, has always been an ideological echo of this nation-formation process. Nations include both national bourgeoisie and the working class of that nation.

What Mzala thus brought to the fore was the importance of appreciating that the working class was being exploited by the bourgeoisie of its own nation. Out of this exploitation process the working class of all nations learn of their common fate as a class. 'Proletarian internationalism,' argued Mzala, 'and not nationalism, therefore, is firmly connected with socialism and the irreconcilable struggle of the working class against all the bourgeoisie.'

Through this intervention, Mzala essentially punched hole after hole in the ideological confusion that was the Azanian Manifesto. He continued to highlight that 'scientific socialists actually teach the working class that their enemies are the bourgeoisie, including their own national bourgeoisie'. For him, a nationalist struggle implied a struggle against imperialism, fascism or racism. 'But to proceed and say that the same nationalist struggle is also socialist in content it is to make real confusion.'[8] He thought this desire for socialism was intoxicating for the 'National Forum gentlemen' and hence their ill-advised assertion that the toiling masses are already struggling for socialism. Mzala considered the painstaking process of national democracy as a pivotal step towards laying a foundation for socialism.

Mzala began the fourth and last part of the series by focusing on the Freedom Charter and the national question. He argued that at no stage had the Freedom Charter pretended that blacks were not oppressed and therefore enjoyed the same rights as their white countrymen. 'The Charter does not underestimate the urge of the oppressed Black people towards the formation of a truly independent national state in South Africa, and their need to exercise the right to self-determination.' According to Mzala, the Charter simultaneously dealt with the present and the future. While it addressed the plight of the oppressed black people, at the same time it also strove to create a single South African nation, 'the most logical development in an economy that has reached the capitalist level of development'.

He articulated the importance of a united democratic movement of the oppressed, in this way more accurately defining the enemy as a system of white supremacy and national domination rather than simply white people. Not every black person is revolutionary, he argued. In other words, being black does not equate to progressiveness. For Mzala, counter-revolutionaries included bantustan leaders like Kaiser Matanzima, Lucas Mangope and Patrick Mphephu, 'even if their pigmentation is blacker than coal'. He continued, 'It might be understandable for some drunk man in a shebeen to shout abuse against the Whites in general, but for someone claiming to be a revolutionary leader not to be able to differentiate White revolutionaries from White racists would be inexcusable.'

Mzala took umbrage at the formulation that sought to separate black and white workers. 'Our new "socialist" teachers of "Azania" should have known … the task of socialists is not to legitimise the separation of Black and White workers by the capitalist. If they did not know this, then they should not have rushed to offer half-baked theories to our people.' In the same vein, he drew attention to No Sizwe's[9] book *One Azania, One Nation*, a book he thought had 'curious' ideas, regarding some of the 'fantasies' contained therein as not admissible in the theory of the national question and its principle of self-determination of nations. 'The working class cannot be a class and a nation at the same time. Nations and classes, while overlapping, are quite distinct categories nevertheless.'

The National Forum Conference had resolved as follows on the land question: 'The usage of the land shall not be [for] the benefit of Azanians only but for the benefit of all Africa, the Third World and the international community as a whole.' Mzala found this formulation quite amusing. 'This approach obviously sounds more evangelical than political,' he wrote. 'Does this suggest that South African land shall be free for use by everybody? Who are these people in Africa, the "Third World" and international community as a whole, who shall benefit from the usage of our land?'

Equally confusing was the economic clause in the Manifesto, which said, 'All proceeds accruing from collective labour shall be distributed according to the needs of each and every individual in Azania'. To Mzala, this was no more than hubris by some 'intellectual gentry'. He wrote, 'This is sheer utopia! These gentlemen were attempting to be more socialist than socialism. This is certainly not what manuals of political economy suggest, and neither is this "Azanian" economic principle applied anywhere in the world.'[10] He pointed out that in socialist societies the product of labour belonged to the working people and not private individuals.

However, Neville Alexander argued that Mzala sought to juxtapose the Manifesto against the Freedom Charter, which is presented as a 'sacred' text 'written' by 'the people' themselves. Alexander argued that such criticism failed to appreciate the context in which the Freedom Charter was formulated. In Alexander's view, both these documents were reflective of particular historical moments, the former being the mid-1950s, the latter the early 1980s. Alexander argued, 'It is, therefore, invidious to suggest, as Comrade Mzala does, that unless a political programme has evolved in the manner of the Freedom Charter, it cannot have any validity.'[11]

Clearly, Mzala remained committed to his responsibilities as an intellectual revolutionary. In fact, this aspect appeared to be taking priority over his soon-to-be status as a husband and a family man. During this period, he penned two more articles in the *African Communist*. In the first, 'On the Threshold of Revolution', Mzala continued to punt his theories on the people's war, arguing that the countrywide uprising in South Africa opened the possibility of arming of the masses and the replacement of the racist state by the people's army.

He was not yielding from his initial argument and postulated: 'It is becoming almost impossible during this period of our struggle to discuss the strategy and tactics of the South African revolution without coming up against the question of "The arming of the Masses" and taking a stand either for or against.' Mzala was convinced that the revolution had reached a decisive turning point where events such as the Nkomati Accord and the militant protests by the people against the Botha Constitution were a clear demonstration that 'the mass movement has reached another peak'.[12]

In the last article for the year, 'Education for Revolution', published under his *nom de plume* Sisa Majola, Mzala argued that the liberation movement's educational policy should be to produce trained cadres operating within an organisational framework and under the discipline of the movement in order to further the objectives of the revolution. In this article, Mzala was responding to a raging debate following Eric Stilton's article in the *African Communist* on the function of education in the liberation struggle. He argued that revolutionaries should not see the purpose of education as only acquiring a certificate. 'Our education policy, and that of a free South Africa equally, is not aimed at satisfying the distorted childhood desires of those who seek the good life irrespective of the conditions of the oppressed people and the exploited classes.'[13]

IV

Mpho's life with Mzala was, in the meantime, on fast-forward. Before Zwide was conceived, they were planning to marry in June 1986, but on discovering Mpho's pregnancy they had to change those plans. With Zwide having arrived, Mzala asked Mpho to bring her older son Sizwe to live with them. Shortly after he was born, Sizwe had been smuggled into South Africa to stay with his paternal grandparents. Mzala did not want Zwide to grow up without knowing that he had an older brother. So it was that Sizwe was eventually smuggled out of South Africa to Zambia.

As always, Mzala was in a hurry to get things done. Even when Mpho's mother pleaded with them to delay the wedding because she wanted to arrange a better dress for Mpho, Mzala would have none of it. Mpho tried to convince him, but he retorted, 'I want to wed you and not the dress.' 'But we don't even have the rings,' Mpho pushed. 'A ring is not necessary,' was Mzala's response. All Mzala wanted was to marry his queen. Mpho was defeated. Mzala thought it would be too time-consuming for Mpho to be running around hunting for dresses and other things for the wedding – it was already December 1986, and he was due to fly to England the following year.

He was hands-on in organising the wedding, insisting on slaughtering a beast because their marriage would be bringing the two families together. In the Zulu culture, slaughtering is regarded as a form of a communication with the ancestors. Not that Mzala believed in ancestors; he was still very much in touch with his Christian upbringing. But still, this symbolic gesture remained important to him as an African. Eventually, he arranged a goat for the wedding.

Mzala ensured that both sets of parents met before the wedding, presumably for *lobola* negotiations. It was easier for Mpho's parents who were in exile already, but slightly more difficult for his own parents who were coming from South Africa. At that point, Mpho's mother was in Botswana, while her dad was in Zimbabwe. With the exception of his sister Phasha, Mzala's siblings, including Titi and Dumisani, were present at the wedding. True to his wishes, both families were brought together by their love.

V

After the wedding, Mpho and Mzala lived a normal family life in Zambia. Mpho has fond memories of this period. Sizwe was dropped off at school in the morning and Mpho remained home with Zwide during the day while Mzala was at work. They were getting to know each other as husband and wife. Mpho recalls this as 'a beautiful moment'. Mzala's approach to building a family was refreshingly unique for Mpho. He did not suffer the patriarchal trappings of many young men his age. For him, building a home and family was a joint responsibility. However, his political priorities did not change now that he had a young family. He insisted on the need to always appreciate why they were in exile. 'Wherever we stayed,' Mpho recalls, 'the first thing that we did when we got in was to make a plan should anything happen. We are still at war and how do we escape.' It was for this reason that they stayed in areas where they would not be noticed.

Due to her linguistic abilities – she spoke fluent Nyanja, one of the Zambian local languages – Mpho easily assimilated. And because of her light complexion, many locals mistook her for a local person of mixed race. They called her *mzungu wamufedero* (a white lady). She fully embraced her new identity and even dressed like the locals. As a form of disguise, she often went to sell a few items at the local school so that she wouldn't be recognised as a refugee. Both she and Mzala mingled freely and built relations within the community. Out of necessity, Mzala thought it important to teach Mpho to drive in case she needed to use the car while he was not around. One day Mpho needed to rush Zwide to the clinic and found that she suddenly could not drive the car. Thanks to the relationships they had struck up with their neighbours, one of them quickly intervened to help.

When they moved to Zambia in September 1986, Mzala was already making plans to go abroad. Soon the date was confirmed for April 1987. At this stage, Mzala was furiously working on the Buthelezi book. His sister, Titi, by then based in the ANC Presidency's office in Lusaka, had access to resources and sometimes intervened. 'I assisted him with the typing of the manuscript.' Patrick Msomi, who stayed within walking distance from Mzala, would often visit his old friend, and recalls that although Mzala was now a family man with a wife and two boys, his fire was still burning. He was writing the book on Buthelezi and Msomi says he did not mind being killed. The writing of this book posed dangers for Mzala and invited enemies determined to defend Buthelezi and protect his reputation. It was very possible that Buthelezi's supporters may resort to violence. 'I am ready for them,' he would tell Msomi.

By the time he left for London, Mzala was satisfied that his family had adjusted to life in Lusaka, but still he made arrangements with a man he had befriended, the owner of a local bar some distance from where they stayed. It was by means of the friend's phone that Mzala called Mpho every week. 'I would go there on Saturdays to talk to him over the phone because that was the only phone available.'

VI

By the end of 1986, Mzala had written several articles demonstrating his voracious appetite for engaging with ideas. In the first part of the year, he had also written the article 'Nation and Class in the South African Revolution' for the *African Communist*. In this article he questioned the call for unity of black and white democratic organisations. He asked, 'On what policy should we base our propaganda and agitational work in the mobilisation of the White population for liberation?' Mzala was keen to determine whether such an exercise was worthwhile. He was convinced that an appeal to 'humanitarian sentiments' as the basis of the movement's faith that the white community was part of the human race and thus would see the 'evil' and 'inhuman' nature of the apartheid system would fall flat.

In advocating for class analysis, he posited: 'That relations among men are determined first and foremost by the position they occupy in the production process is a proposition that is generally recognised by all Marxists.' Mzala called for an objective approach. 'We must make a concrete historical analysis of the existing class and national relations in South Africa, and from this basis we can examine the attitudes of various classes and strata to the national question.'[14]

Mzala was still convinced that his ideas on the people's war were the most tenable and, in the same year, wrote the article, 'The Beginning of People's Power', for the *African Communist*. Here he asserted that the growth of people's communes in the townships coinciding with the collapse of apartheid institutions opened the way to the practical implementation of the reforms outlined in the Freedom Charter. He maintained his thesis, as articulated in previous writings, that conditions were ripe for a popular struggle in South Africa, including arming the people. He argued, 'A crisis of unprecedented scale has descended upon South Africa.' To him, the popular uprising inside the country was rendering the apartheid system unworkable. The country was ungovernable and 'at no other time has the apartheid power revealed such bankruptcy of both ability and strategy to survive'.[15]

Mzala was unrelenting on this question. In September 1986, he penned another article for *Sechaba*, 'Building People's Power'. The emphasis was still on the practical and immediate reasons to discuss the theory of state and revolution in South Africa. 'One such reason,' he argued, 'is the emergence of liberated districts in various parts of our country and establishment of rudimentary organs of people's power where apartheid structures have been destroyed.' The establishment of 'street-level infrastructure' had convinced him that the political communication between the civic organisations and individual households was now activated. People inside the country no longer regarded democracy as 'an abstract projection into a remote future' but rather as something concrete that they were practising daily. The emergence of organs of people's power was for him 'proof that our people do not trust any government other than their own'.[16]

During the same period, Mzala paid tribute to one of South Africa's foremost activist writers, Alex La Guma, who had died in October of the previous year. Alex was the son of James La Guma, a stalwart of the ANC and the SACP credited as the chief architect of the 'Black Republic' thesis.[17] He began the article, 'Culture, the Artist and Liberation', by referring to his conversation with Cosmo Pieterse in Dar es Salaam while La Guma was still alive.[18] Referring to Pieterse he wrote, 'I gathered that as far as he was concerned, Alex La Guma, thus far, had made the greatest mark in the history of revolutionary literature in South Africa.'

Mzala was equally at home discussing art as he was when dealing with revolutionary theory. In fact, he made no differentiation between the two. He presented what he argued to be 'the premises from which a scientific revolutionary must move when evaluating culture, art and the role of the artist in the struggle for liberation'. He reasoned:

> The premises of bourgeois sociology and of its aesthetics in particular starts with the existence of culture and artistic creation in the minds of human beings, and equally ends with its cultural expression in education, music, poetry, sculpture, theatre, painting, cinema, sport and so on. This standpoint does not explain to us where culture comes from, what factors determine its evolution and revolution. This school of aesthetics takes for granted what it is supposed to explain; it takes the very subject matter of 'Culture and Art' to be its own ultimate cause.

For Mzala, it was critical to appreciate that, in a society divided by class, where the class that owns the means of production controls the labour power, 'culture ... is exploited in the interests of the capitalists'. Consequently, when discussing art, it is important, he claimed, not to limit the debate to 'the alienation of culture from the people in general' but rather to locate 'the cultural worker's relationship with the product of his labour in capitalist society'.[19]

Mzala closed the year with a two-part series on his favourite subject: the people's war. The article was title 'Umkhonto WeSizwe: Building People's Forces for Combat War and Insurrection' and published in the December edition of *Sechaba*. In it he claimed, 'The passage of political power from the racist minority to the democratic majority will ultimately be decided by the material strength, and military force is the key element of that strength.' Mzala was adamant that the war – from the perspective of the liberation struggle – should not be obscured by other revolutionary tactics. 'That is why one of the immediate and principal objectives of our military programme is to build a people's army in South Africa.' In advancing his people's war perspective, Mzala presented a holistic approach when it came to reading the balance of forces, historical lessons (including those of MK), resolutions of previous conferences, and current developments inside the country.[20]

The second part of this article appeared in the January 1987 edition, where he continued by responding to the question: What is to be done? In answer to this, he presented two scenarios:

> One angle is that of an arm-chair critic or abstract theoretician, who sits somewhere in the safety and seclusion of his compartment, with a ready paper and ink in hand, quick to pass judgment about events in which he himself might not even have to participate. The other angle is that of an actual practitioner, who is faced with the task of relating theory to

practice, who has to see both the single tree and the whole forest, and who plans for activities whose results he cannot predict with precision.

Clearly seeing himself as an 'actual practitioner', he declared, 'We shall adopt the latter approach, because we are basically not writers of history but makers of it.' He then proceeded to outline his argument located in key historical events such as the June 16 uprisings and key theoretical perspectives that underpinned his argument. Mzala expressed the rationale behind why the vanguard should always lead. Arguing that the ANC was a genuine liberation organisation of the people, he submitted, 'To play this vanguard role, the ANC is obliged to be part of the people during all occasions and also to enjoy their confidence in the process of its leadership.'

As ever, Mzala was determined to see the ANC shift the terrain of the struggle to within the country. He was convinced that there would never be a more opportune moment to crush the racist apartheid regime. He concluded, 'The ANC has never subscribed to the tendency that absolutely postpones all armed activity until a "perfect" point is reached in political organisations.'

CHAPTER 8

Towards people's war and insurrection

I

In April 1987, Mzala began the next and final journey of his short but eventful life. On a warm summer day, he arrived in England to pursue aspects of the revolution that were close to his heart. This was at the height of a turbulent and controversial period in Britain, a country under the spell of Thatcherism and its free-market economy.[1] Although Britain had taken an anti-communist position, it admitted many undocumented South African asylum seekers, including those known to be members of the SACP.[2] Thus, communists like Mzala could still move in and out the country and freely organise. Of course, Thatcher held conservative views – her attitude towards the ANC was 'dismissive'[3] – but still, by allowing entry to political activists without the threat of imprisonment, Britain was regarded as more liberal compared to other European countries. Thus, well-known revolutionaries such as Karl Marx lived in London from 1849 until his death in 1883. So, too, did Vladimir Lenin, whose stay stretched between 1902 and 1905.[4] However, according to Elaine Unterhalter, while political activists were allowed, Britain did not prevent political harassment and they were excluded from certain jobs and educational opportunities.

While the main reason for Mzala's move from the ANC's research department in Lusaka, where he had become close to Oliver Tambo, to London was the finalisation of his book on Buthelezi, he had other ambitions, among them pursuing his studies. At the back of his mind was also the objective of working on Tambo's biography, a project he had already started with Tambo.[5] Once in London, however, he did not lose focus of his primary duties as a revolutionary.

As far as Buthelezi's book was concerned, Mzala was concerned that some comrades were reluctant to see it published. Jeremy Cronin indicates that this project 'did not enjoy support from all quarters of the ANC' since there were those who harboured the view that Buthelezi was 'essentially one of us' and therefore should be handled with 'kid gloves'.[6] But Mzala had managed to secure a publisher in London, Zed Books.[7] That he was not deterred and instead forged ahead with the project speaks to his resolve to pursue his convictions. Unlike contemporaries, such as Joel Netshitenzhe, who was considered modest and hated 'to be in the limelight', Mzala was the opposite. He was assertive – to such an extent that others thought him brash in the way he expressed his opinions as an 'intellectual' without any fear.

John Daniel was central to the production of the book. A Pietermaritzburg-born, internationally respected researcher and academic, Daniel came to prominence as a student activist, having served two terms as president of NUSAS. Having been deported from Swaziland, where he had held a position at the university, he was now an editor at Zed Press.[8] Zed agreed to publish Mzala's book on one condition: 'as long as it was not a mere hatchet job and was not libellous'.

Mzala's original submission was, however, quite the contrary and 'full of colourful libels'. It became clear to Daniel that if Zed were to be involved, Mzala needed to come to London to work through the manuscript in detail and add further research. So it was that funds were raised for Mzala to be based in London for a year, and he was offered the use of the library at the International Defence and Aid Fund. Daniel says, 'They threw away the original draft and started over,' with Mzala spending hours in the library. He worked very closely with Daniel, who was helpful, but also subjected Mzala to his red pen, reducing some of the chapters that were simply too long.

Before jetting off to London, Mzala had done a lot of research for the book, mostly in historical archives, including newspaper articles and Buthelezi's speeches. When he rekindled his acquaintanceship with Dumisani Nduli, who was now also studying in England, he told him that the speeches he had received from their mole in Ulundi had assisted greatly in writing the book. While at the ANC's research unit in Lusaka, Mzala had found more archival material in the ANC history department and was able to speak to many older comrades, who provided additional material on Buthelezi. One of those comrades was Johnny Makhathini, with whom he recorded interviews that provided more important historical material. Makhathini had apparently known Buthelezi from an early age.

II

In London, Mzala stayed with Sonia and Brian Bunting, spending most of his time on the typewriter and with his books. The Buntings were stalwarts of the SACP, with Brian editing its journal, the *African Communist*. They remembered Mzala as a 'brilliant' but 'very undisciplined' person who 'questioned everything'. The undisciplined aspect pertained to his 'unhealthy' diet, which went against the orders of his doctors. Mzala also defied the doctors' orders not to travel to the United States in the autumn of 1990. Later, he discharged himself from hospital to visit Tambo. Nevertheless, Brian was struck by Mzala's intelligence and versatility. He said Mzala learnt how to use a word processor in a single day, even though he had never seen one before. 'He was the most extraordinary person I've ever known.'

Given his candid nature, Mzala was not everyone's cup of tea. If he had a different opinion, he addressed the matter immediately, forthrightly and without fear, with Oyama Mabandla describing him as a 'loud' participant in debates. Coupled with his independent streak, Mzala had little time for egos. Hence, even though he was regarded by some as 'among the cream of the Soweto generation recruited to the SACP through efforts of [Jack] Simons, [Mark] Shope and others', others, such as British historian Stephen Ellis, thought Mzala was 'eccentric' and not a major influence in the SACP or a major theorist but 'just a promising younger member'.[9]

Upon arrival in London, Mzala was immediately integrated into SACP structures. He worked in the international committee and served on the editorial board – which included the likes of Essop Pahad – of the *African Communist* under the supervision of Brian Bunting. Since his first article published in 1978, Mzala had been a prolific contributor to the publication. As a permanent staff member, he was responsible for the 'African Notes and Comments', using Jabulani Mkhatshwa as his penname, Jabulani being his real name and Mkhatshwa his clan name.[10]

Mzala benefitted from this proximity to the Buntings and other senior comrades. He grew particularly close to Brian and Sonia, says Ronnie Kasrils: 'I believe they made a huge impression on him, and he grew greatly in stature and capability under Brian's tuition.' Essop Pahad says they were all happy to have Mzala on board since they regarded him as a 'rising intellectual'. They thought his arrival in London was wonderful because now they could have direct contact and he could hold discussions with the entire editorial board.

Mzala's love for debate and discussions was regarded as a strength by the board. More importantly, says Pahad, was his willingness to get 'involved in theoretical discussions, especially around the theory and practice of Marxism-Leninism'. Mzala was unafraid to state his views, 'even if it seemed to be at odds with what other people might be thinking', and his commitment, passion and clarity on the South African struggle excited communists in London. In order to integrate him, Mzala was assigned to a party unit. There was little challenge since he was already an active member of the ANC and had rekindled his close working relationship with Francis Meli, the editor of *Sechaba*.

Before they finally met in London, Patric Tariq Mellet (Patric de Goede) knew Mzala only by reputation. 'He had a similar reputation and was regarded as a popular leading voice, too, like Chris Hani.' Mellet was initially surprised that Mzala had turned up in London, but he soon discovered why when Mzala began to frequent their semi-clandestine printing press. They were assigned to the same SACP cell, known as 'the family'. In 'the family' Mellet was known as Oscar. The cell included Norman Levy, Aziz Pahad, Stephanie Kemp, Manny Brown and Norman Kaplan.

The SACP operated on a need-to-know basis. 'So, you only knew the other communists in your cell or previous cells in which you served and then you knew some of those in the more senior structures,' recalls Mellet. Tasks included writing articles for SACP publication, for which comrades used *noms de guerre*. Mzala – well known, at least to the younger generation – was now emerging as one of the leading writers and thought leaders in the movement. Says Mellet, 'Jabulani Nxumalo was widely known as Mzala long before coming to London,' and Nduli believes that his arrival in London, together with Sello Moeti, strengthened the SACP's writings.

III

In London, the ANC had two offices. The first was a four-storey building at 28 Penton Street, which the ANC had occupied since 1978, and from where President Tambo operated. The building served as the organisation's headquarters and the nerve centre for international solidarity work. The place was bombed by apartheid security agents in 1982, the morning Tambo was due to address an anti-apartheid demonstration in Trafalgar Square.[11] Luckily, there were no casualties. The other office was in Caledonian Road, which housed the Department of Information and Publicity (DIP) headed by Gill Marcus. All manner of anti-apartheid materials were printed and disseminated from here, and it was there that Mzala's book was also being finalised.

Having arrived in June 1986, Celeste Naidoo had spent almost a year in London by the time Mzala arrived. She was in her early twenties and attached to the DIP, Marcus having awarded her a bursary to study printing at the London College of Printing. Poloko Nkobi, Tom Nkobi's daughter, a master's student at Essex University, invited Naidoo to a pub to meet someone. Being a non-drinker, Naidoo reluctantly agreed. A humbly dressed guy was sitting by himself in the dingy pub. He asked Naidoo for her name and he introduced himself as Mzala. Naidoo was in awe. She had heard of Mzala and read some of his writing. Mzala appeared unusually shy for someone who expressed such bold views on many issues. He chatted casually to Poloko and did not talk much to Naidoo. 'Of course, I was not going to say much. It was the great Mzala I was talking to.' The meeting lasted less than an hour. 'I just know I was in awe. I just sat there and I looked at him and listened to what they had to say. I don't think I contributed. You don't talk to somebody so great.'

Naidoo was struck by Mzala's humility. 'He was absolutely humble.' She saw someone who was humane and did not have to try hard to be humble. Two days later, Naidoo met Mzala with John Pampallis, and this time she was able to have a conversation. Mzala began to frequent their printing offices and would spend time with Marcus discussing the book.

Mellet and Mzala took a liking to each other. Mellet also found Mzala easy-going. 'Unlike most of the other ANC intellectuals, who were aloof and stood apart from the rest of us and generally mixed only with their strata of equals, people like Chris Hani and Mzala, and SACTU comrades like Zola Zembe engaged with the average Joe Cadre.' Mzala's ability to connect with ordinary people drew him to many. Mellet thinks it was because he 'spoke the language of working people and helped people to engage in discussions of complex political and economic matters in a different way without dumbing-down people or dismissing people if we did not have high-brow words and grammar in expressing ourselves.'

Mellet would spend his day working at the printing press, churning out millions of sheets according to deadlines, a task that was both difficult and tiring. Because the printing press was also in Islington and not that far from the ANC office in Penton Street, Mzala would often pop in with a cheerful, smiling face, and always offered to help. He was down to earth and all he wanted was to engage in ideas. 'He would grab and unwrap paper and stack it up to help with the make-ready before a print run. Then, during the down time, he would put some document in your hand and ask for your opinion and critique,' says Mellet. Sometimes, 'he would engage in a discussion by presenting a thesis and the beginnings of a critique on its contradictions and would genuinely ask us what we thought were the flaws and how we would address these. There was nothing patronising about it.'

Comrades were pleasantly surprised that Mzala took their input seriously and incorporated them in his final versions. Says Naidoo, 'He asked you your thoughts on a particular subject and he gave you a sense of worth of your contribution, never mind how little it was worthy to be heard.' He would tell story after story, but would listen to others' stories too. His stories, recalls Mellet, had 'a parable-like quality. He loved seeing the humorous edge in life. It wasn't so much a matter of joking but rather being able to see the humorous side to human idiosyncrasy.' Wherever he was, he made people smile and laugh and saw people as multidimensional. Says Mellet, 'He was able to discern class differences within the liberation movement and purposefully tried to disrupt these self-imposed barriers of them and us.'

With one eye forever winking, recalls Naidoo, although a very serious activist and a dedicated communist, 'there was this humane side about him; he could walk in, he could tell a joke and laugh'. Naidoo fondly recalls his warm and welcoming personality. 'He was very articulate and a great philosopher ... and yet he was able to talk to anybody. He didn't have arrogance and was able to have a conversation with somebody like me.'

Mzala integrated into the ANC community in London with ease. Although thought to be candid and pugnacious by some, those close to him, like the Buntings, adored him. He impacted people positively and was able to motivate those around him. 'In life you will face challenges but you will overcome,' he would tell Naidoo whenever she was down. Such words would make her feel positive about life again. 'He didn't talk about it; he made it a reality for you.' Naidoo had also been roped into the production of Mzala's book. She recalls the book being sent to the lawyers and coming back with more changes. 'I worked on it with Gill [Marcus] so we picked up on it, retyped it, fixed the pages, etc.'

Mzala's friendship with Nduli, now a master's student of Shula Marks at the University of London, was useful. Mzala was keen to pursue his studies further and the same year, 1987, he registered for a Master of Philosophy degree at Essex University under the supervision of Harold Wolpe. Wolpe, a stalwart of the SACP, was now a professor of Sociology at the university. Mzala was able to use his qualifications obtained in the Soviet Union and the GDR to facilitate admission. Between 1976 and 1978, he had studied Political Economy at the Lenin School in Moscow before continuing at Ernst College in Karl Marx Stadt in the GDR in 1979.[12] Pallo Jordan says Mzala had also earned a scholarship to study in the United Kingdom (UK). 'Many regarded him as one of brightest among the post-76 intake into MK and the ANC.'

But bringing his young family over to the UK preoccupied Mzala's mind. He called the pub in Lusaka every Saturday to talk to Mpho. In October 1987, she and the boys finally joined him in London. At that point, Mzala was juggling a number of tasks, including his studies, revolutionary work and taking care of his family. Fortuitously, Mpho had a support structure in London in her parents. Jonas Gwangwa was in London to work on the film *Cry Freedom*, an epic drama based on Donald Woods's autobiographical accounts of being enlightened by Steve Biko.[13] At some point, the young couple stayed with Mpho's parents before getting their own place.

IV

With his responsibilities escalating, Mzala remained committed to writing for *Sechaba* and, most importantly, about the people's war. He had rekindled his friendship with Francis Meli and, in the month that he arrived in London, *Sechaba* published his article 'Towards People's War and Insurrection'. Even at this stage, when the possibility of negotiations between the ANC and the regime were widely anticipated, Mzala still regarded arming the people as important. While acknowledging the correctness of the movement's strategic perspective regarding the armed struggle as 'secondary to the principal task of building up political revolutionary bases', he thought the people's war approach remained critical.

He considered the current mass uprising in the country, which had seen the working class 'acting either independently or in community with students', to be distinct from the 1976 uprising but rather an outcome of this strategy of the movement, and used this to bolster his call for a new approach towards the people's war. 'It is these events among others,' he argued, 'which called for the search for a new approach in our military planning and activities.' He argued that, under prevailing conditions, the 'armed insurrection' was now possible. For him, anything less was a conservative approach that failed to read the situation correctly.

> A conservative approach to armed struggle in South Africa has at times manifested itself in the inability to accept this new development of insurrectionary conditions, and in the failure to reckon with the fact that the only scientific approach to military strategy under the present circumstances will proceed from the fact that we have in South Africa today, side by side, existing together, simultaneously, the possibilities of preparing both for the protracted guerrilla warfare and armed insurrection.[14]

By October 1986, the US Congress had passed its Comprehensive Anti-Apartheid Act, which the Ronald Reagan administration hoped to use to persuade the South African regime to move away from its apartheid policy.[15] Up until then, the US, particularly between 1981 and 1985, had played a typically imperialist role in exercising global hegemony in defence of capitalism and its primitive forms of accumulation. The policy was also largely informed by Cold War machinations. Thus, Reagan supported the apartheid regime's hostility towards African states, particularly those in the southern African region.[16]

During this period, internal debates around peaceful settlement were spilling out into the open. But the idea of a negotiated settlement was not new – the ANC was holding secret meetings with the National Party as early as 1984. Pressure from Western countries had compelled the apartheid regime to introduce some piecemeal reforms but these were rejected by the ANC. In 1983, Reagan had sent his emissary Robert Cabelly with the aim of convincing the ANC to accept PW Botha's reforms.[17]

It is this context that prompted Mzala to write 'United States policy towards South Africa' published in the June edition of *Sechaba*. Like so many others, for the next couple of years Mzala would spend time thinking about various permutations while articulating the ANC's policies. This is how he opened his first article on negotiations:

> Only a few years ago, no one in the government circles of the United States (or even Britain) cared for a minute about the viewpoint of the ANC concerning the nature of the changes that must occur in South Africa. As we endured and fought against the most inhuman oppression over the years – when our people suffered mass removals, when some died of torture in detention or were merely butchered in the streets by the fascist army and police – no leader of American government bothered about our hopes for South Africa.[18]

Mzala was wary of the imperialists' tactics and sudden interest in the ANC and peaceful transition. He posited: 'Let us begin by looking at the genesis of this whole development, analyse the circumstances influencing the evolution of the United States policy towards South Africa, examine the imperialist policy, and then leave it to the reader to answer the question whether or not the imperialist can abort our revolution.' He ascribed the developments to the people's uprising in South Africa. 'Between September 1984 and January 1985,' he wrote, 'the country had already become so ungovernable that out of the 32 town councils, 29 of them had become inoperative.' More than 240 black councils resigned either voluntarily or 'were forced to do so by the militant detachment of the people'. During the period leading to the State of Emergency, over 3 000 people had lost their lives.

For Mzala, the uprising coincided with the resurgence of the ANC as the leader of this revolutionary process. This had basically plunged the apartheid regime into a crisis of power and illegitimacy. The racist government had lost control of the black townships, and Mzala concluded that there was no longer any prospect for it to reassert its authority in these areas. The ANC was the only genuine liberation organ of the people, and thus, Mzala argued, a viable alternative to the crisis of power in South Africa.

But he remained unapologetic about the armed struggle. 'The ANC had made no secret of its strategy for the armed seizure of power by the people in South Africa. And it intends to lead a government that shall establish people's democracy. We represent people who have been robbed of their birthright, who have no state of their own, who enjoy neither liberty nor rights which citizens in a democratic order are entitled to.'

He felt that the sudden interest by the imperialists was driven by fears of the inevitable outcome in South Africa. The US could sense that, unless it 'intervenes' in the crisis of apartheid and positions itself as a 'leader of the inevitable process of change from apartheid', South Africa would slide toward the kind of revolution whose scope would threaten imperialist interests in the region and the world. What the US was doing, according to Mzala, was attempting to manage the ANC's implementation of the Freedom Charter.

Mzala was, therefore, using this article to warn the movement against the dangers of downplaying imperialist manoeuvres whose primary motives were accumulation. South Africa was regarded as an area of 'profitable investment' and 'a source of high profits', with the US having tangible assets with direct or indirect investment totalling '$13 billion, second to Britain with 15 billion'. In the context of the Cold War, Mzala argued that South Africa was an important country, with 75 per cent of oil and 44 per cent of total foreign freight to and from NATO countries passing round the Cape. Therefore, according to Mzala, US policymakers did not see the region for what it objectively was, but rather as an area of conflict between the East and the West. Hence, they were keen to prevent any social revolution that would bring into government a political party or organisation hostile to American interests.

Mzala was unambiguous in characterising the US's change of tack as fundamentally as an economic calculation rather than informed by social justice. And so, now that contradictions between the capitalist mode of production and the apartheid political institutions had emerged, change had to be considered. The crude form of imperialist exploitation – apartheid – had outlived its usefulness for capitalist accumulation and alternative methods were being considered. A democratic government was desirable, but one that would not tamper with the interests of big business and their friends in the Global North. Mzala was concerned that the ANC could be co-opted and used as a tool for this objective.

He regarded the attitude of the US and statements by big business in South Africa 'condemning apartheid policies as the cause of this economic crisis' as a vindication of the correctness of the movement's analysis. He argued:

> [This] also proves just how correct our analysis has always been when we insisted that racialism is only a tool used by the bourgeoisie to extract super-profits; when it no longer ensures this, the bourgeoisie do not hesitate to look for new ways to adapt their system, to opt for an end

to 'a political system in which over 80% of the population are denied basic individual political rights on the basis of race'.[19]

When Mzala identified an issue, he would spend time analysing and researching it in the context of the policies of the movement. This is the same attitude he applied in analysing the interest of the US in the South African developments. He followed this up with the article 'Can the Imperialists Abort our Revolution?' in the July edition of *Sechaba*. This analysis was a continuation of his previous article. For him, the apartheid regime was not only an internal colonising force, but an extension of global imperialism.

He saw the 'greatest shortcoming of the successive policies of the United States towards South Africa' was their regard for the apartheid regime as the principal vehicle for change in South Africa. This flaw was premised on their assumption that apartheid could go beyond itself and commit suicide, he argued. Mzala had no doubt that the apartheid regime had sufficiently demonstrated its inability to lead any meaningful change. Importantly, it remained an illegitimate government that had to be overthrown. 'This regime (particularly now),' he argued, 'has lost all political means to govern the Black people, and now relies solely on its ability to command the military forces.'

It thus was illogical for Mzala that the US had taken the stance it did, blaming the ANC for violence. On the contrary, it was in fact the apartheid regime that was building up its army, which was already the most powerful on the continent. 'From the viewpoint of actual history in South Africa, the source of violence in the country is the apartheid system itself. As long as apartheid exists, violence is bound to be a permanent feature of South African political life.' On the other hand, Mzala portrayed the ANC as fighting a just war; until 1964, when it was forced by circumstances to pick up arms, the ANC had been a peaceful organisation taking a stand against an aggressive oppressor.

Mzala was thus urging the ANC not to abandon the armed struggle until the apartheid regime ceased the use of violence. 'It is therefore unlikely, not now and in the foreseeable future,' he argued, 'that the ANC can be persuaded by the United States policy to abandon the use of violence unless the apartheid regime first ceases to use violence both as a system of political rule and as a means of defending the oppressive regime.' He accused the US of double standards in ignoring the fact that the apartheid regime was essentially an illegitimate government.

The West was using the ANC's alliance with the SACP as rationale for its lack of intervention, but it is precisely this reasoning that, Mzala said, demonstrated their bias. 'This concern with the South African Communist Party is not genuine,' he wrote; 'it is merely an artificial excuse created to avoid the responsibility of the United States, as one of the main economic supporters of South Africa, to force her to abandon her inhuman policies and practice'. He was consistent in his thesis that the US's interests were informed by its narrow capitalist interests. Capitalism was another reality Mzala thought should be considered when dealing with the South African revolution. 'South African people do not only suffer from national oppression by the colonial system, but are also exploited by capitalism as a system of production.'

Mzala was also urging the movement not to abandon the Freedom Charter, particularly clauses such as 'All shall share in the country's wealth'. He declared:

> I foresee no circumstances that can arise in South Africa leading to the ANC abandoning this economic policy, for what will be the use of centuries of struggle and so much sacrifice if at the end people cannot control the wealth of their own country? A revolution without a radically democratic economic policy, detailing concrete measures for transforming the country's economic ills and bringing to an end mass exploitation and hunger, such a revolution is not worth a single alphabet of the word 'revolution'.[20]

These interventions by Mzala were, to an extent, a form of lobbying for a left perspective within the movement. It was through such perspectives that the interests of imperialism in South Africa were exposed. There were contending views in the ANC, expressed in the very same journals. Eventually, in his absence, Mzala's views were ultimately defeated. Almost three decades into democracy, the wealth distribution in South Africa still reflects apartheid patterns of ownership. Thus, Mzala's question as to what would be the use of the struggle and sacrifice if the people cannot control the wealth remains pertinent.

Mzala was still not done. In the August edition of *Sechaba* he continued with his scrutiny of the US with the article 'People's Power or Power-sharing? United States Policy in South Africa'. In this article he argued: 'The belief within the US State Department is that interests of the South African Communist Party are served by an inflexible attitude on the part of the Pretoria regime towards negotiation with the ANC, and by the ANC's focus on increasing military pressure on South Africa.' To Mzala, this was a complete misunderstanding of the ANC and what it was that united its members. Thus, he asserted that the SACP could not reject negotiations in principle. To illustrate this point, he went back to the 1962 programme of the SACP: 'The Party does not dismiss all prospects of non-violent transition to the democratic revolution.' However, he quickly emphasised the conditions under which the Communist Party based this principle:

> [This] prospect will be enhanced by development of revolutionary and militant people's forces. The illusion that the White minority can rule forever over a disarmed majority will crumble before the reality of an armed and determined people. The possibility would be opened of a peaceful and negotiated transfer of power to the representative of the oppressed majority of the people.[21]

So it was that, with these articles, Mzala entered the fray on the negotiated settlement. Of course, by 1987, the genie was out of the bottle, and it was apparent that a 'peaceful and negotiated transfer of power' as envisaged by the SACP was increasingly becoming a likely scenario in South Africa. A month before this article was published, in July 1987, a delegation of South Africans from a broad political spectrum had met the ANC in Dakar, Senegal. It was at this meeting that the 'ANC for the first time in public committed itself to a negotiated settlement to end the political conflict in South Africa'.[22]

Still, Mzala could not fathom this process outside the prism of people's war, insisting that the position of the ANC was well known and aligned to that of the SACP. He argued, 'To suggest that the ANC would, under the present circumstances, place the disarmed people on the altar of negotiations with a fascist regime is to insult the ANC, and to question its sincerity and sense of responsibility to the leadership of the South African oppressed people.' Mzala was no fool. He was not debating simply for its own sake; rather, he was addressing a perspective he felt was in danger within the ANC.

In the article he reverted to points raised previously on the process of the transfer of power to the people. He stated that a People's Assembly 'that can set about drawing up a new constitution for South Africa (after the draft has been thoroughly discussed by the masses in all their walks of life) can only be that which has been invested with supreme authority and power to do so, one that is vested with the sovereignty of the people'. Although he respected the negotiations process, he was adamant that it should be about nothing else but the transfer of power from the racist minority to the democratic majority.

Mzala did not trust the imperialists' commitments to the power transfer, and therefore attached a lot of meaning to narrow concepts such as 'power-sharing'. He perceived this to be an attempt by the US to engineer a deal suitable to its interests. For him, 'power-sharing' was a misguided approach to the country's problem. 'It is a concept that may appear "logical" and "fair" only to those who are not at all acquainted with the history of our country, and the source of our national oppression.' To his understanding, the South African struggle was following a path similar to those of other formerly colonised nations on the continent.

Without succumbing to a narrow exceptionalism about South Africa, he appreciated the country's unique form of colonisation, characterised as 'colonialism of a special type' (CST) by the SACP. The CST thesis noted the existence of a large settlement of colonisers who had severed ties with their countries of origin and had since constituted themselves into 'an internal colonising nation within the same geographical boundaries'. But Mzala was clear that this still did not change the fact that black people had been colonised and were fighting for their right to self-determination. A truly independent South Africa would join and be accepted into the OAU.

Because the apartheid regime with its imperialist handlers would do anything in its power to derail the revolution, Mzala did not discount the possibility of the regime creating 'a third force'. Part of the trick, argued Mzala, was for the US 'to get the apartheid regime to declare its intention to hold negotiations, even long before it can be prepared to negotiate the transfer of power, and if the ANC refuses to participate, to get together puppet forces of the Muzorewa type, and go ahead and fix a neo-colonial solution for South Africa'. In this regard, he warned the liberation forces to be vigilant against the imposition of a neo-colonial solution:

> Such a neo-colonial solution, however, is bound to collapse even before it takes off, because the present uprising and war of liberation in South Africa is not led by those puppet forces; moreover, the people of South Africa are politically conscious enough to know who are their genuine leaders, and they equally know what they want.[23]

Indeed, some attempts along these lines were made, resulting *inter alia* in a low-intensity civil war in what are now KwaZulu-Natal and Gauteng provinces. Mzala's foresight extended to the issue of minority rights, which would be a significant issue during the negotiations. To this end, he invoked the Freedom Charter's clause that 'All national groups shall enjoy equal rights'. Thus, he envisioned a South Africa aligned to the principles of the Freedom Charter where 'all people shall enjoy equal rights whatever their colour, race or creed'. He saw no reason for the white section of the population to fear anything in a free South Africa based on the Freedom Charter, which stipulates that 'South Africa belongs to all who live in it, Black and White'.

V

Mzala's writing spree continued, and towards the end of 1987 he penned the article 'The two stages of our revolution' in the third-quarter edition of the *African Communist*. Writing as Sisa Majola, he argued that the attainment of socialism was 'determined by the historical coincidence of subjective and objective factors'. He was clear that there were no short cuts to socialism. He thought the new experience of the emergence of organs of people's power in various districts of South Africa presented an opportunity for the struggle. He argued: 'as much as we shall teach these organs, so also must we be prepared to learn from them'. In his view, the greatest virtue of a communist is his 'ability to identify with history, rather than to identify history with himself'.[24]

In the fourth-quarter edition – writing as Mzala – he paid a seventieth birthday tribute to Oliver Tambo in the article 'How the ANC was Revived by the Youth League'. Here Mzala revealed his admiration for the bravery of the young generation of the 1940s. He posited: 'Yet there are moments when history demands "glasnost" or openness – bringing everything into the open, hiding nothing, no matter how painful, so as to overcome inertia and stimulate the extraordinary potential of the people to renovate their organisation and life.' He regarded Tambo's generation as pioneers who had introduced a radical dimension to the movement, providing new political insights and setting unprecedented strategic perspectives for that epoch. 'Like their predecessors,' he wrote, 'they considered the ANC to be the principal vehicle for all liberation efforts; but unlike them, they were impatient with the ritual employment of tactics such as deputations, passing of endless resolutions and the holding of annual conferences.'

It is easy to imagine Mzala being inspired by the radicalism of this generation. Just like him, these young leaders were brave and impatient with the leadership of the ANC. Clearly, he admired the impetus this generation brought, an impetus that transformed the ANC into a fighting mass organisation. That this was attained against the backdrop of conservatism in the ANC, with leaders like AWG Champion adopting a hostile attitude towards the youth as they perceived their stance to be undermining to the leadership, was important to him. The conservatives had even warned then ANC President Dr AB Xuma that his association with these youngsters would lead to his downfall. Mzala wrote: 'The experience of the youth in the 1940s seems to confirm the view that fear of the youth is the beginning of conservatism.' Against this background, Mzala detailed how Tambo – together with comrades like Congress Mbatha, both schoolteachers – convened a meeting in Diagonal Street in Johannesburg where the Congress Youth League Manifesto was first drafted. These revolutionaries, for Mzala, never behaved like a splinter group motivated by vanity and petty opportunism.

Apart from the radicalism of this generation, Mzala also praised their academic achievements. 'Almost all of its prominent leaders, with the exception of Walter Sisulu … had either completed matric or had been to university.' Some had been expelled from the University of Fort Hare for their political activities, including Oliver Tambo, who was expelled in 1942. This is yet another parallel between Mzala and those leaders. 'A brilliant student,' he continued, 'Tambo had completed his matric with a first class pass in 1938, setting an academic record by obtaining the best result in the whole of the Transvaal, black and white students considered together.' This piece thus also revealed that Mzala had been researching in depth Tambo's rise within the movement, the goal to write a biography. He brought in Anton Lembede – another great leader of this generation, with whom Mzala would later be compared. He had this to say about Tambo's complementary role to Lembede:

> Lembede, considered by many to be the most daring thinker and dynamic personality of that generation of young leaders, died in 1947 at the age of 33 after obtaining BA, LLB, MA degrees. At the time of his death he was working for a doctorate in law and was able to speak seven languages fluently, including German and Dutch. By 1946 he had been elected to the National Executive Committee of the ANC. He and Tambo formed a dynamic partnership, guiding the youth of the time as organised within the Congress movement.[25]

Mzala tried hard to paint a picture of Tambo and his generation as not just adventurist but rather visionaries who were determined to breathe some life back into the ANC. To demonstrate this point, he portrayed the organisation like this: 'In December 1940, when Dr Xuma was elected ANC president, only 41 delegates had turned up at the annual conference; 21 of them voted for Dr Xuma and the remaining 20 for Rev. ZR Mahabane. When he became president, Dr Xuma found the organisation without treasury.' With the help of the Youth League, argued Mzala, Dr Xuma turned the organisation around, initiating the drafting of a new constitution; the membership increased, and members of the Communist Party were involved in the drafting of policy documents.

However, Mzala still contended that the ANC was not a mass organisation at that stage. Inspired by the 1946 mineworkers' strikes that attracted over 70 000 workers, Mzala credited Tambo, now elected to the Provincial Executive Committee of the ANC, as the person who moved the first motion at the ANC annual conference in 1947. According to Mzala, Tambo called for the boycotting of all government structures, particularly the Native Representative Council. Notwithstanding the narrow nationalism that characterised the Youth League in its formative years, Mzala praised Tambo for his vision and ideological shift in 1949 when he was already a member of the National Executive Committee and vice-president of the Youth League. He argued:

> Oliver Tambo was among the first group of Youth Leaguers to develop respect and recognition of the role of the Communists in the South African liberation struggle. This did not necessarily come about through the reading of Marxist classics or communist literature – it was the product of experience and an honest disposition, which enabled him to broaden his outlook and grasp the significance of all the major streams that have contributed to the present greatness of the ANC.[26]

Demonstrating his research credentials for his pending project that would be Tambo's biography, Mzala also reflected on Tambo's early childhood and upbringing. 'Tambo's desire was to be a medical doctor,' he wrote, 'but after his expulsion from Fort Hare, his keen interest in the natural sciences was overshadowed by a growing concern with the liberation of the black people in South Africa.' He concluded:

> I have met Oliver Tambo on many occasions, mostly in a formal [setting]

> as a president of the ANC. There have been occasions, however, when I met him informally, as Tambo the man, like on Sunday, 12 July 1985, when we came back from the Second National Consultative Conference. That was one of the happiest moments in his life. We sat for hours discussing the Conference and other related issues. He was not in his suit and tie on that day, but in his gym attire, for he insists on doing his exercises. As a member of the Soweto generation, I draw confidence from the fact that the Tambo of the Youth League still maintains constant touch with the youth of today, gauging his own standpoint against theirs.[27]

Indeed, authors of biographical accounts often choose a subject that inspires them, but this presents them with certain limitations, sometimes leading to inherent biases that obscure contradictions of life – the good and bad. That is the case here, with how Mzala portrays Tambo as faultless, and so the article reads like an obituary. Tambo was showered with high praise that essentially reduced him to an angel, with not a single flaw or mistake identified. For example, Mzala praised Tambo's character, and argued that, unlike many of his colleagues, he had never taken his political responsibilities lightly. 'To him the struggle for liberation was a cause worth a life's commitment.'

It is not clear where Mzala's admiration of Tambo stemmed from. Some have argued that Mzala's interest could have been triggered by the fact that they shared a birthday. It is likely that Mzala saw himself through Tambo. Whatever the case, through this celebratory piece on Tambo, Mzala unearthed fascinating aspects about the ANC's president that had hitherto not been revealed to the public. However, sometimes the biographer's inspiration is negative, as we will see in the next chapter, when Mzala deals with Buthelezi, a figure for whom he had very little regard.

CHAPTER 9

Chief with a double agenda

I

In February 1988, having been in London for almost ten months, Mzala's book, *Gatsha Buthelezi: Chief with a Double Agenda*, was published by Zed Books. This exposition of Buthelezi's controversial political life immediately caught the public's imagination and news spread like wildfire, turning Mzala into a household name within the ranks of the movement and academic circles. According to Patric Tariq Mellet, 'On the left within the movement who opposed the Bantustan system and narrow ethno-nationalism this book made Mzi a celebrity.' However, 'there were others in the movement who were close to Buthelezi and other Bantustan figures that frowned on the book' and the sentiments espoused by Mzala. 'They were rather mute, though,' with Mellet regarding some as remnants of the 'Gang of Eight' expelled in 1975 – those who regarded themselves as 'ANC-AN (African Nationalist)'.

As expected, the book was received with hostility in Inkatha circles and Buthelezi threatened legal action against Mzala and those distributing the book.[1] Given Buthelezi's propensity for litigation, Zed Books had been cautious in publishing the book. As Celeste Naidoo revealed, lawyers had been involved well before the publication of the book. 'Two sets of British lawyers' had been retained to examine the book before publication, and amendments were made according to their recommendations. Ultimately, the lawyers gave assurances that it was 'unlikely that the published book would be actionable in terms of the British law of defamation'.[2]

Uncertainty nevertheless remained about releasing the book in South Africa. According to Chantelle Wyley and Christopher Merrett, 'Although the South African law is based on British legislation, the publishers were unsure of the attitude of South African judges, who were felt to be system supporting. In any event Zed's agents in South Africa, David Philip Publishers, were subjected to direct threats of a defamation action in the event of local distribution. This intimidation forced the publisher and agents into a decision not to release the book in South Africa.'[3]

II

This no-holds-barred book began provocatively with the chapter 'A Man of Peace? Ask the Students!' based on the 1983 killings of students at the University of Zululand (Ngoye). The chapter outlines the students' resistance against Bantu Education and Inkatha's collaboration with the apartheid system. It describes in graphic detail how innocent students were butchered by marauding Zulu impis following their attempts to prevent Buthelezi from coming onto the campus.

The central thesis of the book was Buthelezi's rise to power, his role in the South African political landscape and his collaboration with the apartheid regime. Mzala claimed that Buthelezi was a creation of apartheid, a system he continued to tolerate, while those who opposed the system were hounded and jailed. He also argued, 'It was not automatic that Gatsha should become the chief of the Buthelezis since his elder brother, Mceleli Buthelezi, claimed that position by virtue of his being the first son of the first wife of Chief Mathole.' Mzala suggested that Buthelezi got the post because he pledged support for the Bantustan system.

> As this was a particularly difficult time for the government, with the African people rejecting Bantu Authorities, it needed chiefs who would pledge their support for this Act, even if their subjects were hostile to it. Consequently, the Native Commissioner of Mahlabathini called Gatsha for an interview. The meeting was minuted, and Gatsha was made aware that a copy of the minutes would be sent to the Chief Native Commissioner and to Dr Eiselen. The government wanted him to pledge his support for the Bantu Authorities system in view of the fact that the Buthelezi tribe was rejecting it. He pledged his support, and went further to promise that he would try his best to persuade his tribe

to accept it as well. He was subsequently appointed by the government to head the Mahlabathini Tribal Authority.[4]

Mzala also argued that there was no practice that enjoined Zulu kings to choose a Buthelezi as prime minister. 'Chief Buthelezi,' said Mzala, 'has on numerous occasions claimed that his present leadership position in KwaZulu is a hereditary traditional right, that it was not one created by the bantustan constitution.' Mzala cited Buthelezi's speech when addressing the Foreign Affairs Committee of the British House of Commons in May 1986:

> I was born to occupy a leadership position in South Africa ... I am a leader by hereditary right and follow in the footsteps of my father, grandfather and great-grandfather, who in turn followed in the footsteps of their forebears to the time of the founding father of KwaZulu, King Shaka ... I and my forebears have always occupied influential positions as prime ministers ... to successive Zulu Kings.[5]

Mzala indicated that, three years earlier, Buthelezi had stated the same claim at a prayer meeting in Imbali township, Pietermaritzburg:

> I am an hereditary chief in a long line of succession of those who have filled the position of Prime Minister to Zulu kings. It is in response to this demand of my ancestry that I took up my political role in KwaZulu. That role was preordained for me long before apartheid emerged in this country. I was a chief in my own right before the National Party ever dreamt of the current homeland policy objective.[6]

Mzala, however, challenged Buthelezi's use of the title 'prince' or (*mntwana* in its Zulu translation) as there were many in the Zulu royal family who had not claimed the title. Mzala cited speeches by Buthelezi and a sympathetic book by Wessel de Kock that referred to him as 'a prince of the Zulu nation, a scion of the royal house'. Furthermore, Buthelezi's biographer, Ben Temkin, argued Mzala, 'likewise includes at the end of his book an appendix reportedly written by Zami Conco, which claims that "the correct form of address that should be used in addressing Buthelezi is *Mntwana*, meaning Infanta or Prince, a title given to all direct descendants of the Zulu kings"'.

Mzala stated that the assertions in Temkin's book that 'Buthelezi is a direct descendant of the Zulu kings, hereditary prime minister to the Zulu king' were wrong. Wrote Mzala, 'Temkin is wrong in regard to Buthelezi's direct monarchical descent, and hence the claim that he should be referred to as *Mntwana* or "Prince" is wrong too.' According to Mzala:

> It is true that Chief Buthelezi is related to the Zulu royal family through his mother who was the daughter of King Dinizulu.[7] But that in itself adds up to nothing in his claim to hereditary leadership as prime minister of the Zulus. Chief Buthelezi's mother was not the only daughter of King Dinizulu. There were nine in all. The first daughter of King Dinizulu was Princess Phikisile, who was the mother of Dr Pixley Seme, the founding member of the ANC. Dr Seme never considered himself a claimant to 'premiership' in the Zulu traditional hierarchy. The second daughter was Magogo, Gatsha's mother.[8]

Of course, Mzala was wrong in claiming that Princess Phikisile was the mother of Dr Pixley Seme. In fact, Princess Phikisile was Seme's wife – an error that many, including Buthelezi, latched on to discredit Mzala's book. This error, however, does not render Mzala's arguments completely ineffectual. Mzala's argument was that none of the sons of King Dinizulu's daughters had used the title Prince or *Mntwana* other than Buthelezi. 'The title of *Mntwana*, which literally translated means "child", was used in Zulu tradition to refer to the children of the king. Chief Buthelezi is not the child of a king. The usage of this title is therefore without traditional or customary foundation.'

On the question of the premiership role of the Buthelezis, Mzala argued that while it was true that Chief Mnyamana was the premier chief during the reign of King Cetshwayo, he did not inherit this title. 'He was appointed to it by the king in recognition of certain of his leadership qualities. Each Zulu king appointed a chief councillor or premier chief, but it was certainly not always a Buthelezi chief who was so appointed.'

> The premier chief during the reign of King Shaka was Ngomane, who remained King Shaka's 'Prime Minister' long after the death of Shaka's mother, Nandi. Ngomane was not a Buthelezi but an Mthethwa. Then came King Dingane, whose premier chief was Ndlela ka Sompisi. He, too, was not a Buthelezi but an Ntuli. After King Dingane, the kingdom was led by King Mpande, who appointed Masiphula ka Mamba as the premier chief. His surname was Ntshangase and not Buthelezi. It was only when Cetshwayo was king of the Zulus that a Buthelezi featured

– Chief Mnyamana. Cetshwayo was the last king of the sovereign Zulu kingdom as founded by King Shaka, and before it was divided into various chiefdoms by the British.⁹

According to Mzala, Zulu history did not point to any established tradition 'that obliges kings to appoint chiefs from particular tribes for the so-called role of premier. The premiership is not [a] hereditary title. Chief Buthelezi's claim is therefore not substantiated by history.' To his credit, though, as recently as 2021, following the demise of King Zwelithini, Buthelezi has sought to clarify this assertion that his prime minister role was not hereditary. This is, however, contrary to his earlier claims, as detailed by Mzala.

Mzala concluded the book by highlighting that 'Chief Gatsha Buthelezi is a complex and paradoxical man. Looking back over the years at his political actions and statements, a distinct and irreconcilable double agenda seems discernible in a number of critical areas.' He painted Buthelezi as a key figure in the implementation of the Bantu Authorities Act in Natal, a period that, he argued, gave rise to the KwaZulu bantustan.

Mzala also repudiated Buthelezi's assertion that he was a member of the African National Congress (ANC). He argued that there was no known record or 'substantial oral evidence' that revealed Buthelezi as having been a member of the ANC.

> If he was, he was not an active member. At Fort Hare University he did not play an active role in the ANC Youth League, the dominant campus political force. He supported some of its campaigns, but he was never a major political figure in the student body. After graduation, he was not active in the great political campaigns of the 1950s such as the Defiance Campaign, the Congress of the People, or the campaign against the Bantu Education Act.

Again, this is another disputable point as many ANC leaders, including former presidents Luthuli and Mandela, have mentioned Buthelezi as a former member.

Unlike his mother, Mzala claimed, Buthelezi did not come out in public support of the resistance of the women of Natal to the imposition of the pass laws on women.

Alongside this record of inactivity, there is little substance to his claim that he 'stomped the length and breadth of Natal' in opposition to Bantu Authorities. Instead his priority in the early 1950s seems to have been to convince the government in Pretoria that he was worthy or politically reliable enough to be elevated to the chieftaincy of the Buthelezi tribe. Any involvement in national politics could have spoiled his chances of attaining the political elevation he so badly wanted.

Mzala argued that prominent leaders of the ANC in Natal, such as Archie Gumede, MB Yengwa and Johnny Makhathini, have stated that Buthelezi was never an ANC member. Apart from his association with individuals who were members, no contemporary of Buthelezi's remembered him belonging to any branch. Mzala conceded, though, that 'Buthelezi has not himself made this claim, but others have done so'.[10] Citing war-talk speeches by Buthelezi against the UDF and COSATU, Mzala concluded: 'With such sentiments one is forced to ponder what notion of democracy lies within such a philosophy and to consider once again the question posed at the beginning of Chapter One: What man of peace is this?'

III

Back in South Africa, the book received rave reviews from the progressive press. The *Weekly Mail* of 13 October 1988 ran an article titled 'Attempting to Pin Down a Man of Ambiguity'. First acknowledging 'the fraught relationship between the ANC and Inkatha', the paper described Mzala as 'a considerable scholar' and that ...

> ... this is no ephemeral polemical treatise. It is, in the main, a reasoned, informative, well-researched and tightly argued attack on a political opponent. Even the target of such works will concede this is a genre with valuable historical antecedents. Perhaps the key to Mzala's contribution is that he takes his subject very seriously. His conclusion is implacably hostile – he is essentially concerned to debunk the notion that Buthelezi is a 'man of peace' – but it is reached via substantial argument, both empirical and interpretative.[11]

The articles also highlighted that 'for Mzala, it is Buthelezi's actions which have made him persona non grata with the ANC and other organisations committed to the Freedom Charter, rather than the mere fact of his participation in the homeland system'. Noting Mzala's sensitivity in dealing with Zulu history, the article stated, 'Throughout the book, but especially in the first half, Mzala is at pains to treat Zulu history with great respect. (In fact, he is not above indulging in a touch of pastoral idealism about pre-colonial times himself.)'

Some articles were, however, scathing of Mzala's book. One by Nomavenda Mathiane – 'The Hatchet and the Snow' – in *Frontline* of February 1989 argued that Buthelezi was 'now the most biographed living South African' and juxtaposed Mzala's book against Jack Shepherd Smith's *The Biography*.

> Although Mzala's book on Gatsha Buthelezi is fraught with sordid statements in its attempt to run him down, it is however a well researched document. In a country thirsty for unbiased history, it is a pity that Mzala's book is wrapped up in such hate that it defeats the purpose of destroying some of the myths the colonialist historians recorded. This reduces the possibilities of it ever becoming a respected African history book.[12]

Mathiane continued:

> From the onset one is tempted to ask – who is Mzala? Why does he choose to hide in anonymity? Since he apparently lives in Lusaka with the ANC, he cannot be in fear of Inkatha. Does he lack the courage of his convictions so much that he gives in to a word which is especially meaningless even for a pseudonym? Mzala means cousin, what are we meant to read into that?[13]

Once Mathiane was done questioning Mzala's name and motives, she went back to the book itself.

> There is no doubt that the book is a work of an academic and historian. And yet from the very first page it poses strange questions. There is a very un-African feeling about much of the book. It is unusual in African tradition to slander even a worst enemy with such vitriol. And yet we should perhaps accept that African tradition is changing. One proof is the way that the book is being received around the townships of Durban and Pietermaritzburg. People there are directly affected by his [Buthelezi] reign and there his unpopularity is much greater than in Soweto or Lusaka, where it is an ideological or academic matter. Among literate people there, Mzala's book is the biggest excitement for years.[14]

Mathiane questioned some of Mzala's assertions and defended Buthelezi's right to be called a 'prince'. 'In the Zulu traditions,' she argued, 'the offspring of a prince or princess are treated as royalty and called princes or princesses.' She continued, 'Mzala, arguing that Gatsha should not be called "prince" ("*umntwana*"), says that this is not done even by the English. So what? Are the English the standard by which people measure themselves?' She also took issue with Mzala's argument that Buthelezi's brother Mceleli was the rightful heir apparent to the chieftainship.

> Mzala says that Gatsha schemed to the chieftainship, stepping on his relatives' toes. He implies that Gatsha's elder brother Mceleli was meant to be chief. In fact this is not a one way issue. It has been a subject of dispute. One traditionalist faction maintains that the first son is always the heir, but the other school alleges that the son of a princess takes precedence over an elder brother who is the son of a commoner. Even Mzala admits that the clan paid lobola for Gatsha's mother, but he seems unaware that this makes Gatsha's case very strong![15]

Mathiane said that, upon reading in Mzala's book that Mceleli has been banished to the northern Transvaal, she did her own investigation only to find that 'Mceleli is actually employed as a security guard at Gatsha's official residence, Kwaphindangene'. She thought Mzala petty for pointing out that Buthelezi named the commission that was conducted by Professor Schreiner as the Buthelezi Commission and not the Schreiner Commission. 'What is wrong with that? Does that affect the findings of the commission?'

Mathiane concluded, 'Putting aside the writer's passion to destroy Chief Buthelezi, the book gives a spellbinding analysis of black history up to the latter day.' This effort by Mathiane did not win her friends in Ulundi.[16] A letter to the editor in *Frontline* of 3 April 1989 by J Masango of Ulundi accused her of bias in her review of a 'Marxist twaddle'. 'Ms Nomavenda Mathiane's review of the Buthelezi's biographies [*sic*] does not convince us that she herself is completely without bias.' In the letter, Masango accused Mzala of distorting Zulu history by trying to discredit Buthelezi's lineage. This was perceived as a plot by 'international Marxists like Nobleman Nxumalo (Mzala)'.[17]

Another letter in the same edition of *Frontline*, by Jack Shepherd Smith, accused Mathiane of 'almost contemptuously [being] dismissive of Inkatha' and Buthelezi of being a true leader of the Zulus.[18] Suzanne Vos, who later became Inkatha's representative in the democratic parliament, also leaped to Buthelezi's defence following Mathiane's claims that some joined Inkatha for 'expedience'.[19] Mathiane says it did not just end with the letters to the editor; Buthelezi, in fact, issued her with a letter of demand for her review. It's only when someone told Buthelezi that he was unlikely to get anything from her since she did not have money that he dropped the lawsuit. 'I have not been so happy to be known that I'm poor,' she says with a laugh.

Mzala was not, however, one to back down from any challenge. He welcomed the criticism and responded to Mathiane's review by means of a letter to the editor in *Frontline* of 3 April 1989: 'The most conspicuous thing since the publication of *Chief with a Double Agenda* is the silence. If Chief Buthelezi is slandered, why does he not sue in his normal fashion? It is because the book is the truth. Unfortunately, Nomavenda Mathiane seems not to understand this when she leaps to the Chief's defence.' On Mathiane's questioning his name, Mzala asked why she did not enquire from the ANC whether such a person existed? 'Well, my name is Mzala. I am a member of the African National Congress. I am an African of Zulu ethnic origin. For me the name "Mzala" is as meaningful as any other – Shaka, Moshweshwe, Sekhukhune, Hintsa, Lenin or Hitler – all of whom were known by single names for one reason or another.' Continued Mzala:

> I am a descendant of Zwide ka Langa. My surname is therefore Nxumalo or Ndwandwe. King Zwelithini is my cousin since his mother is my aunt. The late King Bhekuzulu opened for me my first Post Office Savings Account just few days after I was born. When I was a young boy, and met the King on several occasions at my grandfather Chief Masikizela's home, he told me many stories about the history of the Zulus. Yet even he is not spared criticism in the book, for his acceptance of the system of Bantu Authorities.

Mzala reiterated his claims on the use of 'prince' or *umntwana*. He argued that this was accorded to people bearing the surname 'Zulu'. 'Give me an example of a single Buthelezi who is referred to as prince? Not one! Now, give me any other surname than Zulu from whom there have been princes? Nobody!' He concluded: 'The fact that I met Chief Buthelezi and interviewed him in London proves that I was not on a slander campaign, but sought the facts even from the horse's mouth.'[20] Nevertheless, it is difficult to believe Mzala's version of events here. Apart from the fact that Buthelezi disputes being interviewed by Mzala, as it will emerge later, citing that they only met after the book was published, Mzala's own admission is that when he met Buthelezi in London he did not infom him that he was writing this book, and neither did he reveal his true identity. Thus, it is a little disingenuous to suggest that he met and interviewed Buthelezi in order to verify certain details for the book prior to publication. Mzala's book continued to make headlines in South Africa. Even when Buthelezi's biography was reviewed, *Chief with a Double Agenda* was inevitably mentioned. Two book reviews by Martin Williams and Lakela Kaunda in the *Natal Witness* in February 1989 mentioned Mzala's book. Juxtaposing the two books and asking the question, 'How are we to know who is telling the truth?' Kaunda concluded: 'For all his political bias, Mzala's book is well-researched and rich in historical information. Smith gives us nothing new and his book sounds more like a response to Mzala.'[21]

Mzala's close associates within the movement received the book with great excitement. *Dawn* carried the article 'In Lieu of a Book Review, a Book by One of Us' by Grant Moloto. The article began by introducing Mzala as 'a cadre of Umkhonto we Sizwe, and a former law student at Ngoye University. He has been writing articles of considerable interest in *Sechaba* and the *African Communist*.' Moloto went on to describe his encounters with Mzala:

> I discerned a dynamic personality. He would always have an issue of revolutionary interest to discuss and apply his mind to penetrate it. *Gatsha Buthelezi: Chief with a Double Agenda*, a well-researched and quite readable book, is fruition of such penetration into issues. The title of this book is apt and reflects adequately its balanced and enlightening contents.[22]

Joel Netshitenzhe recalls that when the book was released it was broadly appreciated because it sought to engage with questions about a great puzzle.

> Among other things, it helped clarify issues about one of the great conundrums of the liberation struggle: how an individual and an organisation who had emerged from the loins of the liberation movement seemed to have totally changed course to embrace the worst excesses of the apartheid regime's machinery of repression; when that metamorphosis happened and why; whether this applied to some or all of the Inkatha leaders; whether at a macro-level there were still some commonalities such as the demand for the unbanning of liberation

organisations and the release of political prisoners; the issue of ethnicity and the role of the royal house, and so on.

However, Netshitenzhe believes that Mzala had his own strong feelings about Inkatha and Buthelezi and his project could easily have been a hatchet, propagandist job. 'But whatever weaknesses the book may have, it was well-researched, with facts and analyses that were truly insightful.'

Sue Rabkin is one of those who were delighted. 'I was very proud of the book produced by one of us and that he actually managed eventually to put pen to paper. We were very pleased, all of us. We were very proud to be associated with that.'

IV

Although the book was not officially released in South Africa because Zed's distributors had been threatened, the book was hot property. University libraries and bookstores 'obtain[ed] copies ordered via European book distributors and library suppliers'. Privately owned copies were widely circulated and photocopied. Some of the copies came 'from book stores in South Africa's neighbouring states, and it seems that a flourishing cross-border trade developed'. Over and above this, the ANC had 'undertaken to assist Zed in distributing the book, taking responsibility for about 8 000 copies of the print run of 12 000'. According to Pallo Jordan, the ANC distributed many of these among its international supporters and its own membership and, for the next couple of years, the book entered the country mainly in the 'backpacks of Umkhonto we Sizwe soldiers'.[23]

There were other methods used to get the book into South Africa. According to Dumisani Nduli, Khaba Mkhize – a journalist for the *Natal Witness* – took some copies of the book from London 'to distribute among prominent journalists in South Africa'. Other colleagues who were with Mkhize took copies for Oscar Dhlomo and other top Inkatha leaders in Ulundi. Before John Pampallis returned to South Africa after years in exile, John Daniel brought him a box of books, which he took with him. Pampallis distributed the books 'to academics and student leaders' at the University of Natal where he was employed. When the ANC was unbanned, it became easier to distribute the book. Pampallis thinks the book is what made Mzala well known outside the ANC, especially in KwaZulu-Natal.

As expected, Buthelezi was extremely unhappy with the book and made numerous attempts to block it and have it removed from library shelves. When these attempts to suppress its distribution in South Africa resulted in a restraining order from the courts, says Jordan, 'that confirmed the correctness of Mzala's analysis to many'. Publications that reviewed it, like *Frontline* magazine, were instructed to publish a letter from Buthelezi's lawyers, Friedman & Friedman Attorneys. *Frontline* published the memorandum under the headline 'Buthelezi Biography' in June 1989. This is how the letter read:

> We refer to your edition of *Frontline*, dated April 1989, and the letter published therein by Mzala in which he refers to his book 'Chief With A Double Agenda.' We act for Dr MG Buthelezi who has instructed us as follows: 1) Our client considers the book with the heading 'Chief With A Double Agenda' by Mzala, to be defamatory of him and he has instructed us to institute legal action immediately if the book is distributed in South Africa, which at present it is not. 2) Our client refuses further to reply to such a book which he holds in contempt. Our client has instructed us to request you to publish this letter in your next edition of *Frontline* magazine.[24]

When the book eventually hit South African shelves, Buthelezi lived up to his threats, issuing legal letters to university libraries. These letters stated, 'If you do not remove the book from your shelf and/or if you distribute the book and/or lend it to others, you will be sued for damages.' Although some retail outlets managed to obtain copies through the usual channels, they were subsequently coerced to remove it. 'Some South African booksellers, however, managed to sell it under the counter.'[25]

Mzala's book caused a huge public debate in South Africa. Buthelezi's attempts to muzzle it only served to accomplish the opposite, as even the apolitical became curious about the book. Buthelezi was vigilant in ensuring that the book was not in circulation in South Africa, and as soon as he sniffed that it was available in institutions such as the University of Natal, he pounced. Through his lawyers, on 26 April 1991, he threatened legal action. 'We understand that your University Library is in possession of the aforementioned book and has made it available for distribution among those who require it.' The lawyers further argued that their clients believed the book to be defamatory and 'if you do not remove the said book from your shelf and/or if you distribute the book and/or lend it to others, you will be sued for damage'.

Natal University's deputy librarian, Christopher Merrett, put his foot down. In his reply on 6 May 1991, he claimed to have 'no power or inclination' to remove the book and that the university was committed to 'academic freedom and freedom of information'. He also began lobbying other university libraries across the country. Buthelezi was, however, unrelenting. On 13 May 1991, his lawyers insisted that while their client was 'committed to *genuine* academic freedom,' Mzala's book, written 'by a man who chose not to reveal his true name or identity on the book' was 'not just any book'. They further raised concerns on the 'haste with which members of the media were alerted'.

On 17 May 1991, university authorities succumbed to pressure and issued instructions to the university libraries to withdraw the book from circulation 'pending further legal advice about the alleged defamatory content'. This, naturally, raised the ire of academics and Merrett, acting in concert with colleagues such as John Wright, fired a letter to the Joint Academic Staff Association (JASA) on 20 May 1991, demanding that JASA raise the matter urgently with university authorities. These academics were concerned that bookstores such as Adams' Bookshop in Durban campus were put under pressure by Inkatha to remove the book from stock.

The Black Students Society in Natal University entered the fray by means of a letter to Vice Chancellor and Principal Professor Booysen on 25 June 1991 by General Secretary Earl Mailula. The student community was 'appalled' by the removal of the book and called upon the university 'to return the book to the shelves, stock more of this book so that students, academic and scholars' could access it. On 12 July 1991, the university eventually announced restoration of the book after receiving legal counsel that affirmed its view that the book was in line with its policy that 'even if critical of public figures, should be available in a University library for critical study by the scholarly community'.

Buthelezi's lawyers' concern about the media was not misplaced. The story soon made headlines. The *Saturday News* led with the article 'University Bans Buthelezi Book' and the *Natal Witness* led with 'Varsity Withdraws Buthelezi Biography'. This resulted in angry reactions from the academic fraternity, who condemned 'Buthelezi's action as an attempt at censorship which infringed academic freedom'.[26]

The *Natal Witness* followed up with an editorial that stated, 'The unequivocal determination of the universities to maintain their academic freedom is one of the most stalwart bastions that democracy has'.[27] Headlines abounded: 'Buthelezi puts legal screws on biography by ANC exile' (*Natal Witness*, 10 May 1991), 'Libraries told to "ban" book on Buthelezi' (*New Nation*, 10 May 1991), 'Buthelezi on the shelf. And he doesn't like it' (*Weekly Mail*, 10 May 1991), 'A volley from Ulundi' (*Sunday Times*, 12 May 1991), 'University bans Buthelezi book' (*Daily News*, 8 June 1991), 'Varsity withdraws Buthelezi biography' (*Natal Witness*, 8 June 1991), 'Buthelezi biography booted off the shelves' (*Weekly Mail*, 14 June 1991). All these headlines served simply to popularise the book and, by extension, the author. Some began to ask questions about Mzala.

However, Buthelezi remained vigilant through his lawyers, demanding the right to reply to what their client perceived to be biased reporting. They demanded the *Natal Witness* accord them equal space to put the matter in 'its correct perspective'.[28] In the *Daily News* of 13 June 1991, Buthelezi's lawyer, Jenny Friedman, penned an opinion piece titled 'Buthelezi committed to real academic freedom' in which she claimed that the withdrawal of the book had 'nothing to do with censorship'. But this claim was not left unchallenged by means of letters to the editors, including one from Professor Paul Maylam, who argued that Friedman's article was 'riddled with dubious and dangerous assumptions'.

Inkatha's mouthpiece, the *Ilanga* newspaper, subsequently ran a story headed 'Propagandists at Work', in which the university's academics were described as 'ANC's fetch and carry boys'.[29] Buthelezi himself never relented as witnessed in his policy speech to the KwaZulu legislative assembly in March 1991, where he reiterated his claims that Mzala's and, later, Francis Meli's books were defamatory and been referred to his lawyers. Legal action would have commenced, he claimed, had both authors not died.

V

To this day, Buthelezi insists that this book was nothing but a propaganda tract, notwithstanding the fact that numerous scholars have described it as objective and balanced. He is of the view that it was never a mere academic dissertation. 'Mzala was employed by the ANC as a Researcher and was a member of the South African Communist Party. His instruction was to write a propaganda tract that could destroy Buthelezi and Inkatha. And that is what he did.' Buthelezi blames the ANC for 'the floodgates of propaganda', which he claims were opened against him and his party when they …

... dared to disagree with the ANC's mission-in-exile on the use of armed struggle and the call for economic sanctions against South Africa. Having worked with Mr Oliver Tambo for years as a loyal ANC cadre, having taken up leadership of the KwaZulu Government on his and Inkosi Luthuli's instruction, and having founded Inkatha with Tambo's approval in order to reignite political mobilisation on South African soil, I had no reason to anticipate that the ANC would turn against me.[30]

Buthelezi's continuous use of the phrase 'ANC mission-in-exile' is what Cassius Lubisi characterised as his attempt 'to position himself as a national liberation leader in South Africa. With the ANC, SACP and PAC banned, Buthelezi tried to take upon himself the mantle of the liberation movement. He adopted ANC symbols and language as a tactic for building a personal base. He presented the ANC as the "ANC Mission in Exile", and Inkatha as the "ANC Mission in South Africa".'[31] Essentially, this sought to create a narrative that the ANC, as represented by its exiled leadership, did not exist inside the country and thus Buthelezi was 'the true heir of the ANC' inside the country.[32]

Nevertheless, Buthelezi insists that when the ANC refused to abandon the principle of non-violent struggle, in October 1979, 'an ideological split opened between us'. He claims that within months the ANC's leaders began a vicious campaign of vilification against him:

> I was leading an organisation with more than a million card-carrying members. It was felt that I should be dispossessed of my support base, lest the ANC lose its hegemony. In the words of SACTU [South African Congress of Trade Unions]: 'Gatsha must be isolated from the people ... He must be forced into a position where he is a leader without a support base and Inkatha is a movement without a leader.'[33]

Buthelezi believes that the best way to isolate him was to attack his credentials and paint him as an enemy of the people. He argues that Mzala, as a young activist, stepped into this context. 'At the age of 19, he went into exile and began devouring propaganda texts of the ANC, SACP and communist leaders. He proved an excellent candidate for indoctrination and, at 22, was sent for "advanced ideological training".' He continues:

> Soon he was working in Tanzania for the ANC's Radio Freedom, which

habitually demonised me and Inkatha, warning that the ANC was 'coming with bazookas' to deal with me. Radio Freedom and *Sechaba*, for which Mzala wrote, were key platforms through which I was attacked. The indoctrinated Mzala was doing his job well.[34]

Buthelezi says it was on this basis that Mzala was tasked to write a book intended solely to defame and draw into question his credentials as a member of the Zulu royal family, traditional leader and political leader.

Thus he was tasked with writing a comprehensive propaganda tract claiming that I and Inkatha were collaborating with the apartheid regime. To ensure that this tract was published as a book, the ANC made an undertaking to a London publisher, Zed, to distribute 8 000 copies. This would be the largest first print run of any book Zed had published. Accordingly, copies of the book were distributed to UmKhonto we Sizwe soldiers, who brought it into South Africa.[35]

VI

Buthelezi says he never consented to Mzala writing this book. 'In fact, I never even knew he was writing it until it was published. He never interviewed me towards it or sought my point of view, and never checked any information with me. This is consonant with the purpose of the book, which was to disseminate lies about me and damage my credibility.' He says it was only after the book had been published that he spoke to Mzala.

Even this, he argues, was not done in good faith. 'On a visit to London, the ANC Office sent me a message that someone by the name of Shabalala, if I remember well, wanted to interview me. I met the so-called Mr Shabalala. I faintly remember that he engaged me on the issue of my position as the Zulu Monarch's Traditional Prime Minister (uNdunankulu we Ngonyama noZulu).' Jordan's recollection is that at a lecture Buthelezi delivered at the Royal Commonwealth Society, Mzala, then a student in the UK, questioned Buthelezi closely about the assertion that the Buthelezi clan traditionally provided the prime minister to the Zulu monarch. To his chagrin, says Jordan, Buthelezi conceded that this was not the case.

Dumisani Nduli says that Shula Marks had invited him to a talk by Buthelezi and he, in turn, informed Mzala about this event. After all, they had been engaging on Buthelezi since their days in Swaziland. Although

Nduli was unable to attend the talk, Mzala later informed him that he had confronted Buthelezi on the accuracy of his claims that the prime minister role was hereditary. Mzala said he referred Buthelezi to Chief Mankulumana kaSomaphunga, 'a direct descendent of Zwide, [who] was a Ndwandwe (also known as Nxumalo)'.[36] However, Buthelezi says:

> I explained that although my great-grandfather Mnyamana Buthelezi was King Cetshwayo's Prime Minister and commanded all the Zulu Regiments and my father Mathole Buthelezi was Prime Minister to King Solomon Maphumzana ka Dinuzulu and the Zulu Nation, that the position was not hereditary. My late father was named as Traditional Prime Minister of the King in Eshowe by King Solomon kaDinuzulu during the visit of Prince Edward, the Prince of Wales, in 1925. I was appointed to that position by my late first cousin, King Cyprian Bhekuzulu kaSolomon, when he gave me the responsibility of organising preparations for the unveiling of King Shaka's tombstone in 1954. I made it clear that the position was not hereditary.[37]

Buthelezi says it was many years later that the Mr Shabalala with whom he discussed these matters 'was discovered to be none other than Jabulani Nobleman Nxumalo *alias* Mzala'. Mzala told Gail Gerhart that, although he had grown up in KwaZulu and gone to school there, including attending the University of Zululand, he had never met Buthelezi in person until their encounter in London. He said he posed a question from the floor while Buthelezi was giving a lecture. After the lecture, Buthelezi invited him for a drink and they spent an hour in conversation. Mzala introduced himself by a false name and did not mention that he was writing a book on Buthelezi. However, he used the opportunity to explore some of Buthelezi's views on his past actions.[38]

In recent media interviews, Buthelezi emphasised the point that his position as prime minister was not hereditary. However, Lubisi points out that Inkatha mouthpiece, the *Clarion Call*, argued that Buthelezi's position was indeed hereditary. The publication argued: 'The leaders of the Buthelezi clan, the largest in the Zulu nation, have been Prime Ministers to a succession of Zulu Kings. As such Chief Buthelezi is the traditional Prime Minister of the seven million Zulu nation and the senior advisor to His Majesty the King of the Zulus.'[39]

Buthelezi says he has performed the duties of 'uNdunankulu weNgonyama nesizwe sika Zulu' (the Prime Minister of the Zulu nation) under his late cousin King Cyprian Bhekuzulu kaSolomon. 'I do not have space to name these duties except to say that even all the funeral arrangements for King Cyprian Bhekuzulu kaSolomon kaDinuzulu were made by myself in that capacity.' He says he continued to carry out those duties under King Goodwill Zwelithini kaBhekuzulu. Buthelezi says he has for years been saying publicly that the King 'has the prerogative of appointing his own Prime Minister, emphasising that such a position is not hereditary'.

However, it was impossible for King Zwelithini to discontinue Buthelezi's services even if he wanted. Buthelezi had subordinated the king to the KwaZulu government and thus it was himself rather than the king who reigned supreme. With Inkatha and the KwaZulu government 'inseparable', Buthelezi had not only 'neutralised the king' but was now in control of both entities.[40] Hence, when the apartheid regime advanced the notion of a monarchy with executive powers, similar to that of Swaziland, Buthelezi objected and instead argued that the king must remain above politics. This essentially meant that, through the KwaZulu government, Buthelezi controlled the budget of the king. 'In the eventual power struggle, Buthelezi emerged dominant. Through the 1980s, the king remained subordinate to his uncle, a figurehead to be deployed at opportune moments as a romantic symbol of Zulu unity.'[41]

VII

Buthelezi says he found the entirety of the book defamatory. 'It would take an enormous amount of ink to identify every lie in this book and counter it with the facts. It denigrates my entire family, from my great-grandfather down. My character, lineage, actions and motives are ripped to shreds by lie after lie after lie.' He does, however, spell out some of the examples he found problematic about the book:

> Mzala questioned my hereditary leadership position, claiming that I was not my father's legitimate heir, but that the true heir was my half-brother, Mceleli Bongwefile, who was the son of my father's sixth wife, Nozigqoko Zulu o KaManekwana, from the Gazini section of the Zulu family. This has no basis in fact.

He continues:

> In accordance with the Code of Zulu Law, when an Inkosi requests his people to contribute to lobolo for his wife, he thereby contracts himself that his heir will come from the House of that particular wife, and she automatically becomes the mother of the Clan. When King Solomon offered his sister, Princess Magogo, to marry Inkosi Mathole Buthelezi, my father, Inkosi Mathole asked the whole Buthelezi Clan to contribute cattle for the Princess's lobolo. The status of the Chief Wife is announced publicly on the day of her marriage. Accordingly, on my father's instruction, on the day of his marriage to Princess Magogo, my mother, the Principal Induna for our Clan, Shameni Khumalo, publicly announced that the Princess was Inkosi Mathole's Chief Wife.[42]

Buthelezi says he grew up at the palace of his uncle King Solomon, KwaDlamahlahla. When his father, Inkosi Mathole, died on 10 December 1942, he was fetched on the instructions of his family. 'According to Zulu custom, I had to stab the ground where Inkosi Mathole's grave was to be dug. The stabbing of the ground was an indication to all and sundry that I was the heir.' He proceeds to highlight that he was only 14 years old when he performed this task and that his half-brother, Mceleli, was already a young man who was courting girls. 'He never raised any voice that he had any claim to the Buthelezi Ubukhosi [chieftaincy]. Eleven years later, when I was installed as Inkosi of the Buthelezi Clan in 1953, Mceleli was present, and he never raised any claim or objection.'

According to Buthelezi, he took over the position at the time when he was to do law articles with Mr Rowley Arenstein, a lawyer who defended ANC cases and later became the longest-banned person in South Africa. He says it was Inkosi Luthuli and other leaders of the ANC who urged him to listen to his mother Princess Magogo, who wanted him to abandon his articles to take over his position as Inkosi of the Buthelezi Clan.

By then, Buthelezi says, he had been expelled from the University of Fort Hare as a member of the ANC Youth League after a demonstration against the then Governor-General of the Union of South Africa, Mr Gideon Brand van Zyl, who was visiting the university. 'From that time,' he argues, 'I was shadowed by the Security Police wherever I went. So when I was installed as Inkosi, the Secretary for Native Affairs installed me as an "Acting Inkosi", because the government of the day could not forgive me for my involvement in a demonstration against the Governor-General and they knew that I was a member of the ANC. The fact that I was close to leaders of the ANC, including Inkosi Luthuli, was also no secret.'

Buthelezi says it was only in 1957 that the government grudgingly gave him full recognition as Inkosi of the Buthelezi Clan. 'And, again, Mceleli raised no objection.' He points out that, in his haste to dispute that he is 'a Prince of the Zulu Royal', Mzala glaringly errs by suggesting that Dr Pixley ka Isaka Seme was a son of a Zulu princess like him but was never called a prince. 'Yet this is another of the glaring fallacies in his propaganda tract, for Dr Seme was in fact married to a Zulu Princess.' Indeed, Seme was married to King Dinuzulu's daughter, Princess Phikisile Harriet, also known as Phikisinkosi or Phikisiwe, according to Buthelezi. 'Dr Seme was my uncle,' says Buthelezi, 'because my mother, Princess Constance Magogo Mantithi Thombisile Ngangezinye, was the daughter of King Dinuzulu – in other words, she and Phikisiwe were sisters.'

Buthelezi asserts that Seme 'was the founder of the African National Native Congress, later named the African National Congress (ANC). He was later elected the fifth President-General of the African National Congress.' When Seme had an eye operation, he would send for Buthelezi 'to write in long-hand his correspondence that he sent to various people; he dictated his letters to me'. Buthelezi was doing this while in matric and considers it his 'first mentorship in the politics of the ANC, from the very founder of the African National Congress'.

He then emphasises: 'Like me, Dr Seme's children were all regarded as Princes, and his daughter Princess Helen Ziphi Teressa Mamama as a respected member of the Zulu Royal House. Incidentally, her funeral ... was attended by no less a personality than the Honourable Dr Zweli Mkhize, a senior leader of the African National Congress and our Minister of Health.'

VIII

For Buthelezi, the glaring error on Seme reflects how 'unreliable this propaganda tract is. It is nothing more nor less than a tissue of lies which Jabulani Nobleman Nxumalo pieced together to defame and demonise me, on behalf of the external mission of the ANC.' He says Mzala's attack on his hereditary position was a precursor to this attack on his leadership of the KwaZulu government. 'He claimed that I was working with the apartheid regime by operating within the system, as though I had taken it upon myself to become leader of KwaZulu, in order to obtain some sort of favour from the regime.' He emphasises the point that he took up the leadership of

KwaZulu on instructions from his 'leaders in the ANC' and 'I fulfilled the mission I was given to derail the apartheid system from within'. To draw Mzala's version into question, Buthelezi says:

> At the time he wrote this book, foreign intelligence services were keeping a close watch on South Africa. They knew who I was and there was no doubt about my credentials as a freedom fighter. Accordingly I was warmly received by Heads of State including Zambia's President Kaunda, Tanzania's President Nyerere, Lesotho's Prime Minister Jonathan, Nigeria's President Obasanjo, Ethiopia's Emperor Haile Selassie, Swaziland's King Sobhuza II, Lesotho's King Moshoeshoe II, the UK's Prime Minister Thatcher (who even came to visit me in Ulundi), German Chancellor Kohl, the Netherlands' Prime Minister Den Uyl, America's Presidents Carter, Reagan and Bush – the list goes on. President Tolbert of Liberia conferred on me the Knight Commander of the Star of Africa, and President Giscard d'Estaing of France conferred the National Order of Merit. I was received in the Vatican by no less than 3 Popes who, as Pontiffs, also doubled up as Heads of the Vatican State.[43]

Buthelezi says these milestones disprove Mzala's theory as that of 'a 31-year-old paid Communist propagandist [who] claimed that I was nothing more than a puppet of the apartheid regime'. It was the ANC, together with the Luthuli family, argues Buthelezi, that when his 'mentor' Inkosi Albert Luthuli passed away, asked him to deliver a eulogy at his funeral. He continues:

> When the OAU [Organisation of African Unity] bestowed a posthumous award on him, Mama Nokukhanya Luthuli asked me to accompany her to Maseru to accept the award and speak on her behalf. The award was handed over by His Majesty King Moshoeshoe II. This was in the presence of several Heads of State. I was then also invited to attend the memorial day of King Moshoeshoe I at his grave at the Thaba Bosiu Mountain.

To confirm his acceptance by the ANC leadership, Buthelezi says that on a subsequent visit to Lesotho he was invited to inspect the site after the apartheid regime bombed several ANC residences causing a number of deaths of some ANC exiles. 'I was accompanied by the ANC representative in Lesotho, Mr Ndlovu, with a group of members of uMkhonto we Sizwe.

Later, after 1994, Mr Ndlovu became South Africa's High Commissioner in Lesotho.' He says even when FW de Klerk announced Mandela's release in Parliament, 'he thanked me by name for having persuaded him to make that decision. When Mandela addressed his first mass rally, he publicly thanked me for all I had done to secure his release'.

Buthelezi continues to cite many incidents that he says debunk Mzala's assertions that he was an apartheid puppet.

> At the unveiling of Mr Oliver Tambo's tombstone, in front of all the Rivonia Trialists and almost the whole Cabinet at the time, the ANC's Mr Cleopas Nsibande spoke about being sent by Mr Tambo and Inkosi Luthuli with a message to me, not to refuse the leadership of KwaZulu if the people asked me to lead. They knew that I opposed the homeland system, but they believed that I could undermine the system from within – which is exactly what I did by refusing to take nominal independence, which would have turned KwaZulu into a Bantustan.[44]

Buthelezi claims that when Nsibande died, former President Kgalema Motlanthe, speaking at his funeral, confirmed what Nsibande had said. 'Until the end of his life, Mr Nsibande went every Monday morning to Luthuli House to appeal for reconciliation between the ANC and the IFP because he knew the truth about me.'

Motlanthe's version is that the ANC's then Secretary-General Walter Sisulu sent a message for Buthelezi, through Nsibande, a 1956 Treason Trialist, to participate as Chief Minister of KwaZulu. Nsibande was to convey the message to Buthelezi's sister who was married to Dr Dotwana in Benoni. Motlanthe says it is correct that Nsibande repeated this story during Tambo's unveiling, where he pleaded with the ANC to reconcile with Buthelezi. While he was the secretary-general of the ANC, Motlanthe says Nsibande would 'ambush' him on the Buthelezi question every Monday before the meeting of officials. However, what is crucial for Motlanthe is that the communication between the ANC and Buthelezi and other leaders occurred in a specific context. Motlanthe states:

> Walter Sisulu in particular approached those people who were going to play some role with the simple agenda of saying you are not the creators of these homelands, it is the regime which has created these homelands. Our people live there and they are now being placed under jurisdiction of homelands. So your role is to use the limited political space you have to preach the message of the unity of the African people.[45]

Nevertheless, Buthelezi regards himself as part of the liberation struggle. When Nigerian President Olusegun Obasanjo visited Mandela on Robben Island as part of the Commonwealth Eminent Persons Group, says Buthelezi, he asked Mandela about him, and Mandela told him, 'Buthelezi is a freedom fighter in his own right'. Similarly, he claims that when Mozambique's President Joaquim Chissano heard his 'condemnation of apartheid', he asked Oliver Tambo who he was. Tambo told him, 'That is our man.' Buthelezi claims that many ANC leaders, like Stalwart Simelane, Joshua Zulu and Wordsworth Luthuli, joined Inkatha upon release from Robben Island because Mandela had instructed them to work with him.

> Mandela himself refused to sever relations with me, for he knew the truth that I was working to undermine the system from within on the instruction of Tambo and Luthuli. Mandela and I continued to correspond throughout his incarceration. Some of our letters are published in his own book, *Conversations With Myself*. In her biography, *491 Days*, Mrs Winnie Madikizela-Mandela writes, 'Buthelezi … was one of the greatest fighters in his day … He was entrusted with fighting the system from within. And that is what people do not know.'[46]

After citing all these examples, Buthelezi asks, 'So who was telling the truth?' He muses: 'Was it all these leaders (as backed by the overwhelming body of history), or was it Mzala? Because the two are not compatible. If what Mzala wrote was true, then Mandela, Luthuli, Tambo, Kaunda, His Majesty the King, my own father, and a whole raft of prominent leaders must have been lying.'

Notwithstanding his self-adulation, Buthelezi's statement is incongruent with public articulation of many prominent ANC leaders. In his political report to the 1985 ANC Kabwe Conference, Oliver Tambo admitted that they had kept in contact with Buthelezi, but things did not proceed as they expected. Tambo said that they had hoped that 'this former member of the ANC Youth League' would use 'the legal opportunities provided by the Bantustan programme to participate in the mass mobilisation' to 'focus on the struggle for a united and non-racial South Africa'. Tambo reported that, owing to the understandable antipathy many comrades had towards working within the bantustan system, 'the task of reconstituting Inkatha therefore fell on Gatsha Buthelezi himself who then built Inkatha as a personal power base far removed from the kind of organisation we had visualised'.[47] Tambo's report highlighted that, instead, Buthelezi dressed

Inkatha in ANC colours 'because he knew that the masses to whom he was appealing were loyal to the ANC ... [Later], when he thought he had sufficient of a base, he also used coercive methods against the people to force them to support Inkatha.'

This report – as well as some of the statements from respected ANC leaders such as Govan Mbeki, as it will emerge briefly – make it implausible to locate Mzala's work entirely in the realm of propaganda. While Mzala worked for the ANC's propaganda platforms such as Radio Freedom, his work must be tested against historical fact. As early as 1978 Mzala had presented a cogent analysis on Buthelezi's politics in his *African Communist* article. What must be analysed are Mzala's assertions in this article that Inkatha was founded to safeguard and perpetuate the bantustan policy and entrench Buthelezi's position in KwaZulu. Was this fact or fiction? Mzala consistently raised such issues about Inkatha until the release of his book, ten years later.

Pallo Jordan believes that, like many others, Mzala was uncomfortable about the tactical arrangements some in the ANC thought were possible with Buthelezi and Inkatha. Because Mzala was steeped in Zulu orature, including history, 'he was very conversant with the dynastic disputes among the Zulu royals, including Cetshwayo's succession, as well as Gatsha's own succession'. This, says Jordan, put Mzala in a position to challenge many of the false claims Buthelezi had made about Zulu history, and specifically the place of the Buthelezi clan. He continues:

> By the time Mzala wrote and published his book, Gatsha's actions had demonstrated that he had an agenda decisively different from the ANC's. He had become the most active African figure opposing sanctions, thus undermining a key ANC strategy; he was actively engaged in the repression of the UDF and other progressive forces in Natal; as it later emerged, he was the principal ally of the far-right in the apartheid security forces, assigned the role of a 'Counter-Gang', to militarily repress the movement in Natal and the then PWV [Pretoria-Witwatersrand-Vaal triangle].

In various quarters within and outside liberation movement circles, according to Jordan, Mzala's book was regarded as a sound riposte to the claims of Buthelezi and Inkatha.

IX

There was consensus across various sectors, including those who were harsh in their review, that the book was well researched and deserved to be distributed. In some quarters it received rave reviews. For example, in his 1989 review, John Brewer posited that Mzala's 'insider' status did not detract from the book but rather 'is its most appealing quality'. Argued Brewer: 'A pleasant feature of Mzala's study, given the deterioration in the relationship between Buthelezi and the ANC, is that the author's partisanship has not resulted in a loss of objectivity and balance, for it is written with fairness that would certainly have been absent had the roles been reversed.'[48] In his 1990 review, Mokubung Nkomo described the book as 'providing a well-documented background briefing on the rise of Chief Mangosuthu Gatsha Buthelezi'.[49] He concluded that the book was 'well researched and well reasoned', which put Buthelezi into perspective and 'casts a penetrating light into an important actor'.[50] Among the respected scholars who reviewed the book in academic journals was Shula Marks 'Review article: Inkatha and contemporary politics' in the *Journal of Natal and Zulu History* (1988), and Norman Etherington 'Buthelezi and the South African revolution' in *Southern African review of books* (1988).

In their 1991 paper, Chantelle Wyley and Christopher Merrett noted: 'Reviews in academic journals, as well as those written by serious political analysts, leave one with no doubt that this is a study worthy of distribution and careful scrutiny.' In dealing with Buthelezi's attempts to block the book, they ask, 'Is it one word, a sentence, a paragraph, a page, or a chapter that is causing offence? And if it is causing offence, is it untrue? Even if it is untrue, is it not in the public interest that it be made known?'

Years later, Merrett continued to argue that no attempt had been made to sue Mzala and yet 'the book has remained as elusive as any formerly banned under draconian apartheid regulations'. Although it was eventually returned to library shelves after universities protested, 'it has never been freely available in South African bookshops'.[51] Buthelezi believes that Mzala's book was one in a barrage of vilification that formed part of a deliberate campaign against him.

In fact, in April 2002, former President Mandela himself admitted to what they had done, saying: 'We have used every ammunition to destroy [Buthelezi], but we failed. And he is still there. He is a formidable survivor. We cannot ignore him.' Today, however, with the benefit of history and all the facts, it is impossible to view Mzala's book as anything other than what it is: a propaganda tract.[52]

Buthelezi says that when Wyley and Merrett published their paper in 1991 the propaganda of the past was still intact, the ANC and IFP still locked in 'a low-intensity internecine civil war, with thousands of lives being lost'. He disputes that Wyley and Merrett's paper should be considered a final authority by discounting everything that had been revealed in the past 29 years. In fact, he says, he is 'quite flummoxed' by Wyley and Merrett's questions. 'How can it possibly be in the public interest for lies to be widely disseminated?' Hence, he feels it was right that he sought to take legal action.

> Anyone who had been attacked like that would do the same. It was not a matter of objecting to criticism, but a matter of trying to stop outright lies. Unfortunately, Mzala passed away before legal action could be finalised. After his death, because it was not clear who owned the book, the court process could not proceed.

More than 30 years after the book was published, Buthelezi is still pained to know that his 'family must suffer this kind of humiliation of having to be slandered into perpetuity. Unfortunately, many young academics and foreign students who come across this book have no basis to understand it as propaganda, so it is still taken as gospel truth by many academics, journalists and teachers.' Buthelezi says the book 'has even informed the content of reputable websites, like sahistory.com – which has refused to engage us on a discussion of the facts. This does tremendous damage to the record of history and to my own legacy.'

X

Those who still clearly have an agenda against him, says Buthelezi, use Mzala's book to prop up their own vitriol and lies. Buthelezi and his party are dead set against having anything named after Mzala. Buthelezi believes the renaming of the ANC's AbaQulusi Region after Mzala Nxumalo has caused serious tension between the ANC and IFP.

> We have no problem with the ANC honouring their heroes. But, in this case, there is an unresolved issue. The leadership of the ANC has never distanced itself from Mzala's lies about me. This drives a wedge

between our organisations, for there is no reason that old propaganda should be allowed to persist when the truth is known.

For this reason, Buthelezi believes that 'this book in fact remains at the centre of discussions between our two parties ... If we are to heal the wounds of the past, the truth about the past must be acknowledged'. Even now, Buthelezi is steadfast in his assessment of Mzala's book:

> Mzala's mission was to defame me. He accomplished that. Whether or not he was 'a revolutionary icon and hero' does not change the fact that he did a hatchet job on Mangosuthu Buthelezi. With all that I have done for my country, it cuts me to the heart to be unjustly labelled an enemy of my people.

XI

ANC and SACP stalwart and Rivonia Trialist Govan Mbeki painted a different picture from the one Buthelezi portrays about himself. In his book *Sunset at Midday: Latshon' ilang' emini*, he describes Buthelezi as a self-centred individual who was prepared to work with the oppressors to satisfy his insatiable ambition for power. Contrary to Buthelezi's assertions that he sought to utilise his positions to undermine apartheid, Mbeki argued that in 1957 Buthelezi 'was appointed a chief by the government in terms of the Bantu Authorities Act because he was willing to serve in the Nationalist government structure'.

A year after Buthelezi's installation as chief of the Buthelezi clan, Mbeki served on a small ANC committee led by President-General Albert Luthuli to devise a plan for the organisation in the bantustans. Among the points of discussion was the role played by the chiefs under the Bantu Authorities Act, 'and Buthelezi's role in particular as a member of the ANC acting within the Bantustan system'. With his experience in the Eastern Cape and the Transkei Bunga, Mbeki advanced that 'Buthelezi would not be able to use his position within the government's dummy institution to promote the freedom struggle'. Mbeki was convinced of his position. He told the committee, 'It is extremely unlikely that he [Buthelezi] would be able to destroy the apartheid structure from the inside.' Luthuli, however, held a contrary view. He believed 'that Buthelezi might prove a successful opponent of apartheid acting within the system'. Luthuli advanced an interesting reason:

Moreover he maintained that Buthelezi should remain inside it on the grounds that if he retired someone less friendly to the ANC cause might take his place. That someone would be Buthelezi's brother, Mceleli, from his father's first wife, with whom the chief was in dispute over the right to assume the chieftainship of the Buthelezi tribe.[53]

This insight by someone who was close to Luthuli and ANC processes contradicts Buthelezi's assertion that his brother Mceleli was never in consideration for the chieftainship. Although Buthelezi is correct to claim proximity to Luthuli and being a member of the ANC, Mbeki revealed that Luthuli was blindsided by Buthelezi who had already given assurance of his loyalty to the apartheid regime. Accordingly, the Minister of Native Affairs, Dr Max Eiselen, wrote to the Chief Native Commissioner that '[he] would appoint Buthelezi chief if he showed more "tangible expression of his obedience and loyalty" to the Department of Native Affairs as well as to the Paramount Chief, Cyprian, who had already accepted the Bantu Authorities Act'.[54]

When Buthelezi was summoned by the Native Commissioner at Mahlabathini and was read the letter, he 'responded that he was "complying with the system", and that he would do his best to explain the Bantu Authorities Act to his tribe and to persuade them of its merits'. Upon his report to Eiselen, the Native Commissioner received a response: 'The Native Commissioner is to be complimented for his handling of the situation … Chief Buthelezi should continue in his efforts to convince the tribe of the desirability of the acceptance of the provisions of the Bantu Authorities Act, 1951.'[55]

According to Mbeki, this route taken by Buthelezi was drastically different to the one by 'Chief Luthuli himself when, earlier in the decade, he had been forced by the government to choose between holding his position as chief of Amakholwa in the Stenga district and being president of the ANC. Luthuli had opted for the ANC, becoming the people's chief, whereas Buthelezi willingly allowed himself to become a government chief.' Mbeki says Buthelezi was of the view that the apartheid regime should not have left room for the Bantu Authorities Act to be voluntary. Rather, Buthelezi said, '[my] suggestion is that it should be made compulsory like Bantu Education and other Acts of Parliament'.[56]

Although Buthelezi is correct when he says it was the ANC that cajoled him to form a political party, this was met with strong opposition internally. Mbeki posits that the ANC underestimated the capacity of the apartheid-created institutions:

They continued to believe that people who were not affiliated to the ANC could be trusted to fight apartheid from inside the apartheid-created institutions. This confidence led to a situation in which MK cadres being infiltrated into the country were instructed to call on Buthelezi. But the chief minister of KwaZulu Bantustan was playing a different game from that of the ANC in exile.[57]

Mbeki also reveals that it is Buthelezi himself who distanced Inkatha from the ANC. In a letter to Mary Benson, a civil-rights campaigner and author, Buthelezi claimed that he was acting on his own when he set up Inkatha. 'You know and I know that SASO [South African Students Organisation] was not spawned [by] the ANC. You know and I know that the BPC [Black People's Convention] was not spawned by the ANC. You know and I know that Inkatha was not spawned by the ANC.' Buthelezi argued that it was a political vacuum that forced him into political action.

> My whole political life was launched by the old ANC. I took up the position at Nongoma and then later at Ulundi because that was the judgement of the ANC's leadership ... if that leadership passes into political oblivion because of a faulty analysis and constant misconception of the South African struggle, then I will be released from a life-long commitment to do what I set out to do and not falter along the way.[58]

In her response, Benson expressed shock and told Buthelezi that, 12 years after he assumed leadership of KwaZulu, there had been no sign of Inkatha confronting the apartheid regime. She argued:

> In face of all the repression, the massive detentions, the torture and deaths and the terrible suffering of the people dumped in homelands, one never hears of genuine resistance from Inkatha – nor of its members being arrested or detained as are members of the equally non-violent UDF. And whereas the latter are banned from holding meetings, Inkatha can do so freely.[59]

Thus, Mbeki concluded, Buthelezi's role in the liberation struggle should not be judged by his own statements and what the media reported about him as these were attempts 'to build him as the chief spokesman of the African people'. 'Rhetoric aside,' argued Mbeki, 'he embodies Verwoerd's original conception of the Bantustan leader as a key element in the grand design of apartheid.'

For Mbeki, the true character and role of Buthelezi must be examined against the backdrop of his action on popular uprisings, especially in the 1980s. Ordinary people on the ground saw and understood his role in their oppression. Even attempts to locate Inkatha within the liberation movement by using ANC symbols and colours did not suffice. Still, these political manoeuvrings were insufficient, and Buthelezi and his party continued to lack credibility among the masses. Hence, the mourners showed him the door at Robert Sobukwe's funeral.

Consequently, Buthelezi took every opportunity to position himself as close to the ANC. When the ANC acceded to his request for a meeting in London in 1979, it was agreed that the meeting would be confidential. However, as Mbeki puts it, 'secrecy did not suit Buthelezi's purposes'. Upon his return from London, he briefed the media about the 'secret meeting'. It is precisely this behaviour that 'led to a rupture between the ANC and Inkatha'.

Oliver Tambo was forced to issue a statement to clarify the ANC's position. Subsequently, Buthelezi became brazen in his condemnation of the movement, including opposing Mandela's release. Contrary to his assertions about his role in persuading FW de Klerk to release Mandela, Mbeki revealed that when the Release Mandela Campaign began in 1980, the Inkatha National Council took the following resolution:

> National Council considers the 'Release Mandela' campaign an ill-conceived gimmick, albeit an exceptionally clever and deliberate ploy to undermine present day black leaders and bring about unbridgeable divisions in the black community. The campaign is even more ominous as it appears to be internationally orchestrated and could thus be a signal to an international onslaught against [the] black man's self-determination in this country.[60]

This was not the first time Buthelezi opposed Mandela's release. As early as 1973 he had expressed misgivings about the call to release political prisoners like Mandela. In a three-day 'multiracial conference' in East London on 9 November 1973, attended by all the bantustan leaders of the six homelands with the exception of Bophuthatswana's Lucas Mangope and initiated by the Progressive Party, the acting president of the Natal Indian Congress, MJ Naidoo, tabled a motion calling 'for the immediate release of Mandela' and all other 'silent leaders'. This did not go down well with Buthelezi, who until then 'had been treated by the white delegates as the star of the conference'. Apparently, he 'reacted angrily' and perceived the motion as denigrating to him 'as an inauthentic leader' and portrayed him as 'a stooge, in the presence of [the] "world press"'.[61]

Mbeki says the release of Mandela and other political prisoners was a threat to Buthelezi and his bantustan counterparts.[62] During this period the ANC was gaining popularity. As history would demonstrate later, Mandela and the ANC proved to be far more popular than the bantustan leaders who have been confined to the scrapheap of history. Mzala's book thus contributes to this history and so it is perceived as unpalatable by Buthelezi and his ilk.

Although Mzala's book is not devoid of error in content – and perhaps in methodology – it remains the only comprehensive critical analysis of Buthelezi.

CHAPTER 10

Aids: Misinformation, racism and the imperialist connection

I

In January 1988, just before the release of his book on Buthelezi, Mzala had been deployed by the SACP to the editorial board of *Problems of Peace and Socialism*, also known as the *World Marxist Review* (WMR), in Prague, Czechoslovakia. It was during this period that he became known as an SACP member.[1] Subsidised and edited by the Communist Party of the Soviet Union (CPSU), this monthly theoretical journal was produced by communist and workers' parties from around the world. It was published from Prague in about 37 languages and had a circulation of over half a million in the 1980s.[2] The journal boasted editors from 69 communist parties across the world and was read in some 145 countries.[3]

Having been on the WMR editor's council for about 10 years, Essop Pahad was now keen to return to London. Brian Bunting also felt that he was getting too old to continue editing the *African Communist*. Mzala was thus identified as a suitable replacement for both Pahad and Bunting. Says Pahad:

> For many of us in the Party, we were very keen that the next editor of the *African Communist* should be a young African because it was important

for the Party to demonstrate it was acceptable to a much larger section of our people. But it was also important to demonstrate the Party itself had young Black intellectuals, young Black thinkers, who could make a contribution to the serious theoretical debates.[4]

The SACP was determined to correct the perception that too many of its leading intellectual thinkers were white. Thus, to remove this stigma, it was considering its next moves carefully to identify young African Marxist-Leninist intellectuals. Pahad says it was important for these young intellectuals to emerge so that they could impact not only on the thinking of the Party, but also the thinking of the ANC and the wider movement. This was critical because the SACP had enjoyed a sound reputation not only within the ANC-headed movement but 'in the world communist movement'. As Pahad prepared to leave the WMR, there was the inevitable discussion around his replacement. Mzala's name came up strongly and eventually there was consensus that he should be the 'representative of the South African Communist Party on the editorial council of the *World Marxist Review*'.

With close to 10 years' experience in the editorial council, Pahad had a better understanding of the requirements of an SACP representative. He knew how the editorial council looked to the SACP, especially since there were so few representatives from Africa. It was thus important for the WMR to have representation from an African party. Pahad says, 'I felt very strongly that Mzala fitted very well for the *World Marxist Review*.' One of the major requirements for a representative on the editorial council included the ability to engage theoretically when articles were presented. Also, the person was expected to review and organise international seminars and participate in a way that enhanced them. For Pahad, 'Mzala fitted the bill'. So it was that a decision was taken that Mzala replace Pahad in Prague.

II

Immediately after his book was published, Mzala, Mpho and the children moved to Prague – but not for long. Upon arrival, Mzala underwent a battery of mandatory medical tests. Some of the tests came back unfavourable and, on the recommendation of their health authorities, the Communist Party of Czechoslovakia asked the WMR and the SACP to withdraw Mzala. The SACP felt that the decision was repugnant. 'To my utter anger,' says Pahad; 'I never got angry at a socialist country, and we always defended them willingly. Whatever happens, we defended the Soviet Union and the other socialist countries. That's how we were brought up. But what they did, I think, was outrageous.'[5]

In the absence of the medical records, the nature of the test undergone by Mzala that returned unfavourably remains unclear. However, speculation was rife that the tests included that for HIV – conjecture that has been repeated by many, both privately and publicly, without any substantiation. For example, in his book *Armed and Dangerous: From Undercover to Freedom*, Ronnie Kasrils writes that Mzala 'died in London of Aids in 1990 at the tragically young age of 33 but was never sexually promiscuous'.[6] Mzala's family say this speculation is both 'nonsensical' and baseless since they had access to Mzala's medical records. Nevertheless, leaders such as Pallo Jordan, Kasrils and Pahad all indicate that Mzala was 'diagnosed' HIV positive. None of them has ever seen Mzala's medical records, however. Thus, their views must be treated as conjecture.

Pahad and close comrades, especially Brian and Sonia Bunting, deliberated on the matter at great length. 'It was a great blow that the Czechoslovakian Party and authorities behaved in the way they behaved.' Due to their attitude towards socialist countries, the SACP did not want to be melodramatic about this uncomradely turn of events. Pahad says, 'We all decided that Mzala must come back to London, and he will work in the Party in London.'

Apart from the problematic attitude of the Czechoslovakian authorities, Mzala also found the weather in Prague miserable. The city, too, was limiting when it came to his other interests and activities, including his academic work. He found himself cut off from comrades he was working with closely. Mzala was still writing for *Sechaba*, and had a number of projects to pursue with Francis Meli, not to mention Brian Bunting and the *African Communist*. Mpho says, 'Being in Prague was too much and he could not be doing the commuting from Prague to London all the time.'

Another aspect that Mpho highlights about their experience in Prague is the cultural and practical challenges. 'There was also a language barrier for Sizwe, myself and Zwide.' So their stay in Prague lasted only three months; in fact, after only six weeks Mzala went back to England to prepare for the family's return. By October 1987, Mpho and the children were back in London. They stayed briefly with the Buntings before finding their own place and a school for the children.

Although he had been looking forward to the WMR experience, Mzala took the setback in his stride. Celeste Naidoo says that the deployment to the WMR was like a coup for Mzala. He was excited about it. Pahad believes it was a great shame that he couldn't stay because Mzala would have grown tremendously from the experience. Pahad points out, 'He would have been able to have that contact with representatives from Communist and Workers' Parties from throughout the world, including from the socialist countries.' He continues, 'That would have helped him to deepen his own understanding of Marxism-Leninism, but also a much deeper understanding of the world communist movement.'

Typically, Mzala did not allow this setback to dampen his spirits. On the contrary, it seemed to energise him to take on even more work. Says Pahad, 'That's the strength of Mzala, that should be a lesson for all of us, that when something drastic happens, something terrible happens to us, we should not allow that to destroy our personalities and our commitment.' Unlike most of us, Pahad says, this experience did not seem to put Mzala into a state of depression where he didn't do anything. 'In fact, Mzala was the opposite of that.' But Jordan says Mzala returned from this experience with a negative view of those parties, and full of questions about the character of the 'socialist states'.

> Ironically, in his questioning he turned to one of the more rigid members of the CC [Central Committee], [Sizakele] Sigxashe, who offered him Leon Trotsky's 'The Revolution Betrayed'. When I pointed out to Mzala that it was probably Trotsky's most controversial critique of the Stalin-led Soviet Union, he began to search elsewhere for answers. Apparently, while working with Bunting at the *African Communist*, they received an essay from two authors based in Harare, that was penned in opposition to an article on Leon Trotsky by one of the regular contributors to that journal, 'Dialego'. He leaked it to me for my comments, because the other members of the editorial board did not want the article published.

Jordan found the piece by the Harare-based authors, Themba and Mathole, rather superficial in many respects and was inspired to put his own pen to paper in response to Dialego (the pseudonym of British political scientist John Hoffman). The *African Communist* also refused to publish Jordan's 1989 letter in which he essentially challenged Dialego's negative assessment of Trotsky's role. Dialego had argued that, while most communists today would no longer accept the view as espoused by Stalin that Trotsky was 'an agent of fascism', few would deny that 'throughout his life Trotsky hindered rather than helped the struggle for socialism'.[7] Hoffman eventually became one of Mzala's PhD promoters. In his response, rejected by the *African Communist*, Jordan accused Dialego of relying on his own partisan construction of Trotsky's views. He posited that Dialego did not 'think it worthwhile to let us in on Trotsky's thinking'.[8]

In a later edition, the *African Communist* conceded that Dialego's piece had attracted a number of responses. The editors said they welcomed 'controversy and comment', but that they reluctantly decided against publishing the responses. The journal said it was 'disappointing' that the responses failed to engage the question of Trotskyism in South Africa before concluding that it was not its task to undertake the reappraisal of Trotsky and Trotskyism but rather to develop Marxist-Leninist thought in Africa.[9]

This experience did not go down well with Mzala. He considered it part of ongoing attempts in the movement to suppress discussion. He later confirmed to Gail Gerhart that when Jordan penned a critique against Dialego on some Trotskyist ideas, the *African Communist* refused to publish his letter. Said Mzala, 'Later one of the replies came out in Ibo Mandaza's journal in Harare, *Southern Africa*.' Mzala said Jordan told him that he had to get his piece published elsewhere because the ANC and party journals wouldn't have aired it.[10]

III

Back in London, Mzala continued where he had left off before his short-lived stint in Prague, and pretended to be undeterred by the negative experience. Nevertheless, he still made his first contribution to the WMR through the article 'The Volcano of the People's Wrath', published in the July 1988 edition.[11] Although disappointed by the turn of events in Prague, he did not lose focus on the bigger revolutionary objective and internationalist character of the struggle.

At this stage, Mzala began to work closely with Johnny Sachs, a South African medical scientist in the same SACP cell as Mzala. Sachs's scientific research was on HIV/Aids. Mzala got involved in Sachs's scientific world, and this culminated in two articles – 'Aids: Misinformation and Racism' and 'Aids and the Imperialist Connection' – in the 1988 October and November editions of *Sechaba*. There was clearly no social problem too big or small for Mzala to tackle head on.

The time Mzala spent researching the disease and its implications for the national liberation movement is evident in his writing. In the first article, Mzala observed that in less than 10 years, a deadly and previously unknown disease had come to represent what had probably become the major health crisis of the time. 'This disease is Aids – Acquired Immune Deficiency Syndrome,' he wrote, 'a name rarely out of the headlines, and a disease that has already outrivaled past scourges such as cholera, bubonic plague, syphilis and influenza.' This is how he opened the article:

> The mass media constantly report millions of people infected by the virus, called the Human Immunodeficiency Virus (HIV), many of whom are expected to die within the next five years or so, by which time twice the original number of people will have been infected.[12]

He indicated that by April 1988 more than 115 countries had reported over 85 000 cases to the World Health Organization (WHO), with the media estimating that more than 10 million people worldwide were infected. Like many other topics Mzala addressed, he demonstrated in-depth research, analysis and respect for the subject and, serious about unravelling some of the latent facts about the subject, used his usual fables to elucidate his point. He wrote, 'Science fiction writers could not have devised a more frightening disease if they tried: an artificial pestilence that kills [the] maximum number of people and which is incurable.' As frightening as these figures were, Mzala's character was to understand any problem comprehensively without succumbing to what might amount to misinformation and propaganda.

Part of understanding any challenge is to appreciate the politics and inherent internal contradictions. Thus, Mzala delved into the politics of the disease. He found it disconcerting that the media portrayed the disease as having originated from black people. 'Ordinarily persons of these continents,' referring to Europe and America, 'have been made to believe, and some of them are convinced, that they are victims of a health problem brought from outside their territories by immigrants, or through contact with Black people.' Mzala largely blamed scientific speculation for this public opinion. He indicated, for example, that in 1983 a certain Dr Gallo published a letter in the British medical journal *The Lancet* containing the first suggestions that the Aids virus had originated from Africa. For Mzala, it was from such theories that the belief, rationalisation and racist prejudice against black people emanated.

Even governments with reputations for progressive foreign policies also got infected (or exposed) by the demon of racism; they, too, compelled all Africans in their countries to have screening tests for Aids, and yet the same was not done to White European tourists, especially from the United States. In this instance, financial rather than medical considerations prevailed; still, it was, in effect, racism.[13]

Mzala also observed how even lobbyists in Britain fell for the racist trap, insisting that Africans coming into the country should be tested for HIV infection before they could enter. He cited the Whitehall Report leaked to the *Sunday Telegraph* in September 1986, which suggested that visitors from Africa 'could be subject to compulsory tests'. He also highlighted a piece in the *Daily Telegraph*, which he said, almost in a state of frenzy with racist rhetoric, referred to the 'invading Black hordes', and warned that 'in a few days' time, hundreds of students from Zambia, Uganda and Tanzania will be arriving in this country. A significant proportion of them – possibly up to 100% – could be [Aids] carriers'. Mzala noted that even South Africa had joined the frenzy of testing African mineworkers from other African countries while excluding white mineworkers. Through this article Mzala scientifically traced the origins of the disease and argued that it was not 'specifically an African disease'.

What troubled Mzala mostly about the developments around HIV/Aids was the clear lack of understanding of the essence of the disease, particularly when it came to screening. He felt that some of the tests were not foolproof. Again, he invoked scientific data to demonstrate that some samples and tests conducted in Africa were false positives. He concluded, 'A detailed analysis of the results of blood tests in Africa, therefore, seem to dispel the popular myth, which has been claimed by many believers in Europe and America, that the HIV originated in Africa and then spread to the West.'

Discernible from his writings is that Mzala was searching for answers and clues about this disease. It is unsurprising, therefore, that he – as he always did – immediately followed with another article in the next instalment of *Sechaba*. In the November 1988 edition, Mzala penned the article 'Aids and the Imperialist Connection' in which he detailed several theories that had been advanced about the origin of Aids.

The problem with reports about [Aids] is that they start at the end of the story, not at the beginning. No serious and informed attempt has yet been made to question why such a deadly virus could suddenly spring from 'nowhere' and infect millions of people within a relatively short time.[14]

Mzala, like many scientists, including social scientists, was grappling with the growing number of questions about the virus, and there were very few answers. Among the questions he posed were:

> Where was the virus all the time? Was it there among human beings or certain animals, but lying dormant until it was triggered by something? If so, why did the animal kingdom (including human beings) not develop antibodies to it during its latent stage? How did the virus get into the blood of certain animals, how did it cross the species barrier and infect human beings? And why have scientists and medical researchers not found any animal infected with HIV?

Mzala's typically inquisitive mind was in overdrive, posing question after question as a dialectical method to get closer to the truth.

He argued that it would be useful to answer these questions. 'This is not to suggest that doctors should stop combating the epidemic and merely stand around wondering where the virus came from.' Nevertheless, he was keen not to neglect the important question on the origins of the disease. In his research he interrogated studies by the Southeast Asia Treaty Organization (SEATO), which had conducted experiments in the 1960s to induce cancer in monkeys. He found the similarities between the disease of these monkeys and human Aids striking. Mzala also perused the report of a 1970s' military project in the United States that he claimed corroborated the findings of SEATO.

Like an expert medical scientist, Mzala cited studies on immune deficiency by the California National Primate Research Center and began to hint that there could have been 'less noble' motives behind these studies, that HIV could be a laboratory product. He argued:

> There is evidence to suggest that two different viruses can be genetically combined to create a new one, a process known in genetic engineering as phenotypic mixing (swapping of genes). The newly-created virus may take some properties from both parents and possess infecting capabilities in a far wider range of species than the individual parent.

At this stage, Mzala was gobbling up any information that could offer clues about his newly found area of interest. To back up his case, he cited a report from the London *Sunday Express* of 26 October 1986, in which some scientists expressed an opinion that more than one virus may have combined to give rise to human Aids. Inevitably, this led him closer to what he could have wanted to know about the ideological enemy, the imperialist United States and its Central Intelligence Agency (CIA). In this article, Mzala pointed his finger at the CIA and its 'germ warfare'. He argued, 'It is common knowledge among politically conscious people that in the 1970s the Cuban government alleged, on the basis of its successful infiltration of the CIA, that the United States government was planning to infect Cuban pigs with African swine fever, in the hope that the Cuban population would eat contaminated pork.'

It is on these bases that Mzala entertained possibilities of germ warfare. 'Was this a result of experiments of human beings by those keen to develop germ warfare?' He did not rule out possibilities of a laboratory experiment that went wrong. Admitting that no laboratory can guarantee the absolute security of its work in germ experimentation, he cited the Marburg virus incident in 1976 when laboratory workers in Frankfurt an der Oder, a city in East Germany, contracted a disease from their working environment leading to the deaths of some workers. Hence, he laid the blame for the rise of previously unknown infections on the ecological disruption and human invasion of the animal environment. He wrote, 'A series of new diseases has come about because of the experiments with animals ... but also more specifically because of the work on the germ warfare that goes on within military establishments and laboratories.' By locating the origins of HIV in the laboratories of the military-industrial complex, it made it easier to point a finger at the imperialists.

Although he admitted that there was inconclusive evidence that HIV was developed in the laboratories of the US military establishment, he still believed that sufficient facts existed to suggest that Aids-like viruses were being created through genetic engineering within these establishments. This led him to conclude that:

> Our task is not to make wild and irresponsible statements, even if they are against the class forces that are hostile to us. Serious analysts, we believe, should not be alarmists. But, on the basis of facts, we can proclaim that the international community needs to develop a sensitive awareness of the proceedings within military laboratories, as well as within those civilian laboratories where dangerous germs are being created.[15]

The research Mzala had been conducting with Sachs was visible. Pallo Jordan is of the view that during this period Mzala developed scepticism about the disease. He says, 'As with so many such illnesses there had been all sorts of speculation about its origins.' He continues, 'At one point it was rumoured to have originated in the US prison system – and as such was said to have infected the male homosexual community first. Later, there were speculations of cross species infection – from animals to humans.' When information about Wouter Basson (South African Defence Force chemical expert), Lothar Neethling (former head of forensics for the South African Police) and others involved in apartheid's chemical and biological warfare programme leaked, Jordan says Mzala was convinced that some in the ANC had been deliberate targets.

It emerged during the Truth and Reconciliation Commission (TRC) hearings that apartheid security forces, led by the likes of Neethling and Basson, used chemical and biological warfare against anti-apartheid activists. Mzala's intervention would become a point of reference post-apartheid as the country battled the world's biggest HIV epidemic, with an estimate of over seven million people living with the virus in 2018.[16] To some, Mzala is considered the 'ANC's first public Aids-sceptic' mainly due to these two articles.[17] He was nevertheless the first within the movement to publicly engage this matter. Because of the context and period the articles were written, it is unsurprising that the posture in his analysis on the emergence of the disease took an anti-apartheid, anti-imperialist perspective.[18] In reality, just as in many organisations globally, Mzala's articles revealed that the ANC was still trying to understand the disease.

Elaine Unterhalter, who shared what she describes as 'a tiny corridor of an office' with Mzala at the Research on Education in South Africa (RESA), recalls a long and distressing conversation they had one day about HIV after Mzala had published the two articles. Unterhalter says Mzala pointed out that the 'big pharma' was not simply benign and the issue thus had to be understood in the context of Africa's colonial history. The controls over health, he argued, were linked to the control over people. 'These were compelling arguments, and he had many facts, figures and stories,' writes Unterhalter. 'I was shaken because I had only a simple way of thinking about illness and treatment, and the numbers and suffering involved. I could not connect the many accounts of the ravages of the virus with the larger political economy background.'[19]

IV

From the day Mzala met and married Mpho, his life revolved around his family. Most people who interacted with him during this time express their admiration for his commitment to his family. Amid soaring political and academic responsibilities, Mzala remained a dedicated and present husband and father. Says Patric Mellet, 'He was a family man who loved his wife and children very much.'

> He was a clean-living, incorruptible Seventh Day Adventist [SDA] communist soldier and family man. His thoughts and actions were all orientated around working people across the spectrum, black and white. For people like me and our working-class families that is how we want our heroes to be. Mzala was a working-class hero.

When Mzala's daughter was born in 1988, they were waiting for Mzala's parents to visit them in London – hence he named her Balindelwe, loosely translated as 'being awaited'. Titi says he told her that 'he named both his children after his parents because the first son is Zwide meaning my father and then the second-born, a girl named after my mother Balindile, because they were expecting them'. Because of this love and commitment to his family, Mzala encouraged Mpho to complete her studies on a full-time basis while he worked from home, taking care of the children. So he, while finalising his master's degree, stayed at home with Zwide and Balindelwe while Sizwe and Mpho were at school. Mpho says that while he was handy in taking care of the children, including dropping Sizwe off at school, she dreaded the sight that confronted her when she got home. 'I knew that when coming back, I will find the whole house a mess. But I didn't mind.'

Mzala regarded Saturday as a family day to rest, and avoided attending engagements apart from family errands. Occasionally, Mpho left the house under the pretext that she was taking the children out to play, but she had discovered a Seventh Day Adventist church. Religion had been a taboo subject in Mpho's exile life. Unbeknown to her, however, he had been raised in the same church. One Saturday, Mzala decided he was going to tag along and was shocked when Mpho confessed that this is where she had been going on Saturdays. Henceforth, observing the Sabbath became part of their Saturday ritual.

Apart from close family members and friends like Patric Mellet, not many were aware of Mzala's commitment to his faith. Later, when

Mzala's younger brother Dumisani, who was also studying in the United Kingdom, revealed that Mzala was a Christian, some comrades like the Buntings scoffed at the suggestion. They were convinced that Dumisani was 'completely wrong in saying Mzala continued to be Christian'. Based on their intimate friendship, including the fact that Mzala had stayed with them at some point, they believed that, like themselves, Mzala was a materialist and 'certainly not a church-goer'.[20]

Mpho says it was in London that their relationship matured, and they were able to openly talk about matters such as religion. In December 1989, when Mzala's mother – a committed and staunch SDA member – visited, Mzala was quick to refer her to Mpho when she enquired about the nearest church. Like Mzala, she was pleasantly surprised that her daughter-in-law attended the same church. This common factor played an important role in building the relationship with mother and daughter-in-law. Mpho says that, due to his open embrace of both religion and communism, they found Fidel Castro a useful political role model. 'I even bought two books actually because he knew that I admired Fidel Castro.'

In the *New York Times* interview published on 24 January 1989, Mzala confirmed his recent focus on reading about both Castro and religion. He spoke about Karl Marx's perspective that 'religion is an opium of the masses' before highlighting that Lenin had to address the same question, 'not only as a theoretical question but as a practical question. He sought to emphasise the unity of peoples towards the actual building of socialism, irrespective of their ideological viewpoint.' He continued:

> Let me quote something that is often said by our General Secretary, Comrade Joe Slovo. He says there are two good people that he has found in the world and that is a good Christian and a good Communist. And I have been reading a lot of material as well, like Fidel Castro on religion, and he seems to adopt the same position.[21]

By referring to Slovo as 'our General Secretary' Mzala was no longer concealing his SACP membership. It was apparent that, although he was a committed communist and a member of the SACP, he was still firmly rooted in his Christian beliefs, imbued in him by his parents. He could see a positive trend in the convergence of Christianity and communism and hence he found comfort in the views of communist leaders like Lenin and Castro. Characterising this convergence as a 'really potentially great social movement', he argued: 'The Communist movement on the one hand and the Christian movement, which ... was originally a very solid, anti-private-property movement, a movement that was persecuted by the ruling class.'

Mzala's erudite perspectives on Christianity demonstrated the deep insights of someone well versed on the topic of Christianity, while at the same time he was determined to ground his beliefs in the concrete material conditions. He postulated that the founding fathers of the Christian Church found themselves in dungeons and persecuted by the Roman emperors 'precisely because their notion was that of sharing, was that of humility, was that which was directed toward the deprived and the underprivileged in society'.

V

Although focused on his studies, Mzala had established a working routine that did not neglect his family and primary revolutionary responsibilities. He was spending most of his time writing and, when not, he was attending political activities, including speaking opportunities. Says Essop Pahad, 'We could send him to different conferences, seminars, knowing that Mzala wouldn't let you down.' Sometimes he would be double-booked, recalls Mpho, and he would write a speech and ask her to present it.

His main contribution in the *African Communist* at this time was the 'Africa Notes and Comment' column, which appeared under one of his pseudonyms, Jabulani Mkhatshwa. Until that point, the column had been written by several different individuals under various names, such as Du Bois and Ahmed Azad. These articles demonstrated Mzala's versatility as a researcher, writer and analyst. He engaged with developments in Africa with ease, providing insights relevant to the movement and progressive forces. His analyses were dialectical and premised on the large body of work he had already produced.

In his first article 'Senegal: What Manner of Democracy? Economic Aid: Till Debt do us Part; Mozambique: Amnesty for the Bandits', Mzala painted a picture on the latest developments on the continent. He accused Senegalese president Abdou Diouf of 'pretence' after having 'preached a doctrine of political tolerance and national unity' when he addressed a conference that brought together delegations from the ANC and white Afrikaans-speaking academics from South Africa. After having basked in the media limelight that portrayed Senegal as 'a democratic country concerned with reconciliation and justice', in less than a year, argued

Mzala, 'this pretence of democracy' was destroyed when Diouf imprisoned opposition leaders following elections characterised by opposition parties as 'a tragedy and farce'. In his analysis, Mzala grappled with the question that continues to haunt Africa to this day: the external debt obligation. Citing that, by 1988, African countries had an external debt estimated at $200 billion, Mzala argued that this debt was not purely a financial nature but rather that it had 'a clearly defined political dimension'.

In the second part of the article Mzala addressed a matter closer to the movement, after the Mozambican People's Assembly passed a law that granted amnesty to bandits backed by South Africa 'if they voluntarily surrendered themselves to the authorities'. Mzala had spent time in Mozambique as a soldier of MK until the country signed the Nkomati Accord with apartheid South Africa. The Accord rendered ANC efforts and Mzala's concept of people's war difficult. Yet, in his analysis, Mzala was still supportive of Frelimo and the People's Assembly decision. In his view, the problem was not the activities of the Mozambique National Resistance Movement (RENAMO) but rather the source of its existence, the apartheid regime. Hence, he concluded, 'Not until the apartheid regime is overthrown can the situation in Mozambique return to normal.'[22]

In the next edition of the *African Communist,* Mzala's article 'Angola: A Military Defeat for the Racists' focused on the defeat of the South African army at Cuito Cuanavale. Mzala was in a buoyant mood and regarded the developments as an indication of 'a significant deterioration in the situation from the racist's point of view'. He felt that this represented 'a dramatic shift in the military balance of power'. He outlined the aggressive encroachment of the SADF, working with rebels of UNITA, into the Angolan territory. They had not bargained for the 'humiliating defeat' that awaited them. He wrote:

> Underestimating the revolutionary forces, the arrogant racist troops attempted to break Cuito Cuanavale's defence through the use of their long-range artillery. In response, a courageous and well-coordinated counteroffensive was launched by the Angolan Cuban forces which decisively pushed back the racist troops almost to the border of Namibia.

The second part of the article focuses on the twenty-fifth anniversary of the OAU, what he called the 'silver jubilee'. Admitting that the struggle for the total liberation of Africa from colonialism was not yet complete, he nevertheless extolled the OAU's commitment to the liberation mission.

'Yet, despite these problems' – referring to the lack of African unity that dogged the organisation – 'it can truly be said that when judged in historical terms, the OAU has legitimate grounds to pride itself on growing qualitatively.' Thus, through his column, Mzala demonstrated his versatility as a revolutionary fighter not only for the national liberation in South Africa but also as a pan-Africanist and internationalist. In the same article he posited that for Africa, more than any other continent, the anti-apartheid struggle was of immediate political, moral and material concern to the broader working masses. He argued, 'Indeed, Africa's energies can best be concentrated if, and when, the Namibia and South African problem has been resolved.'[23]

In the same edition, Mzala reviewed Francis Meli's book *South Africa Belongs to Us: A History of the ANC*. Mzala regarded it as 'an important historical development' that the history of the ANC had been written by an ANC member. At the time of the writing his book, Meli was the editor of *Sechaba* and a member of the ANC's NEC. Sadly, when he died in 1990, Meli was mired in controversy after it was alleged that he had spied for South African Military Intelligence.[24]

Mzala's perception of Meli's book was informed by what he regarded as 'critical observers of the South African liberation movement', whom he thought had been, to a certain extent, justified to accuse South African revolutionaries of lacking an intellectual culture. 'When comparison is made with the Vietnamese,' he asserted, 'it is noted that most of their leaders ... wrote about their revolutionary experience.' Mzala argued that the ANC had paid a price for this neglect with the 'mushrooming of a number of so-called experts on the ANC outside of the ANC itself, most of whom are marketing theories that show very little understanding of the ANC and its history'. Nevertheless, Mzala believed that the book left many questions unanswered, questions that only an ANC historian with the privilege of looking from within could unravel. Thus, he concluded, 'Meli may need to give us this benefit in a second edition or a second volume of the book.'[25]

In the second-quarter edition of the *African Communist*, Mzala presented a comprehensive review of Mikhail Gorbachev's *Perestroika: New Thinking for Our Country and the World*. Writing as Sisa Majola, Mzala welcomed Gorbachev's stance on human morality that 'transcends class antagonisms and their legacies'. After all, since its foundation the Soviet Union, he argued, had 'rendered moral, material and diplomatic support to the forces fighting for social progress, national independence, peace and democracy.'[26]

VI

Mzala's zest for life, energy and enthusiasm can be understood through his prolific production of a large volume of work during this period. His words to Lungile Pepani while in the GDR in 1979 – 'There's no time to rest, mzala' – can be fully appreciated through his work during this epoch. Although some may have thought of him as 'loud' and that most of his writings were 'party hack', that could be understood in the context of what Mzala believed to be 'jealousy' on the part of certain comrades because of his proximity to the leaders. Yet another substantial and more scholarly work by Mzala emerged at this time in the form of a chapter in *The National Question in South Africa* edited by Maria van Diepen. This chapter came out of a conference paper he presented at the University of Amsterdam in 1986.

In this piece Mzala dealt with his academic research interests and argued, 'The national question in South Africa is a controversial issue in relation to both theory and practice.'[27] He discussed critiques of concepts such as 'colonialism of a special type' and the 'two-stage theory' that had come under the spotlight. For Mzala, the national question had received adequate attention from within the movement, inspired by Marxist theories, and in his view, the thesis of the South African liberation movement, as represented by the ANC–SACP alliance, on the national question was a creative application 'of the most advanced theoretical principles of social change'. He considered this application as having been inspired by an internationalist perspective of the working-class movement, but fundamentally and by a concrete study of indigenous conditions, and thus 'it represents a contribution to the development of Marxist theory and practice'.

Mzala's articulation of the concept of the 'nation' in the context of Marxism is interesting in that he sought to apply Marx's thinking to the nation-formation process and accompanying problems of national oppression. 'If, as Lenin argued,' he wrote, 'nations proper emerged in society during the capital epoch as an inevitable product, an inevitable form, in the bourgeois epoch of social production then the decisive role in the inception of the national form of social development was the economic factor, the common economic life.' Mzala sought to first set the scene of the South African scenario, where race was another dimension to the question. To this end, he linked the emergence of the labour movement in the country to the first generation of white artisans who immigrated to South Africa and having belonged to labour and social organisations in their countries of origin.

For Mzala, the articulation of a coherent argument on the South African national question had to be grounded in the arrival of the white settler colonial community that ultimately became an internal colonising force, uniting to form the Union of South Africa in 1910. This in turn, according to Mzala, compelled the scattered African tribes to unite, culminating in the formation of the ANC in 1912 in an attempt to forge their own nationhood. With the two hostile camps formed inside the country, Mzala then traced the emergence of non-racialism to the role of communists. He considered the formation of the International Socialist League (ISL) a turning point in labour movement politics in South Africa. For the first time in the history of white labour organisations they pledged solidarity with the African quest for freedom. Out of the ISL, the Communist Party of South Africa would emerge in 1921 and, with its close relationship with the Third International (Comintern), the right to self-determination was elevated. Mzala argued, 'For the first time the national question was transferred from being a specific country's problem into a global problem of emancipating oppressed peoples and colonies from the yoke of imperialism.'[28]

Indeed, the Comintern's intervention through the 'black republic' thesis would be crucial to the national question. With this, argued Mzala, the Communist Party was enjoined 'to struggle by all methods against every racial prejudice in the ranks of white workers and to eradicate entirely such prejudices from its own ranks'. The national and class struggles are thus central, since, in the context of South Africa, 'the black working class, which is not only oppressed as part of the nation but also exploited by capital, is the most uncompromising enemy of race and class oppression'.[29]

Those who spent time with Mzala during this period say he radiated joy and happiness when debating the national question. Mellet recalls Mzala's views on the subject as uncompromisingly linked to 'ensuring an uninterrupted move towards socialism' along similar lines as the Cuban revolution. Of course, he emphasised that Mzala was never dogmatic and so he did not envision or entertain that the South African revolution would be a carbon copy. As far as Mpho is concerned, 'when you talk about the national question, you are talking about Mzala'. This was his passion and commitment. Of all the unending discussions that went well into the night, Blade Nzimande says the national question is 'what was foremost to Mzala'.[30]

This was not a new-found passion for Mzala, of course, but a commitment developed early on in his life. He was keen to understand and present part of the solution to the South African national question. Thus, he read and cited a wide range of scholars. In a letter to the editor of *Sechaba* in December 1984, Mzala did not hold back when a debate of the South African identity ensued. In the end, he argued:

> To suggest that people need only call themselves 'South African' is to ignore the reality that South Africans are composed of Indians, Coloureds, and even, for that matter, Zulus, Xhosas, Sothos, etc. Our democratic Republic will definitely develop the positive aspects of my Zulu culture, language and so on, so that I, together with those of my ethnic group, can contribute a cultural flower to the banquet of South African culture.[31]

Nzimande says Mzala was taking the discourse on the national question to new heights. 'He was doing some parallel research on the origins of the southern African Bantu people. And he had lots of notes.' He was spending time doing research at the British Library because 'his preoccupation was to refute ethnicity and tribalism' and, to achieve this objective, he deemed it necessary to trace the origins of the Bantu people from around the tenth century. 'He would tell me the stories about his discoveries,' recalls Nzimande, his primary objective being 'to refute this thing of Zulu tribalism'.[32] His central thesis was that 'a tribe, or an ethnic group is a historical creation. It's not an inherent thing. It gets formed over years but originally, there were no tribes like Zulus and everything.'

VII

Mzala's varied interests – be they his family, academic or social life – all coalesced around his revolutionary objectives and commitments. Comrades at the printing press were working long hours, from early morning until late at night, living in an underground South African bubble in one of the world's super-cities, London. Mzala would often join them and, whenever possible, would lend a helping hand. However, his objective was to find people who could discuss politics so he could take a break from his punishing writing schedule. 'If he saw that we had to work late he would work late so that we had company travelling and waiting for buses or trains in the wintry weather,' says Mellet.

He was truly a brother as well as a comrade and he genuinely cared about people. He came to London at a time when one of our comrades Sello Moeti (Michael Lebese) got ill and rapidly went downhill. It affected our morale greatly. Sello was one of those guys (actually a lot like Mzala) that did not smoke, drink alcohol or take medications. He was a health fanatic who would not even take aspirins. ... Mzala showed great care for Sello.

Towards the end of 1988, Mzala had completed his master's degree at Essex University. Shula Marks, another South Africa-born historian, encouraged Mzala to pursue a PhD. In 1989, initially under Harold Wolpe, he began a thesis focusing 'on ethnicity as a factor in South African politics'.[33] Not long after he registered, Mzala moved to the Open University where he had two promoters. One was James Anderson, based at the Open University. Mzala would later describe him as the one who did not 'know much'. The other was Rhodesia-born John Hoffman from Leicester University, whom he held in high regard. Hoffman was a regular contributor to the *African Communist* as Dialego. Mzala's research topic was on the national question, and the working title of his thesis was 'Ethnicity and the Problems of Nation-Formation in South Africa'.

It is with Hoffman that Mzala published an academic article, 'Non-Historic Nations and the National Question: A South African Perspective', in the journal *Science & Society*. The article was a response to Ephraim Nimni's 1989 piece titled 'Marx, Engels and the National Question'. Mzala and Hoffman argued that Nimni's failure to 'identify the development of nationhood with the battle for self-determination and democracy means that he is unable to identify nations in any kind of critical and materialist way'. In their view, South Africa's national liberation struggle could not be coherently sustained unless there was a clear differentiation 'between the authentic South African nation with its right to self-determination and inauthentic "non-historic nations" which have been used as building blocks of apartheid strategy'.[34] This provides a glimpse into Mzala's scholarly interest. Having already contributed a chapter to Van Diepen's book on the national question and, through this work and his 'theoretical heavy' PhD, Mzala was keen to demonstrate the serious problem of ethnicity in South Africa.

But the reason Mzala ended up at Open University was largely due to his fractious relationship with Harold Wolpe. While it was a privilege for any young comrade to work under Wolpe's tutelage, his relationship with Mzala is said to have been a difficult one. At some point Mzala was employed at RESA, an initiative begun by Wolpe in 1985. The focus was on education for a post-apartheid South Africa, and one of the project's first papers, in 1988, was on the Soweto school uprising of 1976.[35]

At the heart of the tension between Wolpe and Mzala was the national question – the issue of race, in particular. Their difference pertained to the interpretation of the concept of colonialism of a special type (CST) as put forward by the SACP in its 1962 programme, *The Road to South African Freedom*. The central thesis of the CST concept was on the internal colonial force of an oppressor white minority that occupied the same territory as the oppressed black majority.[36] Comrades such as Blade Nzimande, Jeremy Cronin and John Pampallis, who were close to both Wolpe and Mzala, confirm that theirs was a 'difficult' relationship due to these theoretical divergences. Nzimande stated, 'I think it was around theoretical issues, in particular disagreements on [CST].' Pampallis confirmed this notion, adding that 'Mzala was quite dismissive of Harold's work'. Cronin admitted that there was 'quite a tough falling-out' between the two. Another activist and student and colleague of Wolpe, Thozamile Botha, also acknowledged the arguments the two had. Mzala, as a scholar of the national question, is said to have felt that Wolpe downplayed the role of race and elevated class in the debate.[37]

Another dimension to the difficult relationship is explained by John Daniel. He indicated that Wolpe gave Mzala 'a hard time' when he began his doctorate. Apparently, Wolpe had wanted Mzala to take a particular course and also to drop the rigid line he had adopted on the national question. Wolpe would have students prepare papers and then critique them in tough sessions, and 'one of these ended in Mzala walking out'. This is how he ended up at the Open University where he had already established some contacts.[38] Prior to his departure, Mzala had told Howard University's historian Robert Edgar, who was visiting London at the time, that Wolpe was a rigid Marxist, and he was having to cope with that. Edgar shared many of Mzala's interests, particularly history and current developments in South Africa. On their train ride to London, Mzala was open with him about his tribulations with Wolpe. Mzala told Edgar that even Botha, also based at RESA, was experiencing major differences with Wolpe.[39]

Steven Friedman notes that, because the two men had different life experiences, the disagreement may have been deeper than just a difference over CST. Whereas white communists like Wolpe emerged from a middle-class background 'whose university education enabled them to hold teaching posts, write for journals and read the new European Marxism', Mzala's praxis was grounded in the MK camps and ANC underground, thus making him an organic intellectual. Elaine Unterhalter told Friedman that 'by the time Mzala arrived at RESA, he had "had a lot of terrible experiences in MK" and was also ravaged by illness – he was engaged in a political and personal battle for survival.' On the other hand, she noted that Wolpe did not face challenges in the movement in the way Mzala did. To this day, debates on race and class within the movement continue.

By now, Mzala had become well known as a fierce and uncompromising character. He never backed down or changed his mind easily; instead, as Vusi Mavimbela recalled from their days at the University of Zululand, 'he stuck to his arguments with ferocity and tenacity of a bull terrier and often left injured souls on the debating floor'. Even though his disagreements with Wolpe could be based on principles, it is highly unlikely that he walked away based on this disagreement alone. Nevertheless, the fellowship grant he received from the Open University during this period enabled him to relax about money, and may have contributed to his decision.

However, Unterhalter writes about the challenges many black comrades faced in their interactions with white liberal intellectuals. She is of the view that 'the different race and class experiences of South Africa and London, twisted personal and professional relationships away from the solidarity we tried to build in other ways'. She remembers Mzala as someone who had a wonderful talking style. 'His eyes sparkled,' she says. 'He picked up an idea and played on it, like a musical instrument.' Unterhalter recalls his many stories that, although serious, were 'told with a light touch'. She regrets not raising obvious questions she should have asked at the time. She writes:

> I had a small car and was a nervous driver. We were on our way to a meeting at Harold Wolpe's house and the petrol gauge read empty. The choice was to go to look for petrol and be late for the meeting, or to try to get to the meeting but possibly run out of petrol. 'Take the risk,' Mzala said. 'Turn off the engine as you go down the hills.' He had once been in a plane, he said, with other comrades that had to make a forced landing in Libya. They had to fasten their seatbelts and hope. It was okay, he said. They bumped, the plane juddered, but they landed. I felt reassured (and we got to the meeting). Maybe it was his tone. There was too much I did not ask. Why had they been forced to land in Libya? What had happened next?[40]

Daniel stated that Mzala was still involved in 'so many things that it's a wonder he can do them all'. This included 'a lot of work on the *African Communist*'. His ability to write 'very quickly' was an advantage and Daniel was convinced that Mzala was serious about becoming an academic. Fuelled by his burning passion to read and write, it is understandable that Mzala would fancy academia as a career choice. His perception of the university was 'spotty', according to Daniel, and he still couldn't believe that people could be paid to just study and teach.

VIII

It is in London that Mzala had the best time in exile. Although working hard for the movement, for the first time in years many people who were important to him were close by. His wife and his children and two of his siblings were all around, as were close comrades, like Meli. Mzala was pursuing his dream to become an academic while writing for the journals of the movement, and his insatiable appetite for debate saw him contribute articles even to the mainstream media. In London he flourished amid a broad-church movement, with many currents of varying proportions.[41]

Reflecting about this moment, Patric Mellet portrays Mzala as a figure who existed within a context of many opinions and ideological variations in the ranks of the movement. Yet Mzala never lost his ideological convictions, with many of his interventions grounded in Marxism-Leninism. Whereas the generation of the 1970s and 1980s had a plurality of thoughts, says Mellet, there was a healthy tension in the movement and hence an influx into the ANC from the BCM, disillusioned New Unity Movement members and other ideologies.

Mellet recalls that there was a growing tendency towards liberation and black theologies in the churches and mosques. 'The younger generations looked at Latin America, other parts of Africa and Southeast Asia rather than having an orthodox Eastern European dogmatic approach nor a European/North American approach.' Mzala embraced this development and befriended many comrades across the ideological landscape, among them comrades such as John Lamola, who was pursuing a PhD in Philosophy and Theology at Edinburgh University. Mzala would take long train rides from London to Edinburgh just to discuss critical theory and liberation theology with Lamola. As a Marxist-Leninist and Christian, the question of Marxism and religion was important to Mzala personally.

Mellet observed a number of ideological currents that were as old as the ANC. A 'narrow ethno-nationalism', which could be traced to the 1960s, pre- and post-Morogoro Conference, was one of the strong poles in London. He thinks another strong and dominant pole was that of the 'national liberationists who, unlike the nationalist orientation around notions of a sub-Saharan African race, were focused on countering colonialism and imperialism to avoid neo-colonial outcomes to the struggle'.[42] Amid these ideological currents, Mzala never kept quiet but rather made his views known in meetings with comrades. Mellet reflects:

> [Mzala] was a class-conscious proponent of socialism and was anti narrow ethno-nationalism, seeing these as only a slight variation on Verwoerdian politics of multiple nations and Bantustanism. Mzala stood firmly against the multi-nation thesis in the national question debate. He was also not entirely orientated towards the two-nation theory. He was more of a proponent of a no-nation/nation-in-the-making thesis.[43]

For Mellet, Mzala's engagement in the struggle for national liberation was focused mainly on understanding the nature of imperialism, colonialism and the dangers of neo-colonialism. To this end, winning all forces and building maximum unity of the alliance towards national liberation while keeping colonialism and imperialism at bay to ensure independence were important to him. This is how Mzala perceived the notion of building a better life for all, and he was anxious about the need to intensify the struggle. At this stage, the ANC and the regime were already engaged in talks, with political prisoners like Govan Mbeki and Harry Gwala having been released in 1987 on 'humanitarian grounds'. They were soon joined by Walter Sisulu and seven other political prisoners in 1989.[44]

As Mzala observed the movement entering new terrain, Mellet remembers that he worried about the possible rise of reactionary tendencies that could marginalise progressive forces within the movement. He was acutely aware that such developments could set the socialist struggle back in many ways. He was concerned that the ANC was being manipulated, that it 'was pushing us too quickly towards a negotiation scenario'. Part of his concern was what he perceived as 'a death blow to the aims and objectives' of national liberation as articulated in the 1930s by the likes of Moses Kotane, Cissie Gool, James La Guma and John Gomas. Says Mellet:

> Mzala was convinced that the downfall of the ANC as a national

liberation movement was being engineered from the inside with support from without. His discussions on the national question, land question and economic question were electrifying and he made it easy to understand as he understood the language of the common men and women.

IX

It was during this period that Harry Gwala visited London. He had been released from his second stint in prison in November 1988, following political pressure from various organisations and medical specialists. Gwala, suffering from a debilitating motor-neuron disease that had robbed him the use of his arms,[45] hit it off immediately with Mzala. 'He found a wonderful soulmate in Mzala,' who was much younger than him, recalls Essop Pahad. Pahad believes Gwala, whose bodily movements were now seriously restricted due to his illness, had a lot in common with Mzala. 'He was coming from the heart of the fire in the struggle against the IFP and the violence,' says Pahad, 'so Harry used to take very tough positions with respect to the IFP.' With Mzala's radical stance on Buthelezi and Inkatha, they had a lot in common.

According to Mellet, part of the reason why Gwala ended up in the UK had to do with bad health combined with security considerations, and so the movement deemed it necessary for Gwala to seek medical treatment that side. 'Mzi looked after him in London.' One of the people who convinced Gwala to seek medical treatment outside the country to see whether his hands could be fixed was Blade Nzimande. Nzimande felt the regime was already on the back foot and many people were going outside to meet with the ANC. Also, Nzimande was going on a sabbatical to Oxford University, and this made things easy for him to leave with Gwala. Apart from spending time with Mzala, Gwala's schedule was hectic, meeting many people and spending time with Oliver Tambo who was recuperating in London after his second stroke.

Pahad's recollection is of Mzala and Gwala spending a lot of time together. Mzala helped Gwala settle in London because 'it's not easy when you just come to a strange country' and, says Mellet, his darkroom at the liberation printing press became a secure private interview room for Mzala and Gwala. 'Mzi always needed to keep his finger on the pulse of South Africa and I think that he may have been writing a book on Harry's life.' Mzala's interest in writing Gwala's biography culminated in numerous interviews where he used 'both video and audio equipment and was said to have produced a manuscript'.[46] Nzimande confirms that Mzala conducted a lot of recorded interviews with Gwala in 1989 while they we in the UK.

Like Mzala, Gwala was a well-known theoretician in the SACP. Prisoners on Robben Island, says Pahad, relied on Gwala 'for guidance on the theory and practice of Marxism-Leninism and on the theory of revolution in South Africa'. During both his spells of imprisonment, Gwala played a pivotal role in driving political education. He would later remark that political education in prison 'was a matter of do or die' and 'we had no problem with the restrictions imposed on us because we carried out our political activities'.[47]

Mzala found Gwala a useful companion who supported his thoughts on numerous topics of interest, such as the 'question of the relationship between the national liberation struggle and the working-class struggles'.[48] Mzala and Gwala fed off each other in terms of what Pahad considered 'a really militant attitude towards IFP and the violence across town and what we needed to do to really intensify the unravelling struggles in South Africa'. Their militancy propelled them to begin a process of setting up SACP units.

> If I am not mistaken, they did set up some party units, which [were] not necessarily sanctioned by those who are responsible for the setting up of the units inside the country. But that's what led to some of the problems with some of our comrades in the Party. Because sometimes, Harry Gwala would have felt that they have been marginalised, from the underground Party structures inside the country.[49]

Everyone felt that Mzala was wonderful for Gwala. The union was also beneficial for the leadership of the movement since, through his interactions with Mzala, they got to understand Gwala's thoughts. As Gwala continued to seek medical help, he expanded his search for help to East Germany and the Soviet Union. In the end, none of the facilities could help him.[50]

Many comrades had first-hand experience of the Eastern bloc, including what some considered Mzala's unfair treatment in Prague. Still, Gwala remained an ardent supporter of the socialist countries. Pahad says they maintained an idealistic commitment to the socialist bloc. 'You know, we couldn't see anything wrong with the socialist countries.' Gwala's sojourn to Britain and later to the Soviet Union coincided with the perestroika (restructuring) period in which Soviet leader Mikhail Gorbachev initiated the reforms of glasnost (openness) in an attempt to revive the ailing economy and address corruption.[51]

When Gwala visited East Germany and the Soviet Union, the fissures were already palpable. 'You could begin to see some disintegration taking place,' says Pahad. These countries were in great difficulties; 'You could see the collapse coming,' Pahad said. 'The Soviet Union was collapsing.' Yet, on his return to London, Gwala was full of passion and optimism. 'He used to come to our flat and we would invite other people, both British and South Africans, to come and meet with him.' When Pahad predicted the inevitable and imminent collapse of the socialist republics, Gwala 'got angry with me and, by the way, he never forgave me for that,' chuckles Pahad.

Years later, when Pahad was working full-time in the ANC's headquarters, he bumped into Gwala in the corridor. 'Comrade Pahad, why did you tell me that the GDR was going to collapse?' Pahad retorted, 'But, Comrade Harry, did it not collapse?' 'Yes, but why did you tell me?' he said. Pahad laughed and read the interaction as Gwala's way of saying he would have preferred to remain in the dark. While the collapse was inevitable, Pahad says Gwala never forgot the 'fantastic' treatment the socialist countries gave to ANC and SACP comrades.

Amid his search for a cure for his debilitating disease, Gwala maintained his constant engagements with Mzala. Says Pahad, 'My own view is that Harry Gwala respected the depth of theoretical understanding of Mzala. I think that was important because it wasn't easy to satisfy Harry Gwala.' Nzimande was not only close to both Mzala and Gwala but spent this period with them. 'Mzala had such love and respect for *umuntu omdala* [Gwala].' Sometimes, the three would sit for hours at Oxford or in London, discussing everything, but especially the possibility of a transition at the time. And the violence in KwaZulu-Natal.

CHAPTER 11

Negotiations: Thank God things are moving

I

From the mid- to late 1980s, South Africa was well on its way towards a negotiated settlement. The 'war-weary' apartheid regime was in crisis, facing a plethora of challenges, among them the economic crunch and popular uprisings. Secret talks had begun with ANC leaders in exile before the momentum shifted to involve incarcerated leaders such as Nelson Mandela.[1] By 1989, negotiations were an important part of the political debate. Having been at the coalface of the national liberation struggle for many years, it is reasonable to expect that Mzala would have been preoccupied by the question of negotiations.

His two articles in *Sechaba* in the middle of 1987 – 'United States Policy towards South Africa' and 'Can the Imperialists Abort our Revolution?' – revealed his thoughts on the topic. These developments would see Mzala moving around, engaging and representing the ANC in the debate. Typically, he was very much involved in influencing policy direction through debates and writing in the publications of the movement as well as the popular media. Comrades who were with him during this period remember how he engaged animatedly with the topic. Patric Mellet recalls this period with fondness. 'We discussed what should be non-negotiables.'

Mzala believed the movement should never engage in negotiations of the round-table, multi-party type, he says.

> He wanted a two-sided table. All enemy forces on one side and a united front of all opposing forces including PAC etc. on the other to prevent a divide and rule scenario. He wanted it to be non-negotiable to fragment a unitary state in any form whatsoever. He would have opposed the nine provinces break-up which aligns closely with the Bantustans and with the social engineering carried out by the British to deal with what they called the 'Native Question'.[2]

Mzala would warn Blade Nzimande against complacency and that the movement needed to be careful how it approached the question of negotiations. He was wary that the regime could unban the movement and, once all its leaders re-emerged, would then 'chop our heads off when we are all inside'. One of the dangers that Mzala did not spend time writing about was the right-wing element that would later threaten civil war, a development that created a dangerous situation for the movement inside the country. These elements played a significant role in creating instability during the transition period, which included the assassination of Chris Hani. Nevertheless, Mzala would emphasise the need to apply tactics of social democracy, recalls Nzimande. 'We mustn't have a long transition, Mzala,' he would say. 'Even if it's a negotiated one, we must not have a long transition, because if we have a long transition, the revolution may be aborted completely.'

Ronnie Kasrils says that, although Mzala was not opposed to the idea of negotiations, there were justifiable concerns that the movement could be walking into a trap, and that negotiations could be a ploy of the regime and its Western supporters to disarm and deradicalise the ANC. It was no surprise to Kasrils that such questions would arise from within the ranks of the movement. He says this required patient explanation and that is exactly what the Tambo leadership provided. Argues Kasrils:

> Bear in mind that from the outset the MK Manifesto had expressed the hope that civil war could be averted if the whites were prepared to negotiate a transition to democratic change. Mzala's generation had been schooled in the concept of politics being primary with armed struggle the means to reinforce a political settlement. Of course, by 1990 there were heated debates as the struggle began to change course.

The caveat was that the liberation movement had to remain vigilant, keep our gunpowder dry so to speak, [to] ensure that mass mobilisation and organisation would strengthen our position at the negotiation table.[3]

Kasrils says it was important to be sceptical, as Mzala and the likes of Chris Hani were, 'but then so had Tambo been when as early as 1988 he had begun to formulate the Harare Declaration about a negotiated strategy'. To Mellet's mind, Mzala, like Chris Hani, did not oppose the negotiations but cautioned that there was naivety in the movement and that many in the movement had been actively whittling away its integrity as a national liberation movement. However, Mellet thinks of the developments within the movement at that time as 'a quiet palace coup', which resulted in a 'Velvet Revolution' replacing the national liberation struggle. He says Mzala would express that some leaders often exaggerated the extent of the traction garnered during the negotiation.

II

It is apparent that the dominant view in the movement considered negotiations a viable option. Mzala did not hold back his views and took to all available platforms to express his own interpretation of the ANC's positions. Hence, he penned two articles for the June and August 1989 editions of *Sechaba*. In the first discussion article, 'Omelettes Cannot be Made without Breaking Eggs', Mzala did not mince his words about the need to crush the apartheid regime. Building on his 'people's war' argument, he posited, 'Complete victory in the South African revolution will depend on whether or not the working class has been sufficiently organised and significantly armed to provide the decisive force when the apartheid system has to be finally crushed into ruin.'

He was unwavering in his belief that the working class remained the motive force for the South African revolution. 'The outcome of the struggle,' he said, 'will depend on whether the working class is the leader or disciple of the alliance of classes that is presently waging the struggle against apartheid.' Throughout his debates at various moments of his life, Mzala continuously located the working class at the centre of the South African struggle. Like a prophet who could foretell the danger lurking, he opened the article by posing two critical questions:

Will the working class allow itself to be used merely as the storm troops and then have the struggle called to a halt while the representatives of the other classes declare their preference for a partial victory and a negotiated deal with racism? Will the outcome of the present revolutionary events leave the working class at the helm or outside state power of the post-apartheid South Africa?

Mzala stated that 'these are not rhetorical or idle questions', but rather informed by his reading and interpretation of the prevailing conditions. Some 30 years later, left-leaning individuals and activists of the Communist Party are still lamenting the marginalisation of the working class in the post-apartheid South African power structure. The debate on state and popular power rages on within and outside the SACP. But what seemed to be irking Mzala most was what he characterised as the 'mystic theory of talks' enunciated by 'a few theorists' within the ranks of the movement who 'think that what is needed and possible under the circumstances is a partial victory; that the apartheid regime cannot be defeated but has produced a stalemate, which means that the ANC has to effect as peaceful a deal as possible between the apartheid regime and the revolutionary people'.

With the negotiated settlement at the centre of the debate within the ANC-headed movement, *Sechaba* and the *African Communist* were laden with articles on this matter. Typical of its broad-church character, the views of ANC cadres and leaders differed. Hence, Mzala stated, 'If the articles that have appeared in *Sechaba* during 1988 can be used as an index of the strategic thinking among some theorists, then a compromising and almost capitulationist tendency can be observed in the views of Brenda Stalker, Theresa and Alex Mashinini.'

Brenda Stalker was one of the pseudonyms of Sylvia Neame, a former political prisoner and member of the SACP. Her other pseudonyms included Theresa and Theresa Zania.[4] As already indicated earlier, Alex Mashinini was Tshidiso Mokhoanatse. Brenda Stalker had penned a series of articles in *Sechaba* in which, among other things, she responded to Thando Zuma and Ronnie Kasrils. Mzala vehemently disagreed with Stalker's conclusion. She had pooh-poohed his pet subject of a people's war. Stalker argued that, based on the events that took place in Lusaka in 1985, where a delegation of top business personnel met the ANC leadership, as well as a similar meeting in Dakar, Senegal, in 1987 where Afrikaner intellectuals engaged the ANC, that 'such talks could represent a step towards eventual negotiation with the government or a sector of it'.[5]

In the January 1989 edition of *Sechaba*, this time writing as Theresa, she differed with Kasrils's take on the need to develop a 'revolutionary army'. Theresa questioned the logic behind the belief that the 'creation of a revolutionary army is our most crucial task'.[6] Again, Mzala took issue with this view and aligned himself with Kasrils, arguing that the 'question of victory concerns the practical methods of achieving that victory, and so relates to the need to build a revolutionary army'. Mzala also argued:

> Theresa does not look forward to the overthrow of the apartheid regime; rather she theorises, like Brenda Stalker, about the ANC entering 'into certain compromises with the ruling class, and even with the apartheid regime, in regard to questions concerning the central state and even regions' so that we could continue the process of democratic transformation of the country 'in essentially peaceful forms'.[7]

Mzala had similar issues with Alex Mashinini, another 'theorist on these ideas about the need for the ANC to compromise'. He argued, 'Mashinini's recent theme is no longer people's war and insurrection but partial victory and the call for the ANC to walk proudly on a red carpet towards a negotiated settlement.' Even in his writings, Mzala's combative and forthright debating strategy came through. The sharp-tongued Mzala did not hesitate to drive his point home. Mashinini had argued that the talks with the business community and Afrikaner intellectuals were a new element to the ANC's strategy and tactics that would lead to a negotiated settlement. Mzala's retorted, 'To Mashinini, it was quite new.' As far as Mzala was concerned, this was just another 'mystic theory'. In the final analysis, he was adamant about the need to continue to 'propagate among the people and within the liberation movement the idea of the arming of the masses as the most important condition for victory'.

In the August edition of *Sechaba*, Mzala's article 'Negotiations and People's Power' continued to focus on negotiation. Throughout his life, from the days when he was confined to Ngoje after his numerous expulsions from school, Mzala consumed the media to keep abreast of local and international politics. It is not surprising, therefore, that this article was largely triggered by criticism in three newspapers: *Die Beeld* (an Afrikaans-language newspaper), *African Confidential* (a London-based newsletter on politics in Africa), and *Newsweek* (a weekly news magazine in the United States). Among the sins these publications committed was to characterise the ANC as a 'terrorist gang' that had now been cornered following recent developments in the Soviet Union and in southern Africa.

Their views were that the ANC must abandon its 'violent' approach, and that it had been forced into negotiations with government.

Mzala dismissed these analyses with contempt, characterising them as akin to reading 'a magazine horoscope'. He maintained that, for the ANC and its allies, the question of negotiations was not problematic in principle, contrary to the media's provocative suggestions. He argued:

> The issue is not whether or not, by taking a stand on this issue, we are deciding to be a 'freedom movement' or 'terrorist gang'. If negotiations in Angola and the settlement of the Namibian question can be anything to go by, then the ANC has gone on record as acclaiming the processes leading to imminent independence of Namibia, and even volunteering to abandon its military camps in Angola, in the belief that it will not then be held responsible for any excuses the Pretoria regime may make for aborting the processes leading to Namibian independence. This is what we have done, not merely claimed.[8]

Mzala's view was that the media was making mischief in their preoccupation with negotiations and, in the process, 'making all manner of speculations about the fate of the South African liberation struggle'. He regarded this as 'an orchestrated' campaign coordinated at various levels of opinion-making. 'It has even been joined by the British prime minister, Margaret Thatcher,' he wrote, 'who has made known her views about the circumstances under which the ANC and the apartheid regime can be brought to the negotiating table.'

Mzala characterised the images 'constructed' by the media as 'strange and even surprising, full of illusions and guesswork', especially for ANC members. He accused the media of failing to understand the ANC's strategic outlook and its policies, which, according to his view, was a crucial starting point to comprehend the South African liberation struggle. This antagonistic relationship between the media and the ANC would persist post-apartheid, with successive presidents – from Nelson Mandela to Thabo Mbeki and Jacob Zuma – all accusing the media of being used as a tool against the black majority government.[9] Mzala's views on the media were informed by its coverage of the ANC against the organisation's own internal discussion, strategy and policy position. In this regard, Mzala was thus one of the early ANC pioneers to accurately identify the true character of the media in the liberation of the oppressed majority. Because of its location in capitalist structures of power, even post-apartheid, the media continue to reproduce the views of the dominant powers.[10]

Among the salient features pinpointed by Mzala in his article was the misrepresentation of the ANC's policy position on negotiations, thus exposing the media bias. He went on to analyse the experiences of other struggles, the attitude of the apartheid regime, and the failure of British policy on southern Africa under Thatcher. He situated his views on the transfer of power on the fact that the ANC was 'a revolutionary movement' and, as such, its 'political business is not to reform South African society but to transform it from the social foundation'.

To this end, Mzala emphasised that in order for the ANC to achieve its revolutionary objectives it should continue to demand the complete transfer of power to the people. This, according to Mzala, could be achieved through 'universal suffrage, complete freedom, and also the immediate overthrow of the racist government, to be replaced by the people's government'. For Mzala, anything less would be tantamount to capitulation and reformism. 'Unless the liberation struggle definitely ends with the transfer of power to the people,' he concluded, 'there is no instrument to guarantee that the misery experienced during pre-liberation days would be ended in all its forms.'

Of course, Mzala and his fellow hardliners were eventually proven wrong. During the initial phase of the talks, the ANC took a hard-line approach and refused to abandon the armed struggle unless the government met its terms, but eventually it capitulated, as Mzala would put it. On 6 August 1990, the ANC and government issued a joint statement in which the ANC announced the suspension of armed activities.[11] The ANC tried hard to sell the 'ceasefire' package, but it was not universally accepted within the ranks of the movement; Joe Slovo admitted that about '90 per cent of ANC supporters thought the decision was a sell-out'.[12] Nevertheless, the ANC argued that the suspension did not mean abandoning the armed struggle.

It is a matter of historical record now that this was indeed the end of the armed struggle and Mzala's dream of a people's war. While MK played an important role in organising and training self-defence units when communities were under attack from state-sponsored violence, this did not amount to the people's war Mzala had envisaged. The perspective pursued by Mzala and his fellow people's war protagonists was roundly rejected by the ANC during negotiations.

Nevertheless, in 1989 Mzala was on a warpath, as reflected in the article 'The Battle of Income: Symbol of our Armed Struggle' that appeared under Comrade Mzala in the *African Communist*. In this article, which was later picked up by the mainstream media back home, Mzala argued that the defeat of Dingane on 16 December 1838 'has come to have a new meaning for the people of South Africa since the launching of Umkhonto we Sizwe in 1961'.[13] As we see later, this article was used to infer that the ANC will do away with days such as the Day of the Vow, important to the Afrikaner community.

Still, in 1989, as Jabulani Mkhatshwa, Mzala penned three 'African Notes' and comments in the *African Communist*. In the first edition, he wrote about developments in Kenya in 'From Wananchi Declaration to MwaKenya'. He also spent time on the new political situation in Sudan.[14] In the second edition, he wrote about UNITA's fate in Angola and the Fifth Frelimo Party Congress in Mozambique before turning his attention to developments in Burkina Faso by posing the question: 'Is it Glasnot or counter-revolution?'[15] In the third edition, of Margaret Thatcher's tour to Africa, he wrote, '[She] came, she saw, but was conquered.' He also wrote about the corruption of Zaire as 'the most corrupt record in post-independent Africa' and on the new constitution in Nigeria, which he hoped could be a 'creation of a socialist alliance'. The struggle of the Saharawi people has been an important part of the ANC-headed movement. Thus, in this edition, Mzala wrote about what he regarded as a 'reality that cannot be ignored'.[16]

In the same edition, writing as Sisa Majola, he penned 'The Current Crisis and the Growth of our Revolution' in which he provided a comparative analysis of the States of Emergency in 1960 and 1986. Arguing that since the formation of MK and looking back at the growth of the liberation struggle and considering the crisis enveloping South Africa, he wrote, '[We] shall find it necessary to admit, without making ourselves victims of our own propaganda, that victory over the apartheid forces is definitely within our grasp.'[17]

III

The year 1990 would turn out to be one of Mzala's most productive years. With his health waning and an escalating work schedule, it speaks to his tenacious character that he produced such an incredible amount of work. Perhaps this bears testimony to one of Gail Gerhart's observations: that things such as sleeping and other mundane activities never bothered him. He was strong-headed and primarily focused on his goals. He may not have known that he was living with a terminal illness, or perhaps he simply ignored this fact. Of course, the feelings expressed to his siblings that he was not going to live a long life were based on being killed rather than dying of an illness. However, his activities in 1990 do not suggest that he was anticipating it to be his last full year.

On the contrary, he was pushing hard to finalise his PhD and making plans that included moving across the Atlantic with his family to take up a fellowship at Yale University. Perhaps he was driven by his mantra, 'There's no time to rest, mzala.' By the time the year ended, Mzala had appeared on television shows and on a number of public forums as an ANC analyst. He had delivered conference papers and public lectures in the United States, written memorandums and a series of articles for *Sechaba* and the *African Communist*, as well as opinion pieces for the South African media. He had been cited in numerous publications as ANC spokesperson or analyst, with his articles in the *African Communist* increasingly cited in the media back home. Mzala also crossed swords with his nemesis Buthelezi and his Inkatha party. This period certainly entrenched Mzala's status in the broad liberation movement as one of its emerging intellectuals.

His hectic schedule came on the back of historic events back home. The year began with the speech by the last apartheid president, FW de Klerk, in which he announced the unbanning of liberation organisations and the release of Mandela. When the year ended, Mandela and many other political prisoners were free, Tambo had returned home after 30 years in exile, and the ANC had held its first Consultative Conference inside the country in three decades.

As Mzala adhered to his punishing schedule, he also began to broaden his horizons and was casting his net wide. Perhaps this was not his own doing but a revolutionary sacrifice and commitment to the struggle of the people of South Africa. But even under these circumstances, he still did not neglect his family duties – something on which he prided himself. His ideas were now frequently captured by the South African media, and he was by now regarded as an authority on the political developments in the country. The media used him to gain insights into the ANC's thinking. Clearly, Mzala's political future was on an upward trajectory.

In January 1990, he participated in a debate at the Oxford Union involving the Democratic Party's leader, Dr Denis Worrall. The debate was covered by *The Argus* and Mzala was introduced as 'an opposing speaker' and 'ANC political analyst'. According to the article:

Mzala said the ANC remained committed to bringing about change through negotiation, but could not be expected to 'give room' to the president, understand or wait for him while apartheid and injustice continued and while preconditions for negotiation remained to be met.[18]

Although political changes were widely anticipated, it was still a momentous occasion when De Klerk announced the unbanning of political parties and the release of political prisoners on 2 February 1990. South Africa's major news wire for foreign and domestic news, the South African Press Association (SAPA), issued a comment by the ANC on the same day based on Mzala's interview 'on satellite television, which was carrying live excerpts from Mr de Klerk's speech at the opening of Parliament'.[19] While Mzala regarded the unbanning of the ANC as an 'important signpost on the way to freedom', he still insisted that De Klerk meet all the preconditions laid down in the Harare Declaration the previous year. Described as a senior ANC political analyst, Mzala regarded the decision as a response to international pressure. However, he was confident that the ANC 'might' now be in a position to hold discussions with the government 'to remove this obnoxious system of apartheid'.[20]

The same month, Mzala was part of the delegation of ANC leaders visiting Sweden, where a call was made for sanctions to remain in place. Back home, the visit was covered by the *Cape Times*, which noted that Walter Sisulu welcomed the lifting of the ban on political organisations but called for economic sanctions to be maintained. The article went on:

> The analyst, who goes only by the name of 'Mzala', said the ANC was 'absolutely committed to a negotiated solution for South Africa'. The next step, now that the ANC had been unbanned, was facing the question of a new constitution for South Africa and the dismantling of the present one. Responding to a question from the interviewer, 'Mzala' confirmed that his gut reaction to Mr de Klerk's announcement was 'thank God things are moving'.[21]

In April, Mzala penned an article for the South African weekly, *New Nation*, where he drew from a special meeting of ANC members in Britain to present an analysis of the 'present political situation in South Africa'. Characterising Britain as 'one of the few ANC regions which, like Zambia and Tanzania, has a large community of ANC members, including veterans who left the country in the early 1960s', Mzala stated that the special meeting had been convened to discuss the current situation in South Africa and the significance of the NEC's decision to confirm the return of members and leaders from exile. He wrote:

> Present at the meeting were both full-time activists as well as ANC students studying in Britain. Among some of the well-known ANC members who were present at the meeting were Albie Sachs, a leading South African constitutional lawyer; Francis Meli, member of the ANC's NEC and former editor of *Sechaba*; M.D. Naidoo, former Durban lawyer and leader of the Natal Indian community; and Sipho Pityana, secretary of the International Reception Committee.[22]

In reporting about this meeting, Mzala portrayed the ANC as an organisation whose decision-making processes were imbued in its democratic character. This meeting, according to Mzala, regarded as important the need to continue mobilising the international community to support the liberation struggle and to isolate the apartheid regime, while on the other hand reorganising the democratic movement inside the country. However, he considered the situation in the country as 'political equilibrium'. This, he said, meant that the liberation movement had reached a stage where it could not be defeated, yet was still not strong enough to completely dislodge the apartheid regime and seize power 'through a people's insurrection'.

Mzala also reported concerns expressed by members on De Klerk's meeting with British prime minister Margaret Thatcher, which they believed 'was aimed at co-ordinating strategies to create conditions which make the revolution either impossible or difficult to achieve in South Africa'. According to Mzala, they were also wary of the 'attempt to create prefects', with De Klerk as the principal and his cabinet as the teachers. 'Like in any school situation,' he wrote, 'the principal would then expect that it should be the prefects, the leadership of the liberation movement, who should go around stopping violence between the people and the vigilantes, which have been created and armed by De Klerk's government.'[23]

As an increasingly prominent ANC voice in the media, Mzala spoke and commented on a wide array of issues, but negotiations still preoccupied his mind. In May 1990, he followed up with an opinion piece in the *New Nation*: 'A Response to Mounting People's Pressure'. Reflecting on a recent meeting between the ANC and the government in Cape Town, he argued that there were already conflicting interpretations from various political tendencies on the implications of the meeting. The first tendency accused the ANC of capitulation to De Klerk's strategy of co-opting them into a reformist scheme designed to derail revolutionary transformation. The other tendency, represented by the right-wing Afrikaner movement, regarded De Klerk as selling out the 'aspirations' of the Afrikaners. Mzala considered this meeting in a historical context as having broken 'new ground in the politics of South Africa, because for the first time since 1652, a white government made a public acknowledgement that the political business of the country's administration could no longer be the exclusive domain of a white parliament'.

Arguing that the principal historical problem in South Africa had been the continued exclusion of blacks from the political decision-making process that affected their land and lives while fundamentally subjected to laws decided by unrepresentative institutions, he posited:

> No serious student of South African history, unless filled with prejudice, can therefore deny that the meeting symbolises the beginning of a new era in South African politics, whatever the substantial achievement of its deliberations and conclusions. Never again can the government pretend that the politics of South Africa can be concluded within the whites-only chambers. Never again can the government pretend that a meaningful constitution for the country can be decided upon without a go-ahead from the ANC.[24]

Mzala defended the leadership of the ANC and argued that they were 'no puppets'. 'Mandela and Slovo,' he wrote, 'can never be compared to [Lucas] Mangope and [Lennox] Sebe. They are people's leaders in every sense of the word and they have never pretended to be anything else but revolutionaries.' He indicated that De Klerk was under pressure and whatever their 'hidden agenda might be', Mzala argued, the process had 'acquired a momentum of its own, and there is no way in which [De Klerk] or anyone else can stop it'.

Behind the scenes, Mzala – building on his many arguments articulated in various platforms – was already articulating what the new South Africa ought to look like. According to Mellet, Mzala believed that we should have an elected National Assembly on a constituency basis, where the candidates for election must come from those constituencies and were accountable to the people of the areas wherein the candidate lived. Mzala felt that a second house should complement the National Assembly and that it should be a People's Council of voluntary, unpaid representatives. Mellet says they had long discussions on legal reforms and constitutionalism.

[Mzala believed that] the National People's Council should draw representatives from local People's Councils and from membership-based civil society organisations across the different sectors in society. The Nation People's Council would be a watchdog over government and the National Assembly and because these representatives would be unpaid volunteers they would not have vested interests, and an institutionalised dynamic of guarding liberation gains to root out delinquency and corruption [and] to ensure that the majority poor would be ably served.

Mzala remained sceptical about the true intentions of the apartheid regime and its allies. According to Mellet, he was alive to the reality that, as early as the 1980s, 'big business in South Africa, a number of Western governments and counter-insurgency ideologues in the South African and foreign security intelligence agencies had already come to the conclusion that a new dispensation needed to be negotiated'. Mzala verbalised his concerns to close associates about the possibility that some within the movement could already have been co-opted to the imperialist agenda.

Another development that worried Mzala greatly was the mushrooming of civil society organisations whose source of funding was linked to corporate philanthropy and Western governments. Many of these non-governmental agencies were quickly becoming politicised. According to Mellet, Mzala was not convinced that this was as a result of hard underground work, and he felt that not all the agencies were led by forces friendly to the liberation movement. 'He saw it as contested ground where we barely held the upper ground in the balance of forces.' Although the ANC had had a close relationship with many progressive civil society organisations during the anti-apartheid struggle, things could quickly change post-apartheid. Nevertheless, Mellet says Mzala cautioned about the need to not get caught up 'in our own propaganda but to be logical and clear thinking in analysing the balance of forces'. Mzala was unhappy that the liberation movement was going into negotiations in a situation where the enemy was far from being 'worn out'.

The negotiations continued apace during a hugely significant epoch that saw a number of important changes in the global balance of force, including the fall of the Berlin Wall. These events significantly impacted development in South Africa's own balance of forces. In fact, the fall of the Berlin Wall had a trigger-like effect on southern Africa.[25] Thandeka Gqubule-Mbeki, who met Mzala later in 1990, recalls that it was in this global context that their meeting took place. She says the ANC was going through a lot of turmoil and ideological debates about the fall of the Wall, which led to the questioning of socialist ideas by many members. Gqubule-Mbeki thinks this led to a sense of defeat for socialists like Mzala, but paradoxically with hope that something was about to come. However, at this early stage of negotiations, Gqubule-Mbeki says Mzala was already verbalising concerns about 'the cauldron, the mix of ideas and practices in the ANC against the backdrop of fluid, world and global events that had dramatic impact on the political balance of forces at home'.[26]

IV

In his unique ways of articulating ANC policy positions, there was an air of bravery about Mzala. The way he put himself out there as an uncompromising ANC radical was in the mould of well-known firebrands such as Chris Hani, Winnie Mandela and Harry Gwala. In the context of a very volatile political situation, this was a courageous as well as a dangerous a move. But Mzala had demonstrated from a very young age his fearless streak when it came to confronting injustices.

With his forthright political attitude, Mzala had already accrued enemies both inside and outside the movement. His biography on Buthelezi had not made him popular, particularly in his home province of KwaZulu-Natal, a stronghold of Inkatha. Also, within the movement his pugnacious style had made him foes and friends alike. And, just like all uncompromising revolutionaries, Mzala was in constant danger from the apartheid's security agents. But still he did not relent. He was, however, vigilant and wherever they stayed, says Mpho, they always had an escape plan should anything happen. Mzala was always cognisant of the reality that 'we were still at war'. Nevertheless, he remained feisty in his political engagement, and during this time he went back to battle with his old adversary Buthelezi when he took him on together with the *Ilanga* newspaper. Mzala accused the paper of using his name to lend credence to one of its stories, based on documents purported to be written by him.

Ilanga had reported that a letter, supposedly written by Mzala, and some documents from Kagiso Trust, were brought to their offices by an unknown man. 'According to the letter, "Mzala" could no longer keep quiet about the truth of what was happening in Kagiso and he had decided to hand over the documents to *Ilanga* to expose the truth.'[27] According to

Ilanga, the man had come to their offices on 3 July 1990 and delivered a letter addressed to the editor. 'Once we had read the covering letter,' wrote the paper, 'there was no room for doubt that we had in our hands one of the most remarkable documents that could surely surface at this crucial time in the country's history.'[28] In its previous issues in June, the paper had published three articles: 'Kagiso, the UDF and the EEC millions', 'Kagiso Funds used to Recruit for Umkhonto?' and 'Biting the Hand that Feeds'.

The 'leaked' documents purportedly confirmed the allegations previously made by *Ilanga* accusing Kagiso Trust of funding 'projects which promoted the ANC, thus betraying the mandate of the funders'. This prompted a response by Kagiso's executive director Achmat Dangor, through an open letter, which clarified that projects controlled by government and its structures like the homelands were excluded from their funding. He was also reported to have said on the publication of Kagiso documents:

> It is sad to note how a person of Buthelezi's personal stature is being associated with cheap propaganda tricks based upon documents purloined from our organisation. We believe that the documents *Ilanga* has could only have been obtained through electronic interception of our telefax communication or illegally obtained from one of our offices. Only the State's security apparatus has the sophistication to do either or both of these things.[29]

As the reportage continued, Mzala entered the fray, and threatened to sue. On 9 July 1990, the *Natal Witness* reported, 'A leading member of the African National Congress in London has instructed his lawyers to take legal action against Inkatha's Zulu-language newspaper *Ilanga* and against Inkatha leader Mangosuthu Buthelezi for a letter bearing his name which appeared in the paper last week.'[30] On the same day, Umtata Capital Radio reported: 'A top ANC official is taking legal action against the Inkatha-owned newspaper, *Ilanga*, because of the publication of a letter which the ANC official says is fraud.'[31] The report also mentioned that at the root of the row was Inkatha's anger that Kagiso Trust was not giving the organisation any money. Continued the report: 'Now Mzala says he is taking legal action against *Ilanga*, and Inkatha leader Mangosuthu Buthelezi, because of the letter bearing his name, which he says is a fraud.'

Although his hands were full, Mzala – out of principle and conviction – would not let Buthelezi and *Ilanga* get away with using his name. It is difficult to comprehend why the person who purportedly dropped the documents claimed he was Mzala or why the paper believed that Mzala, exiled, would come all the way from the UK to drop the documents at its offices.

V

Mzala's reputation as an authority on ANC policy positions was gaining traction inside the country. In articles such as 'ANC sal met Geloftedag wegdoen' (ANC will do away with the Day of the Vow), published in the Afrikaans-language *Patriot* of 27 July 1990, Mzala's *African Communist* article was used to understand the ANC's position. Celebrated on 16 December during apartheid, the Day of the Vow was considered one of the most important days in the history of the Afrikaners. The story goes that, as the Voortrekkers (early Dutch-speaking migrants into the interior) prepared for the Battle of Blood River on 16 December 1838 against the Zulu people, they took a vow before God that they would build a church and that they and their descendants would observe the day as a day of thanksgiving should they be granted victory.[32]

Speculation was rife within the Afrikaner community on what the future ANC government might do about minority groups and their cultures. Mzala's article was used as the basis for this newspaper's conclusion that it was false hope to think that this day would be preserved in the new South Africa. Referring to the Battle of iNcome (Blood River), Mzala's article was cited by the newspaper: 'There are many lessons that can be learnt from the Battle. The importance of the date is in it that the founders of Umkhonto we Sizwe ... chose the day for the start of the armed struggle. The dead of I'Ncome [*sic*] ... rose under the new banner of Umkhonto we Sizwe.' According to the newspaper: 'Speaking about the Battle itself, Mzala writes: "The Afrikaners were in an impenetrable fortress where the natural barrier of the river compensated for a lack of military ingenuity."'[33]

During this period, Mzala's appetite for engagements had not waned. Instead, his horizons were widening and he was increasingly using the media as a platform for the battle of ideas to express the views of the movement on South Africa's revolutionary trajectory. In November 1990, through an opinion piece titled 'Patriotism and Positivity what SA Needs Now' in the *Cape Times*, Mzala accused Professor Hermann Giliomee of 'underestimating the dramatic and fundamental way in which

South African politics shall have changed' by the time the elections came around. Giliomee had expressed an opinion that there would be 'genuinely competitive elections' in South Africa, with a showdown between the ANC and the National Party (NP).

In typical style, Mzala described Giliomee's views as 'amusingly' speculative. Locating the NP's strength in 'whites-only' race politics while 'more than three quarters of the country's population was excluded from central parliamentary politics', Mzala argued: 'The future South African elections Giliomee is speculating about will include, for the first time, all adult blacks, not just "qualified blacks" as Constitutional Minister Dr Gerrit Viljoen might want.' He continued:

> There is just no way in which an ANC leadership or delegation to negotiations would accept the argument for a qualified franchise for blacks without the risk of forfeiting its leadership role within [its] traditional constituency. Certainly not when the NP itself came to power in 1948 by relying precisely on the vote of these 'unqualified' whites, the majority of whom were Afrikaners.[34]

Of course, Mzala's perspectives were informed by his practical application of politics as an activist and intellectual of the ANC-headed movement. By the time the 1994 general elections came, not only was Giliomee's question a non-issue but so was the outcome. Notwithstanding the state-sponsored violence that characterised the build-up to the elections, the main question was not if but by what margin the ANC would win. When the counting was done, the ANC had convincingly thumped all pretenders to the throne, winning a massive 62 per cent of the votes, with the NP a distant second with a paltry 20 per cent and the IFP further behind in third position with little over 10 per cent.

But Mzala had the presence of mind to know that the ANC's stay in power was not permanent and would depend on its track record in government and its ability to remain the people's choice.

> Our immediate and practical political concern should be the building of a new South African constitution, as the fundamental law of the country. Such a constitution should not, and will not, be the expression of any partisan political tendency. It will be neither an ANC nor an NP constitution. By definition the constitution should embody the aggregate aspiration of all citizens irrespective of their racial or ethnic

affiliation. It is only on the basis of such a constitution that true national unity and equality will be placed on a secure legal basis in South Africa.[35]

Mzala placed the constitution above any party-political interests. He was also not blinded by loyalty to the ANC, and understood that evolving political conditions would lead to new challenges that might necessitate the development of new political forces and alliances. He wrote:

> Governments come and go. The ANC may win the first post-apartheid elections only to be outvoted from government by a new alliance of political forces in five or 10 years time (as was the case with the Sandinista government in Nicaragua), yet our new South African constitution, like our new flag, will have to belong to that solemn category of the new nation heritage which shall be the pride of all South Africans, black or white, and whatever their political affiliations.[36]

Mzala was convinced that this was a perspective that 'should bind us and evoke the genius within us, towards the realisation to this paramount matter: the building of a just national unity'. He expressed irritation with the frequent reference to South Africa's multi-ethnicity because 'it proceeds from simplistic assumptions that the existence of ethnic variety implies politicised ethnicity and that correspondingly, it means ethnic political polarisation and tension'. As seen in this input, Mzala's world of politics and academics often collided. He was fundamentally advancing a clear political position informed by his academic research on the resolution of the national question.

Unsurprisingly, another academic article – titled 'Is South Africa in a Revolutionary Situation?' – emerged in the September 1990 edition of the *Journal of Southern African Studies*. In this article, written before Mandela's release, Mzala reviewed three books: *South Africa Between Reform and Revolution* by Alex Callinicos, *Popular Struggles in South Africa* edited by William Cobbett and Robin Cohen, and *After Apartheid: Renewal of the South African Economy* by John Suckling and Landeg White. The article demonstrates Mzala's appetite for reading and his commitment to scholarly engagement. In providing a detailed review of all three volumes, Mzala argued that, while it had become 'near impossible' to keep a track record of all currently published research on South Africa, scholarly debates remained important for the revolution. Argued Mzala: 'The importance of engaging in this exercise cannot be underestimated, so long as it is not pursued merely for academic interest.' He continued: 'This means that the liberation movement and some of the researchers within it, should be actively engaged in these debates, not merely as observers, but as formulators of policy which may, in future, become the government policy in the post-apartheid South Africa. Herein lies the significance of the endeavours that have gone into the writing of these books.'[37]

VI

In addition to his other – and increasing – writing commitments, Mzala still produced five articles for the *African Communist* in 1990. Except for the article 'The Bantustan System is at the Centre of Natal Violence', the remainder were for the 'Africa Notes and Comments' column. In the first article, Mzala wrote on developments in Algeria, based on his reading of the media and information shared by political activists. Using the National Liberation Front's behaviour as a lens through which to understand the crisis, he concluded that whether the 'crisis' situation would be resolved depended on whether the 'broad democratic slogans' would be backed up by 'fair distribution of the wealth produced by the Algerian people'. For Mzala, a truly democratic reform was one that emerged out of the people's own democratic perspectives.

In the same article he analysed the 'violation of ceasefire by UNITA' in Angola. He was unsurprised by the actions of UNITA, based on the well-documented sell-out tendencies of its leader, Jonas Savimbi. In his analysis of Ethiopia's peace talks with Eritrea, Mzala emphasises the role of the Workers' Party of Ethiopia, which he said 'submitted a thesis to the parliament calling for talks with the secessionists without any preconditions whatsoever'. Moving deftly from one country to another, he closed the article by analysing the Sudanese coup, arguing that the fallen government of Sadiq al-Mahdi had been coming to a realisation of the importance of making peace with Sudanese People's Liberation Army led by John Garang. Thus, he was perturbed by the new coup leaders' 'negative and irresponsible attitude to the conflict in the south' and their intent on uniting the Sudanese people 'behind the pan-Arab banner'.[38]

In the next edition Mzala analysed developments in Benin, Lesotho and Swaziland. When it came to Benin, he discussed the demonstration that threatened to paralyse the government of President Mathieu Kérékou, while in Lesotho he profiled the dastardly act of General Justin Metsing

Lekhanya, who had told a magistrate that in shooting a 20-year-old student he was 'only doing his duty as a citizen'. This incident, according to Mzala, occurred when Lekhanya went to the Agricultural College to see his girlfriend, only to find her with her lover, George Ramone. The General fired two shots at the student with an Israeli Uzi, killing him on the spot. Mzala titled this section 'When shooting is a presidential duty'.

He dedicated the last part of the article to Swaziland, a place close to his heart. Under the headline 'Swaziland: A New Organisation is Formed', he celebrated the formation of PUDEMO, or Insika Yenkhululeko Yemaswati in Siswati. He wrote:

> Although it is generally assumed in the world that Swaziland is a peaceful monarchy exercising a constitutionally democratic form of government through the Tinkhundla system (introduced by the late King Sobhuza in 1978), in fact this is an undemocratic system. Candidates to parliament are not nominated by the people but by the ruling Imbokodvo Party in consultation with the royal family. That is why every Prime Minister in Swaziland has to belong to the Dlamini ruling clan.[39]

In the third-quarter edition, Mzala wrote another 'Africa Notes and Comments', coupled with a profile of Wilton Mkwayi, recently released from a sentence of life imprisonment. His Africa Notes were dedicated to the Namibian independence and developments in Liberia. Although buoyant about the developments in Namibia, he still called for caution, characterising the independence of Namibia as classical:

> Despite the political gymnastics by South Africa over years denying the colonial character of its occupation of Namibia, as well as attempting to foster its own version of independence through puppet administrators, on March 21 this year, Pretoria was forced to perform all the functions and responsibilities of a departing colonising power.

Mzala advocated for total freedom, including the handing over of Walvis Bay, where South Africa maintained a military force and continued to practice apartheid. He concluded, 'Namibia needs Walvis Bay as a child needs its mother's breast.'[40]

Turning his attention to the West African coast, Mzala analysed developments in Liberia under the heading 'The peeling of a banana republic'. Peaceful protests in the country had quickly developed into armed skirmishes with President Samuel K Doe, who had himself come to power through a military coup that overthrew President William R Tolbert Jr, and was now facing a taste of his very own medicine. Mzala read the reaction of the US army stationed in Liberia as an indication that the rebels represented 'interests which are hostile to America'.[41] Of course, these skirmishes later developed into a full-scale war, with US-educated and Libyan-trained Charles Taylor toppling Doe and eventually controlling large portions of the country as one of the most feared warlords. Although he was elected president following a peace deal in 1997, Taylor eventually ended up in The Hague where he was convicted of war crimes.[42]

In the same edition, Mzala paid tribute to Wilton Mkwayi through the article 'Wilton Mkwayi: A Veteran of Revolutionary Campaigns'. Again, Mzala displayed his versatility and passion for history. He considered the liberation struggle in South Africa as having been enriched by the release of leaders such as Mkwayi, who had been serving a life sentence since 1964 following his arrest immediately after the Rivonia Trial. In his article, Mzala meticulously traced Mkwayi's life from early childhood to his involvement in the struggle in the 'fighting fifties', his underground years during the State of Emergency in 1960, up to his arrest and trial. Mzala assessed the implication of the release of leaders of Mkwayi's calibre and concluded, 'Without underestimating the obstacles that still lie on the way, it can be said that South Africa has reached a point of no return in the march of the revolution towards people's power.'[43]

In the 'Africa Notes and Comments' column of the fourth-quarter edition, Mzala penned what would be his last two articles in the publications of the liberation movement. In the first section of the article, 'The First Steps towards Democracy', Mzala explained the postponement of the democratic process in Angola. He argued that this was due to the emergence of UNITA aided by the Portuguese colonial government, and the need to fend off the racist South African regime while supporting the Namibian liberation struggle. This condition, he said, made it 'almost impossible to go about civil affairs as though it were peace time'.

He rationalised Angola's one-party political system, which, he argued, 'stemmed from concrete historical causes rather than a commitment to theoretical principles'. He lionised the MPLA Workers' Party and its leader President José Eduardo dos Santos as having 'given full thought and practical consideration to the building of democracy in the country'. Of course, these assertions would be proven to have been rather optimistic if not idealistic a couple of decades later when Dos Santos's excesses were laid bare after his successor President João Lourenço assumed office in 2017.

Then, under the heading 'Demand for a New Beginning and a New Direction', Mzala turned his attention to Kenya. There had been mass campaigns by various social forces expressing frustration with the government of President Daniel arap Moi. 'In order to thwart the growth of a united opposition movement,' he wrote, 'President Moi's government tried to divide Kenyan people on the basis of religion and regions of origin. Fortunately in these decades Kenyans have learnt that they are one nation with a common history of struggle and a common future.'[44] Through this article, Mzala demonstrates yet again his belief in people's power and irritation with narrow ethnic mobilisation. This is what was at the heart of his academic enquiry.

The article 'The Bantu System is at the Centre of Natal Violence' was the swan song of his illustrious writing career in the journals of the liberation movement, his farewell piece inspired by Alan Paton's famous novel *Cry, the Beloved Country*. Mzala opened the article poetically:

> From Drakensburg to the Indian Ocean, the once great and historic hills now stand desolate, as earth and the human spirit have torn like flesh. Down in the countryside valleys women are scratching the red earth for a livelihood as well as burying their dead. Maize hardly reaches the height of a man. Much as children no longer grow into old age. In Natal, the soil and the Bantustan politics cannot keep the people alive any longer.[45]

Paton's laments, wrote Mzala, 'might as well have been a forecast of the tragedy that has developed in the country forty years later'. He continued, 'The titihoye does not cry here any more, only the sounds of pangas and gunshots provide the lightning to the dark and cloudy sky.' Mzala put the blame for this inevitable disaster squarely on the shoulders of the National Party and its bantustan policy. He said that the violence that characterised Natal had been opportunistically used by the government 'as a pretext for not lifting the State of Emergency, [it] is essentially the climax of the apartheid policy of the bantustans'.

After characterising Inkatha's role in the unfolding calamity, and providing a brief history of the popular rejection of the bantustan policy in Natal in the 1950s, Mzala urged the movement to dismantle bantustans.

'It is within the context of these questions that the democratic movement needs to place the call for the immediate dismantling of the bantustan at the head of the agenda of the campaign to stop the vigilantes in Natal.' Of course, the ANC-headed democratic government would only tinker with the bantustan policy when it assumed power in 1994, as the introduction of nine provinces, which included KwaZulu-Natal, was essentially a continuation of this policy and the violent infrastructure established during this period persists to this day. Political violence in this province is pronounced and, more than 30 years since Mzala made his call, the worst public violence witnessed since the dawn of democracy took root here after the arrest of former president Jacob Zuma in July 2021.

VII

By the latter part of 1990, Mzala was fighting the biggest battle of his life. His health was quickly deteriorating and those close to him claim he was trying different treatments to stay alive. Although a committed Marxist-Leninist, he did not abandon his African and Christian roots. Interestingly, Patric Mellet links the natural medicine to his church. 'He came from a staunch Seventh Day Adventist family where there is much emphasis on natural medications, vegetarianism and non-use of drugs, alcohol and cigarette smoking.'

It was not just the natural medicine that interested Mzala; his diet, too, had changed. According to Celeste Naidoo, Mzala was on a garlic diet. Apart from enjoying his usual coffee, says Naidoo, he was 'eating garlic soup'. Brian Bunting commented that Mzala was on an all-vegetarian diet without protein, and that wasn't healthy. Blade Nzimande also recalls that Mzala had stopped eating meat and that Harry Gwala would tease him. 'What kind of a man are you who doesn't eat meat?' Gwala would ask before responding to his own question: 'You will get sick because you don't eat meat.' Nzimande was convinced by Mzala's argument when it came to African medicine. 'To me some things made sense,' he says, 'just like today I am making sense now, as Minister of Higher Education, Science and Innovation, about our indigenous knowledge systems.' For Nzimande, some of these African herbs have become part of our modern medicine, part of the pharmaceutical industry.

Robert Edgar, with whom Mzala spent several days at his home in the United States, says he was struck by his healthy diet, which included drinking fruit juice. Also, while in New York, Thandeka Gqubule-Mbeki says she found his eating habits 'funny':

> He used to be a fussy eater, so I would ask him, why do you not eat this and not eat that? And then he will tell me of the politics of the food industry, what's good for you, what's not good for you and I became aware that he's not well and that this journey was partly a personal journey and this urgency was a sense that he was running out of time.

Naidoo can still picture him walking up and down in the lounge of his London flat with 'cloves of garlic'. Patric Mellet also found the garlic story funny. 'One of his habits was to walk around with whole cloves of garlic in his jacket pockets.' He continues, 'Now garlic has an overpowering aroma and there would be me and Mzala travelling in a bus in London packed with commuters and standing room only and he would haul out a garlic and proceed in eating it like it was a chocolate bar.' Mellet was not convinced by Mzala's garlic theories though:

> Of course, with a mix of socialist and Seventh Day Adventist zeal, he would at the same time be passionately trying to convince me that garlic and a Mexican spirulina would answer any health issue. I was spellbound when it came to all of his other subjects, but this subject was one of those that did not convince me. His manner of making his case, however, was as intellectually polished as his other passions.

Mellet argues that Mzala's 'big thing' for natural medicine – as well as his radical political thoughts – may be traced to his religious background. However, some comrades, like Nzimande, never experienced Mzala's religious side. 'I never knew much about his religious side,' he says. 'He never showed his religious side to me.' But Mellet remains fascinated by Mzala's down-to-earth approach, even to intellectual discourse. It seems this time he was no longer the Mzala of Ngoye who vociferously pushed his points home. At this stage of his life, although still up to debate, he was calmer. He was now more appreciative of the use of simple language as progressive and never anti-intellectual. Thus, he regarded the opposite as 'a fascist trait'. Mellet says, 'He expected everyone to back up their arguments with solid data and argument. Most of us saw him as Comrade Commissar. Our teacher. I certainly learnt much from him.'

VIII

Mzala's love for reading and writing from early on is one aspect of his life that he carried all the way through. During this period, with exiled comrades now able to return, many in London were either preparing to leave or had already left. Celeste Naidoo was one of those who did not hesitate to grab the opportunity when it arose in 1990. 'Soon as I hear that we can go home I phoned my parents' to ask for their assistance. Mzala, however, still had unfinished business abroad, including his academic commitments.

Mzala was also 'assigned' to return home and was advised to pack, but he did not take kindly to this 'inappropriate' approach, regarded it as 'peremptory' and lacking consideration of the academic work he was undertaking in London. He also felt that the approach was too casual, especially as it was put to him by someone in the organisation he did not respect. So Mzala's response was that he was not ready.

When Nzimande returned home from his sabbatical in 1989, Mzala was clear on what needed to be done. Having carefully studied the Russian Revolution, Mzala thought it vital to borrow from Lenin's 1905 book, *Two Tactics of Social-democracy in the Democratic Revolution*. In this book, Lenin presented his thoughts on the Russian Revolution and the need to appreciate the character of the motive force of that revolution, the role of the working class in it, the revolutionary prospects, and the tactics arising from the analysis. Lenin conceptualised the revolutionary-democratic government of the proletariat and the peasantry and the path of transition from the bourgeois-democratic to the socialist revolution.[46]

This was a framework that Mzala thought could be useful for the South African revolution. He told Nzimande that the task was to read and engage with Lenin's work, and explicitly declared this as the 'tactic for this period we are [in] because clearly we are in a transition'. These were the lenses through which Mzala analysed the South African revolution. He was demonstrating clarity of purpose on what needed to be done inside the country once organisations like the SACP were unbanned. One of the things he informed Nzimande about was that 'when the Boers are forced to unban the Party, we will rebuild the structures of the SACP inside the country'.

Mzala was excited about the possibility of returning home as soon as he was done with his academic work. 'No, mzala, I'll come back,' he told Nzimande. Once Nzimande was back home, they kept in constant communication telephonically, and Nzimande would continue to pose the question of Mzala returning every time he felt things were moving in the country. With both the ANC and SACP congresses approaching, the political landscape was developing rapidly and Nzimande was yearning to engage politically with Mzala during this transition. He was looking forward to Mzala's return and must have been hopeful when Mzala was nominated as a delegate representing the London constituency for the 1990 ANC conference.

CHAPTER 12

Dazzled by capital: The ANC and the transition to democracy

I

When Mzala arrived in the United States in October 1990, a lot had already transpired in relation to the South African national liberation struggle. Political parties had been unbanned in February, followed by the release of Nelson Mandela (after 27 years in jail) and other political prisoners. Formal negotiations between the ANC and the government had started in May, leading to agreement for full-scale negotiations.[1] This was followed in August by the 'suspension' of the armed struggle by the ANC, Mzala's dream of the 'revolutionary army' that would 'overthrow' the racist apartheid government through a 'people's war' now hanging by a thread.

South Africa was a hive of activity with high-profile delegations – from the United Nations, for instance – touching down in the country. Within a few months, Tambo and his family also arrived back in the country. But, while Mandela was emerging as a global superstar preaching reconciliation, a low-intensity civil war was unfolding in Mzala's home province of Natal. Ater a long absence, the ANC and its allies were working hard to rebuild structures inside the country. In July, the SACP had emerged publicly for the first time since it was declared illegal as the Communist Party of South Africa (CPSA) in 1950, and an interim leadership was elected.[2] What could have been Mzala's mood and views in the context of these developments while he was outside the country?

It is apparent that Mzala was in no hurry to return home. With his PhD almost done, he was now preparing himself to spread his wings even further across the Atlantic, where he planned to take up a fellowship in the United States. Mzala had been in contact with professors Gail Gerhart and Tom Karis, to whom he had been introduced by John Daniel. Daniel was convinced that Mzala was serious about becoming an academic, a point he would later emphasise in his discussions with Gerhart.

Best known for the four-volume book series, *From Protest to Challenge: A Documentary History of African Politics in South Africa 1882–1964* published in the 1970s, both Gerhart and Karis had a keen interest in South Africa. Karis had written the first two volumes in the series with Gwendolen Carter. Gerhart had written extensively about South Africa, dating back to the 1960s when she completed her PhD at Columbia University on the Pan Africanist Congress. Karis, a former foreign service officer who was a critic of US policy on South Africa, was a leading historian of the South African liberation movement. Both were now senior research fellows at Yale University's Southern Africa Research Program (SARP). Based at Yale, the programme had been inaugurated in 1977 to focus on southern African issues.

Daniel had been cajoling Mzala to spend some time in the United States, so when an opportunity to attend a conference with Joe Slovo arose, Mzala grabbed it with both hands, against his doctors' orders. Both Slovo and Mzala were scheduled to speak on the future of socialism at the Monthly Review conference in New York in October 1990. Mzala was also invited to speak at many other platforms. Although his in-laws were now back in the US, this was Mzala's first trip to the country, and he spent almost a month in formal and informal discussions with scholars and activists with an interest in South African history and politics. Apart from attending and presenting at the conference, he attended numerous seminars and presented guest lectures.

At this point, Mzala had not been approached by SARP but immediately expressed interest when that possibility was raised. Upon learning that Neville Alexander was also in the programme, Mzala indicated his willingness to meet and talk to him, especially on the Azanian Manifesto that Alexander and his colleagues had written in 1983. In 1984, while he was in Swaziland, Mzala had written a pamphlet exposing some of the Manifesto's theoretical incoherencies; in 1985, he expanded on this in a four-part series of articles in *Sechaba*.

Mzala told Gerhart that he had read almost everything Alexander had written.[3] His desire to meet Alexander was realised. Years later, reflecting on the Azanian Manifesto and Mzala's harsh rebuttal, Alexander spoke about their meeting. 'To my regret,' he wrote, 'I met Comrade Mzala only briefly at Yale University in 1990 or 1991 and found him to be a very different person from the apparatchik that peers from underneath the cloak of scholarship he presents in this forgettable pamphlet.'[4]

II

Among the individuals who vividly recall this moment and encounter with Mzala is activist and veteran journalist Thandeka Gqubule-Mbeki. Gqubule-Mbeki was at Columbia University doing a master's degree in Journalism, after colleagues such as Anton Harber and Shaun Johnson at the *Weekly Mail,* along with her father, decided to send her back to school. 'So I got to Colombia and had the time of my life doing my master's and doing extra subjects in the Department of Political Economics,' she says. She was studying under and rubbing shoulders with the likes of Claude Ake and Achille Mbembe.

One of the first people Gqubule-Mbeki met in the US was Senti Thobejane who introduced her to the South African 'crowd' in New York. Thobejane, a graduate of the Solomon Mahlangu Freedom College in Tanzania, had been sent by the ANC to study for a master's degree in radiation science. While in the US, he became an acquaintance of the historians Tom Karis and Gwendolen Carter who were, in turn, connected to many other South Africans. Gqubule-Mbeki says they were 'a magnet for South Africans in exile and also those who had come to study'. She continues:

> One day in the train Senti introduced me to Mzala Nobleman Nxumalo and I had read his book when I was covering the stuff in the township and the stuff in the East Rand and in the big rallies in Inkatha in Natal, which I used to follow *uMntwana* [Buthelezi] around when I was covering. I almost died when I met him.

Mzala's intellect and humbleness drew Gqubule-Mbeki even closer. They began spending time together in discussions and political debates. During this period, says Gqubule-Mbeki, many leading figures of the liberation struggle, like Pallo Jordan and Chris Hani, were also in the US on various missions. Having met Jordan the previous year in Paris while covering the 'talks about talks' as an intern for *Libération* newspaper in France, Gqubule-Mbeki had become acquainted with him. 'I think I abandoned my books for a few weeks just to be a groupie. But I learnt so much.' Mzala introduced Gqubule-Mbeki to the New York left and his friends from the Marxist school, which she later frequented for various sessions.

Although she found Mzala fascinating and full of ideas, Gqubule-Mbeki recalls that 'he was intense. It took a lot to even make him lighten up, everything was urgent, everything was serious, everything was earnest.' Karis observed that, despite his fierce intensity, Mzala had a relaxed and warm personality. Reflecting about that period, Gqubule-Mbeki says:

> You meet very few people who are that gentle but that earnest. He was in a hurry to impart everything he had learnt and to see it manifest in the world. We had ideas of justice, a concern for the country, and a love for information and in detail and joining the dots and a prolific reader and an amazing, beautiful mind and he was the kindest soul you can meet, curious about everything.

She chuckles when she recalls that 'he wasn't neat'. Gerhart also described him as a man 'so totally in a world of ideas that he's rather negligent when it comes to practical things like eating, sleeping, and carrying an umbrella when it's raining'. John Daniel, says Gerhart, described him 'rather like a contemporary of Anton Lembede'. While in New York, Gerhart recalls, he attended the entire conference in the same shirt. Karis later recorded that Mzala went with Robert Edgar to the University of Virginia for a measly $100, out of which he had to pay expenses, leaving him with $70 clear. But Mzala gave no indication of concern about such matters.

Gqubule-Mbeki is grateful for the time she spent with Mzala, 'listening to him, sitting on the streets and cafes of New York, listening to him and Gail Gerhart and argumentative but never offensive'. While Mzala was fond of debates and not one to retreat, Gqubule-Mbeki noted that his arguments were always posed as a question and she found this fascinating. His arguments were 'polemical, but not obnoxious, always prodding you to think differently. And he would ask you, if you were to think of it this way, you know what would happen.' Mzala was reading across genres and one of the areas he encouraged Gqubule-Mbeki to read about was food and the dynamics of this industry. They interacted and mingled with the South African community, including spending time in Aubrey Nkomo's flat, where his wife Barbara entertained them. One day, recalls Gqubule-Mbeki, 'a number of us sat on the floor just listening to Chris [Hani] and Mzala vibe'.

At the time that Mzala travelled to the United States, his in-laws, Violet and Jonas Gwangwa, were living in New Jersey. Gqubule-Mbeki says Mzala took the opportunity to visit them and, as usual, he brought along with him a group of others. Senti and Gqubule-Mbeki were spending most of their time with Mzala, and she thought he was almost asexual. Dating and so on was never in his mind. 'But the way he would be so concerned, as if he is gender blind.' Top of his mind were seminars and lectures that he recommended to Gqubule-Mbeki, with motivation on the exact aspect of the debates they had that the seminar would resolve. 'His love of ideas and imparting [them] was second to none. Even the people that he hung out with, it was because of his intrigue with the ideas that he hung around people like Gail Gerhart [and] Tom Karis.'

III

Outside of the conference, Mzala spent most of his time with Gerhart and Karis. He stayed with Gerhart for several days, and although she had known of Mzala for some time because of his writings and through Daniel, she was still in awe after meeting him for the first time. She described him as a slight man of about 5 foot 5 inches (about 1.65 metres) and of nondescript appearance, except for having lost most of his front teeth. What he lacked in physical stature he compensated for with his intellectual acumen. Daniel had described him to Gerhart as 'a gifted intellectual who has enormous potential to develop into an influential leader of his generation', praising him for his 'sterling character, modesty and integrity'.

Gerhart concedes that the advanced billing by Daniel predisposed her to look for these positive qualities when they eventually met. 'I did find them,' she wrote, 'and much more besides, in spite of arming myself with a certain wariness in anticipation of meeting someone so evidently a darling of the hard left.' She continued:

> What I found was a charmingly candid, very undogmatic, extremely thoughtful and shrewd man, socially shy but intellectually self-confident, who spoke so knowledgably and articulately about South African politics that one could publish his verbal commentaries virtually unedited and they would stand as substantial contributions to current debates and analyses.

Karis agreed with Gerhart that Daniel had not exaggerated.

Both Gerhart and Karis recorded some of their discussions with Mzala, perhaps in the process capturing his only unwritten raw thoughts. It appears these engagements were cathartic for Mzala, allowing him a rare opportunity to freely express emotions he had bottled for a very long time about various aspects of the liberation movement. As Gqubule-Mbeki posits, he appeared like someone who was in a hurry to share as much as possible as if he was running out of time. In one of the discussions immediately after arriving in New York, Mzala had a detailed, no-holds-barred conversation with Gerhart and Gqubule-Mbeki about himself and his academic interests. It was clear that at this stage, like many PhD journeys, doubts were creeping into his mind. Even though he had drafted all the chapters, he had been stalling because he was wondering whether he should conduct some empirical research in South Africa. Of course, time would not permit this, as the thesis was due in less than six months. He seized the opportunity and lobbied Gerhart and Karis to read his draft and provide comments.

What stands out about this period is that it gives us insights into Mzala's thoughts on an array of issues. He was very critical of the ANC's leadership. He later would justify his views, mainly shared in private sessions, on the grounds that they were deliberate and 'trying to shock' and bring to the fore a reality to which the public was not privy. Using hand gestures to drive the point home, he argued that in the future and if some people were to have it their way, only the 'official' sanitised history of the movement would be known. Although he was not exaggerating, his objectives were to expose certain problems and weaknesses in the liberation movement so that people like Gerhart should not settle for the 'benign-official-pretty picture' of history. He thought it was necessary to dig under the surface and behind the propaganda images.

Mzala did not want books about the ANC's history to be 'cheerleading types'. Most fundamentally, he wanted his children to read a genuinely objective history. While still alive to the importance of not bringing the organisations into disrepute as part of the code of conduct one pledged when joining the SACP and ANC, Mzala said he felt a great urge to be truthful, to look for the objective reality and to avoid a cover-up mentality. Indeed, while in the US he spoke candidly about certain practices within the ANC.

Mzala believed that, while there were many strengths to the ANC – or it would not have survived this long and pushed the apartheid regime to the brink of defeat – he felt that there were plenty of reasons for the people of

South Africa to be militant even if they had never heard of the organisation. Mzala did not think that the ANC could claim sole responsibility for the popular militancy – in fact, he thought that would be 'ridiculous'. Although he never referred to notes during these discussions, he appeared to have mentally organised his thoughts. Among all the themes he shared, Oliver Tambo was central.

IV

Shifting his focus to OR Tambo as a subject for his fellowship, Mzala said that this was still confidential. He appeared to have learnt from Adelaide Tambo's mistakes in handling the book on Tambo's speeches. Apparently, she had not consulted Tambo, who was 'a very consultation-oriented person'; according to Mzala, 'he was especially irate about inclusion of speeches that showed up [an] embarrassing alignment with Joshua Nkomo/ZAPU'.[5] The book *Oliver Tambo Speaks*, compiled by Adelaide Tambo, was eventually published some 14 years later. Mzala thought that the biography was a different thing, which Tambo was not opposed to. On the contrary, Mzala said Tambo was in fact one of the individuals who encouraged him to write the book.

Mzala revealed that to get Tambo's commitment to anything it was crucial to get it pushed through the 'presidential council', a subcommittee of the organisation's NEC. Thus, around 1987, just after the seventy-fifth anniversary of the ANC, Mzala penned a tribute to Tambo in the *African Communist* on the occasion of his seventieth birthday – an article that would demonstrate Mzala's interest in Tambo as a subject. He told Gerhart that during this period, mainly in Lusaka, Tambo dictated 18 tapes, working alone and apparently with considerable forethought and organisation. Tambo seemed to have written down his thoughts first before recording them. Amid his numerous commitments, Mzala had been transcribing the tapes and becoming even more impressed and inspired by Tambo. 'You could transcribe the tapes almost without editing,' he told Gerhart.

Although the tapes only covered the period up to 1942, Tambo was willing to resume the project after the ANC's December conference. Mzala was buoyant about the fact that Tambo wanted him to write the biography but, according to Mzala, Tambo remained apprehensive because he wanted confidentiality, allowing him to record critical views pertaining to people still living. Tambo's view was that it might be healthier for the biography to be published posthumously. Mzala concurred that 'there must be candour and confidentiality', otherwise the project 'would be useless'. Nevertheless, Mzala demonstrated his preparedness and a clearly mapped out plan for this project, mindful of the potential difficulties it entailed. Thus, he informed Gerhart that he felt he had very good rapport with Tambo, who had 'singled him out as special'.

> ORT's [Tambo's] memory is very clear, but he has days when he doesn't feel well and his speech becomes hard to understand, and he can't work. Then a few days later he's much better. Tapes of him speaking now will be slower and more difficult to understand, but definitely usable. To do a long talking job will require a long period in London and great flexibility. He designed the topics discussed in the tapes done so far.[6]

Mzala agreed with Gerhart's advice that future interviews should be more of a dialogue as opposed to Tambo's current approach of recording what he thought was worth recording. Indeed, a semi-structured interview would be more beneficial because it would allow the interviewer to probe certain aspects beyond what the subject preferred to say. Nevertheless, Mzala was visibly excited by the prospect of writing Tambo's biography. Nzimande recalls that this was one of the books that Mzala really wanted to write.

Thandeka Gqubule-Mbeki, present at the discussion between Mzala and Gerhart, says he talked a lot about Tambo's project when he was in the US. 'The biography on OR Tambo he really loved.' Upon return from the US, Mzala fell ill and had to be hospitalised around February 1991. On 14 February, he pleaded with Mpho that he needed to see Tambo because 'he had started writing the biography'. Says Mpho, 'So we went. I had to smuggle him out of the hospital.' They took a cab from the London hospital to Tambo's home. It could be this encounter that Dali Tambo was referring to when he described Mzala as having been terribly thin when he last saw him.

V

Although Tambo was central to Mzala's talk, the main theme he sought to drive home on the first evening with Gerhart was the ANC's inability to provide sufficient 'encouragement to critical or objective thinking'. He felt that the ANC had failed to encourage 'democratic procedures', and posited that many of them just 'learnt to wear blinkers, digest and repeat a line given to them. Did Mandela say this? Then you repeat it.' There was a lot of name-dropping, according to Mzala, where senior comrades were often used to legitimise decisions. He reserved his best praise for Jordan. 'One person who has the needed critical sense is Pallo Jordan.' He referred to the piece Jordan had brought to him in which he had challenged Dialego's negative assessment of Trotsky 'because none of the ANC organs would have it printed'.

However, Mzala contextualised the problem by relating it to the underground environment in which the ANC found itself after it was banned in the 1960s. This situation gave rise to the undemocratic behaviour that Mzala was now decrying. He maintained:

> Democracy had to be sacrificed to achieve unity, or this is how it was perceived. An inner circle formed around Tambo, and this group formulated the line. At first the line was obvious, but later it wasn't so obvious what it should be; the possibilities for disunity were high, and so discipline and [a] no-questions attitude began to take hold. Gradually this hardened as those in control became concerned with keeping control, and not losing their positions of power.[7]

Mzala hastened to qualify that this statement referred to the people around Tambo and not a criticism of Tambo himself. He continued to credit Tambo for holding the organisation together during difficult times in order to present a united face to the world. However, Tambo and the organisation, he argued, had paid a heavy price for this in the sense that it led to lack of democracy. Mzala thought that the people in power were not interested in improving the organisation's capabilities, especially in areas such as intelligence gathering, research, military strategy and its implementation. 'One might see the function of age,' he said, 'but it's better seen as one of longevity and a desire to hold onto positions gained at an early stage.'

It is possible that this view represented a general frustration of Mzala's generation, the 1976 generation, which felt that the leadership was getting comfortable in exile. This was the crux of their dissatisfaction at the 1985 Kabwe Conference, a discontent partly captured in Mzala's article, 'Cooking the Rice inside the Pot'. Across the decades, the younger generation within the ANC had always vocalised their discontent and impatience with the leadership, dating back to the 1944 generation that had formed the ANC Youth League (ANCYL). This generation was not happy with the ANC's strategy at the time and fought hard to imbue some revolutionary vigour through their 1949 Programme of Action that culminated in the launch of the first defiance campaign.[8] Even the current generation of the ANCYL is impatiently advocating for economic freedom and a generational mix in the deployment of young people to strategic democratic institutions.

Mzala continued to argue that when new people came into exile bringing new ideas and questions – the generation of comrades such as Thabo Mbeki, Pallo Jordan, Francis Meli and Sizakele Sigxashe – troubling challenges were supressed in the name of 'maintaining ANC traditions'. The age of the organisation was invoked as a way of reinforcing this suppression. Mzala did not see the logic to some of the so-called 'tradition' arguments; he considered this as just a cover for unwillingness to entertain new thinking, which implied new people:

> A tone of veneration was supposed to be used when speaking to the power-holders. When speaking of [Alfred] Nzo, one refers to him as 'the SG' [secretary-general]. And one had to go through these people to get to Tambo, although Tambo sometimes on his own jumps over these people when he sees a situation that requires his intervention.[9]

By the time of the post-Soweto influx, he said, the power structure in the organisation had hardened, with the 'clique' having established a modus operandi among themselves. They had 'learnt how to reproduce a type of underling who was to their liking', a 'yes man' and a 'choir'. In this regard, Mzala characterised four types of the younger generation in the ANC.

The first type, he said, comprised those who were noticed, chosen and promoted by the leadership because of their loyalty and unquestioning attitude. 'In return for their loyalty,' he pointed out, 'they are praised and built up into "little idols". If they ever once begin to ask questions or show less than 100% personal loyalty, then they are unceremoniously dumped.' Mzala made example of Welile Nhlapo (also known as Welile Mkhize) whom he described as 'an outstanding youth leader in SASO before 1976'. Because the ANC needed credible people from this group, Nhlapo was made head of the youth section. 'We all assumed at the time of the Kabwe Conference that he would get a seat on the NEC, but he was just dumped and instead his deputy Mandala Manzini was nominated … At first Mkhize looked obedient – but later he had begun to ask questions.'

Mzala identified the second type as a group of loyal individuals, partisan to the ANC as an organisation but critical of the leadership. In the main, he said, this is the post-1976 group that went into MK. 'Some became discontented because of stagnation in [the] camps when nothing seemed to be happening. If they expressed this discontent, they were regarded as a threat, and the favoured method of silencing them was to accuse them of being agents.' Although suspicious caution was necessary because the agent problem was real, this was also a useful method to silence dissent. Others were not accused of being spies, he posited, 'but were squelched by being accused of being "anti-leader", which was considered a very bad label to have pinned on you'. He continued:

> In Angola there were some people who were imprisoned by the movement for eight years and nothing was ever proved against them; when they were let out they demanded explanations and never got any. The Angola mutiny was the clearest case of demonstrating the problem of lack of democracy in the ANC. People in this category that got too dangerous would be attacked in *Sechaba*, etc.[10]

When one traces Mzala's history in the movement through his actions and writings, it becomes clear that he belonged to this group. As a product of 1976, Mzala was not one to be silent. This was against his character. He sided with comrades who were critical of the leadership and openly punted the 'people's war' strategy. Not many comrades had the courage to tell the organisation that it was 'building pyramids in Egypt'. For this, he was one of those comrades labelled an 'agent'. The way he left the country did not make things easy for him. Dumisani Nduli recalls a group that tried to label Mzala a spy, using some dubious argument that he was seen carrying a phone when students torched the administrative building at the University of Zululand in 1976.

Mzala classified the third type as those who were 'just there' and made no waves. At public meetings, they shouted 'Viva!' and 'Down with X!', sang the national anthem – but later in the shebeens, after they had a few beers, they complained bitingly, called leaders nasty names. In the shebeens and bars, the first type – the 'blue-eyed boys' – were berated with names worse than spies and were seen as yes men by this third type. He said one of the milder epithets was 'the members of the members' because, while they were members of the ANC, they could be regarded as 'special' members. He thought of this third group as people who were brought in at Morogoro and Kabwe as appointed delegates to do the bidding on behalf of the bosses. The second type 'consolidated' themselves by gaining recruits from the third type. Of course, just as the ANC membership is not homogeneous, these types varied, depending on context and location in term of ANC regions.

Mzala characterised the fourth type as those people who had recently come out of prison. He saw them as closest to the second type:

> They are critical of lack of democracy. Some of them are veterans of the Angolan camps and have carried that grievance with them. In prison there was actually more democracy and much more open discussion, in spite of the Rivonia 'elders' not being all that attuned to it (with the partial exception of Sisulu).

For Mzala, none of the four types extended to cover those in the movement who had been genuine 'mischief-makers', critics who were not serious about achieving the organisation's goal.

He used the Kabwe Conference to demonstrate his point. The Angolan delegates had organised themselves to try to sway the conference, he said. 'They wanted to challenge delegates who weren't elected but got credentials anyway ... When they tried to raise questions on how delegates had been accredited, they were met with a "choir" of boos, etc., well orchestrated.' Mzala contended that, since the unbanning and the release of political prisoners, many more openly 'heretical' ideas were being expressed in meetings. He thought the leadership no longer had control and thus could not silence the critics. He was simultaneously predicting and advocating that the present power-holders were 'simply caretakers and that in December there will be quite a cataclysmic change. December won't be anything like Morogoro and Kabwe, where things were tightly controlled.'

By 'December', Mzala was referring to the first consultative conference of the ANC to be held inside the country. He was basing this prediction on the reaction after the Groote Schuur meeting where 'branches berated [Secretary-General] Nzo for not consulting about what positions the ANC would take, and not reporting back afterwards'. On 4 May 1990, the apartheid government and the ANC met; in what later became known as the Groote Schuur Minute, an agreement was reached on a common commitment towards the resolution of violence and intimidation, commitment to stability and peaceful negotiation process.[11] According to Mzala:

> There were angry people at the London branch meeting when he [Nzo] came there later; they said, 'we are not just journalists waiting to take

down notes on what the line is now'. Earlier when Walter Sisulu came to Lusaka the first time, he was bombarded with a storm of protest and complaints against the leadership about the lack of democracy.[12]

After a detailed talk, to which Gerhart and Gqubule-Mbeki listened attentively, Gqubule-Mbeki entered the discussion. In agreeing with Mzala's observation on a potential revolt, she said similar dissatisfactions were expressed at a big Natal meeting after Groote Schuur where questions on the democratic process were posed. She observed the emergence of a clash of cultures. On one hand, the leadership in exile had developed a particular style of leadership, largely influenced by the concrete conditions of being an exile organisation. On the other hand, activists inside the country, steeped in the tradition of the MDM and UDF, were clear on democratic process and accountability. According to Gqubule-Mbeki, the older generation from exile and those from Robben Island lacked the democratic experience of the UDF.

Hence, when Nzo appointed Winnie Mandela to head the Department of Social Welfare without broader consultations, he did not anticipate the 400 letters of protest from ANC branches. Apparently, Nzo had consulted the inner circle, as was the practice in exile. Gqubule-Mbeki pointed out that the organisation of social workers led by Leila Patel made various complaints about the fact that Winnie Mandela was not a practising member of the profession, that their views had not been solicited, and that 'no one in the ANC hierarchy has even asked them about all the thinking and planning they have been doing as professionals about the way social problems should be approached in the new [South Africa]'. This illustrates the expectation and trust people had placed on the ANC. Their experience of oppression at the hands of a brutal apartheid regime had awakened a culture of civil activism.

VI

Mzala was thus pinning his hopes on the December consultative conference. 'There is going to be a huge shake-up,' he predicted, believing that the powerful would include the likes of Mosiuoa 'Terror' Lekota and some ex-prisoners. 'It won't be like the last two conferences,' he said, referring to Morogoro and Kabwe. But there would be a demand for democracy mainly due to the experiences of 1985 in Kabwe, which he still resented. Mzala considered the traditions arising out of the UDF's premise of accountability to members as a possible catalyst for change. No one, he said, would tolerate delegates being there who weren't elected, and the 'doctoring' that had been experienced in the past.

Mzala believed that Tambo would be remote from politicking and felt that Mandela didn't know the exile 'co-optees' of the NEC. He stated, more as a wish than analysis, that '[these] unknown people can never be elected in December because the conference will be preponderantly insiders [and] not exiles'. At the same time, Mzala was keen for those inside the country to learn and understand much more about the exile ANC. He was being deliberately frank and Gerhart felt that the reason for this was Gqubule-Mbeki's presence. He mentioned several times, said Gerhart, that 'he was painting a picture of the ANC in exile that she had never heard before and apparently found quite shocking'.

Though still out of the country, he was nevertheless convinced that the picture the people at home had of the ANC was far removed from reality. This, coupled with the fact that exile returnees had not yet had the time to learn about activists inside the country, made for a complex situation. Still, he was convinced that it was imperative that the ANC elect an 'internally based' leadership at the conference, 'people who have the feel of the situation on the ground which the exiles can't have'. He also thought that, up until then, only a small proportion of the exiles had returned.

Of course, history would prove Mzala wrong, as many exiles participated in the conferences and emerged to occupy senior leadership positions, but he would not to be the last to raise this concern. ANC critics across ideological lines have lamented the malign influence of exiles on the organisation's culture, couched as it was in secrecy and a lack of internal democracy because of its exile years.[13] Some have located this 'lack of internal democracy' in the organisation's continued adherence to Leninist principles such as 'democratic centralism' and the desire for 'absolute party discipline' on the part of members.[14] To date, there are still calls to even rethink Marxism along democratic lines. Thus, the 'vanguardist Marxism' associated mainly with hierarchical communist parties and adopted by national liberation movements like the ANC is now considered obsolete by some in the quest for more internal democracy.[15]

VII

As the night wore on, Mzala dished out insights on the ANC that not many had brought to the fore up until then. In his frank assessment of the revolution, Gerhart was struck by his 'unpompous' and 'undefensive' attitude. He did not pretend to know it all, but was forthright and honest in his engagements, gracefully accepting facts he was unaware of. Throughout his exile years, Mzala had developed a penchant for critical thinking even where it went against the grain. By means of his forthright engagements, including his writing, he was prepared to rock the boat. He was not confined by the need to toe the party line at the expense of the truth. Obviously, up until then he had kept some of his most robust criticism of the ANC to himself and some of his close confidantes. For some reason, he had considered the platform to engage Gerhart and others in the US as an opportunity to reveal some of his harsher views about the movement.

As he continued with his critique, he used SOMAFCO as a point of reference, expressing doubts that the acclaimed school had lived up to its purpose of providing a good 'alternative education'. He argued that the college had not taught people critical thinking or how to be objective. In 1985, Mzala had argued that the educational approach of the liberation movement should be to produce trained cadres who would advance the objectives of the revolution. This included producing people who would use their education to improve the conditions of the oppressed and exploited classes.[16]

Repeating a similar view now, he argued that the 'alternative' of SOMAFCO was just a counter-ideology that had not prepared students to be serious and objective intellectuals so badly needed. In that sense, he argued, SOMAFCO had not been any different than what it was supposed to combat. In fact, stalwarts like Harold Wolpe, Seretse Choabi and Henry Makgothi were also critical of the school for not being what it was intended to be. 'An example was the work programme where students were supposed to do weeding, etc., on grounds. What was this for? There was never a coherent policy linking practical dirty work to [the] ANC ideal.' However, he singled out Senti Thobejane – studying in the US at the time – as one of the few bright lights, 'but mainly the graduates just vanish and make no contribution'.

Returning to the question of the UDF, he laid the blame squarely on the shoulders of the exile ANC for its inability to correctly read the emergence of this organisation. He thought the ANC leadership was unsure how to view and relate to the UDF. 'Major errors were made,' he said, with leaders such as Govan Mbeki, without substance, believing that the UDF's structures were very weak and, as such, had no actual popular base. Mzala disagreed with Mbeki's views on his appraisal of the UDF's strength and his conclusion that, as such, the influence of Indians and non-Africans became disproportionate.

For Mzala this lack of leadership was manifesting itself in various facets of the organisation, including the slowness in setting up structures on the ground after the unbanning. This led to complaints from veteran leaders such as Govan Mbeki about resources being concentrated in Johannesburg. Instead of letting the Rivonia Trialists languish, argued Mzala, they should be sent to areas where there were no organisers. He was told by some people in northern Natal that in their area neither the ANC nor Inkatha had ever come to organise, and these were people who were likely to join whichever party came to them first.

Instead of using the preparations for the December conference as an excuse for lack of time, he felt that this was precisely the time to mobilise the people around the ANC's objectives. Thus, he invoked the speech by Joe Slovo in Cape Town where he said negotiations were not a substitute for popular struggle. And yet, argued Mzala, Slovo and the ANC were in fact 'acting like they believe it is'. Mzala lambasted the ANC for not having a plan in place for popular struggle, let alone armed struggle, to keep the pressure on. 'In fact, Slovo speaks like he believes there can be a resolution with the government through the "elites",' and this displayed a mentality of people who 'are in a historical waiting room'.

As the tirades continued unabatedly, Gerhart began to ponder whether Mzala was not expressing a long-term grievance that the ANC had never taken seriously the strategy of building towards a popular insurrection. From the early 1980s, Mzala had been one of the leading advocates of the people's war. According to Gerhart, when he worked in the frontline states of Swaziland and Mozambique in the early 1980s, he became fed up with the lack of commitment to this strategy. At one point in Swaziland, said Mzala, 'we did something very revolutionary; we downed tools', and told the leadership in Maputo that 'we are not going to stay in place unless there's more serious effort made to build underground structures in preparation for an uprising'.

As far as Mzala was concerned, the ANC was unprepared for the actual uprising. He said there was a time in late the 1970s to early 1980s when there ought to have been a strategy to capitalise on the groundswell of mass unrest. 'They thought that blowing up SASOL and a few episodes like that were so terrific, but something much greater was actually required.' He drew comparisons to the Zimbabwean, Namibian, Mozambican and Angolan struggles where the war was successfully carried into the country as a guerrilla struggle. But in South Africa, he argued, 'we never succeeded in achieving this'. For example, on the Zimbabwean struggle he said there was a time when Robert Mugabe made it clear that the fighting would continue at the same time as the negotiations, down to the last possible moment, so as to strengthen the revolutionary side. He also indicated that at some point Tambo alluded to the example of Vietnam, where fighting and talking went on simultaneously, and that it would have to be the same in South Africa. 'But MK failed to get anywhere near this.'

When the clock passed 1 am, Mzala's audience was weary, having listened to him attentively for some hours. But he was not done. Mzala ascribed the leadership failure to implement mass insurrection as resolved at the Kabwe Conference to the role of South African business. He accused business leaders of convincing the ANC that there was no link between capitalism and apartheid, and they promised to help put more pressure on government. The leadership, said Mzala, was swayed by this seemingly compelling proposition, which was 'dazzling', 'infatuating' and 'so gratifying'.

Gerhart was still wide awake, and asked whether he thought it was not a case of the ANC trying but failing due to lack of capability to make headway against a much more powerful foe. Mzala responded with a firm no. 'That's too generous an interpretation,' he retorted. He was convinced that the leadership had almost abdicated its responsibility by elevating sanctions as the primary strategy to defeat the government. He thought the leadership had prioritised sanctions more than the armed struggle, especially in the context of FW de Klerk's admission that they were hurting, as opposed to PW Botha, who downplayed their impact. He continued:

> Businessmen actually visited the leaders in prison and made promises that they would support majority rule. The leaders were impressed, flattered, too easily won over without analysing what these people were up to. They abandoned the idea of a military struggle and settled for the dubious idea [of] business helping them come to power. Businessmen also went to court the exiles, of course. The leaders were 'dazzled' by this ...

To his mind, this was only possible because MK had failed to make war a reality for the whites. 'Thabo Mbeki and Johnny Makhathini had begun to believe that the armed struggle was futile,' and hence, when feelers from the government came, they were receptive. 'The feelers were reinforced by the businessmen', with frontline state leaders like Kenneth Kaunda playing a prominent role, which eventually included an initially reluctant Robert Mugabe. Mzala stated, 'This culminated in the Harare Declaration, one case where the ANC did get out in front of the regime with an initiative of its own.'

Nevertheless, Mzala still regarded as 'delusional' the notion that the government's retreat was because of ANC pressure. He likened this suggestion to the organisation falling 'victim to its own propaganda'. On the contrary, Mzala attributed the change of tack by the NP to the argument by influential businesspeople, such as Tony Bloom, that apartheid and economic growth were incompatible and so a new system had to be found. Salient in Mzala's harsh appraisal of the leadership was a sense of irritation at either being outmanoeuvred or betrayed. While he believed this to be the NP's strategy, his problem was that 'the ANC has accepted this too naively' with no 'clear conception of what end objectives we are being manipulated towards by the Nationalists. We are still just reacting to their moves, which are much more calculated than our own.'

He maintained that the ANC's research department – which he thought had always been a sham and hardly researched anything – was unable to play a meaningful role in this process, blaming this subjective weakness for the lack of information and intelligence about the government. He felt that there had been no attempts to formulate future scenarios and hence the movement was falling too readily for the government's machinations. It was precisely this weakness that made him believe that there would hardly be any open debates on policies in December, because 'they won't be prepared for it with an analysis'.

VIII

Another matter that continued to aggravate Mzala was the ongoing violence in Natal. This would be among the topical issues at the December conference in his absence. When Gqubule-Mbeki raised a concern that the leadership did not seem to have a strategy in response to the ongoing war and behaved instead as if they wished it would just go away, as though it was simply an annoying inconvenience, Mzala rejoined: 'Yes, it's a great inconvenience spoiling their otherwise clear run to the finish line.' He agreed that the leadership assumed that everyone would just change, and the violence would just go away. Part of the weakness, he thought, was that the movement had been caught off guard by the violence and so had no long-term vision how to handle it.

It seems that Mzala wished for the fighting to escalate towards a social revolution. He believed that there was a misperception within the ANC leadership that the war in Natal was a vestige of the past rather than a harbinger of the future. He agreed with Harry Gwala, whom he said had already warned the leadership that the violence could spread. The leadership's belief that the violence could be resolved through a deal with Buthelezi seemed unreasonable to him. Mzala felt that the ANC's strategy was simply to bide time and, at the right moment, the leadership could eventually win over Buthelezi and other homeland leaders.

However, he saw a division between what he called the 'Rivonia men' and the 'exile NEC' on how to deal with Buthelezi because Mandela, in particular, felt that Buthelezi should be accommodated since he carried the full weight of the Zulus. Not surprisingly, Mzala found this idea ludicrous. Gwala and Govan Mbeki were opposed to Mandela's view on Buthelezi and hence, when Mandela was booed at a rally in Durban, Gwala felt vindicated, said Mzala. He thought Mandela sounded silly when he used all of Buthelezi's praise titles, and was happy that Mandela was stopped from going to Ulundi to meet Buthelezi.

Mandela confessed that, on his release, his inclination was to immediately meet with Buthelezi and resolved their differences – an idea he took to the NEC in Lusaka and 'was voted down'. Mzala ascribed Mandela's attempts to bring Buthelezi into the fold to his own roots as a 'chief'. Mandela, however, based his views on Buthelezi's role as an ANCYL member at Fort Hare University, where he had regarded him as one of the 'movement's upcoming young leaders'. Also, Buthelezi's consistent calls for Mandela's release and what Mandela considered Buthelezi's 'resolute' opposition to apartheid and his refusal to allow KwaZulu to become an 'independent' homeland are what had swayed Mandela.[17] While it is factually correct that Mandela was indeed a chief, it was conjectural to use this as basis for his attempts to win over Buthelezi.

Nevertheless, Mzala believed that it was not only Mandela who held such views on Buthelezi. People such as Moses Mabhida and Johnny Makhathini, while they represented the left and right in the ANC, agreed that Buthelezi was potentially co-optable and that the ANC should gear its strategy to this end. The idea that Buthelezi was greeted by the ANC leadership with much fanfare whenever he came to London, as if he was royalty, irked Mzala. 'They were really enamoured of him.'

IX

During the discussions, Mzala constantly referred to Tambo. Even in moments of cynicism about the movement and its leadership, Mzala always spoke glowingly of Tambo. At every opportunity, he sang his praises and regarded him as the glue that held the movement together. He was quick to point out that Tambo did not share the desire of anti-democratic individuals to sideline critical thinkers, such as had been done at Kabwe. Mzala kept track of the inside politics by befriending NEC members, citing for instance Cassius Make (Job Tabane) as a friend. Mzala carefully cultivated his contacts in the NEC and, because of his contacts in 'high places', he would occasionally get to see minutes of NEC meetings. This enabled him to know about special internal NEC commissions. For example, he said that there had been no less than five commissions concerning charges of 'tribalism' in the ANC.

Another NEC member, John Nkadimeng, had also informed Mzala that in one of the meetings Tambo had expressed the view that they needed to keep critical thinkers in order not to stagnate. Tambo insisted on allowing critics and that they should not be stigmatised and characterised as 'anti-leader' for being critical. Mzala was greatly impressed by this, as well as that Tambo was able to relate to young, critical minds since, as a young ANC member, he had been much the same. To this end, he was appreciative of Tambo's attempts to maintain a rapport with younger members and not become isolated from them. He said that, while some of the Black Consciousness generation were loyal to the ANC after they joined it in exile, they remain critical thinkers.

Mzala cited Mongezi Stofile's example. Stofile, a former president of SASO, shocked people when he stood up in a meeting where Tambo was speaking to the youth members and openly challenged the ANC policy on holding talks with Buthelezi. This was in 1979, at around the same time Mzala wrote his first critical piece on Buthelezi and Inkatha. When others tried to stop Stofile, said Mzala, telling him that it was an aberration to criticise Tambo to his face, Tambo invited Stofile for a chat.

During that chat, Mzala said Tambo used his experience as a member of the ANCYL in the 1940s where they took the same stance towards their elders. To prove his point, Tambo produced Mandela's handwritten autobiography where he discussed the ANCYL period. He wondered aloud whether Mandela would be able to build such rapport with the youth. Mzala was looking forward to meeting someone like Terror Lekota, whom he regarded like 'a real up and comer' just like Peter Mayibuye (Joel Netshitenzhe). He thought Netshitenzhe was among the most promising of the young people in the ANC, someone who would go places. By that time, and at the age of 34, said Mzala, Netshitenzhe had been on many important committees.

X

At the New York conference on the future of socialism, Joe Slovo had addressed the question of what had created the gap between socialist reality and socialist aspiration. Was the promise false from the start or had it simply remained unfulfilled? Writing in the conference report, Mike Morris observed that the conference took place in the context of 'very few optimistic scenarios for socialists in the USA'. 'This lacuna,' he observed, 'perhaps explained the somewhat surprising adulation accorded to Slovo's presentations.'[18]

Slovo's adulation extended beyond the conference to the media. In the article 'Old Marxist Returns, with Hope for South Africa' in *The New York Times* of 17 October 1990, Slovo was described as 'an avuncular white man lionized in South African black townships as a symbol of resistance against apartheid, a committed Marxist with an ideology that many thought had collapsed with the Berlin Wall and a politician glad-handing his way across South Africa after years as a clandestine leader'.[19] The *Baltimore Evening Sun* also carried an article, 'Slovo's Vision', in which Slovo was reported as having said he believed the rights to property should be retained.[20]

So, when Thandeka Gqubule-Mbeki expressed scepticism about Slovo's comments at the conference, when he conceded that even he had accepted unquestioningly certain dogmas such as the principle of the 'dictatorship of the proletariat', Mzala leapt to Slovo's defence. 'No,' he said, adding that this was an inaccurate assessment of Slovo. He regarded Slovo as a critical thinker, and even someone like Slovo had felt censored at times. He argued that Slovo complained that some of his articles were suppressed. To Mzala, this was indicative of the fact that at some point the SACP accepted the Soviet line without questioning. He added, 'One was just meant to accept it *in toto* as an article of faith.' This, according to Gerhart, was Mzala's first mention of the SACP. It seemed to her that he had made a conscious decision to avoid mentioning it in their conversation. The SACP had jettisoned the concept of 'the dictatorship of the proletariat' at its Seventh

Congress in 1989, presumably with Slovo playing a pivotal role as general secretary.

Because of Slovo's closeness to Tambo, Mzala saw him as the 'ultimate insider' in the ANC. He informed his audience that Tambo had a sense of debt, coupled with a mutual respect, and thus his reliance on Slovo. While he hadn't uncovered the origins of this bond, Mzala felt that it went far back. Not many people in the NEC, he felt, were as close to Tambo as Slovo. Someone he thought came closest was Moses Mabhida, another SACP leader. Indeed, the ANC's alliance with communists was an issue within the organisation for years – before, during and after its time in exile. For example, Tambo had to constantly explain the alliance with the SACP on various platforms, such as when he addressed the National Press Club in Washington, DC, in January 1987.[21] Mzala used Tambo's eulogy at Mabhida's funeral in Maputo as evidence of their affinity. He thought the oration was 'qualitatively' different to many such speeches by Tambo, and markedly different to those of Moses Kotane, JB Marks and Joe Gqabi, for example. 'He spoke about his deep sense of loss; it was a genuine lament.'

Of course, Slovo and his wife Ruth First had a long track record in the liberation struggle. By 1943 they had met and befriended Mandela – Tambo's lifelong friend – at the University of the Witwatersrand, and Mandela had, in turn, met Tambo earlier at Fort Hare University.[22] First and Slovo worked very closely with emerging leaders such as Mandela, Tambo and Sisulu, who would eventually radicalise the ANC and play a leading role in the formation of the ANCYL.[23] In fact, Mzala alluded to this relationship by relating a story of Mandela's note to Tambo, smuggled out of prison before the Kabwe Conference. The note, referring to the special relationship between Mandela, Tambo and Slovo, was read to Conference.

Apparently, the note called for Conference to recognise Slovo's value and his tireless efforts on behalf of the liberation struggle. Mzala saw this as a prelude to Slovo's election to the NEC. Part of Mandela's letter, on behalf of leaders in Pollsmoor Prison and Robben Island Prison, read: '[The] positions taken by Oliver Tambo on various issues and also stressed by Joe Slovo inspired us tremendously. Both drew attention to the vital issues which, in our opinion, are very timely.'[24] Could it be coincidental or simply perfect timing that Mandela happened to write a letter to validate Slovo's role in the struggle to be read during Conference?

To emphasise the special bond between Tambo, Slovo and Mandela,

Mzala referred to the misconception about the formation of MK, which is always attributed to Mandela. In fact, he argued, it was Mandela and Slovo who set up MK. When Tambo handed over the 18 tapes he had recorded about his early life, he emphasised their confidentiality, only for Mzala to discover later that Tambo had played some of the tapes to Slovo and that he was aware of the project. To Mzala, this accentuated how close the two leaders were.

Mzala believed that even when decisions that affected NEC members were made, Slovo was often the exception to the rule. As the influence and growth of the ANC began to gain a foothold both inside and outside the country with the re-emergence of organised labour, schools and community uprisings, the government stepped up its efforts to infiltrate state agents into the movement in exile. With the influx of many young people post the 1976 Soweto uprising came spies and agents of the regime, too. Indeed, this penetration 'not only shook the stability of the movement; it threatened to erode its very foundation – its value system – and was to have repercussions for many years to come'.[25]

Thus, in the early 1980s, a number of individuals were incarcerated by the ANC in Lusaka. Mzala said that, because spies were so rife, some of the detentions were unfair, but at the time it seemed like it was necessary to be super-cautious wherever there was suspicion. Mzala said that the leadership, including Tambo, became so paranoid that he began to wonder whether the NEC had been infiltrated. At that time, Tambo issued special orders to guard the Lusaka headquarters; henceforth no one was to enter the building after hours, including NEC members, who up until then were able to access the building at any time. It was only Slovo and Mabhida, said Mzala, who were not affected by that order. Of course, Tambo's orders were not far-fetched, as years later it would emerge that the infiltration had indeed penetrated the NEC, and members such as Francis Meli, one of Mzala's closest comrades, were exposed.[26]

It is this proximity to communist leaders that Mzala said could have created the impression that Tambo himself was either a communist or pro-communist. But, he hastened to add, Tambo was not a communist. 'Though he has given the left free rein to work within the ANC, with the sky the limit,' Tambo himself did not accept communist doctrine. Hence, Mzala argued that the explanation of Tambo's relationship with these two men must have been founded on some completely different and perhaps much more subjective level.

XI

Slovo's life would be incomplete without Ruth First. They had met at the University of the Witwatersrand in 1946 where they were both students and activists of the then Communist Party of South Africa. Both were militants and intellectuals who would devote their lives to the struggle for equality and justice. First was brutally assassinated by the apartheid regime on 17 August 1982 at the age of 57.[27] However, Mzala did not think First was part of Tambo's inner circle, and not just because she was a woman but because of her completely different personality. Having spent time with First in Maputo in the early 1980s, Mzala admired her as both a scholar and veteran activist. In his 1983 tribute to her, Mzala used her life to explain the ANC's alliance with the SACP in the article 'Why We are with the Communists'.

Almost a decade later, Mzala was still in awe of First's revolutionary commitment, especially considering how she had suffered at the hands of the regime. She had used her skills as a writer to advance the struggle by assisting Govan Mbeki to write *The Peasants' Revolt* and putting together Mandela's *No Easy Walk to Freedom*. For both these books, First wrote a preface and foreword respectively. Still, Mzala thought she was acerbic; because of this, some characterised her as a 'Maoist', an explanation that Mzala thought to be 'untrue' and simplistic. He thought First objected to the whole notion of following the 'line'. She would say, 'Which line?' This amused Mzala so much that he used it one day while examining the New York City subway map. 'Which line?' he jested. 'The Q, the N or the R?' Mzala seemed to agree with First's question on the line and remarked that you always got the line by referring to whatever was being put out by Progress Publishers in Moscow.

According to Mzala, there were certain Moscow lines that First, who was not interested in leadership positions, just did not agree with and she said so openly. For example, she did not agree with the official line to support Mengistu Haile Meriam in Ethiopia, and instead vocalised her support for Eritrean independence. Mzala said First also openly questioned the concept of the two-stage theory in relation to the South African national liberation struggle. While this strategy could work in underdeveloped colonies that had to secure self-determination before they could work on getting socialism, First felt that things were different in South Africa. Because there was no foreign power from which to obtain liberation, the fight for socialism could not wait for the end of white rule but had to be constantly waged, said Mzala. She believed that in South Africa the class struggle was the real struggle, and that any talk of 'national' struggle was wrong. According to Mzala's interpretation, First believed that classes, and not nations, were oppressed, and also that South Africa was an industrial country and so qualitatively different from 'colonies'.

However, Mzala believed that Slovo and First shared one particular trait: both were regarded as 'renegades' in terms of toeing the party line. For example, he argued, in the Party school everyone was taught to believe that there could be 'a non-capitalist road to development' in developing nations. But Slovo came to believe this to be untrue and even wrote a piece in which he argued that in developing nations the level of material and other types of culture were such that socialism couldn't really develop or be sustained. Mzala portrayed Slovo as someone who had no time for romantic visions of socialism or notions of a fast track to socialism. Apparently, the *African Communist* refused to publish Slovo's piece, and he had to get it published in the journal of the British Communist Party, *Marxism Today*, in the early 1970s. During this period, the British party was becoming tinged with Eurocommunism rather than simply following Moscow on everything. Mzala described Slovo as one who was able to put his own 'independent' ideas into *Umsebenzi*, the SACP journal that he edited.

Obviously, by speaking so glowingly about Slovo's and First's characteristics as independent thinkers, Mzala was trying to convey a message. That he lionised them as 'renegades' gives us an insight into his own thoughts about the trajectory of the revolution at this particular juncture. That he was a loyal ANC and Party man was never in doubt, his critical views notwithstanding. He was looking forward to being a delegate at the ANC conference in December. This would have meant being back home legally for the first time since skipping the country in 1976. That the conference was to be held in his home province of Natal must have been an added incentive.

XII

Among the points that Mzala deferred to the second night of discussion was the integration of the Black Consciousness-oriented 1976 generation into the ANC. His focus was now getting ready for the conference. But he still had time during breakfast to reflect on Phil Bonner's paper on the Russian Gang and 'tsotsi'[28] element in politics in the 1950s.[29] Mzala remarked that there were two 'former tsotsis' in the NEC. One was Josiah

Jele, whom he considered quite respectable, dressed properly and had left his tsotsi style behind. The other was Joe Modise, who he thought was still proud of his tsotsi past and spoke 'flytaal'.

After the second night, Gerhart had made numerous observations about Mzala. One such observation was his avoidance of discussing the SACP and offering critical observations as he did so freely with the ANC. Gerhart wondered whether it could be that he felt more bound by his promise not to make any revelations about the SACP? She observed, 'Yet there was nothing in all the rest of the discussion to suggest that he is a person who feels bound by dogma or blind loyalty.' Although Mzala spoke candidly about other people's ambitions for power, Gerhart said his own were only something that one could infer. 'If he has such ambitions,' she continued, 'he never displays them directly. He says he wants to be an academic.'

Furthermore, Gerhart observed that while his remarks could be considered sour grapes that he himself was not in the top leadership, 'when he's talking he comes across as extremely un-egoistic in that he speaks with great apparent sincerity, detachment and candor, and never mentions his own role in doing any of these things'. Perhaps his candour had to do with the views held about Gerhart and Karis themselves – that they were 'serious scholars' and therefore willing to discuss things at a 'deeper level'.'

XIII

Mzala used his talks with Gerhart to prepare his inputs for the conference, repeating most of the points he had raised about both the SACP and ANC, including the characteristic that prior to the developments in Eastern Europe, where socialism was unravelling, both organisations had been the 'uncritical recipients of many Soviet foreign policy positions'. He, however, qualified this point by indicating that this did not mean that 'there was not an internally generated theoretical and ideological response to the problems of building socialism in Eastern Europe, but within the movement there was not a forum for a critical debate about these issues'.

Mzala argued that there were exceptions – as reflected by the SACP pioneering some aspects of 'glasnost in South Africa' – in how the party formulated and conceptualised the relationship between itself and the mass organisations. He used Slovo's rejected article as an example. He regarded this piece as a 'devastating critique of some positions that had been published in Moscow by Progress Publishers on the concept of the non-capitalist road to development'.³⁰ To him, this symbolised the earliest efforts within the South African liberation movement to introduce critical perspectives.

Mzala was still critical of the *African Communist* and regarded its record as an 'unmitigated intolerance of those Marxist positions that were questioning the legitimacy of the Soviet practice'. He presented as a positive development Slovo's 1989 paper 'Has Socialism Failed?', which he thought would have been regarded as 'heretical' a few years earlier. Thus, he thought it was largely the SACP south of the equator that had kept alive the perspective of socialism. He ascribed the failed socialist experiments in Mozambique and Angola to the destabilising effect of South Africa.

He used the argument by Moses Mayekiso (General Secretary of the National Union of Metalworkers of South Africa, NUMSA) that socialism would be possible in South Africa simply because of the way capitalism had been operated. He thought socialists needed to unite in the SACP where 'rigorous and robust debate should take place' and that they had to be 'confident and build a powerful civil society controlled by its own members and independent of any political party. The practices of the trade union movement around mandates, and shop floor control were important lessons for the building of grassroots democracy.'³¹ Almost 30 years later, at its fourteenth National Congress in 2017, the SACP would reaffirm Mzala's view by resolving to work with its 'alliance partners and with a wide range of working class and progressives forces' to play a leading role 'in developing a common platform for a left popular front of working class and progressive forces',³² a posture reiterated by the fifteenth National Congress to build a 'powerful, socialist movement of the workers and the poor'.³³

XIV

Mzala's schedule was hectic, and he was taking every opportunity to network and engage with as many people as possible. He also rekindled his friendship with Robert Edgar, whom he had last seen when he visited London a year earlier. Edgar recalls that they parted on friendly terms in London, and that Mzala informed him that he was planning a visit to the United States, and 'I invited him to stay at my home'. At the time, Edgar was teaching a course on South African history at the University of Virginia as a visiting professor. Mzala stayed with him for several days and accompanied Edgar to Charlottesville to give a guest lecture. Although Edgar has no recollection of Mzala's lecture, he was very impressed with his skills as a teacher. 'He had an impressive intellect.' According to Karis, there were about 70 students, which Mzala thought were very different from the students at City College in terms of their interests.

On 23 October, Mzala was having his last meetings before leaving for London later that same day, tying up the loose ends for his imminent return the following year. One of the meetings was with John Gerhart who worked in the international division of the Ford Foundation. They discussed potential funding for his fellowship, and he emerged from the meeting with a great deal of enthusiasm. He believed that it had gone very well. His plan to return to the US was coming together nicely.

Mzala had left his luggage at Karis's office and he wanted to spend his last moments with Karis and Thobejane. At the ANC's spacious new office, said to have a sense of Madison Avenue about it, Karis used the opportunity to engage Mzala on a few issues. The discussions continued as they walked the streets of New York, scouting for a place to have lunch. He told Karis that he considered the project very important, and was committed to cooperating with him and Gerhart. He was convinced that his trip had been a great success, the high point being meeting Gerhart and Karis.

At the ANC offices Karis had seen a note on the notice board about the death of Francis Meli and that there was to be an autopsy. Meli was close to Mzala, having worked together on numerous projects. It is not clear, though, when and how he received the news of Meli's death, particularly the cloud under which he died. As they walked the streets of New York, Mzala told Karis that the SACP had always looked out to recruit the brightest and ablest. He said it had reached out to the younger generation. 'There are members of the 1976 generation in the Party's Central Committee,' he said, before adding that he wished the ANC was readier to follow the Party's example in this respect.[34]

Mzala thought there had been a lot of misunderstanding when it came to the Party's role in relation to the ANC. He was now anticipating a postponement of the December conference to the following year in order to allow for more preparation. He also confirmed that he was a delegate. With a smile, he added that he did not want to appear immodest, but expected to be elected to one of the structures, although not necessarily the NEC. When Karis brought up the question of the role of COSATU in the ANC, Mzala's response was that labour leaders should have a 'dual role' and must be integrated into ANC structures.

When they eventually sat down for lunch, with Thobejane present, Mzala finally had a chance to read Karis's memo, which was essentially a proposal for a collection of original valuable historical documents that would be inventoried and made available through the Centre for Research Libraries in Chicago. The microfilmed collection would be under Mzala's name and a guide would be produced, similar to the volume entitled *South African Political Materials: The Carter-Karis Collection*. Mzala read the memo over lunch and pronounced his satisfaction. He committed to do everything listed in the memo by the end of November.

As they darted across the street, with Karis restraining himself from asking personal questions lest he appear like a typical American obsessed with the movement, he nevertheless decided to probe about other players. What was Ben Turok's standing in the ANC and regarding the SACP? He was 'a good friend', responded Mzala before indicating that Turok's troubles in the movement went back to the 1950s when he was seen as undisciplined. When Mzala had been invited by Turok to speak at a meeting at his Institute for African Alternatives, he said he was instructed not to go.

At the end, warmly embracing Karis, Mzala said his goodbyes. His mind was on returning to take up the fellowship. His dream about becoming an academic was well on track.

CHAPTER 13

The Lost Prince of the ANC

I

By the end of October 1990, Mzala was back in London. Foremost in his mind, apart from finalising his PhD and the pending ANC conference, was securing the fellowship in the United States. Within a week of his return, he sent a postcard to Gail Gerhart, informing her that he was trying to tie the various strings together 'into a meaningful robe'. In thanking Gerhart for everything, he said his trip to the US had been 'very much' inspiring, particularly his meetings with Gerhart, Tom Karis and Senti Thobejane. He was grateful for the material Gerhart had provided on the national question and other related issues, which he had found useful. Mzala was looking forward to joining his new colleagues and friends the following September, and once more committed to sending the memo on the developments of the ANC's strategy.

The trip had greatly inspired Mzala and he saw the planned fellowship as a critical stepping stone for his ambitions to become an academic. Then, a few weeks after he returned from the US, Mzala developed pneumonia, and his health took a turn for the worse. He spent a short time at a London hospital before being discharged. Meanwhile, Gerhart and Karis were working hard to ensure that the proposed fellowship became a reality. The plan was to motivate and lobby for Mzala to join the Southern African Research Program (SARP). Mzala had made things easy with his brief stay in the United States, where he networked and presented at numerous events.

On 2 November, Karis wrote to the head of the SARP, Professor Leonard Thompson, about an opening that had arisen for a fellow for the 1991–1992 academic year. He was pleased that Thompson had met Mzala when he was in the US. 'He is an extraordinary – in some ways, unique – candidate for the fellowship,' wrote Karis. 'There is much about his personal and political experience that makes him unusually interesting, but what is most relevant for SARP is his commitment to independent-minded scholarship, his record in research and writing, and the fact that he would be at Yale while completing the writing of Oliver Tambo's biography.'

Karis was astonished by the reputation Mzala had achieved in the ANC and the SACP by the age of 35. The fact that he had published numerous articles that were often cited was another factor that Karis found interesting about Mzala. 'I think there is no doubt that his importance as a respected and provocative analyst will continue to grow.' Ever since John Daniel had introduced Karis to Mzala's work, he had been following his work closely. What struck Karis about Daniel's praise of Mzala was his emphasis on his intellectual integrity: 'his appetite for frank discussion, his appreciation for criticism, and his capacity for intellectual re-examination'. Daniel had likened Mzala's addiction to intellectual work with almost fierce intensity to that of Anton Lembede.

Karis was also impressed by Mzala's academic work, including the book on Buthelezi, which, said Karis, 'is a substantial and carefully researched study', and 'remarkably non-polemical'. He invoked Professor Shula Marks's quote on the back cover, which read: 'Mzala has amassed a great deal of new material and has drawn on a wide variety of sources in a clear and balanced fashion.' He found the chapter 'Revolutionary Theory on the National Question in South Africa', in the edited volume by Maria van Diepen, to be 'historical, well-written, well-documented, and mature analysis from the standpoint of Marxism-Leninism'. Karis duly recommended the chapter to Thompson.

Also, Karis found it interesting that someone of Mzala's orientation would devote his attention to examining ethnicity in South Africa as he was doing in his PhD thesis. But, like everyone else, apart from Mzala's piercing mind, Karis was looking forward to Tambo's biography that Mzala was to focus on at SARP. In one of the SARP's Wednesday-afternoon sessions, Mzala had already demonstrated 'how searching and succinct he is' while remaining 'non-polemical in his tone'. Karis concluded by remarking on Mzala's talent as a speaker and respondent to questions as demonstrated during his talk at a 'progressive' synagogue in Manhattan to some 80 students at City College in New York. The manner in which he established a rapport with students from the Black Studies department, who had fired hostile questions on the ANC's non-racialism and its alliance with the SACP, impressed Karis immensely.

The following day, 3 November, Gerhart wrote to Thompson in support of Karis's letter. Again, Gerhart's letter revealed that Mzala's hosts, just like Daniel, regarded him as a man of character, modesty and integrity. His first-hand inside knowledge of the exile movement, including MK, made Mzala a fascinating figure to the historians. That he was already working on Tambo's biography, with Tambo's full backing and cooperation, was a sweetener to the deal. Mzala's passion for history was another standout feature. 'When I showed him Walker Connor's *The National Question in Marxist-Leninist Theory and Strategy*,' wrote Gerhart, 'he pounced on it as if it were the holy grail. Perhaps I was being conned, or am jumping to unwarranted conclusions, but what I think I see in Mzala is a serious and potentially mature scholar trying to crawl out of the straightjacket of a talented young political propagandist.' The fact that Mzala wanted to become an academic in the new South Africa emerged once more.

At this stage of their academic careers, both Karis and Gerhart were experienced enough to make judgement calls on budding scholars. Having written numerous volumes about the politics of southern Africa, there was no need for exaggeration on their part to bring Mzala over. Their interaction with Mzala, over and above examining his work, had not only convinced them that he was a promising scholar but that they had met an exceptionally gifted individual. Their high praises were an objective indication of what Mzala was capable of at just 35 years of age.

II

Mzala's imminent arrival at SARP was highly anticipated and his two would-be collaborators, Gerhart and Karis, were tangibly excited. They continued to exchange correspondence and numerous historical materials with him on a regular basis. In his note of 8 November, accompanying the return of old issues of *Dawn* and the *African Communist*, Karis thanked Mzala for his card and sentiments before stating, 'I can hardly tell you how much Gail and I enjoyed our conversations and how much we look forward to working with you. Best of all, of course, is the prospect of your coming to Yale next September with your family. That will be a wonderful year.' Karis was also excited by the feedback received that the Tambo biography was under way.

It did not take Thompson long to consent to his colleagues' requests. Having also met Mzala, he was delighted for him to join the programme and, hence, on 19 November, he wrote to Mzala, 'cordially' inviting him to become a Fellow of the Program for the academic year 1991–1992. The central feature of the programme was to bring 'distinguished specialists' on southern Africa in different disciplines to participate in the weekly seminars while focusing on their own research and writing.

Before Thompson's letter could even arrive in London, Karis had called Mzala. In a note to Gerhart a few days later, he said Thompson's letter to Mzala was a good excuse for him to call. Obviously, both Mzala and Karis were excited by the news. One can imagine Mzala standing in the lounge of his third-floor flat in London, looking through the window while assuring Karis that he was feeling much stronger and was recovering. That was good enough for both men to move on to their exciting project, with Mzala promising to send the requested information before leaving for South Africa, where he would attend the ANC conference as a delegate in December. Even though his health was not good, he was still hopeful to make it back home.

Mzala also informed Karis that he had spoken to his PhD advisor and both were confident that he would meet the May 1991 submission deadline. The thought that he would be coming to Yale with his doctorate was thrilling. After reacting to the Yale news, he also told Karis, rather enthusiastically, that he had spent four hours with Tambo the day before, but – although they had a 'very good discussion' – he conceded that it had been a long and tiring session. Mzala stated that he had done most of the talking since Tambo wanted to hear in detail about the project, the trip to Yale, the seminars, Thobejane and many other details. According to Mzala, Tambo was 'excited' to hear about everything. Most importantly, Tambo was very positive about the importance of the project. Mzala informed Karis that he explained to Tambo that he had established a 'very non-competitive relationship' with Karis and Gerhart that would be mutually beneficial to all.

A few weeks later Karis wrote again, assuring Mzala that he would find Yale 'marvelously stimulating' and thanking him for the good word he put in for them to Tambo. He also informed Mzala about some useful information he had found on Tambo that should be available at the

University of London. He then mentioned that although he was never in doubt of Mzala's application sailing through, he wanted to remind him that the appointment of a fellow without an advanced degree was a 'rarity'. Thus, the invitation was 'a vote of confidence'.

III

The next time Karis and Gerhart would hear from Mzala would be through his wife, Mpho. In a letter to Karis, Mpho stated that 'Mzala has been going through hazard health conditions'. She revealed he had been struggling to get clearance to attend the conference in South Africa and that 'took too much of his energy', on top of the reality that he been overdue for a rest. This whole turn of events, according to Mpho, had become too emotional and physically draining for Mzala, to the extent that 'he got an attack of acute bronchitis'. He was now convalescing in a secluded place where he was receiving both treatment and rest. Attached to the letter was 'a comprehensive survey of the ANC's military strategy' that Mzala had promised Karis. Mpho also dispatched a similar letter to Gerhart.

Mzala's health was thus taking a turn for the worse. But even in bad health, he was still looking forward to his next role in the United States. While disappointed at having missed the ANC conference, he had not lost sight of the bigger picture. Karis kept in touch with letters and phone calls to cheer him up, but Mzala's health was clearly deteriorating, to the extent that his parents decided to come over to London. When Karis called on 11 February 1991, Mzala's father answered the phone and informed him that Mzala was back in hospital. Karis was 'distressed' by the news. He had wanted to arrange a teleconference between himself, Mzala and Gerhart to discuss their planned conversation with Tambo. Karis and Gerhard had secured a slot with Tambo for March, and they were already finalising arrangements. Part of the plan included spending a week in London so that they could catch up with Mzala too. He closed his 12 February note to Mzala thus: 'Surely you will have recovered by the time we arrive, at least to the point that we can see you.' He informed Mzala of where they would be staying in London, and promised to phone upon arrival. Everyone was hopeful that Mzala would recover soon.

Keen to ensure that there was progress on the Tambo project, Mzala must have been feeling the pressure that his health problems were slowing him down. His commitment to his work was sometimes detrimental to his health, but nothing could stop him once he had decided on a project. Predictably, on 14 February, while back in London hospital, he cajoled Mpho to smuggle him out of the hospital. Whatever protests and rationalisation Mpho tried, they were like water off a duck's back. Mzala held to his opinions with great obstinacy, and was sometimes charming enough to get his way. Without the doctors' knowledge, Mpho called a cab and whisked him away. After the meeting with Tambo, Mzala decided not to go back to the hospital but rather to his flat.

Mzala, however, was not fit enough to be home. His body had endured years of insufficient sleep and little regard to eating properly, and it was buckling under the pressure. It was only a matter of time before Mpho had to call an ambulance to take him back to the hospital. Mzala's younger sister Titi and her twin brother Dumisani were now based in the United Kingdom. Titi says with hindsight that she feels lucky to have had time with him during that period. Mpho's children were all young and, with her in-laws visiting, she couldn't afford to be at the hospital all the time. Titi says they took turns; Mpho would go to the hospital during the day while she looked after the children, and then she would go in the evening. Mpho would wake up early in the morning to ensure that there was food for everyone, and that the children were sorted and Sizwe was dropped off at school. After lunch she would come back to prepare dinner for everyone and pack some home-cooked food for Mzala. Luckily, the hospital was not too far from where they stayed.

Because Mzala had always been so busy and they had been living in different countries, Titi says they had not had time and space to talk and catch up. His hospitalisation afforded them a chance to reconnect, even though it was not an easy time. 'It was not a pleasant time that I spent with him at the hospital; it was one of the most painful times.' Even under the difficult hospital conditions, Mzala remained mentally sharp and his candid nature had not changed. Titi found herself discussing 'very deep things' with Mzala; that was the only time she recalls him talking about so many things. Some were very personal, and 'I don't think I can even talk about [them]'. But they had time to be open about everything.

This was the only time Mzala spoke to Titi about his medical condition. He confided in her that there was uncertainty about the cause of his illness, and it is at this point that the 'poison' theory emerged. To this day, there have been many rumours and speculation about the cause of Mzala's illness. From a very young age Mzala had had a close relationship with his mother, and the sight of watching her son wasting away was thus very traumatic for her. Titi says he was extremely protective of his family and if you wanted to see his wrath you had only to touch his family. He was worried about his sister Phasha, who was the only close family member not around. The thought that he might not survive had begun to cross his mind, and he told Titi that he wished to be taken home to South Africa should anything happen. He made a similar request to Mpho. 'Lovey, if anything happens to me, please, take me where my grandmother is lying.' 'His grandmother was his favourite,' says Mpho.

As the days went by, with Titi sitting on his bed, he would talk until he fell asleep. He would be surprised to find her sitting on the edge of the bed when he woke up, but he would continue where he had left off. His questions about Phasha became frequent; '[All] of you are coming here but when is Phasha coming?' On 22 February, an extremely cold Friday morning, Phasha finally landed in London. The first thing she did was to rush to the hospital. By this time Mzala was too weak to utter any words, but he nevertheless responded and acknowledged her presence.

Later the same day, in the presence of Mpho and Dumisani, Mzala began to drift away. Out of desperation, they both started to pray; it is likely that he could hear their prayers. As they prayed, there were clear signs that his body was shutting down. Soon Mzala stopped breathing. Although his eyes remained open, there was no pulse. Rigor mortis was setting in. Says a sobbing Mpho, 'I was there when he took his last breath. I'm the one who closed his eyes, stretched his body and it was just me and his brother.' Thereafter, Mpho called her in-laws who rushed to the hospital to see for themselves that their son Jabulani Nobleman Nxumalo was no more. Comrade Mzala was dead. And with that, all his dreams to become an academic in the new South Africa and his commitment to write Oliver Tambo's biography evaporated into thin air.

IV

'The South African Communist Party regrets to announce that one of its leading activists, Comrade Jabulani Nobleman "Mzala" Nxumalo, died in hospital in London on the evening of February 22, 1991 after a long illness,' read the SACP's sombre statement issued by Brian Bunting on Saturday, 23 February. The statement described Mzala's upbringing and his education before stating that he held a leading position in the ranks of Umkhonto we Sizwe, the military wing of the liberation movement. 'But his outstanding contribution to the movement was in the sphere of ideas and ideology.' The statement continued:

> He was endlessly fascinated and intrigued by the national question, and wrote and lectured extensively on the relationship between the national and class struggle in South Africa. Asserting that the aim of the South African revolution was to end inequality between the nations, he believed this could only be achieved under socialism.

While Mzala was intensely proud of his Zulu history and culture, he was remembered as someone who believed that the bantustan system stifled the national drive and independence of the African people. Confirming his recent utterances shared with Gerhart and Karis while in the United States, said the statement:

> Though ever loyal to the movement, Comrade Mzala was a fierce critic of bureaucracy and had no patience with fudge or compromise. He was a delegate to the ANC conference in Kabwe, Zambia, in 1985 and presented a number of sharp challenges to the leadership. He was the chosen representative of the London region to the ANC's Consultative Conference in Johannesburg in December 1990 but was prevented by ill-health from attending.

Mzala's death was 'tragically early' for everyone and the statement noted that this 'has deprived South Africa of one of its most brilliant talents at the very period when he was destined to reach the peak of his powers. That he should be snatched from us when he had so much still to give is a grievous loss to the liberation movement.'[1]

As the news of Mzala's death began to spread, those who had not seen him in a while and were not aware of his health battles were shaken. Blade Nzimande was 'shocked and devasted' when he received the news of Mzala's death. Nzimande and Mzala were friends and 'intellectual ideological partners' who belonged to the SACP and ANC. Nzimande had noticed that Mzala was picky about what he ate in London, but he was not worried because Mzala was mentally sharp, robust and physically strong. 'We used to walk fast while debating in the streets of London, getting in and out of the trains' and at no point had he struck Nzimande 'as someone who was on his deathbed'. Nzimande says that when he departed after his sabbatical and teaching at Jesus College in August 1989, Mzala was just fine.

Once Nzimande was back in South Africa, Mzala kept in touch with him through regular and 'lengthy' phone calls, maybe twice every week. He was looking forward to the ANC conference in December. John Pampallis was also back in the country and working with Nzimande at the University of Natal. 'Blade told me.' They might not have been close, but Mzala was someone Pampallis knew very well. 'It was very sad to know somebody who contributed so much' was no more. Pampallis says that because Mzala was a regular contributor to *Sechaba* and *African Communist*, when you read his articles you feel even closer to him.

Ronnie Kasrils was already back in South Africa, but had been forced underground after FW de Klerk had withdrawn his indemnity and was now being hunted by the police. He learnt of Mzala's death with 'great shock' under stressful personal conditions. The news came as a terrible blow because he had not been aware that Mzala had been sick. Says Kasrils, 'I was deeply saddened that I could not attend his funeral. For me it was like losing a family member.' Just as for Kasrils, for Sue Rabkin Mzala's death was a personal blow. She was also back in the country and working at Luthuli House when she received the news of his death. 'It was so sad.' She continues:

> This was someone that I've grown up with and that I had shared a really important period of the struggle with. You're in those situations, being attacked, there are raids, massacres, assassinations. Your lives depend on each other and therefore the level of trust is very deep, and you know the comrades that were in the forward areas were the crème de la crème, all of them including the military. ... the rate of infiltration was nowhere near what it was anywhere else because we were on to you pretty quick if we sniffed anything wrong. So, the relationships that we had with each other, they're still there to this day. I'm in touch with everybody from Maputo, Swaziland, everybody. It's family.

What makes Rabkin even sadder is that, just as it had been with Shadrack Maphumulo, she did not get a chance to say goodbye. 'There were so many comrades that I have to say goodbye to. I don't even want to think about it.' Patric Mtshaulana is one of those simply 'devastated' by the news. He held onto the hope and belief that Mzala's ideas would live forever. Celeste Naidoo describes the experience as traumatic. Although Mzala had not been well when she left London, she had not expected him to die. When someone informed her that Mzala had died she refused to believe it until she read about it in a newspaper. 'I remember phoning Mpho in London to ask her, and the conversation was brief.'

Pallo Jordan says he had known Mzala was not well and had anticipated his passing, but still he 'experienced his passing as a terrible personal loss and as a reverse for our movement that so desperately needed a younger generation of thinkers and strategists'. This was a double blow for Jordan who, just a couple of years previously, had been a principal speaker at the London funeral of Sello Moeti (Michael Lebese), one of his Radio Freedom recruits in Luanda. 'In Angola, Mzala and Sello had been very close friends and the two of them were the principal debaters – between each other, and with others – at [Radio Freedom]. Meeting in London had sealed that bond.'

Mzala's death came at a difficult time for many of his comrades, who were either preparing to return to South Africa or had just arrived and were trying to find their footing. Some, like Raynauld Russon and Sifiso Buthelezi, were still incarcerated. Having been detained by the Swaziland government in 1991, together with the leadership of PUDEMO, Russon only learnt about Mzala's death on his return to South Africa in 1992. 'I was shocked and devastated by his loss. He would have been a pillar of strength for the negotiations team and to support the SACP team in the process.' Nevertheless, Mzala left an everlasting impression on Russon as 'a committed revolutionary who understood the motive forces of the struggle against apartheid and that it was broader than just the national question'. Buthelezi also learnt about the sad news only on his release from prison. 'I was trying to find out his whereabouts' and only discovered about two months later that he had just been buried.

Patrick Msomi had just returned to the country and was working in the ANC's head office when he received the news of Mzala's death. He was devasted. 'I felt like I had a lost a blood brother. He had become my mentor and he was the reason I skipped the country.' From the day they met at the university in 1976, Mzala had been influential to Msomi, sharing all sort of political material with him, and their bond was strengthened when they trained in the same unit in the USSR. 'In Moscow he was my commissar,' says Msomi. 'I couldn't believe that he was dead.'

V

The ANC proposed that Mzala be buried in London, but, says Phasha, after consultations with elders such as Adelaide Tambo and Mendi Msimang,

Mzala's wishes to be interred next to his grandmother prevailed. When it was decided that Mzala would be laid to rest in South Africa, a London region memorial service was held, and a number of people visited Mzala's flat in London to pay their respect. Dr Sibusiso Bhengu was not only a friend to Sethi but fond of Mzala too, having admitted him to Dlangezwa High after his expulsion from Bethal College. He had subsequently befriended Mzala when they were both in Europe. When he arrived at Mzala's place, Phasha says, he just stood at the door for a very long time, lost for words. Such was his sadness at Mzala's death. Tom Karis and Gail Gerhart had taken advantage of their planned trip to London to meet Tambo to also pay their respects to Mzala. They arrived on Friday, 1 March, seven days after Mzala's death. On Sunday, they visited Mzala's apartment where they met his family, including his wife, children, parents, brother and two sisters. On 6 March, they met Brian and Sonia Bunting who reflected about Mzala, including the 'confusion' about his religion.

But to his family, 'there was no confusion at all' about his religion, says Mpho. She thinks Brian and Sonia understood that about Mzala. 'They knew that Saturdays he was not involved, and on Fridays he would actually even come early to make sure that we had a Sabbath session in preparation with the kids.' Even the memorial service displayed this aspect of Mzala's life. 'We had somebody from the church who spoke and a number of the church members that were there, too, at the memorial service.' Mpho recalls that the service was a joint initiative of the SACP and ANC since, like Mzala, SACP members were also ANC members. 'So everybody spoke.'

While en route to the memorial service, John Daniel had a chance encounter with the literary editor of *The Guardian* newspaper who then asked him to write an obituary. Published on Thursday, 14 March, *The Guardian* gave the obituary quite a spread. Daniel had found the process of writing the obituary 'cathartic'. The title – 'Lost "Prince" of the ANC' – was borrowed from a British television drama at the time, *The Lost Prince*, about Prince John, the youngest child of King George V and Queen Mary, who died at the age of 13.[2] The obituary noted that Mzala's death had 'occasioned an outpouring of grief both in exile circles and in South Africa where he was seen as a future leader, the "intellectual prince" of the generation of militants who had entered the ANC since the 1976 national uprising and had changed the course of the country's history.'

Daniel indicated that 'in 1988 ANC President Oliver Tambo invited Mzala to work on his biography. That he should choose a man half his age for the task shows the esteem with which Mzala was held in senior ANC circles.' Daniel recalled that Mzala loved to argue through the night, 'but unlike many big talkers he also often worked through the night producing a torrent of articles under various pseudonyms in both the main journals of the liberation movement and in such scholarly outlets as the *Journal of Southern African Studies*.' After the unbanning of the ANC in 1990, Daniel noted that Mzala had contributed an occasional column to *New Nation*, the South African weekly paper.

For Daniel, Mzala's primary obsession was the national question, which was part of his prospective PhD dissertation. 'He was fascinated by its complexities, and wrote extensively on the nature of national and class struggle in South Africa.' Daniel also noted that Mzala was 'within months of completing what may have been the authoritative work on the subject'. He reminisced about Mzala's recent trip to New York where he 'dazzled the audience with [the] lucidity of his analysis, and appearances on national television and campuses followed'. Sadly, Daniel noted:

> Soon after his return, he became ill with pneumonia, and was unable to attend the ANC's regional conference in London, held as a prelude to the December's National Consultative Conference [in South Africa] ... Despite his absence, Mzala's keynote policy address, read for him by his wife, was adopted with unanimous acclaim.

It is apparent that a comparison between Mzala and Anton Lembede fascinated Daniel. In his tribute to Mzala, he took the opportunity to amplify it.

> In the last weeks of Mzala's life, some were haunted by the spectre of death, 44 years earlier, of Anton Lembede, one of the founders of the ANC Youth League, which brought Mandela and Tambo into the organization. Another Zulu of humble origins, Lembede was the intellectual guru of his time which articulated a new and assertive brand of African nationalism. A prolific writer, he drove 'himself with such energy and carelessness of body that he could hardly be persuaded to sleep.' Mary Benson could well have been writing of Mzala, who simply wore his slight body out.

Mpho agreed with this observation and the comparison to Lembede by revealing that even when his health was deteriorating, Mzala never stopped working himself hard. Apparently, he hated it and felt 'useless' when he was confined to a hospital bed and could not write.³ Daniel concluded: 'At the funeral of Lembede, dead at 33, a speaker said of him: "In the garden of life a bird sang from the highest tree, and then soared away." I can think of no more apt an epitaph for this other young genius.'⁴

To a certain extent, Mzala's death was captured by the South African media. Among the newspaper headlines that reported on his death include: 'SACP Man Nxumalo Dies' (*Natal Witness*, 26 February 1991), '"Double Agenda Author" Mzala Dies' (*Natal Witness*, 28 February 1991), 'Revolutionary Writer Dies in Exile' (*New Nation*, 1 March 1991), 'ANC Activist Mzala Dies in London' (*Sunday Tribune*, 3 March 1991), '"Mzala" to be Buried in Ngoje' (*Natal Witness*, 13 March 1991), 'Mzala's Body Back in SA' (*Natal Witness*, 14 March 1991), and 'Guardian Pays Tribute to ANC's "Intellectual Prince"' (*Cape Times*, 15 March 1991).

The article 'Mzala Laid to Rest' in the *Natal Witness* of 21 March 1991 reported briefly on Mzala's funeral. 'Author, sociologist and prominent ANC/SACP member Jabulani "Mzala" Nxumalo was buried at Ngoje in Vryheid last weekend.' According to the report, speakers at the funeral included Billy Masetlha of the ANC Youth League, Nana Mnandi (regional chair of the ANC Women's League), Geraldine Fraser of the SACP, Sipho Cele of Cosatu Northern Natal and Shakes Cele of the ANC Midlands region.

VI

In 2013, Chris Matlhako posed the question: 'Why should we be concerned about Mzala Nxumalo and his works?' He went on to answer it from a personal perspective.

> For me, who encountered Mzala in my early student days, found his writing skills extraordinarily excellent, penetrating and importantly, the conjectural issues he raised, to have been hugely important at the time. The time of the United Democratic Front (UDF) and its allied structures, coupled with huge debates about the key questions the mass of our people had to engage (non-racialism, non-sexism and a future post-apartheid SA), made such writings and others a must read and contemporary – not to mention instructions on insurrectionary warfare.

With this background in mind, Matlhako considered Mzala as someone who dedicated his energies and capacities to the liberation struggle of the working class in particular. He continued: 'He symbolised the very embodiment of a dialectical relationship between theory and practice.'[5]

The way comrades like Matlhako and many others encountered Mzala makes one wonder about the role he would have played in a post-apartheid democratic dispensation, considering his contribution to the liberation struggle. Of course, it is a matter of conjecture how Mzala would have perceived and navigated the new South Africa, and many of his contemporaries, comrades and friends have their own views on this matter. Some, of course, differ with what they regard as an exaggerated legacy as well as the role he would have played. Some speak with authority, somehow presenting their wishes and feelings through Mzala.

The views range from Mzala being vehemently against corruption, to loathing the current state of the ANC and SACP, to possibly leaving the ANC, to taking up a position on the Central Committee of the SACP and advocating for an independent line. As a materialist, Mzala's posture would of course have been guided by the analysis of concrete conditions. On numerous occasions he clearly stated his ambitions to become an academic. Whatever might have happened, one thing is sure: he would not have kept quiet, for he was loud and unambiguous in expressing his opinions.

Vusi Mavimbela thinks Mzala's chances of surviving within the ANC were slim because he would have clashed with many people. He is convinced Mzala would have been a prime candidate for ostracism and marginalisation. 'But he would have been very critical of both the Communist Party and the ANC because he was always radical. No doubt he would have been very unhappy with both parties.' Sue Rabkin is sure that, because of his intellectual acumen, Mzala would have played 'quite a leading role'. But because he was very outspoken, she suspects he would have rattled a few people and taken radical positions. 'I think he might even have been one in the schools of thought that the Communist Party should stand on its own ticket. I wouldn't have been surprised if he'd taken that position.'

Patric Mellet is adamant that Mzala's voice would have been strongly critical of corruption. But he would have first exposed the political corruption that preceded financial corruption, says Mellet, including drawing links between organised crime and political aims and objectives. He states as a matter of fact that Mzala would have argued that the ANC-headed alliance had reached its sell-by date and 'called on the trade unions, civil society organisations, the SACP and other left formations to create a new alliance rooted in integrity to seek direct support from the public and voters as a left force within our democracy to hold the ANC to account'.

V

In life and in death, Mzala remains one of the foremost critical revolutionary thinkers of the 1976 generation. Jeremy Cronin believes that even though Mzala's intellectual work was embedded within the traditions of the ANC and the SACP, organisations of which he was a member, 'he did not allow this loyalty to become uncritical'. He locates Mzala among the comrades who were 'not prepared simply to recite dogmas or repeat "the line"'. For example, in his 'critical' assessment of Francis Meli's book, Cronin believes Mzala never lost a sense of decorum, engaging 'constructively' with his seniors like Meli.[6]

It is precisely for this reason that someone like Essop Pahad regards Mzala's death as a serious blow to both the SACP and the ANC. 'I have no doubt in my mind that if Mzala had remained alive, he would have become the editor of the *African Communist* ... [At] some point, Mzala would have been elected to the Central Committee of the South African Communist Party.' Pahad is convinced that he would have played an important role in all of the current theoretical discussions, including how to enhance the revolutionary struggle in South Africa.

Mzala was a fierce and committed MK soldier, but it is in the realm of ideas that he made an indelible mark. For someone like Jordan, who was his senior, Mzala made his mark as a critical thinker and intellectual through his prolific writing, while his most notable contemporaries made theirs on the battlefield. Joel Netshitenzhe is among those who think that Mzala's life and his labours still have contemporary relevance. It is indeed the contributions of many men and women like Mzala that has 'spawned' our freedom. A few things about Mzala stand out for Netshitenzhe:

> His fearlessness: in debate; in weighing the pros and cons of given approaches to critical issues; in contributing not only to theory but also to its implementation; and in tackling issues for what they are, not to please any individual or to satisfy the urges of some faction. In other words, South Africa today ... needs Mzalas in their thousands, the better to help the movement extricate itself from the rut in which it is currently trapped.

But what happened to the Mzalas that the movement produced en masse during the most difficult of times? Kasrils imagines that the need for political study, analysis and debate linked to practical implementation is the contemporary relevance of Mzala – the unity of thought and action in the Marxist tradition. As Cronin posits, 'Our movement requires tens of thousands of Mzalas, commissars working away in state departments, parastatals, trade unions, branches, and communities.' Just as it had for Netshitenzhe, what stood out for Kasrils about Mzala was his 'fearless' nature in both battle and debate. It is not wrong to have doubts and then to raise questions in a disciplined manner. However, Kasrils hastens to mention that this does not suggest that people must 'kow-tow' to leaders or have 'blind adherence' to settled positions. Of course, Mzala abhorred the 'cheerleading' type of members who only presented their robust views in shebeens.

It is precisely for this reason that Pahad deems it fit to use Mzala as an example for the current generation of comrades in the movement, encouraging them to spend time reading and understanding the theory of Marxism-Leninism and the national democratic revolution as a basis that informs 'our own practice'. He states that everyone should take a lesson from Mzala's life; the lesson not to be afraid to debate without putting others off, but to put your point strongly while being prepared to listen to others' point of view is another useful skill that Pahad thinks can be emulated. Kgalema Motlanthe concurs with this observation and adds that Mzala's life is a 'powerful example'. He was 'studious' in his approach to the revolution and appreciated the value of 'well-researched arguments, not just politics for the sake of politics'.

According to Pahad, Mzala could re-evaluate his position through debates and thereby learn from others. All are thus lessons that can be drawn from Mzala's life. 'If Mzala had stayed alive for another 10 years, at least, he would have made a most notable contribution to our struggle, and if he had come back to South Africa in 1990, you can rest assured that Mzala would have been employed by the Party [in] a full-time capacity.' Mzala's full-time presence, argues Pahad, would have certainly strengthened the Party.

Thandeka Gqubule-Mbeki reckons that the quality of debate in the country would have been much richer if he had been allowed to freely express himself. 'But one got the sense that he was concerned about the degree to which people were permitted to express themselves.' Her recollections of Mzala include his concerns about ideas that were being pushed to the margin, unexplored and rejected because of the people with whom those ideas were associated. To take a leaf out of Mzala's life, says Kasrils, means being disciplined and basing one's thoughts on careful study and assessment of the 'concrete situation'. He asserts:

Mzala was not anarchistic in his approach to problems but sought serious consideration of the issues and the importance of debate in order to reach the best way forward. Add to this his honesty and integrity, his insistence on service to the people and not one's own individual interests. I have no doubt that he would have been a fierce opponent of the corrupt practices that began to creep into the ANC and government.

VI

Others, like Patric Mellet, believe Mzala would not have survived in post-apartheid South Africa. Mellet seems to have given this some serious thought before responding: 'Chris Hani, Mzala and others represented a fresh modern left voice in MK, the ANC and SACP and posed a threat towards the trends that were moving along trajectories away from the anti-colonialist, anti-imperialist trajectory of national-liberationism as an ideological platform.' Titi agrees that the very same reasons that got Hani assassinated would have endangered Mzala's life. She thinks that, just like Hani, Mzala would have taken a hardline approach that would have threatened both the right-wing elements and moderates within the movement. Bongani Khumalo, Mzala's childhood friend, thought that radicals like Hani and Mzala posed a danger to the system and were hence 'pruned'.

Mellet characterises three tendencies he says were at play in the movement – 'narrow ethno-nationalists, the African social democrats and the liberal democrats' – which he thinks were in competition with each other 'but also with a tenuous degree of cooperation [that] was fast changing the national liberation movement'. He considers Mzala to be among those whose analysis and thinking made him dangerous for the establishment and hence his death would not have been accidental, as proven by Hani's assassination. On Hani's murder, Mellet considers it likely that it was not simply orchestrated by the far right alone. It reminded him of, if not a carbon copy, the assassination of Josiah Tongagara, a popular commander of the Zimbabwe African National Liberation Army (ZANLA), who was also highly respected within ZIPRA, during the British-organised negotiations in Zimbabwe.

Mellet says Mzala thought the three tendencies were using 'left language' to corrupt the struggle and sideline the 'real' socialists.

Ultimately, he argues that Mzala believed that they would sell out the poor and the marginalised. He recalls Mzala's wariness about the transition and summarises some of Mzala's concerns as follows:

> The national democratic struggle for him had to lead uninterruptedly to socialism. A corrupt neo-colonial aspirant middle-class would do everything in their power to thwart the working class in fulfilling that trajectory. Mzi saw what was happening within the late 1980s in the UDF and ANC as being a terrain of struggle between different forces aided and abetted by capitalist vested interests which realised that black majority rule was inevitable. It was strategic to change the battlefields off the street and the bush to a multi-party round table negotiations process and a keeping of what was considered the 'radical socialist element' out of the game.

Mellet argues that hardliners and radical thinkers were sidelined in favour of the moderates; 'Chris Hani was assassinated and had Mzala been with us he, too, would have been killed.' Raynauld Russon is also convinced that Mzala 'was likely to toe a hardline approach similar to Chris Hani and I don't believe that he would have been accommodated in the process'. Mpho confirms that within the movement there were those who could not stand Mzala's politics, and would do everything to block him. Bulunga agrees that it is unlikely Mzala would have survived much longer. 'He would have been killed,' he says. He believes he would have threatened the 'liberal revolution' that the ANC pursued towards the end and post-apartheid. He was well read, sharp and articulate, hence Bulunga believes 'he would have been unstoppable in his argument'. Msomi is convinced that Mzala would have led the SACP, which would have been influential in strengthening COSATU and ANC. But suddenly he pauses before saying: 'They would have killed him like Chris Hani.'

VII

On 27 April 2010, President Jacob Zuma posthumously awarded Mzala the 'Order of Luthuli in Silver for his contribution to the struggle for liberation in South Africa'. In his speech Zuma said, 'Through his sharp mind and pen, Jabulani Nobleman "Mzala" Nxumalo left a legacy of intellectualism, writing about the revolutionary process in the country at the time.' Of course, Mzala had worked under Zuma in the forward areas, particularly during his time in Swaziland, so Zuma knew exactly who and what he was talking about. Ronnie Kasrils welcomes this acknowledgement, but feels that Mzala should receive even more recognition. 'In my view, that should have been in gold, for placing the young patriot among top leaders would have done so much to inspire young people.' Thandeka Gqubulembeki agrees that Mzala should be elevated posthumously as one of the greatest intellectuals the country has produced. 'He was the quintessential revolutionary intellectual; that's what I think he was and self-consciously so.'

However, Pallo Jordan believes that the 1976 intake has received far wider and better recognition than their predecessors. 'There are at least three feature movies, a number of documentaries and, of course, freedom songs about them.' Certainly, age was on the side of this generation; many were fortunate to return to the country at the prime of their lives, thus playing a significant role in the transition to democracy. Joel Netshitenzhe also notes the efforts, particularly in the recent period, to invoke Mzala's name and his legacy, especially on the part of the SACP. But he is mindful that these can never be adequate recognition, not only in relation to Mzala but also to many other eminent cadres of his generation and other generations. He posits, 'The challenge of ensuring balance in such tributes will of course remain; but it can only be resolved in the practical dialectic of thesis, antithesis and synthesis which Mzala himself so keenly appreciated.'

People like Kasrils insist that more needs to be done to honour Mzala's 'passionate' contribution to freedom, arguing that streets and institutions, particularly those relating to the youth and academic study, should be named in his honour. Says Kasrils, 'Mzala exemplifies the best moral conviction and steadfastness of the freedom fighter, the youth, patriot, communist and internationalist. A remarkable and extraordinary MK warrior, who is one of the most glorious young comrades it has been my privilege to have known and worked with.' It is precisely this example that today's youth should emulate. Matlhako concurred that '[despite] his relative obscurity in the annals of the revolutionary history,' Mzala 'remains an exemplary cadre and stalwart of our revolution'. To this end, argued Matlhako, '[his] works and revolutionary activism should inspire any young person given that all that he undertook, was in a mere 35-odd years until his death.'[7]

For Mellet, nothing significant has been done to honour Mzala. He says:

We need young thinkers and doers like Mzala today. He was not rash, nor one for soap box grandstanding and slogans. He was sharp, measured and methodical and practical. He was not against tactical agreements and manoeuvring but knew the difference between this and capitulation. He would be deeply disappointed in the kind of leadership and behaviours in the ANC leadership over at least the last 15 years and disgusted at the corrupt feeding frenzy and bling behaviours. But he would have taken the lead in saying 'don't mourn, mobilise'.

Mzala lived for only 35 years, about 15 of those in exile. Most of those years were dedicated to the liberation of the people of South Africa. Hence, his contributions will linger. In Nikolai Ostrovsky's novel *How the Steel was Tempered*, Pavel 'Pavka' Korchagin visited a spot where his comrades had fallen, gallantly facing the noose after being sentenced to death. He slowly raised his hand and removed his cap, his heart filled with sadness, and said, 'Man's dearest possession is life. It is given to him but once, and he must live it so as to feel no torturing regrets for wasted years, never know the burning shame of a mean and petty past; so live that, dying, he might say: all my life, all my strength were given to the finest cause in all the world – the fight for the Liberation of Mankind.'[8] One cannot help but feel a tinge of sadness when thinking about Mzala's short life.

POSTSCRIPT

Socialism is the future

As over 400 delegates converged in Boksburg, in the outskirts of Johannesburg, for the fifteenth National Congress of the South African Communist Party (SACP) in July 2022, the delegation of the Young Communist League of South Africa (YCL-SA) was vocal in plenary even through its song 'Namanje siyabuzwa ubinzima' (Even now we feel the hardship). In a scene reminiscent of the vocal group of young delegates from Angola who sat in the corner in the ANC's Kabwe Conference in 1985, the YCL delegation was caustic in its demand for the 'state power'. This refers to the resolution of the fourteenth National Congress in 2017 at which the SACP resolved on 'electoral contestation in the affected areas' as part of its resolution on the 'State and Popular Power'.[1] Whenever the opportunity arose, they belted out their popular song: 'sesino 100 years, YCL, namanje ayikho isocialism' (we are now 100 years old as the YCL, but still there is no socialism).

Ensconced within the Gauteng delegation and looking calmly on the unfolding scene, I couldn't help but imagine the Kabwe Conference, where it was the young people who pushed the leadership on various critical issues. What would Mzala have said and what would be his intervention, I wondered. He was vocal and took no prisoners in his engagements, that much we know for sure. So what would have been his tone in this debate? What would he think of the state of his organisations, the ANC and SACP?

Of course, it is unhelpful to even attempt a response on Mzala's behalf. Any response would be presumptuous. The good thing about Mzala though is that, to a certain extent, his work speaks for him. There are lessons on how he approached contentious issues such as the people's war and the national question. And he did this through Marxist-Leninist framework. Although theoretical, his analysis was grounded in practice.

Since his first article appeared in 1978 in the journals of the movement, Mzala employed Marxism-Leninism as a tool of analysis to tackle the South African problem. Inevitably, this amounted to writings on how to build socialism in South Africa. In doing so, he appreciated the importance of concomitantly advancing the national struggle as the basis upon which a class struggle ought to be waged. Whether dealing with his favourite subjects – the national question and advancing the notion of the people's war – the conclusions were the same: it was only through socialism that South Africa's contradictions could be resolved.

Therefore, it would be remiss of a book about Mzala not to spend a few pages reflecting on consolidated views on his writings in relation to his life. To do so, let us take a look at those two topics that epitomised Mzala's life: the national question and the people's war.

The national question

As his wife Mpho posited, 'when you talk about the national question, you are talking about Mzala', and this is indeed one topic that Mzala spent his short life studying. Blade Nzimande concurred that this was a subject 'foremost to Mzala'.[2] Certainly, you will be hard pushed to find an interlocutor in South Africa's liberation movement in the 1980s that was as central to this debate as Mzala.

It was in the South African Student Organisation (SASO) that Mzala began to grapple with this question. Touching on this point in his discussion with Julie Frederikse in 1985, he stated that, in discussing the Freedom Charter in 1976 during the University of Natal's seminar, they concluded that they were striving for an inclusive South Africa 'where black and white will be able to be equals and where we'd have a fair share in the processes of political administration and the wealth of the country'. He argued, '[We're] striving for a non-racial society.'

Thus, it is not surprising that when he penned his first article in the *African Communist* in 1978, 'The Compromising Role of Inkatha', he was already employing Marxism-Leninism to analyse ethnicity and other tendencies that he regarded as 'reactionary'. Eliminating apartheid and white supremacy and establishing national democracy was not the end for Mzala but fundamentally a preparation of 'the road for the advance to socialism'.³ From this point onwards, for Mzala, the resolution of the national question in South Africa was intractably linked to socialism. Hence, in his 1983 article 'Karl Marx and the Colonial Question' in the *African Communist*, he argued that socialism was 'the only way out' in resolving the South African contradictions. 'There can be no true national equality until class division is ended,' he wrote. 'Only socialism can create the conditions in which national division and race discrimination can be abolished.'⁴

Also in 1983, in the article 'Why We are with the Communists' in the *African Communist*, he argued that because the mode of production in South Africa was capitalist, as reflected by the country's highly developed industrial monopolies, 'the transition to socialism' was the 'logical continuation' of the liberation struggle. For him there was no artificial delineation between the national and class struggle. The national question, for Mzala, was essentially a social problem that 'is, in the final analysis, subordinated to the general tasks of the class struggle of the proletariat'. Therefore, 'national liberation could only relax national tensions and therefore provide partial or provisional solutions' and thus 'it was only socialism that guaranteed lasting and fundamental solutions to the national question'.⁵

This was not a fleeting posture for Mzala, but rather how he perceived the problem throughout his life since joining the liberation struggle. In his 1984 article 'A Tale of Two Nations: The Presentation of the National Question in South Africa' he used Leninist principles to analyse inter alia the 'historico-economic conditions of the national question', 'The special features of colonialism', 'The meaning of the right to self-determination' and 'The merging of nations into a single South African nation'.⁶

Consistently, he never lost sight of the fact that the South African economy had 'reached the capitalist level of development'. This prompted him to advocate for class analysis beyond narrow racial discourse in articles such as 'The Freedom charter is our lodestar' in *Sechaba* in 1985 and 'Nation and Class in the South African Revolution' in the 1986 edition of the *African Communist*. In the latter article, Mzala posited that 'relations among men are determined first and foremost by the position they occupy in the production process' and thus '[we] must make a concrete historical analysis of the existing class and national relations in South Africa, and from this basis we can examine the attitudes of various classes and strata to the national question.'⁷

Even in academic enquiry, Mzala's solution to the national question was linked to socialism. In a 1989 book chapter 'Revolutionary Theory on the National Question in South Africa', Mzala perceived the development of nations as having been driven by economic factors. In this regard, nations could not be 'divorced' from their 'essential material root, that is from its social essence in human history'.[8] With this historical emergence of nations, he argued, capitalism used nationalism to submit the class interests of the workers to their class rule. For Mzala, consideration of the socio-economic base of the national oppression and the solution of the national question rested in the victory of the working class, with the ultimate objective being the 'expropriation of the bourgeoisie'.[9]

In another academic article, 'Non-Historic Nations and the National Question: A South African Perspective', penned with John Hoffman in 1989, he used Marxist perspectives to analyse the topic. It is little wonder that Gail Gerhart would write the following after their brief meeting in the US in 1990: 'When I showed him Walker Connor's *The National Question in Marxist-Leninist Theory and Strategy*, he pounced on it as if it were the holy grail.'

Armed struggle: Advancing the people's war

Another area Mzala spent time theorising was advancing the people's war in the armed struggle. For him, the armed struggle in South Africa would only make sense if it involved the people as a whole. Of course, by and large, Mzala and his fellow people's war protagonists ultimately lost this debate, but not before they put up a gallant fight. Like any other debate that Mzala entered, his were not reckless points of a radical guerrilla fighter spoiling for action. They were well thought through, as witnessed in his 1982 series of articles 'Lessons of Our People's War' in *Dawn*.

In these articles he pointed out the painstaking process the liberation movement needed to put in place to prepare for armed struggle. At the heart of the armed struggle were the people. He argued: 'A few people taking to arms do not equal a revolution, unless the decisive masses of the people are already in motion of struggle towards revolutionary objectives, and the armed action is related to it, as a feature of it.'[10] Fundamentally, for him the people's war strategy was aimed at taking the struggle to its logical conclusion of socialism. Importantly, Mzala did not only theorise on this issue, but sought to implement it, as witnessed through his Ingwavuma activities.

One of Mzala's most popular interventions on this matter is his 1985 piece 'Cooking the Rice inside the Pot' in *Sechaba*. At the heart of this article was the need to expedite the people's war inside the country. He was convinced that the ground was fertile for Umkhonto we Sizwe (MK) to plug into the war already being waged by the people back home with no weapons. 'Our people have long ago discovered that what is needed in South Africa is a new society, a new political and economic system, a radical change of all that is existing,' he wrote. Inherent in this posture was not just the toppling of the racist regime but its capitalist economy too and building socialism.

Fundamentally, he thought of the masses as decisive in the revolution as opposed to 'an elite corps of professional revolutionaries'. He argued that it was only a mass movement led by the working class that could deliver the decisive blow to apartheid because they had 'nothing to secure and to fortify in the present South Africa, since the working class has the objective mission to destroy, not just appearances, but, on the contrary, the essence of oppression; not just its form, but the thing itself, the root of the social evil'.[11]

At the centre of his people's war thesis was the 'arming of the masses' because he was convinced that they were the motive force of the revolution – under the leadership of the working class, of course. The deepening crisis in South Africa in the mid- and late 1990s was a signal for him that 'the mass movement has reached another peak'.[12] He was not, however, convinced that it was the liberation movement that was in control of the uprising, but rather that the people were acting independently. He thus considered this as an opportune moment for an 'armed insurrection' and regarded anything less as a 'conservative approach' that failed 'to accept this new development of insurrectionary conditions, and in the failure to reckon with the fact that the only scientific approach to military strategy under the present circumstances will proceed from the fact that we have in South Africa today, side by side, existing together, simultaneously, the possibilities of preparing both for the protracted guerrilla warfare and armed insurrection'.[13]

Even when theorising about negotiation, Mzala still saw the role of the people's war as a significant tactic. He was convinced that the ANC was not going to 'place the disarmed people on the altar of negotiations with a fascist regime'.[14] For Mzala, complete victory in the South African revolution was dependent 'on whether or not the working class has been sufficiently organised and significantly armed to provide the decisive force when the apartheid system has to be finally crushed into ruin'. Mere negotiation with the enemy without a strong military push was a 'capitulationist tendency', he said.[15] He later used the Zimbabwean struggle as an example of where fighting continued alongside negotiations in order to strengthen the revolutionary side.[16]

By 1990, the ANC had already suspended the armed struggle and was negotiating with the regime, with Mzala harbouring some resentment for the ANC's failure to make the war real in South Africa. With hindsight, he thought the ANC was unprepared for the actual uprising, even when material conditions on the ground were conducive for such. 'They thought that blowing up SASOL and a few episodes like that were so terrific, but something much greater was actually required,' he argued. He admired the courage of liberation fighters from neighbouring countries such as Zimbabwe, Namibia, Mozambique and Angola who successfully carried the war into the country as a guerrilla struggle. Sadly, for him, 'we never succeeded in achieving this'.

The lost prince

Celebrating the sixtieth anniversary of Frantz Fanon's death in December 2021, Danny Shaw wrote: 'Fanon's contributions are timeless. As long as white supremacy and neocolonialism remain in the driver's seat of human relations, Fanon's thought will continue to arm the colonized in the Battle of Ideas.'[17] The same can be said of Mzala's contribution to building socialism in South Africa. The manner in which capitalism is practised in South Africa, resulting in myriad socio-economic challenges, chief being the highest levels of inequality in the world, makes Mzala's arguments not only fascinating but compelling.

In South Africa, poverty and opulence live side by side. The ruling capitalist class, still largely white, enjoys some of the highest living standards in the world and indeed even in history. On the other side, the black working class, including the unemployed, lives in abject poverty. This class is among the poorest of people in the world and highly exploited.[18] The way Mzala relentlessly pursued his convictions when it came to the people's war and the national question presents us with a hint of how he would have entered and advanced the current debates on building socialism. It is apparent that he would have been crucial in theorising this, not only from the movement's perspective, but the entire working class and the country.

When he argued for the people's war, he once posited, 'Striking the necessary balance, depending on the concrete situation of a given country, constitutes the art of guerrilla warfare – and art cannot be reduced to scientific formula.'[19] He consistently applied Marxism-Leninism in his analysis and thus argued on the imperative of reading the concrete conditions at any given time. He would almost certainly have translated this approach to the debate of building socialism in South Africa. Most likely, he would have insisted that the art of building socialism could not be reduced to a scientific formula.

It is precisely this analysis that we miss from someone like Mzala in the contemporary revolutionary processes in South Africa. As Joel Netshitenzhe argued, Mzala would have helped the movement deepen its theorisation on numerous tasks that it had to grapple with post the unbanning, such as the negotiation process and the implication of the transition. However, I believe that Mzala would have played a much more meaningful role in advancing socialism in South Africa beyond the transitionary period. It is precisely for this reason that the broader national liberation movement and the country at large indeed lost an intellectual prince in Mzala.

Notes

Foreword

1. Ngonyama's approach was the adoption of the broad interdisciplinary concept of 'memory' and its construction in a public sphere in order to examine ways in which the memories of Mzala Nxumalo in liberation struggle circles have been constructed and kept alive since his passing (see Ngonyama, 2017).
2. KwaZulu-Natal (KZN) was, in fact, formed only later, as a compromise name early in the democratic era. Before 1994, there were officially two entities – the KwaZulu bantustan and the province of Natal. I use KZN here for convenience, except when I refer specifically to the KwaZulu bantustan.
3. See Mare, Gerhard and Muntu Ncube (1989), 'Inkatha: Marching from Natal to Pretoria', in *South African Review 5*, Johannesburg: Ravan Press. Some of the work had earlier been presented as seminars on different academic and political platforms prior to publication.
4. When I met Mzala, I had been recruited (in 1986) to work with the ANC on its project 'Post-Apartheid South Africa' (PASA), led by Comrade Thabo Mbeki at the time. Along with comrades from inside the country, such as Mathole Motshekga and Mike Sutcliffe, we were part of this project, the aim of which was to begin to develop comprehensive ANC policies for the post-apartheid South Africa the ANC would like to see. Comrades in exile who were involved in this project included Pallo Jordan, the late comrades Zola Skweyiya, Harold Wolpe, Miranda Ngculu, Jaya Appalraju, and others.
5. Mzala's PhD research was on the national question, and my research was on the black middle class and petty bourgeoisie and their likely positioning in the liberation struggle.
6. See Nzimande, EB (1991), 'The Corporate Guerillas': Class Formation and the African Corporate Petty Bourgeoisie in Post-1973 South Africa, doctoral dissertation, University of Natal.
7. Essop Pahad later told me he was part of the decision that I be recruited into the SACP.
8. Mzala (1988), *Gatsha Buthelezi: Chief with a Double Agenda*, London: Zed Books.
9. As part of the apartheid government's Pass Laws, Africans in urban areas were required to carry a 'dompas', to allow them to work in cities (see Welsh, 2009).

10. Refer to my article written under the pseudonym Gwala, Nkosinathi (1989), 'Political violence and the struggle for control in Pietermaritzburg', *Journal of Southern African Studies*, 15(3), 506–524, for more insight into some of the struggles around Pietermaritzburg.
11. For more information, see my piece written under the pseudonym Mdluli, Praisley (1987), 'Ubuntu-Botho: Inkatha's "People's Education"', *Transformation*, (5), 60–70.
12. The late Dr Stan Mudenge, Minister of Higher Education in Zimbabwe, did his PhD at the School of Oriental and African Studies (SOAS) in London on the Monomotapa Kingdom, and eventually published a book based on that PhD thesis.
13. In English: Freedom Front Plus (FF Plus).

Preface

1. Ngonyama, P. (2017). 'Comrade Mzala: Memory Construction and Legacy Preservation'. *African Historical Review*, p. 75.
2. Ibid.
3. Ibid, pp 73–74.
4. Ngonyama, P. (2018). 'Comrade Mzala – A revolutionary left-wing intellectual from eNgotshe' (unpublished).
5. Ngonyama (2017: 73).
6. Ngonyama (2018).
7. Gottfried, H. (1998). 'Beyond Patriarchy: Theorising Gender and Class.' *Sociology*, 32(3): 451–468. Cited in Haynes, K. (2006). 'Other Lives in Accounting: Critical Reflections on Oral History Methodology in Action'. Working Paper. Department of Management Studies, University of York, York.
8. Haynes (2006).
9. Ngonyama (2018).
10. Wisker, G. (2001). *Sylvia Plath: A Beginner's Guide*. London: Hodder & Stoughton.
11. Ngonyama (2017).
12. Yeasmin, S and Rahman, KF. (2012). 'Paulo Freire and "critical literacy": Relevance for Bangladesh', *Bangladesh Education Journal*, 11(2), pp 7–14.
13. Denzin, NK. (1978). *The Research Act: A theoretical introduction to sociological methods*. New York: McGraw-Hill.
14. Tyali, SM. (2020). 'Re-reading the Propaganda and Counter-Propaganda History of South Africa: On the African National Congress' Anti-Apartheid Radio Freedom'. *Critical Arts*, 34(4), pp 61–75.
15. Ngonyama (2017).

Introduction

1. Sparks, A. (1990) 'Tambo draws tumultuous welcome on return to S. Africa from exile', *The Washington Post*, 14 December. https://www.washingtonpost.com/archive/politics/1990/12/14/tambo-draws-tumultuous-welcome-on-return-to-s-africa-from-exile/d77e6722-9754-4aef-8373-b63c0bb52f6a/
2. Ibid.
3. Jabulani 'Mzala' Nxumalo, South African History Online (sahistory.org.za). https://www.sahistory.org.za/people/jabulani-mzala-nxumalo

4	*African Communist*, No. 124, 1991.
5	Kaunda, L. (1991). 'Double Agenda Author Mzala Dies', *The Natal Witness*, 28 February, p 2.
6	Angamuthu, Wasantha. (1991). 'ANC activist Mzala dies in London', *Sunday Tribune*, 3 March, p 11.
7	'Guardian pays tribute to ANC's "intellectual prince"'. *Cape Times*, 15 March 1991, p 6.
8	'Revolutionary dies in exile', *New Nation*, 7 March 1991, p 2.
9	'Buthelezi puts legal screws on biography by ANC exile', *The Natal Witness*, 10 May 1991, p 1.
10	Email: 27 August 2020.
11	Pahad, Essop. (1991). 'Hamba Kahle, Comrade Jabulani "Mzala" Nxumalo'. *African Communist*, No. 124, p 64.
12	Ibid.
13	Email: 10 January 2021.
14	Email: 29 August 2020.
15	Email: 30 October 2020.
16	Email: 30 October 2020.
17	Email: 7 October 2020.
18	Zoom interview: 12 October 2020.
19	Ibid.
20	Ibid.
21	*The Natal Witness*, 'Mzala's body back in SA', 14 March 1991, p 1.
22	The International Defence and Aid Fund (IDAF)	South African History Online (sahistory.org.za).
23	Tim Eichler (2014), 'South Africa's negotiated transition to democracy – GRIN' (Accessed: 11 January 2021).
24	Comrade Mzala. (1985). 'Cooking the rice inside the pot', *Sechaba*, January 1985, pp 23–28.
25	The Seven Days War took place from 25 to 31 March 1990; over 200 people are said to be have been killed and over 20 000 displaced. It was reported that 80 people were killed on the first day, 25 March 1990, with special police constables participating in some of the attacks allegedly planned by Inkatha Midlands leader David Ntombela. John Aitchison, human rights campaigner and University of Natal professor, said that according to witnesses, Inkatha members were behind most of attacks on members of the United Democratic Front (See Christopher Merrett, 2013).
26	Ibid.
27	Mzala. 'Negotiations and People's Power', *Sechaba*, August 1989, pp 20–26.
28	Zoom interview: 12 October 2020.
29	Post-apartheid, the ANC is in an alliance with the SACP, the Congress of South African Trade Unions (COSATU) and the South Africa National Civic Organisation (SANCO) – known as the Tripartite Alliance plus one (see Radebe, 2017).
30	Ibid.
31	Telephonic interview: 16 September 2020.
32	Zoom interview: 12 October 2020.
33	MS Teams interview: 11 September 2020.
34	Telephonic interview: 17 September 2020.

35 *The Natal Witness*, 21 March 1991.
36 Ngonyama (2018).
37 Ibid.

Chapter 1

1   See https://www.blackpast.org/global-african-history/apartheid-1948-1994/
2   This collective term is used here to denote Africans, coloureds (people of mixed descent) and Indians.
3   See https://www.blackpast.org/global-african-history/apartheid-1948-1994/.
4   Pampallis, J. (1991). *Foundations of the New South Africa*. London: Zed Books.
5   Khunou, SK. (2009). 'Traditional leadership and independent Bantustans of South Africa: Some milestones of transformative constitutionalism beyond Apartheid'. *Potchefstroom Electronic Law Journal/Potchefstroomse Elektroniese Regsblad, 12*(4).
6   Glyn-Fox, D. 'The Anglo Zulu War Unnecessarily Destroyed The Zulu Nation', chrome-extension://efaidnbmnnnibpcajpcglclefindmkaj/https://www.anglozuluwar.com/images/Journal_22/The_Anglo-Zulu_War_of_1879_Unnecessarily_Destroyed.pdf (Accessed: 21 March 2022).
7   https://en.wikipedia.org/wiki/Louwsburg
8   Ngonyama (2018).
9   Pietermaritzburg Archival Repository (PAR), Secretary for Native Affairs (SNA) 1/1/338, 845/1906, Magistrate of Ngothse writing to Undersecretary for Native Affairs (USN), 14 March 1906, cited in Ngonyama (2018).
10 Nkosi, Zakes. (2016). 'Mzala's Legacy and its Relevance in Contemporary South Africa', Mzala Nxumalo Institute at the University of KwaZulu-Natal, Peitermaritzburg, 24 February 2016.
11 Ibid.
12 Maroleng, C. (2003). 'Swaziland: The King's Constitution', *African Security Studies, 12*(3), pp 45–48.
13 https://fhya.org/uploads/r/historical-papers-university-of-the-witwatersrand-johannesburg-wits/e/d/1/ed128340638ce9c6bc9cdaac-cf10315be228720d47568da6ed9e622fb3f4f03f/WITS_SWOHP_BON_1970_wm_rejected_edited_typescript_from_CH_floppy_disk4_Ndwandwe_Mkhonta_A2760.pdf (Accessed: 7 October 2021).
14 Mngomezulu, BR. (2020). 'The politics of the coronavirus and its impact on international relations', *African Journal of Political Science and International Relations, 14*(3), pp 116–125.
15 https://www.sahistory.org.za/article/general-south-african-history-timeline-1950s
16 Mavimbela (2018).
17 Phasha says her father, Seth Nxumalo, regarded Professor Otty Nxumalo not only a friend but a brother too. Professor Otty Nxumalo is a renowned South African writer of isiZulu books, novels, poetry, essays, short stories and children's books, and has collaborated with others on language and lexicographical works. He is one of the three biographers of His Majesty, King Goodwill Zwelithini kaBhekuzulu (see https://www.mut.ac.za/downloads/publications/MUT-Spirit-6-2017/files/assets/common/downloads/page0021.pdf).
18 Transcript of Mzala interview by Julie Frederikse, London, 1987, 2.AL2460_

A13.441, Julie Frederikse Collection, South African History Archive, p 1.
19   Mavimbela (2018).
20   Institute for Justice and Reconciliation (2017). 'Pathways for Connections: An emerging model for long-term reconciliation in post-conflict South Africa', http://www.ijr.org.za/home/wp-content/uploads/2012/07/Pathways-for-Connections-BIS-Publication.pdf (Accessed: 8 October 2021).
21   Mzala interview by Julie Frederikse (1987).
22   Puzi, ME. (1999). *A history of college libraries in the Transkei from 1882–1994* (Doctoral dissertation).
23   https://bethelcollegehighschool.adventisthost.org/about_us
24   Mzala interview by Julie Frederikse (1987).
25   Ibid.
26   Ibid.
27   Nkosi (2016).
28   Schauffer, D. (2006). 'In Memoriam: Gibson Kente – Interview', *South African Theatre Journal*, *20*(1), pp 303–322.
29   Nkabinde, AC (ed.). (1971). *Inkwazi*. Pietermaritzburg: Lincroft Books.
30   Ntuli, DBZ. (1975). *Ugqozi* (Vol. 1). Cape Town: Van Schaik.
31   Nkosi (2016).
32   Interview: 22 April 2020.
33   Lekgoathi, SP. (2010). 'The African National Congress's Radio Freedom and its audiences in apartheid South Africa, 1963–1991', *Journal of African Media Studies*, *2*(2), pp 139–153.
34   https://www.sahistory.org.za/people/abram-ramothibi-onkgopotse-tiro
35   Tiro, G. (2019). *Parcel of Death: The Biography of Onkgopotse Abram Tiro*. Johannesburg: Picador Africa.
36   https://www.sahistory.org.za/people/sibusiso-mandlenkosi-emmanuel-bengu
37   Mavimbela (2018).
38   Interview: 19 April 2020.
39   Ibid.
40   Ibid.
41   Mavimbela (2018).
42   Sigmund, Paul E. (1991). 'Christianity and violence: The case of liberation theology, Terrorism and Political Violence', 3:4, 63-79, DOI: 10.1080/09546559108427127
43   See also https://www.npr.org/templates/story/story.php?storyId=89236116
44   Transcript of Mzala interview by Julie Frederikse (1987).
45   Thomas, MG, Parfitt, T, Weiss, DA, Skorecki, K, Wilson, JF, Le Roux, M and Goldstein, DB. (2000). 'Y chromosomes traveling south: The Cohen modal haplotype and the origins of the Lemba – The "Black Jews of Southern Africa"', *American Journal of Human Genetics*, *66*(2), pp 674–686.
46   Interview: 30 August 2020.
47   Interview: 16 April 2009.
48   https://www.sahistory.org.za/article/1973-durban-strikes
49   Founded in 1916, Fort Hare produced a number of very prominent political figures, such as Oliver Tambo, Nelson Mandela, Govan Mbeki, Robert Sobukwe and Mangosuthu Buthelezi (South Africa); Robert Mugabe and Herbert Chitepo (Zimbabwe); and Elius Mathu and Charles Njonjo (Kenya). The university also produced pioneering poets, journalists, artists, authors, scholars, medical doctors

and novelists (https://www.sahistory.org.za/place/university-fort-hare-alice-eastern-cape).
50   Nkosi (2016).
51   Joyce, LK. (2018). 'Kente's "How Long?" makes a powerful return to the stage', *IOL*, 24 May 2018, https://www.iol.co.za/entertainment/movies/reviews/kentes-how-long-makes-a-powerful-return-to-the-stage-15117956 (Accessed: 10 October 2021).
52   Schauffer (2006).

Chapter 2

1   Thompson, Leonard. (2001). *A History of South Africa*. New Haven: Yale University Press.
2   Kwhela, GC. (2003). 'Umkhonto Wesizwe's contribution to the defence of the African revolution in Angola', *Journal of Contemporary History* 28(2), pp 107–23.
3   Hare, P. (2005). 'Angola: The end of an intractable conflict', in Crocker, CA, Hampson, FO and Aal, P (eds). *Grasping the Nettle: Analysing Cases of Intractable Conflict*. Washington, DC: United States Institute of Peace Press.
4   https://www.sahistory.org.za/article/general-south-african-history-timeline-1970s
5   https://www.sahistory.org.za/article/national-union-south-african-students-nusas
6   Tambo, Oliver and Tambo, Adelaide. (1988). *Preparing for Power: Oliver Tambo Speaks*. New York: G Braziller.
7   According to Mavimbela (2018), the term was derived from Johannesburg Afrikaans-aligned tsotsi taal, based based on how students from Transvaal responded when asked where they came from. 'Ek kom van Jozi af' (I come from Johannesburg).
8   Mavimbela (2018).
9   Mzala. (1988). *Gatsha Buthelezi: Chief with a Double Agenda*. London: Zed Books, p 51.
10 Ibid, p 230.
11 Ibid, p 116.
12 https://www.sahistory.org.za/article/inkatha-freedom-party-ifp
13 https://www.sahistory.org.za/dated-event/violence-breaks-out-university-zululand
14 Willan, Brian. (2108). *Sol Plaatje: A Life of Solomon Tshekiso Plaatje 1876–1932*. Jacana Media, Johannesburg.
15 Mzala, p 18.
16 https://www.sahistory.org.za/people/denis-theodore-goldberg
17 https://www.sahistory.org.za/people/professor-raymond-suttner
18 Mavimbela (2018).
19 https://www.sahistory.org.za/article/june-16-soweto-youth-uprising
20 https://www.sahistory.org.za/people/hector-pieterson
21 Webster, Dennis. (2019). 'The forgotten massacre of 18 June 1976', https://www.newframe.com/the-forgotten-massacre-of-18-june/
22 Fekisi, L. (2018), 'A comparison of Drum's coverage of the 1976 Soweto student uprisings and the 2015 #FeesMustFall student protests', https://scholar.ufs.ac.za/bitstream/handle/11660/9633/FekisiL.pdf?sequence=1&isAllowed=y

23 https://www.nytimes.com/1976/07/19/archives/black-students-riot-in-south-africa-third-university-is-ordered.html
24 Ndlovu, Sifiso Mxolisi. (2017). *The Soweto Uprisings*. Johannesburg: Picador Africa.
25 Cited in Ndlovu (2017).
26 Gerhart, GM. (1994). 'The 1976 Soweto Uprising' – Wiser Seminar Paper. https://core.ac.uk/download/pdf/39667638.pdf

Chapter 3

1   Saeboe, Maren. (2002). 'A State of Exile: The ANC and Umkhonto we Sizwe in Angola, 1976–1989' (Master's Dissertation, University of Natal).
2   Ibid, p 49.
3   Motumi, Tsepe. (1994). 'Umkhonto we Sizwe: Structure, Training and Force Levels (1984 to 1994)', *African Defence Review*, No. 18.
4   https://www.sahistory.org.za/article/umkhonto-wesizwe-mk-timeline-1961-1990
5   Houston, Gregory F. (2013). *Democracy, Governance, and Service Delivery*. Cape Town: HSRC Press, p 63.
6   Ibid.
7   Ibid.
8   Cherry, J. (2012). *Spear of the Nation: Umkhonto weSizwe – South Africa's liberation army, 1960s–1990s*. Atehns: Ohio University Press, p 48.
9   Motumi (1994).
10 Cherry (2012: 60).
11 Motumi (1994).
12 Ndebele, N and Nieftagodien, N. (2004). 'The Morogoro Conference: A moment of self-reflection', *The road to democracy in South Africa 1 (1960–1970)*, p 582.
13 Saeboe (2002: 37).
14 Ibid.
15 McKinley, DT. (2018). 'Umkhonto We Sizwe: A critical analysis of the armed struggle of the African National Congress', *South African Historical Journal*, *70*(1), pp 27–41.
16 Radebe, Jeff. Address at Mzala Nxumalo's 30th anniversary commemorating his death.
17 Email: 16 February 2021.
18 Houston (2013).
19 https://www.sahistory.org.za/article/umkhonto-wesizwe-mk-exile
20 Houston (2013: 63).
21 Houston (2013: 64).
22 Ngculu, J. (2009). *The Honour to Serve: Recollections of an Umkhonto Soldier*. Cape Town: David Philip.
23 Shubin, Vladimir. (2012). 'Comrade Mzwai', in Lissoni, A, Soske, J, Erlank, N, Nieftagodien, N and Badsha, O (eds). *One Hundred Years of the ANC: Debating Liberation Histories Today*. Johannesburg: Wits University Press, pp 255–74.
24 Manong, S. (2015). *If We Must Die: An autobiography of a former commander of Umkonto We Sizwe*. Pretoria: Nkululeko Publishers.
25 Simons, HJ. (2001). *Comrade Jack: The political lectures and diary of Jack Simons, Novo Catengue*. STE Publishers, Johannesburg, p 95.

26   Saeboe (2002: 105).
27   The term askari was derived from the Arabic word meaning 'soldier' (Abebe 2017). However, Van Zyl-Hermann (2015, p 122) says the term entered South Africa's 'lexicon of terror' in the 1970s to describe a member of the liberation forces who had switched sides, joining the apartheid state's counterinsurgency campaign.
28   Manong (2015: 99).
29   Asheeke, TTPW. (2018). *Uncovering Hidden Fronts of Africa's Liberation Struggle: Black Power, Black Consciousness, and South Africa's Armed Struggle, 1967–1985* (Doctoral dissertation, State University of New York at Binghamton) https://orb.binghamton.edu/dissertation_and_theses/78
30   Simons (2001: 97).
31   Manong (2015: 99).
32   Houston (2013: 65).
33   Simons (2001: 96).
34   Saeboe (2002).
35   Houston (2013: 69).
36   Ibid, pp 69–70.
37   Manong (2015: 93).
38   Ibid.
39   Manong (2015: 94).
40   Ibid.
41   *The African Communist*, No. 136, 1st Quarter, 1994.
42   Radebe, J. (2021). 'Remembering Comrade Mzala: "The world we want, time for change"', https://www.youtube.com/watch?v=v0XU8EkWbfA (Accessed: 28 March 2022).
43   Mann, C. (2020). *Trends in Active-Duty Military Deaths Since 2006*. Washington, DC: Library of Congress.
44   Saeboe (2002: 105).
45   Houston (2013: 78).
46   A lot of the incomers comprised young people – some deemed by the leadership to be too young to become MK combatants. Thus, the decision to develop the Solomon Mahlangu Freedom College (SOMAFCO) was made. See also, Morrow, S, Maaba, B and Pulumani, L. (2004). Education in exile: SOMAFCO, the African National Congress school in Tanzania, 1978 to 1992. HSRC Press.
47   Asheeke (2018: 259–60).
48   Ibid.
49   Asheeke (2018: 260–1).
50   Kasrils, R. (1998). *Armed and Dangerous: From Underground Struggle to Freedom*. Johannesburg: Jonathan Ball.
51   Simons (2001).
52   Suttner, R. (2008). *The ANC Underground in South Africa*. Johannesburg: Jacana Media, p 160.
53   Slovo, J. (1988). *The South African Working Class and the National Democratic Revolution*. Umsebenzi Discussion Pamphlet, South African Communist Party.
54   Magubane, Bernard M. (1979). *The Political Economy of Race and Class in South Africa*. New York: Monthly Review Press.
55   Khumalo, Ngacambaza. (1978). 'The Compromising Role of Inkatha', *The African Communist*, No. 74, 3rd Quarter, p 116.

56 Murphy, C. (1978). 'Militants Eject Zulu Chief from Funeral', *The Washington Post*, 12 March 1978, https://www.washingtonpost.com/archive/politics/1978/03/12/militants-eject-zulu-chief-from-funeral/4f70ebee-a54c-4805-b806-5556c4978a67/ (Accessed: 13 October 2021).
57 Migwe, Khumalo [Mzala]. (1980). 'Black Consciousness and the South African Revolution', *The African Communist*, No. 83, 4th Quarter.
58 Fanon, Frantz. (1961). *The Wretched of the Earth*. Harmondsworth: Penguin.
59 Manong (2015: 98).
60 Gerhart, Gail. (1990). Discussions with Mzala, in Karis-Gerhart Collection of South African political materials, 1964–1990. http://www.historicalpapers.wits.ac.za/?inventoryajax/AJAX/collections&c=A2675/R/ (Accessed: 2 September 2021).
61 Maloka, Eddy. (1994). 'Mzala – A revolutionary without kid gloves', *The African Communist*, No. 136, 1st Quarter, pp 61–66.
62 Riding, A. (1978) 'Politics Aside, Cuba Is Festive for Visiting Young Leftists'. *The New York Times*, 7 August 1978, https://www.nytimes.com/1978/08/07/archives/politics-aside-cuba-is-festive-for-visiting-young-leftists.html?auth=link-dismiss-google1tap (Accessed: 18 April 2021).
63 Maloka (1994).
64 Radebe (2021).
65 https://www.sahistory.org.za/people/jabulani-mzala-nxumalo; also see Ngonyama (2018).
66 Interview: 3 March 2021.
67 Migwe, Khumalo [Mzala]. (1982). 'Further Contribution on the Arming of the Masses', *The African Communist*, No. 89, 2nd Quarter, pp 77–87.
68 Maloka (1994: 61–66).
69 Maloka (1994: 64).
70 Mzala. (1989). 'Omelettes cannot be made without breaking eggs', *Sechaba*, June 1989.
71 Gerhart (1990). Karis-Gerhart Collection.
72 Maloka (1994: 61–66).

Chapter 4
1 Ngculu (2009: 102–3).
2 Email: 30 October 2020.
3 Lekgoathi (2010: 139–153).
4 Brown, K. (2013). 'Agitprop in Soviet Russia', *Constructing the Past*, 14(1). Available at: http://digitalcommons.iwu.edu/constructing/vol14/iss1/4 (Accessed: 9 April 2021).
5 According to Zantsi (2019, p 100), 'Mkatashinga is a Kimbundu word meaning acute pain or difficult situation and it is not really clear why the name was given to the mutiny'.
6 Zantsi, L. (2019). 'Mkatashinga: Narratives of the Mutiny in ANC Camps in Angola (1983/84)', *Journal of Global Faultlines*, 6(1), pp 90–101.
7 Khumalo, Ngacambaza. (1978). 'The Compromising Role of Inkatha', *The African Communist*, No. 74, 3rd Quarter, p 94–99.
8 Ibid.
9 Migwe, Khumalo [Mzala]. (1979). 'Book Review: 'How Long Will South Africa

Survive?" by R.W Johnson, Published by Macmillan', *Dawn*, Vol. 3, No. 7, August 1979, pp 35–37.

10   Migwe, Khumalo [Mzala]. (1979). 'Critical remarks of the question of the terror tactic', *Dawn*, Vol. 2, No. 11, December 1979, pp 10–12.

11   Van der Heyden, U and Schade, A. (2019). 'GDR Solidarity with the ANC of South Africa', in Dallywater, L, Saunders, C and Fonseca, HA, *Southern African Liberation Movements and the Global Cold War 'East'*, De Gruyter Oldenbourg, Berlin, pp 77–102. Available at https://doi.org/10.1515/9783110642964-008.

12   Shubin, VG. (2008). *The Hot 'Cold War': The USSR in Southern Africa*. Pluto Press, London, p 151.

13   Gevisser, M. (2007). *The Dream Deferred*. Cape Town: Jonathan Ball Publishers.

14   ANC PMSC (1979). 'The Green Book: Report of the Politico-Military Strategy Commission to the ANC National Executive Committee', August 1979, http://anc.org.za/show.php?id=79 (Accessed: 27 June 2011).

15   Houston, G and Magubane, B. (2006). 'The ANC political underground in the 1970s', in South African Democracy Education Trust (eds), *The Road to Democracy in South Africa, 2, 1970–1980*. Pretoria: Unisa Press, p 413.

16   Saeboe (2002: 80).

17   Interview: 28 August 2020.

18   Ibid.

19   https://www.sahistory.org.za/people/david-rabkin

20   Gerhart (1990). Karis-Gerhart Collection.

21   Warwick, R. (2012). 'Operation Savannah: A measure of SADF decline, resourcefulness and modernisation', *Scientia Militaria: South African Journal of Military Studies*, 40(3), pp 354–397.

22   Truth and Reconciliation Commission. (1998). *Truth and Reconciliation Commission of South Africa Report*, Vol. 2, ch. 6, para. 419–441.

23   Ibid; see also https://www.news24.com/health24/Experts/forumarchive/they-called-us-terrorists-yet-they-crossed-borders-to-terrorise-and-ambush-mk-20130206

24   https://www.news24.com/health24/Experts/forumarchive/they-called-us-terrorists-yet-they-crossed-borders-to-terrorise-and-ambush-mk-20130206

25   Truth and Reconciliation Commission (1998: Vol. 2, ch. 6, para. 419–441).

26   Ibid.

27   Houston and Magubane (2006: 410).

28   https://www.sahistory.org.za/people/dr-frene-noshir-ginwala

29   Interview: 29 August 2020.

30   https://www.sahistory.org.za/people/sunny-girja-singh

31   Interview: 29 August 2020.

32   Truth and Reconciliation Commission (1998).

33   *Dawn*, Vol. 5, No. 11, November 1981, pp 16–20.

34   Comrade Mzala. (1983). 'Why we are with the communists'. *The African Communist*, No. 93, 2nd Quarter, pp 66–73.

35   Migwe, Khumalo [Mzala]. (1983). 'Karl Marx and the Colonial Question', *The African Communist*, No. 94, 3rd Quarter.

36   Comrade Mzala. (1980). 'Armed Struggle in South Africa'. *The African Communist*, No. 82, 3rd Quarter, pp 65–73.

37   Comrade Mzala. (1981). 'Has the Time Come for the Arming the Masses?'. *The African Communist*, No. 86, 3rd Quarter, pp 83–94.

38   Interview: 30 August 2020.
39   Mantashe, G. (2016). "Do we still have leaders who can save the ANC from itself?". *Sunday Times*, 30 October. https://www.timeslive.co.za/sunday-times/opinion-and-analysis/2016-10-30-do-we-still-have-leaders-who-can-save-the-anc-from-itself/ (Accessed: 17 April 2021).

Chapter 5

1   'Swaziland: Africa's last absolute monarchy', *Deutsche Welle*, 14 July 2014.
2   Moloi, T. (2016). 'The Role of "Freelance" Underground Operatives in the Struggle for Liberation in South Africa: The Case of Eastern Transvaal, 1980–1990', *Oral History Journal of South Africa*, Vol. 4, pp 82–91.
3   Callinicos, L. (2004). *Oliver Tambo: Beyond the Engeli Mountains*. Cape Town: David Philip.
4   Gevisser (2007: 342).
5   Simpson, TW. (2009). 'The Bay and the Ocean: A History of the ANC in Swaziland, 1960–1979', *African Historical Review*, 41(1), pp 90–118.
6   Mavimbela (2018).
7   Temko, N. (1987). 'Switching sides: Young blacks leave ANC for arms of Pretoria. South African police keep an eye out for disenchanted dissenters', *Christian Science Monitor*, 11 March 11 1987, https://www.csmonitor.com/layout/set/tabletkiosk/1987/0311/ofect.html (Accessed: 18 April 2021).
8   Interview: 26 November 2020.
9   Maloka (1994).
10   Karis-Gerhart Collection of South African political materials, 1964–1990. http://www.historicalpapers.wits.ac.za/?inventoryajax/AJAX/collections&c=A2675/R/ (Accessed: 2 September 2021).
11   Maloka (1994: 61–66).
12   This 'common' university had been established in 1964 with its headquarters in Lesotho. In later years, it split into the National University of Lesotho, the University of Botswana and the University of Swaziland (now the University of Eswatini) (see Agachi, 2019).
13   Ibid.
14   Minter, W. (1991). 'South Africa: Behind the violence: "black-on-black", the "third force", and the real Gatsha Buthelezi', *Christianity and Crisis*, 50(19), pp 418–421.
15   Miya, S. (2011). 'Zulu queen mother reburied', *The Witness*, 9 May 2011. https://www.news24.com/witness/archive/Zulu-queen-mother-reburied-20150430 (Accessed: 30 April 2021).
16   *Mail & Guardian*. (1994). 'Zwelithini Nods To An Old Buthelezi Enemy', 9 September 1994. https://mg.co.za/article/1994-09-09-zwelithini-nods-to-an-old-buthelezi-enemy/ (Accessed: 3 May 2021).
17   Maloka (1994: 61–66).
18   https://www.upi.com/Archives/1984/03/31/South-Africa-Swaziland-reveal-secret-accord/8059449557200/
19   https://www.sahistory.org.za/sites/default/files/archive-files2/mem19820715.026.021.000.pdf
20   Russon, R. (1994). 'Southern Africa: Consolidation or fragmentation: Territorially, nation states and the border question – The case of Swaziland.' Paper presented

at the Association of African Political Sciences (AAPS) Conference, Dakar, Senegal.
21 Maloka (1994: 61–66).
22 Ibid.
23 Ibid.
24 http://www.thepresidency.gov.za/national-orders/recipient/jameson-nongolozi-mngomezulu
25 Badat, S. (2013). *The Forgotten People: Political Banishment under Apartheid*. Leiden: Brill Press; see also https://www.sahistory.org.za/people/mbalekelwa-mngomezulu
26 Named after the ANC president who had died on 21 July 1967, the Luthuli Detachment was made up of units of Umkhonto we Sizwe operatives and the Zimbabwean African People's Union (ZAPU) guerrillas. They crossed the Zambezi River from the Zambian banks of the river into Rhodesia in 1967 and were engaged in battles until late 1968. Their objective was to march across Rhodesia to South Africa to set up underground operations to politically mobilise South Africans in different sections of the country (see https://www.sahistory.org.za/dated-event/luthuli-combat-detachment-crosses-zambezi).
27 Truth and Reconciliation Commission (1998: vol. 2, ch. 6, paras 351–354).
28 Houston, G, Pophiwa, N, Sausi, K, Dumisa, S and Seabe, D. (2013). 'Documenting the legacy of the South African liberation struggle: The national liberation heritage route – Unsung heroes and heroines of the liberaton struggle project', https://repository.hsrc.ac.za/ (Accessed: 17 April 2021).
29 Griffiths, Ieuan L and Funnell, DC. (1991). 'The Abortive Swazi Land Deal'. *African Affairs*, *90*(358), pp 51–64. http://www.jstor.org/stable/722639
30 Bennett, TW and Peart, NS. (1986). 'The Ingwavuma land deal: A case study of self-determination', *BC Third World LJ*, *6*, p 23.
31 Ndlovu, SM. (2018). 'Sowing the seeds of political mobilisation in Bantustans: resistance of the cession of the KaNgwane Bantustan to the Kingdom of Swaziland', *Journal for Contemporary History*, *43*(1), pp 43–69..
32 Maloka (1994: 61–66).
33 Matlhako, Chris 'Che'. (2013). 'A personal reflection on attraction(s) to the works of Mzala Nxumalo', Umsebenzi online, Vol. 12, No. 39, 7 November 2013.
34 https://www.sahistory.org.za/article/umkhonto-wesizwe-mk-exile
35 Truth and Reconciliation Commission (1998: vol. 2, ch. 6 paras. 351–354).
36 http://www.thepresidency.gov.za/national-orders/recipient/jameson-nongolozi-mngomezulu
37 Migwe, Khumalo [Mzala]. (1982). 'Lessons of Our People's War – Part 2', *Dawn*, Vol. 6, No. 3, March 1982, pp 15–19.
38 Migwe, Khumalo [Mzala]. (1982). 'Lessons of Our People's War – Part 3', *Dawn*, Vol. 6, No. 4, April 1982, pp 23–27.
39 Mzala (1983: 6–73).
40 Majola, Sisa [Mzala]. (1984). 'A Tale of Two Nations: The Presentation of the National Question in South Africa', *The African Communist*, No. 97, 2nd Quarter, pp 40–52.
41 The National Forum was formed in June 1983 from institutions that claimed to be to the left of the ANC. They comprised organisations such as the Azanian People's Organisation (AZAPO), AZAPO's student wing Azanian Students' Movement (AZASM), Society of Young Africa (SOYA), Action Youth, Cape

Action League and several others (see https://www.sahistory.org.za/archive/national-forum).
42 Maloka (1994: 61–66).
43 Ibid.
44 Comrade Mzala. (1984). 'Latest Opportunism and the Theory of the South African Revolution: A critique of an Ideological Trend Against the Freedom Charter'. Lusaka: Publisher unknown.
45 The official title is the Agreement on Non-Aggression and Good Neighbourliness between Mozambique and South Africa.
46 Erasmus, G. (1984). *The Accord of Nkomati: Context and Content*. Johannesburg: SAIIA.
47 McKinley (2018).
48 Maloka (1994: 61–66).
49 Daniel, J. (presumed). (c. 1988). *Why the need for anonymity* [unpublished manuscript]. Bessie Head Library, Pietermaritzburg, South Africa.
50 *The African Communist*, No. 98, 3rd Quarter 1984.

Chapter 6

1 Baillie, GK. (1999). *Printmaking at the Dakawa Art and Craft Project: The Impact of ANC Cultural Policy and Swedish Practical Implementation on Two Printmakers Trained During South Africa's Transformation Years* (Doctoral dissertation, Rhodes University).
2 Morrow, Seán, Maaba, Brown and Pulumani, Loyiso. (2004). *Education in Exile: SOMAFCO, the ANC School in Tanzania, 1978 to 1992*. Cape Town: HSRC Press, pp 143–44.
3 Hilda and Rusty Bernstein Papers, 1931–2011 http://www.historicalpapers.wits.ac.za/?inventory/U/collections&c=A3299/R/ (Accessed: 11 May 2021).
4 Ibid.
5 Manghezi, A. (2004). 'Solomon Mahlangu Freedom College: Symbol of international solidarity', in Anti-Apartheid Conference, University of KwaZulu-Natal, Durban (October 2004), pp 10–13.
6 Nkosi (2016).
7 As it will emerge later, when criticising the leadership's reluctance to expedite the people's war in South Africa, Mzala used this phrase to critique the over-emphasis of exile.
8 Of course, Mzala was not the first African intellectual revolutionary to use this phrase. Paying homage to Kwame Nkrumah in May 1972, Amílcar Cabral used the phrase. He wrote: 'True, imperialism is cruel and unscrupulous, but we must not lay all the blame on its broad back. For, as the African people say: "Rice only cooks inside the pot."' (see Manji, F., and B. Fletcher. 2013. *Claim No Easy Victories: The Legacy of Amilcar Cabral*. CODESRIA). It is therefore not clear whether Mzala was borrowing from Cabral or the African adage as invoked by Cabral.
9 *The African Communist*, No. 98, 3rd Quarter 1984.
10 https://www.sahistory.org.za/article/township-uprising-1984-1985 (Accessed: 7 June 2021).
11 Nyawuza. (1985). 'Response to Comrade Mzala', *Sechaba*, April 1985, p 19.
12 Mashinini, Alex. (1985). 'Preparing the fire before cooking the rice inside the

pot', *Sechaba*, April 1985, pp 20–30.
13 Macmillan, H. (2009). 'The "Hani Memorandum" – Introduced and annotated'. *Transformation: Critical Perspectives on Southern Africa*, 69(1), pp 106–129.
14 Manong (2015).
15 Ibid, p 231.
16 Mavimbela (2018: 165–6).
17 Gerhart (1990). Karis-Gerhart Collection.
18 Ibid.
19 Ibid.
20 Simpson, T. (2016). *Umkhonto we Sizwe: The ANC's armed struggle*. Penguin Random House, Cape Town; see also https://omalley.nelsonmandela.org/omalley/index.php/site/q/03lv03445/04lv04015/05lv04016/06lv04025/07lv04027.htm (Accessed: 7 June 2021).
21 Mavimbela (2018: 168).

Chapter 7

1 Zwide kaLanga was king of the strong and powerful Ndwandwe (Nxumalo) kingdom from about 1805 to around 1820; he was eventually defeated by King Shaka, the founder of the Zulu nation.
2 'Brief Biographical sketch and CV of Mzala', Karis-Gerhart Collection of South African political materials, 1964–1990. http://www.historicalpapers.wits.ac.za/?inventoryajax/AJAX/collections&c=A2675/R/ (Accessed: 2 September 2021).
3 Nxumalo, JM. (1992). 'The National Question in the Writing of South African History: A Critical Survey of Some Major Tendencies', Front Cover, *Jabulani*.
4 Alexander, N. (2008). 'An illuminating moment: Background to the Azanian Manifesto'. In *Biko Lives!* (pp 157–170). New York: Palgrave Macmillan.
5 The Freedom Charter is a unique document in which the people of South Africa formulated their vision of an alternative society from the oppressive and exploitative apartheid state. It was adopted on 25 and 26 June 1955 at the Congress of the People in Kliptown, Soweto. The Congress was attended by some 2 844 delegates from all over the country, as well as allies of the ANC, including the South African Indian Congress, the South African Coloured People's Organisation and the South African Congress of Democrats. (See https://scnc.ukzn.ac.za/doc/hist/freedomchart/freedomch.html [Accessed: 18 June 2021]).
6 Comrade Mzala. (1985). 'The Freedom charter is our lodestar', *Sechaba*, July, pp 2–17.
7 Comrade Mzala. (1985). 'The Freedom charter is our lodestar', *Sechaba*, August, pp 29–32.
8 Comrade Mzala. (1985). 'The Freedom charter is our lodestar', *Sechaba*, September, pp 28–31.
9 No Sizwe was Neville Alexander's pseudonym. He was also associated with the National Forum and the writing of the Azanian Manifesto.
10 Comrade Mzala. (1985). 'The Freedom charter is our lodestar', *Sechaba*, October, pp 22–31.
11 Alexander (2008: 166).
12 Comrade Mzala. (1985). 'On the threshold of revolution'. *The African Communist*,

No. 102, 3rd Quarter, pp 66–77.
13. Majola, Sisa [Mzala]. (1985). 'Education for Revolution', *The African Communist*, No. 103, 4th Quarter, pp 30–39.
14. Majola, Sisa [Mzala]. (1986). 'Nation and class in the South African revolution', *The African Communist*, No. 105, 2nd Quarter, pp 40–48.
15. Majola, Sisa [Mzala]. (1986). 'The beginning of people's power', *The African Communist*, No. 106, 3rd Quarter 1986, pp 55–66.
16. Mzala. (1986). 'Building people's power', *Sechaba*, September 1986, pp 8–15.
17. https://www.sahistory.org.za/people/alex-la-guma
18. Mzala described Pieterse as a noted South African poet and dramatist living in the United States where he was a university lecturer. He was in Tanzania to run an Art and Theatre workshop at SOMAFCO.
19. Comrade Mzala. (1986). 'Culture, the artist and liberation', *The African Communist*, No. 107, 4th Quarter 1986, pp 71–82.
20. Mzala. (1986). 'Umkhonto WeSizwe: Building people's forces for combat war and insurrection – Building people's power', *Sechaba*, December 1986, pp 19–28.

Chapter 8

1. Gamble, A. (1994). *The Free Economy and the Strong State: The politics of Thatcherism*. Macmillan International Higher Education.
2. Unterhalter, Elaine. (2022). 'The national question and exile: Remembering Mzala in London'. Forthcoming.
3. Bale, T. (2015). 'In life as in death? Margaret Thatcher (mis) remembered'. *British Politics*, *10*(1), pp 99–112.
4. Unterhalter (2022).
5. Karis-Gerhart Collection of South African political materials, 1964–1990. http://www.historicalpapers.wits.ac.za/?inventoryajax/AJAX/collections&c=A2675/R/ (Accessed: 2 September 2021).
6. Cronin, J. (2009). 'The Role of the revolutionary intellectuals: the life of Comrade Mzala', in *The Poverty of Ideas: South African democracy and the retreat of Intellectuals*. Johannesburg: Jacana Media, pp 98.
7. See 'Brief Biographical sketch and C.V. of Mzala', Wits William Cullen Library.
8. 'Obituary John Daniel (1944–2014)', http://transformationjournal.org.za/01_Obituary.pdf (Accessed: 13 June 2021); see also *Julie Frederikse. (2014).* 'John Daniel: Activist, exile and a truly inspiring academic', *Mail&Guardian*, 31 July 2014, https://mg.co.za/article/2014-07-31-john-daniel-activist-exile-and-a-truly-inspiring-academic/ (Accessed: 13 June 2021).
9. Karis-Gerhart Collection of South African political materials, 1964–1990. http://www.historicalpapers.wits.ac.za/?inventoryajax/AJAX/collections&c=A2675/R/ (Accessed: 2 September 2021).
10. 'Brief Biographical sketch and C.V. of Mzala', Karis-Gerhart Collection.
11. Kamana, Caroline. '28 Penton Street – African National Congress (ANC) in London Headquarters'. https://www.layersoflondon.org/map?l=eyJmcmVlX-3RleHRfcXVlcnkiOm51bGwsInNlYXJjaF9wYWdlIjoxLCJjYXRlZ29yeV9hb-mRfdGVybV9maWx0ZXJzIjp7InRlcm1faWQiOm51bGwsImNhdGVnb3J5X2lk-IjoxfSwiYWN0aXZlX2xheGVyX2dyb3VwX2lkcyI6W119&m=eyJjZW-50ZXIiOlsiMS41MDc0LDAuMTI3OF0sInpvb20iOjEwLCJsaWdodHNwZX-QiOm9hbHNlfQ%3D%3D&record=6433 (Accessed: 12 June 2021).

12 'Brief Biographical sketch and C.V. of Mzala', Karis-Gerhart Collection.
13 Carchidi, V. (1994). 'South Africa from Text to Film: "Cry Freedom" and "A Dry White Season", in Simons, JD (ed.). *Literature and Film in the Historical Dimension*, Gainesville: University Press of Florida Press, pp 47–61.
14 Mzala. (1987). 'Towards people's war and insurrection', *Sechaba*, April 1987, pp 2–6.
15 Thomson, A. (1995). 'Incomplete Engagement: Reagan's South Africa Policy Revisited', *Journal of Modern African Studies*, *33*(1), pp 83–101.
16 Wright, VG. (1989). 'US foreign policy and destabilisation in Southern Africa', *Review of African Political Economy*, Vol. 45/46, pp 159–168.
17 https://www.sahistory.org.za/article/negotiations-and-transition
18 Mzala. (1987). 'United States policy towards South Africa', *Sechaba*, June 1987, pp 3–10.
19 Ibid.
20 Mzala. (1987). 'Can the Imperialists Abort our Revolution?', *Sechaba*, July 1987, pp 7–13.
21 Cited in Mzala (*Sechaba* August 1987: 23–28).
22 Liebenberg, I. (2017). 'Dakar 1987 – Reflections on a conference', Researchgate, https://www.researchgate.net/publication/319837060_Dakar_1987_-_Reflections_on_a_conference (Accessed: 4 September 2021).
23 Mzala (*Sechaba* August 1987: 23–28).
24 Majola, Sisa [Mzala]. (1987). 'The two stages of our revolution', *The African Communist*, No. 110, 3rd Quarter 1987, pp 39–51.
25 Comrade Mzala. (1987). 'How the ANC was revived by the Youth League'. *The African Communist*, No. 110, 3rd Quarter, pp 50–62.
26 Ibid.
27 Ibid.

Chapter 9

1 Ngonyama, Percy. (2012). 'Mzala: A Short Intellectual Biography'. Department of Historical Studies, University of KwaZulu-Natal (Howard College Campus).
2 Wyley, C and Merrett, C. (1991). 'Universities and the New Censorship: Mzala's *Gatsha Buthelezi: Chief with a double agenda*', *Critical Arts*, *5*(4), p 99.
3 Ibid.
4 Mzala (1988: 5).
5 Ibid, p 103.
6 Ibid.
7 This is how the name of King Dinuzulu kaCetshwayo is spelt in Mzala's book.
8 Ibid, p 104.
9 Ibid, p 105.
10 Ibid, p 66–67.
11 *Weekly Mail*. (1988). Book review: 'Attempting to pin down a man of ambiguity', 13 October 1988.
12 Mathiane, N. (1989) 'The Hatchet and the Snow', *Frontline*, 1 February 1989.
13 Ibid.
14 Ibid.
15 Ibid.
16 Ulundi was the capital of the KwaZulu bantustan.

17	Masango, J (1989). 'Marxist twaddle', *Frontline*, 3 April 1989.
18	Smith, JS. (1989). 'Nonsense Nomavenda', *Frontline*, 3 April 1989.
19	Vos, S. (1989) 'Buthelezi biography', *Frontline*, 3 April 1989.
20	Mzala. (1989). 'Horse's mouth', *Frontline*, 3 April 1989.
21	Kaunda, L. (1989). 'The Biography', *Natal Witness*, 9 February 1989.
22	Moloto, G. (1988). 'In lieu of a book review, a book by one of us', *Dawn*, Vol. 1, No. 1, pp 25–30.
23	Wyley and Merrett (1991: 99).
24	Friedman & Friedman Attorneys. (1989). 'Buthelezi Biography'. *Frontline*, June 1989.
25	Wyley and Merrett (1991: 100).
26	Wyley and Merrett (1991: 103).
27	Ibid.
28	Ibid.
29	Wyley and Merrett (1991: 104).
30	Email: 27 August 2020.
31	Lubisi, C. (1993). 'Buthelezi and the "Zulu Kingdom"'. *The African Communist*, (134), p 65.
32	Karis, TG and Gerhart, GM. (1997). 'A Documentary History of African Politics in South Africa, 1882–1990: Nadir and Resurgence, 1964–1979'. *From Protest to Challenge*, 5. p 258.
33	Email: 27 August 2020.
34	Ibid.
35	Ibid.
36	Mzala (1988: 105).
37	Email: 27 August 2020.
38	Gerhart (1990). Karis-Gerhart Collection.
39	Lubisi (1993).
40	Mbeki, G. (1996). *Sunset at Midday: Latshon 'ilang 'emini!*. Nolwazi, p 90.
41	Lynd, H. (2021). 'The Peace Deal: The Formation of the Ingonyama Trust and the IFP Decision to Join South Africa's 1994 Elections', *South African Historical Journal*, pp 1–43.
42	Email: 27 August 2020.
43	Ibid.
44	Ibid.
45	Interview: 24 June 2021.
46	Email: 27 August 2020.
47	Tambo and Tambo (1988).
48	Brewer, J. (1989). 'Mzala, *Gatsha Buthelezi: Chief with a double agenda*. London: Zed Press, 1988, 240 pp', *Africa*, 59(2), pp 254–255.
49	Nkomo, M. (1990). 'Gatsha Buthelezi: Chief with a Double Agenda', *Canadian Journal of African Studies*, 24(1), pp 129–132.
50	Ibid, 131–3.
51	Merrett, C. (2013). 'A Tale of Two Books', *Natal Witness*, 8 November 2013, p 9.
52	Email: 27 August 2020.
53	Mbeki (1996: 87).
54	Ibid.
55	Cited in Mbeki (1996: 88).
56	Ibid.

57 Mbeki (1996: 88–89).
58 Cited in Mbeki (1996: 89).
59 Ibid.
60 Ibid, p 92.
61 Karis and Gerhart (1997).
62 Mbeki (1996).

Chapter 10

1 Karis-Gerhart Collection of South African political materials, 1964–1990. http://www.historicalpapers.wits.ac.za/?inventoryajax/AJAX/collections&c=A2675/R/ (Accessed: 2 September 2021).
2 Kapinos, A. (2020). *'An Oasis of Free Thought' in Prague: Problems of Peace and Socialism and the End of the Thaw, 1968–1969.* (Doctoral dissertation, The University of North Carolina at Chapel Hill).
3 https://en.wikipedia.org/wiki/Problems_of_Peace_and_Socialism
4 Interview: 18 September 2020.
5 Ibid.
6 Kasrils (2004).
7 Dialego. (1988). 'What is Trotskyism?'. *The African Communist*, 4th Quarter, pp 68–78.
8 Jordan, ZP. (2017). *Letters to my Comrades: Interventions & excursions.* Jacana Media, Johannesburg.
9 Editorial Notes. (1989). 'The controversy around Trotskyism'. *The African Communist*, No.118, 3rd Quarter, pp 5–7.
10 Gerhart (1990). Karis-Gerhart Collection.
11 Mzala. (1988). 'The Volcano of the People's Wrath', *World Marxist Review*, Vol. 31, 7 July, pp 121–127.
12 Mzala. (1988). 'Aids – Misinformation and Racism', *Sechaba*, October 1988.
13 Ibid.
14 Ibid.
15 Ibid.
16 UNAIDS, http://aidsinfo.unaids.org/ (Accessed: 24 August 2021).
17 Gevisser (2007: 731).
18 Kenyon, C. (2008). 'Cognitive dissonance as an explanation of the genesis, evolution and persistence of Thabo Mbeki's HIV denialism'. *African Journal of AIDS Research*, 7(1), pp 29–35.
19 Unterhalter (2022).
20 Karis-Gerhart Collection of South African political materials, 1964–1990. http://www.historicalpapers.wits.ac.za/?inventoryajax/AJAX/collections&c=A2675/R/ (Accessed: 2 September 2021).
21 Crossette, B, Kifner, J, Riding, A, and Rohter, L. (1989). 'In Asia, African and Latin America: A Banner for Revolution'. *The New York Times*, 24 January 1989.
22 Mkhatshwa, Jabulani [Mzala]. (1988). 'Senegal', *The African Communist*, No. 115, 3rd Quarter, pp 65–73.
23 Mkhatshwa, Jabulani [Mzala]. (1988). 'Angola: A military defeat for the racists', *The African Communist*, No. 115, 4th Quarter, pp 79–84.
24 Trewhela, P. (2009). *Inside Quatro: Uncovering the exile history of the ANC and SWAPO.* Jacana Media, Johannesburg.

25	Majola, Sisa [Mzala]. (1988). 'To Whom Does South Africa Belong?', *The African Communist*, No. 115, 4th Quarter, pp 93–98.
26	Majola, Sisa [Mzala]. (1988). 'Perestroika and class struggle', *The African Communist*, No. 113, 2nd Quarter, pp 91–108.
27	Comrade Mzala. (1989). 'Revolutionary Theory on the National Question in South Africa', in Van Diepen, M (ed.). (1989). *The National Question in South Africa*. London: Zed Books, pp 30–55.
28	Ibid.
29	Ibid.
30	Interview: 15 April 2020.
31	Mzala. (1984). Letter to the editor. *Sechaba*, December 1984.
32	Interview: 30 November 2020.
33	Gerhart (1990). Karis-Gerhart Collection.
34	Hoffman, J and Mzala, N. (1990). '"Non-Historic Nations" and the National Question: A South African Perspective'. *Science & Society*, *54*(4), pp 408–426.
35	Burawoy, M. (2004). 'From liberation to reconstruction: Theory & practice in the life of Harold Wolpe'. *Review of African Political Economy*, *31*(102), pp 657–675.
36	South African Communist Party (SACP). (1981) [1962]. 'The Road to South African Freedom. Programme adopted at the fifth national conference of the communist party held inside the country', in *South African Communists Speak: Documents from the History of the South African Communist Party 1915–1980*. London: Inkululeko Publications.
37	Friedman, S. (2015). *Race, Class and Power: Harold Wolpe and the radical critique of apartheid*. Pietermaritzburg: University of KwaZulu-Natal Press, pp 85–87.
38	Karis-Gerhart Collection of South African political materials, 1964–1990. http://www.historicalpapers.wits.ac.za/?inventoryajax/AJAX/collections&c=A2675/R/ (Accessed: 2 September 2021).
39	Email: 27 August 2021.
40	Unterhalter (2022).
41	Suttner, R. (2008). *The ANC underground in South Africa to 1976: A social and historical study*. Johannesburg: Jacana Media, p 208.
42	Email: 3 October 2020.
43	Ibid.
44	Maharaj, M. (2008). *The ANC and South Africa's negotiated transition to democracy and peace*. Berghof Transitions Series 2. Berlin: Berghof Foundation.
45	Dlamuka, MC. (2018). *Connectedness and Disconnectedness in Thembeyakhe Harry Gwala's Biography, 1920–1995: Rethinking Political Militancy, Mass Mobilisation and Grassroots Struggles in South Africa* (Doctoral dissertation, Department of History, Faculty of Arts, University of the Western Cape), p 232.
46	Ibid, p 34.
47	Ibid, p 173.
48	Interview: 18 September 2020.
49	Ibid.
50	Dlamuka (2018: 275).
51	Sylvest, JM. (1999). 'Glasnost: The Pandora's box of Gorbachev's reforms', https://scholarworks.umt.edu/ (Accessed: 3 June 2022).

Chapter 11

1. Doxtader, E. (2001). Making rhetorical history in a time of transition: The occasion, constitution, and representation of South African reconciliation. *Rhetoric & Public Affairs*, 4(2), pp 223–260.
2. Email: 3 October 2020.
3. Email: 30 October 2020.
4. http://www.historicalpapers.wits.ac.za/?inventory/U/collections&c=A2729/I/6364 (Accessed: 30 August 2021).
5. Stalker, Brenda. (1988). 'Crisis in our country'. *Sechaba*, May 1988, pp 18–26.
6. Theresa. (1989). 'The People's Struggle', *Sechaba*, January 1989, pp 26–30.
7. Mzala (*Sechaba* June 1989: 11–18).
8. Mzala (*Sechaba* August 1989: 20–26).
9. Radebe, MJ. (2020). *Constructing Hegemony: The South African Commercial Media and the (Mis) Representation of Nationalisation*. Pietermaritzburg: University of KwaZulu-Natal Press.
10. Radebe, MJ. (2022). 'Framing the Poor during Covid-19: Townships and Informal Settlements in South African Online News'. *Communicatio*, pp 1–22.
11. Simpson, T. (2009). 'Toyi-Toyi-ing to freedom: The endgame in the ANC's armed struggle, 1989–1990', *Journal of Southern African Studies*, 35(2), pp 507–521.
12. Cited in Simpson (2009).
13. Comrade Mzala. (1989). 'The Battle of Income – Symbol of our Armed Struggle', *The African Communist*, 1st Quarter, pp 65–75.
14. Mkhatshwa, Jabulani [Mzala]. (1989). 'Africa notes and comments', *The African Communist*, 1st Quarter, pp 65–75.
15. Mkhatshwa, Jabulani [Mzala]. (1989). 'Africa notes and comments'. *The African Communist*, 2nd Quarter, pp 65–72.
16. Mkhatshwa, Jabulani [Mzala]. (1989). 'Africa notes and comments'. *The African Communist*, 3rd Quarter, pp 44–53.
17. Majola, Sisa [Mzala]. (1989). 'The Current Crisis and the Growth of our Revolution', *The African Communist*, 3rd Quarter, pp 31–43.
18. Argus Foreign Service. (1990). 'Limited role for outsiders in SA reform, says Worrall', *The Argus*, 19 January 1990.
19. SAPA. (1990). 'African National Congress Reacts to Address', South African Press Association, 2 February 1990.
20. Ibid.
21. Staff Reporter. (1990). 'ANC wants sanctions to remain', *Cape Times*, 3 February 1990.
22. Mzala. (1990). 'An ANC View', *New Nation*, 5 April 1990.
23. Ibid.
24. Mzala. (1990). 'A response to mounting people's pressure', *New Nation*, 11 May 1990.
25. Daniel, J. (2016). 'The Impact of the Cold War and the Fall of the Berlin Wall on Southern Africa'. chrome-extension://efaidnbmnnnibpcajpcglclefindmkaj/ https://www.kas.de/c/document_library/get_file?uuid=7dd3251f-7488-37c4-50e9-52e15c225130&groupId=252038 (Accessed: 17 March 2022).
26. Interview: 22 April 2020.
27. Rickard, C. (1990). 'ANC's Mzala takes legal action against Ilanga', *Natal Witness*, 9 July 1990.

28 Ilanga. (1990). 'Further on Kagiso Funding'. *Ilanga*, 5–6 July 1990, p 11.
29 Rickard (1990).
30 Ibid.
31 Umtata Capital Radio. (1990). 'Mzala to Sue', 9 July 1990.
32 https://www.gov.za/ReconciliationMonth2020
33 *Patriot.* (1990). 'ANC sal met Geloftedag wegdoen', 27 July 1990.
34 Mzala. (1990). 'Patriotism and Positivity what SA Needs Now', *Cape Times*, 13 November 1990.
35 Ibid.
36 Ibid.
37 Mzala. (1990). 'Is South Africa in a Revolutionary Situation?', *Journal of Southern African Studies*, *16*(3), pp 563–578.
38 Mkhatshwa, Jabulani [Mzala]. (1990). 'Africa Notes and Comments', *The African Communist*, 1st Quarter, pp 84–93.
39 Mkhatshwa, Jabulani [Mzala]. (1990). 'Africa Notes and Comments', *The African Communist*, 2nd Quarter, pp 77–83.
40 Mkhatshwa, Jabulani [Mzala]. (1990). 'Africa Notes and Comments', *The African Communist*, 3rd Quarter, pp 75–78.
41 Ibid.
42 https://www.history.com/this-day-in-history/former-liberian-president-charles-taylor-found-guilty-of-war-crimes (Accessed: 1 September 2021).
43 Majola, Sisa [Mzala]. (1990). 'Wilton Mkwayi: A Veteran of Revolutionary Campaigns', *The African Communist*, 3rd Quarter, pp 51–57.
44 Mkhatshwa, Jabulani [Mzala]. (1990). 'Africa Notes and Comments', *The African Communist*, 4th Quarter, pp 62–67.
45 Mzala. (1990). 'The Bantu System is at the Centre of Natal Violence', *The African Communist*, 4th Quarter, pp 34–38.
46 Lenin, VI. (1919). *Two Tactics of Social-Democarcy in the Democratic Revolution*. New York: Foreign Policy Association Inc.

Chapter 12

1 https://www.sahistory.org.za/article/general-south-african-history-timeline-1990s (Accessed: 30 August 2021).
2 Ibid.
3 Gerhart (1990). Karis-Gerhart Collection.
4 Alexander (2008: 170).
5 Gerhart (1990). Karis-Gerhart Collection.
6 Ibid.
7 Ibid.
8 Tau, Rebone. (2020). *The Rise and Fall of the ANC Youth League*. Cape Town: Penguin Random House.
9 Gerhart (1990). Karis-Gerhart Collection.
10 Ibid.
11 https://omalley.nelsonmandela.org/omalley/index.php/site/q/03lv02039/04lv02103/05lv02104/06lv02106.htm (Accessed: 23 August 2021).
12 Gerhart (1990). Karis-Gerhart Collection.
13 Macmillan, H. (2009). 'The African National Congress of South Africa in Zambia: The culture of exile and the changing relationship with home, 1964–

1990', *Journal of Southern African Studies*, 35(2), pp 303–329.
14 Lotshwao, K. (2009). 'The lack of internal party democracy in the African National Congress: A threat to the consolidation of democracy in South Africa', *Journal of Southern African Studies*, 35(4), pp 901–914.
15 Williams, Michelle and Satgar, Vishwas (eds). (2021). *Destroying Democracy: Neoliberal capitalism and the rise of authoritarian politics*. Johannesburg: Wits University Press.
16 Majola, Sisa [Mzala]. (1985). 'Education for Revolution', *The African Communist*, No. 103, 4th Quarter, pp 30–39.
17 Mandela, N. (2008). *Long Walk to Freedom: The autobiography of Nelson Mandela*. Hachette UK, London, p 688.
18 Morris, M. (1991). 'The Future of Socialism', *Transformation* (14), p 45.
19 Hedges, C. (1990). 'Old Marxist Returns, with Hope for South Africa', *The New York Times*, 17 October 1990.
20 Lewis, A. (1990). 'Slovo's vision', *The Baltimore Evening Sun*, 17 October 1990.
21 Land Noli. (n.d.). A speech by ANC President OR Tambo, guest speaker at the National Press Club, Washington DC., USA on 28 January 1987. https://www.youtube.com/watch?v=umScRCjRZNo
22 Mandela (2008).
23 Wieder, A. (2013). *Ruth First and Joe Slovo in the war against apartheid*. New York: NYU Press.
24 https://omalley.nelsonmandela.org/omalley/index.php/site/q/03lv03445/04lv04015/05lv04016/06lv04025/07lv04029.htm
25 Callinicos, L. (2012). 'Oliver Tambo and the Dilemma of the Camp Mutinies in Angola in the Eighties'. *South African Historical Journal*, 64(3), DOI: 10.1080/02582473.2012.675813, pp 587–621.
26 Trewhela (2009).
27 Wieder (2013).
28 A tsotsi is a young criminal or gang member, generally in the townships of large cities. Particularly in the 1940s and 1950s, they spoke a specific language – tsotsitaal or flytaal – and wore flashy clothing.
29 Bonner, PL. (1990). 'The Russians on the Reef, 1947–1957: Urbanisation, Gang Warfare and Ethnic Mobilisation', in Philip Bonner, Peter Delius and Deborah Posel (eds.). (1993). *Apartheid's Genesis: 1935–1962*. Johannesburg: University of the Witwatersrand and Ravan Press, pp 160–94.
30 Morris (1991: 59).
31 Ibid, p 62.
32 South African Communist Party (SACP). (2017). 14th National Congress Resolutions. https://www.sacp.org.za/docs/decl/2017/declaration-and-resolutions.pdf (Accessed: 28 September 2021).
33 See SACP (2017). 15th National Congress Resolutions. https://www.sacp.org.za/content/sacp/15th-ntional-congress-declation-adopted-16-july-22 (Accessed: 25 September 2022).
34 Karis, Tom. (1990). Notes on meeting with Mzala, in Karis-Gerhart Collection of South African political materials, 1964–1990. http://www.historicalpapers.wits.ac.za/?inventoryajax/AJAX/collections&c=A2675/R/ (Accessed: 2 September 2021).

Chapter 13

1. http://www.sacp.org.za/main.php?ID=2313
2. https://www.bbc.co.uk/programmes/b0078zs3
3. Mpho Nxumalo: Oral History Interview, Part 2 of 2, London (1991), Islandora Repository, University of Cape Town (UCT) Libraries Digital Collections, http//www.digitalcollections.lib.uct.ac.za/oral-history-interview-mpho-nxumalo-part-2-2.
4. Daniel, J. (1991). 'Lost "prince" of the ANC', *The Guardian*, 14 March 1991.
5. Matlhako (2103).
6. Cronin (2009).
7. Matlhako (2103).
8. Ostrovsky, Nikolai. (1974). *How Steel is Tempered*. Moscow: Progress Press.

Postscript

1. SACP (2017).
2. Interview: 15 April 2020.
3. Khumalo, Ngacambaza [Mzala]. (1978). 'The Compromising Role of Inkatha', *The African Communist*, No. 74, 3rd Quarter.
4. Migwe, Khumalo [Mzala]. (1983). 'Karl Marx and the Colonial Question'. *The African Communist*, No. 94, 3rd Quarter.
5. Comrade Mzala. (1983). 'Why We are with the Communists'. *The African Communist*, No. 93, 2nd Quarter, pp 66–73.
6. Majola (1984).
7. Majola (*African Communist* 3rd Quarter 1986: pp 40–48).
8. Comrade Mzala, in Van Diepen (1989).
9. Ibid, p 51.
10. Migwe, Khumalo [Mzala]. (1982). 'Lessons of Our People's War – Part 2', *Dawn*, Vol. 6, No. 3, March 1982, pp 15–19.
11. Comrade Mzala (*Sechaba* January 1985).
12. Comrade Mzala (*African Communist*, 3rd Quarter 1985).
13. Mzala (*Sechaba* June 1987: 2–6).
14. Mzala (*Sechaba*, August 1987).
15. Mzala (*Sechaba* June 1989: 11–18).
16. Gerhart (1990). Karis-Gerhart Collection.
17. Shaw, D. (2021). 'Frantz Fanon Lives! 60 Years After His Death, Fanon's Ideas Remain the Weapons of the Oppressed', https://towardfreedom.org/story/archives/africa-archives/frantz-fanon-lives-60-years-after-his-death-fanons-ideas-remain-the-weapons-of-the-oppressed/ (Accessed: 28 July 2022).
18. Del Monte, Catherine. (2021). 'Exploring what comes after capitalism in South Africa', *Daily Maverick*, 31 October 2021, https://www.dailymaverick.co.za/article/2021-10-31-exploring-what-comes-after-capitalism-in-south-africa/ (Accessed: 29 July 2022).
19. Migwe (*Dawn*, April 1982).

Selected bibliography

Abebe, D. (2017). 'Ethiopian and Eritrean Askaris in Libya (1911–1932)', *Ethiopian Journal of the Social Sciences and Humanities*, *13*(2), pp 27–52.
Agachi, P.S. (2019). 'Building a higher education sector needs more than high hopes'. *University World News – Africa Edition*. https://www.universityworldnews.com/post.php?story=20190315123120482 (Accessed: 19 April 2021).
Alexander, N. (2008). 'An illuminating moment: Background to the Azanian Manifesto', in *Biko Lives!* (pp 157–170). New York: Palgrave Macmillan.
ANC PMSC. (1979). 'The Green Book: Report of the Politico-Military Strategy Commission to the ANC National Executive Committee', August 1979. http://anc.org.za/show.php?id=79 (Accessed: 27 February 2021).
Angumuthu, W. (1991) 'ANC activist Mzala dies in London', *Sunday Tribune*, 3 March 1991, p11.
Argus Foreign Service. (1990). 'Limited role for outsiders in SA reform, says Worrall', *The Argus*, 19 January 1990.
Asheeke, TTPW. (2018). *Uncovering Hidden Fronts of Africa's Liberation Struggle: Black Power, Black Consciousness, and South Africa's Armed Struggle, 1967–1985* (Doctoral dissertation, State University of New York at Binghamton).
Baillie, GK. (1999). *Printmaking at the Dakawa Art and Craft Project: The Impact of ANC Cultural Policy and Swedish Practical Implementation on Two Printmakers Trained During South Africa's Transformation Years* (Doctoral dissertation, Rhodes University).
Bale, T. (2015). 'In life as in death? Margaret Thatcher (mis) remembered', *British Politics*, *10*(1), pp 99–112.
Bennett, TW and Peart, N.S. (1986). 'The Ingwavuma land deal: A case study of self-determination', *BC Third World LJ*, *6*, p 23.
Bonner, PL. (1990). 'The Russians on the Reef, 1947–1957: Urbanisation, Gang Warfare and Ethnic Mobilisation', in Philip Bonner, Peter Delius and Deborah Posel (eds.). (1993). *Apartheid's Genesis: 1935–1962* (pp 160–94). Johannesburg: University of the Witwatersrand and Ravan Press.
Brown, K. (2013). 'Agitprop in Soviet Russia', *Constructing the Past*, 14(1). Available at: http://digitalcommons.iwu.edu/constructing/vol14/iss1/4 (Accessed: 9 April 2021).
Burawoy, M. (2004). 'From liberation to reconstruction: Theory & practice in the life of Harold Wolpe', *Review of African Political Economy*, *31*(102), pp 657–675.

Callinicos, L. (2004). *Oliver Tambo: Beyond the Engeli Mountains*. New Africa Books, Cape Town.

Callinicos, L. (2012). 'Oliver Tambo and the Dilemma of the Camp Mutinies in Angola in the Eighties'. *South African Historical Journal*, 64(3), pp 587–621.

Cape Times. (1991) 'Guardian pays tribute to ANC's "intellectual prince"', 15 March 1991, p 6.

Carchidi, V. (1994). 'South Africa from Text to Film: "Cry Freedom" and "A Dry White Season", in Simons, JD (ed.). *Literature and Film in the Historical Dimension* (pp 47–61). Gainesville: University Press of Florida Press.

Cherry, J. (2012). *Spear of the Nation: Umkhonto weSizwe – South Africa's liberation army, 1960s–1990s*. Ohio University Press, Athens.

Comrade Mzala. (1980). 'Armed Struggle in South Africa', *The African Communist*, No. 82, 3rd Quarter, pp 65–73.

Comrade Mzala. (1981). 'Has the Time Come for the Arming the Masses?', *The African Communist*, No. 86, 3rd Quarter, pp 83–94.

Comrade Mzala. (1983). 'Why we are with the communists', *The African Communist*, No. 93, 2nd Quarter, pp 66–73.

Comrade Mzala. (1985). 'On the threshold of revolution', *The African Communist*, No. 102, 3rd Quarter, pp 66–77.

Comrade Mzala. (1985). 'The Freedom charter is our lodestar', *Sechaba*, July, pp 2–17.

Comrade Mzala. (1985). 'The Freedom charter is our lodestar', *Sechaba*, August, pp 29–32.

Comrade Mzala. (1985). 'The Freedom charter is our lodestar', *Sechaba*, September, pp 28–31.

Comrade Mzala. (1985). 'The Freedom charter is our lodestar', *Sechaba*, October, pp 22–31.

Comrade Mzala. (1987). 'How the ANC was revived by the Youth League', *The African Communist*, No. 110, 3rd Quarter, pp 50–62.

Cronin, J. (2009). 'The Role of the revolutionary intellectuals: The life of Comrade Mzala', in *The Poverty of Ideas: South African democracy and the retreat of Intellectuals*. Johannesburg: Jacana Media.

Crossette, B, Kifner, J, Riding, A, and Rohter, L. (1989). 'In Asia, African and Latin America: A Banner for Revolution', *The New York Times*, 24 January 1989.

Daniel, J. (1991). 'Lost "prince" of the ANC', *The Guardian*, 14 March 1991.

Daniel, J. (2016). 'The Impact of the Cold War and the Fall of the Berlin Wall on Southern Africa'. chrome-extension://efaidnbmnnnibpcajpcglclefindmkaj/ https://www.kas.de/c/document_library/get_file?uuid=7dd3251f-7488-37c4-50e9-52e15c225130&groupId=252038 (Accessed: 17 March 2022).

Denzin, NK. (1978). *The Research Act: A theoretical introduction to sociological methods*. McGraw-Hill, New York.

Dialego. (1988). 'What is Trotskyism?', *The African Communist*, 4th Quarter, pp 68–78.

Dlamuka, MC. (2018). *Connectedness and Disconnectedness in Thembeyakhe Harry Gwala's Biography, 1920–1995: Rethinking Political Militancy, Mass Mobilisation and Grassroots Struggles in South Africa* (Doctoral dissertation, Department of History, Faculty of Arts, University of the Western Cape).

Doxtader, E. (2001). 'Making rhetorical history in a time of transition: The occasion, constitution, and representation of South African reconciliation', *Rhetoric & Public Affairs*, 4(2), pp 223–260.

Editorial Notes. (1989). 'The controversy around Trotskyism', *The African Communist*,

No.118, 3rd Quarter, pp 5–7.

Eichler, T. (2014). 'South Africa's negotiated transition to democracy – GRIN'. https://www.grin.com/document/286989 (Accessed: 11 January 2021).

Erasmus, G. (1984). *The Accord of Nkomati: Context and Content*. Johannesburg: SAIIA.

Evans, M. (2009). 'Apartheid (1948–1994)'. https://www.blackpast.org/global-african-history/apartheid-1948-1994/ (Accessed: 15 January 2021).

Fanon, Frantz. (1961). *The Wretched of the Earth*. Harmondsworth: Penguin.

Fekisi, L. (2018). *A Comparison of* Drum's *Coverage of the 1976 Soweto Student Uprisings and the 2015# FeesMustFall Student Protests* (Doctoral dissertation, University of the Free State).

Frederikse, J. (1990). *The Unbreakable Thread: Non-racialism in South Africa*. Bloomington: Indiana University Press.

Frederikse, J. (2014). 'John Daniel: Activist, exile and a truly inspiring academic', *Mail & Guardian*, 31 July 2014, https://mg.co.za/article/2014-07-31-john-daniel-activist-exile-and-a-truly-inspiring-academic/ (Accessed: 13 June 2021).

Friedman & Friedman Attorneys. (1989). 'Buthelezi biography', *Frontline*, June 1989.

Friedman, S. (2015). *Race, Class and Power: Harold Wolpe and the radical critique of apartheid*. Pietermaritzburg: University of KwaZulu-Natal Press.

Gamble, A. (1994). *The Free Economy and the Strong State: The politics of Thatcherism*. Macmillan International Higher Education.

Gerhart, GM. (1994). 'The 1976 Soweto Uprising'. Wiser Seminar Paper. https://core.ac.uk/download/pdf/39667638.pdf

Gevisser, M. (2007). *Thabo Mbeki: The dream deferred*. Johannesberg: Jonathan Ball Publishers.

Glyn-Fox, D. 'The Anglo Zulu War Unnecessarily Destroyed The Zulu Nation', chrome-extension://efaidnbmnnnibpcajpcglclefindmkaj/https://www.anglozuluwar.com/images/Journal_22/The_Anglo-Zulu_War_of_1879_Unnecessarily_Destroyed.pdf (Accessed: 21 March 2022).

Griffiths, Ieuan L and Funnell, DC. (1991). 'The Abortive Swazi Land Deal', *African Affairs*, 90(358), pp 51–64, http://www.jstor.org/stable/722639

Gottfried, H. (1998). 'Beyond Patriarchy: Theorising Gender and Class'. *Sociology* 32(3), pp 451–468. Cited in Haynes, K. (2006). *Other Lives in Accounting: Critical Reflections on Oral History Methodology in Action*. Working Paper. Department of Management Studies, University of York, York.

Hare, P. (2005). 'Angola: The end of an intractable conflict', in Crocker, CA, Hampson, FO and Aal, P (eds). *Grasping the Nettle: Analysing Cases of Intractable Conflict*. Washington, DC.: United States Institute of Peace Press.

Haynes, K. (2006). *Other Lives in Accounting: Critical Reflections on Oral History Methodology in Action*. Working Paper. Department of Management Studies, University of York, York.

Hedges, C. (1990). 'Old Marxist Returns, With Hope for South Africa', *The New York Times*, 17 October 1990.

Heywood, M. (2010). 'Civil society and uncivil government'. Cited in Glaser, D (ed.), *Mbeki and After: Reflections on the legacy of Thabo Mbeki* (pp 128–162). Johannesburg: Wits University Press.

Hilda and Rusty Bernstein Papers, 1931–2011 http://www.historicalpapers.wits.ac.za/?inventory/U/collections&c=A3299/R/ (Accessed: 11 May 2021).

Historical Papers Research Archives. http://www.historicalpapers.wits.ac.za/?inventory/U/collections&c=A2729/I/6364 (Accessed: 30 August 2021)

Hoffman, J and Mzala, N. (1990). '"Non-Historic Nations" and the National Question: A South African Perspective', *Science & Society*, 54(4), pp 408–426.

Houston, G. (2013). 'Military bases and camps of the liberation movement, 1961–1990', in *Amathole Municipality: Democracy, Governance and Service Delivery (DGSD)*. Cape Town: Human Sciences Research Council (HSRC).

Houston, G and Magubane, B. (2006). 'The ANC political underground in the 1970s', in South African Democracy Education Trust (eds), *The Road to Democracy in South Africa*, 2, 1970–1980.

Kamana, Caroline. '28 Penton Street – African National Congress (ANC) in London Headquarters', https://www.layersoflondon.org/map?l=eyJmcmVlX3RleHRfcXVlcnkiOm51bGwsInNlYXJjaF9wYWdlIjoxLCJjYXRlZ29yeV9hbmRfGVybV9maWx0ZXJzIjp7InRlcm1faWQiOm51bGwsImNhdGVnb3J5X2lkIjoxfSwiYWN0aXZlWVyX2dyb3VwX2lkcyI6W119&m=eyJjZW50ZXIiOlslMS-41MDc0LDAuMTI3OF0sInpvb20iOjEwLCJsaWdodHNdXQiOmZhbHNlfQ%3D%3D&record=6433 (Accessed: 12 June 2021).

Ilanga. (1990). 'Further on Kagiso Funding'. *Ilanga*, 5–6 July 1990, p 11.

Institute for Justice and Reconciliation. (2017). 'Pathways for Connections: An emerging model for long-term reconciliation in post-conflict South Africa', http://www.ijr.org.za/home/wp-content/uploads/2012/07/Pathways-for-Connections-BIS-Publication.pdf (Accessed: 8 October 2021).

Jordan, ZP. (2017). *Letters to my Comrades: Interventions & excursions*. Johannesburg: Jacana Media.

Joyce, LK. (2018). 'Kente's "How Long?" makes a powerful return to the stage', *IOL*, 24 May 2018, https://www.iol.co.za/entertainment/movies/reviews/kentes-how-long-makes-a-powerful-return-to-the-stage-15117956 (Accessed: 10 October 2021).

Kapinos, A. (2020). *'An Oasis of Free Thought' in Prague: Problems of Peace and Socialism and the End of the Thaw, 1968–1969* (Doctoral dissertation, The University of North Carolina at Chapel Hill).

Karis, TG and Gerhart, GM. (1997). 'A Documentary History of African Politics in South Africa, 1882–1990: Nadir and Resurgence, 1964–1979' (pp 258). *From Protest to Challenge*, 5.

Karis-Gerhart Collection of South African political materials, 1964–1990. http://www.historicalpapers.wits.ac.za/?inventoryajax/AJAX/collections&c=A2675/R/ (Accessed: 2 September 2021).

Kasrils, R. (2004). *Armed and Dangerous: From undercover struggle to freedom*. Johannesburg: Jonathan Ball Publishers.

Kaunda, L. (1989). 'The Biography', *Natal Witness*, 9 February 1989.

Kenyon, C. (2008). 'Cognitive dissonance as an explanation of the genesis, evolution and persistence of Thabo Mbeki's HIV denialism', *African Journal of AIDS Research*, 7(1), pp 29–35.

Khumalo, Ngacambaza [Mzala]. (1978). 'The Compromising Role of Inkatha', *The African Communist*, No. 74, 3rd Quarter.

Khunou, SK. (2009). 'Traditional leadership and independent Bantustans of South Africa: Some milestones of transformative constitutionalism beyond Apartheid', *Potchefstroom Electronic Law Journal/Potchefstroomse Elektroniese Regsblad*, 12(4).

Kwhela, GC. (2003) 'Umkhonto Wesizwe's contribution to the defence of the African revolution in Angola', *Journal of Contemporary History*, 28(2), pp 107–23.

Selected bibliography

Land Noli. (n.d.). A speech by ANC President OR *Tambo*, guest speaker at the National *Press Club*, Washington DC., *USA* on 28 January 1987. https://www.youtube.com/watch?v=umScRCjRZNo

Lekgoathi, SP. (2010). 'The African National Congress's Radio Freedom and its audiences in apartheid South Africa, 1963–1991', *Journal of African Media Studies*, 2(2), pp 139-153.

Lenin, VI. (1919). *Two Tactics of Social-Democarcy in the Democratic Revolution*. New York:Foreign Policy Association Inc.

Lewis, A. (1990). 'Slovo's vision', *The Baltimore Evening Sun*, 17 October 1990.

Liebenberg, I. (2017). 'Dakar 1987 – Reflections on a conference'. Researchgate. https://www.researchgate.net/publication/319837060_Dakar_1987_-_Reflections_on_a_conference (Accessed: 4 September 2021).

Lotshwao, K. (2009). 'The lack of internal party democracy in the African National Congress: A threat to the consolidation of democracy in South Africa', *Journal of Southern African Studies*, 35(4), pp 901–914.

Lubisi, C. (1993). 'Buthelezi and the "Zulu Kingdom"', *The African Communist*, (134), pp 65–72.

Lynd, H. (2021). 'The Peace Deal: The Formation of the Ingonyama Trust and the IFP Decision to Join South Africa's 1994 Elections', *South African Historical Journal*, pp. 1–43.

Macmillan, H. (2009). 'The "Hani Memorandum" – Introduced and annotated', *Transformation: Critical Perspectives on Southern Africa*, 69(1), pp 106–129.

Macmillan, H. (2009). 'The African National Congress of South Africa in Zambia: The culture of exile and the changing relationship with home, 1964–1990', *Journal of Southern African Studies*, 35(2), pp 303–329.

Magubane, BM. (1979). *The Political Economy of Race and Class in South Africa*. New York: Monthly Review Press.

Maharaj, M. (2008). *The ANC and South Africa's negotiated transition to democracy and peace*. Berghof Transitions Series 2. Berlin: Berghof Foundation.

Mail & Guardian. (1994) 'Zwelithini Nods To An Old Buthelezi Enemy', 9 September 1994. https://mg.co.za/article/1994-09-09-zwelithini-nods-to-an-old-buthelezi-enemy/ (Accessed: 3 May 2021).

Majola, Sisa [Mzala]. (1985). 'Education for Revolution', *The African Communist*, No. 103, 4th Quarter, pp 30–39.

Majola, Sisa [Mzala]. (1986). 'Nation and class in the South African revolution', *The African Communist*, No. 105, 2nd Quarter, pp 40–48.

Majola, Sisa [Mzala]. (1986). 'The beginning of people's power', *The African Communist*, No. 106, 3rd Quarter 1986, pp 55–66.

Majola, Sisa [Mzala]. (1988). 'To Whom Does South Africa Belong?', *The African Communist*, No. 115, 4th Quarter, pp 93–98.

Majola, Sisa [Mzala]. (1990). 'Wilton Mkwayi: A Veteran of Revolutionary Campaigns', *The African Communist*, 3rd Quarter, pp 51–57.

Maloka, E. (1994). 'Mzala: A revolutionary without kid gloves'. *The African Communist*. No. 136, 1st Quarter, pp 61–66.

Mandela, N. (2008). *Long Walk to Freedom: The autobiography of Nelson Mandela* (p. 688). London: Hachette UK.

Manghezi, A. (2004). 'Solomon Mahlangu Freedom College: Symbol of international solidarity', in *Anti-Apartheid Conference, University of KwaZulu-Natal, Durban*,

October 2004, pp 10–13.

Manong, S. (2015). *If We Must Die: An Autobiography of a Former Commander of uMkhonto we Sizwe*. London: Nkululeko Publishers.

Mantashe, G. (2016). 'Do we still have leaders who can save the ANC from itself?', *Sunday Times*, 30 October. https://www.timeslive.co.za/sunday-times/opinion-and-analysis/2016-10-30-do-we-still-have-leaders-who-can-save-the-anc-from-itself/ (Accessed: 17 April 2021).

Maroleng, C. (2003). 'Swaziland: The King's Constitution', *African Security Studies*, 12(3), pp 45–48.

Masango, J (1989). 'Marxist twaddle', *Frontline*, 3 April 1989.

Mashinini, Alex. (1985). 'Preparing the Fire before Cooking the Rice inside the Pot', *Sechaba*, April 1985, pp 20–30.

Mathiane, N. (1989) 'The Hatchet and the Snow', *Frontline*, 1 February 1989.

Mavimbela, V. (2018). *Time is Not the Measure: A memoir*. Johannesburg: Real African Publishers Pty Ltd.

Mbeki, G. (1996). *Sunset at Midday: Latshon'ilang'emini!*. Nolwazi.

McKinley, DT. (2018). 'Umkhonto we Sizwe: A critical analysis of the armed struggle of the African National Congress', *South African Historical Journal*, 70(1), pp 27–41.

Merrett, C. (2013). 'A tale of Two Books', *Natal Witness*, 8 November 2013, p 9.

Merrett, C. (2013). 'A small civil war: Political conflict in the Pietermaritzburg region in the 1980s and early 1990s', *Natalia*, 43, pp 19–36.

Migwe, Khumalo [Mzala]. (1979). 'Book Review: "How Long Will South Africa Survive?" by R.W Johnson, Published by Macmillan', *Dawn*, Vol. 3, No. 7, August 1979, pp 35–37.

Migwe, Khumalo [Mzala]. (1979). 'Critical remarks of the question of the terror tactic', *Dawn*, Vol. 2, No. 11, December 1979, pp 10–12.

Migwe, Khumalo [Mzala]. (1980). 'Black Consciousness and the South African Revolution', *The African Communist*, No. 83, 4th Quarter.

Migwe, Khumalo [Mzala]. (1982). 'Lessons of Our People's War – Part 2', *Dawn*, Vol. 6, No. 3, March 1982, pp 15–19.

Migwe, Khumalo [Mzala]. (1982). 'Lessons of Our People's War – Part 3', *Dawn*, Vol. 6, No. 4, April 1982, pp 23–27.

Migwe, Khumalo [Mzala]. (1983). 'Karl Marx and the Colonial Question', *The African Communist*, No. 94, 3rd Quarter.

Minter, W. (1991). 'South Africa: Behind the violence: "black-on-black", the "third force", and the real Gatsha Buthelezi', *Christianity and Crisis*, 50(19), pp 418–421.

Miya, S. (2011). 'Zulu queen mother reburied", *The Witness*, 9 May 2011. https://www.news24.com/witness/archive/Zulu-queen-mother-reburied-20150430 (Accessed: 30 April 2021).

Mkhatshwa, Jabulani [Mzala]. (1988). 'Angola: A military defeat for the racists', *The African Communist*, No. 115, 4th Quarter, pp 79–84.

Mkhatshwa, Jabulani [Mzala]. (1988). 'Senegal', *The African Communist*, No. 115, 3rd Quarter, pp 65–73.

Mkhatshwa, Jabulani [Mzala]. (1990). 'Africa Notes and Comments', *The African Communist*, 1st Quarter, pp 84–93.

Mkhatshwa, Jabulani [Mzala]. (1990). 'Africa Notes and Comments', *The African Communist*, 2nd Quarter, pp 77–83.

Mkhatshwa, Jabulani [Mzala]. (1990). 'Africa Notes and Comments', *The African Communist*, 3rd Quarter, pp 75–78.

Selected bibliography

Mkhatshwa, Jabulani [Mzala]. (1990). 'Africa Notes and Comments', *The African Communist*, 3rd Quarter, pp 75–78.

Mkhatshwa, Jabulani [Mzala]. (1990). 'Africa Notes and Comments', *The African Communist*, 4th Quarter, pp 62–67.

Mngomezulu, BR. (2020). 'The politics of the coronavirus and its impact on international relations', *African Journal of Political Science and International Relations*, *14*(3), pp 116–125.

Moloi, T. (2016). 'The Role of "Freelance" Underground Operatives in the Struggle for Liberation in South Africa: The Case of Eastern Transvaal, 1980–1990', *Oral History Journal of South Africa*, Vol. 4, pp 82–91.

Moloto, G. (1988). 'In lieu of a book review, a book by one of us', *Dawn*, Vol. 1, No. 1, pp 25–30.

Morris, M. (1991). 'The Future of Socialism', *Transformation* (14), p 45.

Motumi, T. (1994). 'Umkhonto we Sizwe: Structure, Training and Force Levels', *African Defence Review* (18).

Murphy, C. (1978). 'Militants Eject Zulu Chief from Funeral', *The Washington Post*, 12 March 1978, https://www.washingtonpost.com/archive/politics/1978/03/12/militants-eject-zulu-chief-from-funeral/4f70ebee-a54c-4805-b806-5556c4978a67/ (Accessed: 13 October 2021).

Murphy, JT. (1927). 'The first year of the Lenin School', *Communist International*, 30, pp 267–269.

Mzala. (1984). Letter to the editor, *Sechaba*, December 1984.

Mzala. (1986). 'Building people's power', *Sechaba*, September 1986, pp 8–15.

Mzala. (1986). 'Umkhonto WeSizwe: Building people's forces for combat war and insurrection Building people's power', *Sechaba*, December 1986, pp 19–28.

Mzala. (1987). 'Can the imperialists abort our revolution?', *Sechaba*, July 1987, pp 7–13.

Mzala. (1987). 'People's power or power-sharing? United States policy in South Africa', *Sechaba*, August 1987, pp 23–28.

Mzala. (1987). 'Towards people's war and insurrection', *Sechaba*, April 1987, pp 2–6.

Mzala. (1987). 'United States policy towards South Africa', *Sechaba*, June 1987, pp 3–10.

Mzala. (1988). 'Aids – Misinformation and racism', *Sechaba*, October 1988.

Mzala. (1988). 'Aids and the imperialist connection', *Sechaba*, November 1988.

Mzala. (1988). 'The Volcano of the People's Wrath', *World Marxist Review*, Vol. 31, 7 July, pp 121–127.

Mzala. (1989). 'Negotiations and People's Power', *Sechaba*, August 1989, pp 20–26.

Mzala. (1989). 'Omelettes cannot be made without breaking eggs', *Sechaba*, Vol. 23, June 1989, pp 11–18.

Mzala. (1990). 'A response to mounting people's pressure', *New Nation*, 11 May 1990.

Mzala. (1990). 'An ANC View', *New Nation*, 5 April 1990.

Mzala. (1990). 'Patriotism and positivity what SA needs now', *Cape Times*, 13 November 1990.

Mzala. (1990). 'The Bantu System is at the Centre of Natal Violence', *The African Communist*, 4th Quarter, pp 34–38.

Mzala, C. (1988). 'Revolutionary theory on the national question in South Africa', *The National Question in South Africa*, pp 30–55.

Mzala. (1988). *Gatsha Buthelezi: Chief with a double agenda*. London: Zed Books.

Natal Witness. (1991) 'Buthelezi puts legal screws on biography by ANC exile', 10 May 1991, p 1.

Natal Witness. (1991) 'Mzala's body back in SA', 14 March 1991, p 1.

Ndebele, N and Nieftagodien, N. (2004). 'The Morogoro Conference: A moment of self-reflection', *The road to democracy in South Africa 1 (1960–1970)*, pp 573–599.

Ndlovu, SM. (2018). 'Sowing the seeds of political mobilisation in Bantustans: resistance of the cession of the KaNgwane Bantustan to the Kingdom of Swaziland', *Journal for Contemporary History, 43*(1), pp 43–69.

Ndlovu, SM. (2017) 'Cultural imperialism, language, and the ideological struggle inside the Soweto classrooms', in South African Democracy Education Trust. *The Road to Democracy in South Africa, Vol. 7: New perspectives, commemorations and memorialization*. Pretoria: UNISA Press.

New Nation. (1991). 'Revolutionary writer dies in exile', 7 March 1991, p 2.

Ngculu, J. (2009). *The Honour to Serve: Recollections of an Umkhonto Soldier*. Cape Town: David Philip Publishers.

Ngonyama, P. (2017). '"Comrade Mzala": Memory Construction and Legacy Preservation', *African Historical Review, 49*(2), pp 72–101.

Ngonyama, P. (2018). 'Comrade Mzala – A revolutionary left-wing intellectual from eNgotshe' (unpublished).

Nkabinde, AC (ed.). (1971). *Inkwazi*. Pietermaritzburg: Lincroft Books.

Nkosi, Z. (2016). 'Mzala's Legacy and its Relevance in Contemporary South Africa', Paper presented at the Mzala Nxumalo Centre, UKZN, 24 February 2016.

Ntuli, DBZ. (1975). *Ugqozi* (Vol. 1). Cape Town: Van Schaik.

Nxumalo, JM. (1992). 'The National Question in the Writing of South African History: A Critical Survey of Some Major Tendencies', Front Cover, *Jabulani*.

Nyawuza. (1985). 'Response to Comrade Mzala', *Sechaba*, April 1985, p 19.

Ostrovsky, Nikolai. (1974). *How Steel is Tempered*. Moscow: Progress Press.

Pahad, E. (1991) 'Hamba Kahle, Comrade Jabulani "Mzala" Nxumalo', *The African Communist*, No. 124.

Pampallis, J. (1991). *Foundations of the New South Africa*. London: Zed Books.

Patriot. (1990). 'ANC sal met Geloftedag wegdoen', 27 July 1990.

Pietermaritzburg Archival Repository (PAR), Secretary for Native Affairs (SNA) 1/1/338, 845/1906, Magistrate of Ngothse writing to Undersecretary for Native Affairs (USN), 14 March, 1906 (cited in Mngonyama draft manuscript).

Puzi, ME. (1999). *A history of college libraries in the Transkei 1882–1994* (MIS Thesis, University of Natal).

Radebe, J. (2021). 'Remembering Comrade Mzala: "The world we want, time for change"', https://www.youtube.com/watch?v=v0XU8EkWbfA (Accessed: 28 March 2022)

Radebe, MJ. (2022). 'Framing the Poor during Covid-19: Townships and Informal Settlements in South African Online News', *Communicatio*, pp 1–22.

Radebe, MJ. (2020). *Constructing Hegemony: The South African Commercial Media and the (Mis) Representation of Nationalisation*. Pietermaritzburg: University of KwaZulu-Natal Press.

Rickard, C. (1990). 'ANC's Mzala takes legal action against Ilanga', *Natal Witness*, 9 July 1990.

Riding, A. (1978) 'Politics Aside, Cuba Is Festive for Visiting Young Leftists', *The New York Times,* 7 August 1978, https://www.nytimes.com/1978/08/07/archives/politics-aside-cuba-is-festive-for-visiting-young-leftists.html?auth=link-dismiss-google1tap (Accessed: 18 April 2021).

Russon, R. (1994). 'Southern Africa: Consolidation or fragmentation: Territorially, nation states and the border question – The case of Swaziland'. Paper presented at the Association of African Political Sciences (AAPS) Conference, Dakar, Senegal.

Saeboe, M. (2002). *A state of exile: the ANC and Umkhonto we Sizwe in Angola, 1976–1989* (MA Thesis, University of Natal).

SAPA. (1990). 'African National Congress Reacts to Address', South African Press Association, 2 February 1990.

Williams, Michelle and Satgar, Vishwas (eds). (2021). *Destroying Democracy: Neoliberal capitalism and the rise of authoritarian politics*. Johannesburg: Wits University Press.

Houston, G, Pophiwa, N, Sausi, K, Dumisa, S and Seabe, D. (2013). 'Documenting the legacy of the South African liberation struggle: The national liberation heritage route – Unsung heroes and heroines of the liberaton struggle project', https://repository.hsrc.ac.za/ (Accessed: 17 April 2021).

Schauffer, D. (2006). 'In Memoriam: Gibson Kente – Interview', *South African Theatre Journal*, *20*(1), pp. 303–322.

Shubin, VG. (2008). *The Hot 'Cold War': The USSR in Southern Africa* (p 151). London: Pluto Press.

Shubin, Vladimir. (2012). 'Comrade Mzwai', in Lissoni, A, Soske, J, Erlank, N, Nieftagodien, N and Badsha, O (eds). *One Hundred Years of the ANC: Debating Liberation Histories Today* (pp 255–74). Johannesburg: Wits University Press.

Sigmund, PE. (1991). 'Christianity and violence: The case of liberation theology', *Terrorism and Political Violence*, *3*(4), pp. 63–79.

Simons, HJ. (2001). *Comrade Jack: The political lectures and diary of Jack Simons, Novo Catengue*. STE Publishers, Johannesburg.

Simpson, T. (2009). 'Toyi-Toyi-ing to freedom: the endgame in the ANC's armed struggle, 1989–1990', *Journal of Southern African Studies*, *35*(2), pp 507–521.

Simpson, T. (2016). *Umkhonto we Sizwe: The ANC's armed struggle*. Penguin Random House, Cape Town.

Simpson, TW. (2009). 'The Bay and the Ocean: A History of the ANC in Swaziland, 1960–1979], *African Historical Review*, *41*(1), pp 90–118.

Slovo, J. (1988). *The South African working class and the national democratic revolution*. South African Communist Party.

South African Communist Party (SACP). (1981) [1962]. 'The Road to South African Freedom. Programme adopted at the fifth national conference of the communist party held inside the country', in *South African Communists Speak: Documents from the History of the South African Communist Party 1915–1980*. London: Nkululeko Publishers.

South African Communist Party (SACP). (2017). 14th National Congress Resolutions. https://www.sacp.org.za/docs/decl/2017/declaration-and-resolutions.pdf (Accessed: 28 September 2021).

South African History Online. 'Jabulani "Mzala" Nxumalo'. Available at: https://www.sahistory.org.za/people/jabulani-mzala-nxumalo (Accessed: 24 February 2021).

Sparks, A. (1990). 'Tambo Draws Tumultuous Welcome On Return To S. Africa From Exile', *The Washington Post*, 14 December 1990, https://www.washingtonpost.com/archive/politics/1990/12/14/tambo-draws-tumultuous-welcome-on-return-to-s-africa-from-exile/d77e6722-9754-4aef-8373-b63c0bb52f6a/ (Accessed: 3 February 2021).

Staff Reporter. (1990). 'ANC wants sanctions to remain', *Cape Times*, 3 February 1990.

Stalker, Brenda. (1988). 'Crisis in our country', *Sechaba*, May 1988, pp 18–26.

Suttner, R. (2003). 'Culture(s) of the African National Congress of South Africa: Imprint of exile experiences', *Journal of Contemporary African Studies*, *21*(2), pp 303–320.

Suttner, R. (2008). *The ANC Underground in South Africa to 1976: A social and historical study*. Johannesburg: Jacana Media.

Sylvest, JM. (1999). 'Glasnost: The Pandora's box of Gorbachev's reforms', https://scholarworks.umt.edu/ (Accessed: 3 June 2022).

Tambo, O and Tambo, A. (1987). *Oliver Tambo Speaks*. Cape Town: Kwela Books.

Tau, Rebone. (2020). *The Rise and Fall of the ANC Youth League*. Cape Town: Penguin Random House.

Temko, N. (1987). 'Switching sides: Young blacks leave ANC for arms of Pretoria. South African police keep an eye out for disenchanted dissenters', *Christian Science Monitor*, 11 March 11 1987, https://www.csmonitor.com/layout/set/tabletkiosk/1987/0311/ofect.html (Accessed: 18 April 2021).

Tiro, G. (2019). *Parcel of Death: The Biography of Onkgopotse Abram Tiro*. Johannesburg: Picador Africa.

Theresa. (1989). 'The People's Struggle', *Sechaba*, January 1989, pp 26–30.

Thomas, MG, Parfitt, T, Weiss, DA, Skorecki, K, Wilson, JF, Le Roux, M and Goldstein, DB. (2000). 'Y chromosomes traveling south: The Cohen modal haplotype and the origins of the Lemba – The "Black Jews of Southern Africa"', *American Journal of Human Genetics*, *66*(2), pp 674–686.

Thompson, LM. (2001). *History of South Africa (Yale Nota Bene)*. New Haven: Yale University Press.

Thomson, A. (1995). 'Incomplete Engagement: Reagan's South Africa Policy Revisited', *Journal of Modern African Studies*, *33*(1), pp 83–101.

Trewhela, P. (2009). *Inside Quatro: Uncovering the exile history of the ANC and SWAPO*. Johannesburg: Jacana Media.

Truth and Reconciliation Commission. (1998). *Truth and Reconciliation Commission of South Africa Report*.

Umtata Capital Radio. (1990). 'Mzala To Sue', 9 July 1990.

Van der Heyden, U and Schade, A. (2019). 'GDR Solidarity with the ANC of South Africa', in Dallywater, L, Saunders, C and Fonseca, HA, *Southern African Liberation Movements and the Global Cold War 'East'* (pp 77–102). Berlin: De Gruyter Oldenbourg.

Van Zyl-Hermann, D. (2015). 'History made human: Confronting the unpalatable past through biographical writing in post-apartheid South Africa', *African Historical Review*, *47*(2), pp115–131.

Warwick, R. (2012). 'Operation Savannah: A measure of SADF decline, resourcefulness and modernisation', *Scientia Militaria: South African Journal of Military Studies*, *40*(3), pp 354–397.

Webster, D. (2019) 'The forgotten massacre of 18 June 1976', https://www.newframe.com/the-forgotten-massacre-of-18-june/ (Accessed: 2 February 2021).

Weekly Mail. (1988). 'Attempting to pin down a man of ambiguity', 13 October 1988.

Wieder, A. (2013). *Ruth First and Joe Slovo in the War against Apartheid*. New York: NYU Press.

Willan, Brian. (2018). *Sol Plaatje: A Life of Solomon Tshekiso Plaatje 1876–1932*. Johannesburg: Jacana Media.

Wisker, G. (2001). *Sylvia Plath: A Beginner's Guide*. London: Hodder & Stoughton.

Wright, VG. (1989). 'US foreign policy and destabilisation in Southern Africa', *Review* of *African Political Economy*, Vol. 45/46, pp 159–168.

Wyley, C and Merrett, C. (1991). 'Universities and the New Censorship: Mzala's *Gatsha Buthelezi: Chief with a double agenda*', *Critical Arts*, 5(4), pp. 98–115.

Yeasmin, S and Rahman, KF. (2012). 'Paulo Freire and "critical literacy": Relevance for Bangladesh', *Bangladesh Education Journal*, *11*(2), pp 7–14.

Zantsi, L. (2019). 'Mkatashinga: Narratives of the Mutiny in ANC Camps in Angola (1983/84)', *Journal of Global Faultlines*, 6(1), pp 90–101.

Interviews

Buthelezi, Mangosuthu. IFP Founder and President Emeritus, Inkosi of the Buthelezi clan, Traditional Prime Minister to the Zulu Monarch and Nation. (Responses emailed to Mandla Radebe: 27 August 2020.)

Edgar, Robert. Professor Emeritus at Howard University. (Responses emailed to Mandla Radebe: 27 August 2021.)

Esau, Cecyl. Former UDF rural organiser in Cape Province and Robben Island prisoner. (Responses emailed to Mandla Radebe: 21 September 2020.)

Gqubule-Mbeki, Thandeka. Journalist and friend. (Interview with Mandla Radebe: 22 April 2020.)

Jordan, Z Pallo. Former Minister of Arts and Culture, ANC NEC member, political activist, analyst and writer. (Responses emailed to Mandla Radebe: 10 January 2021.)

Kasrils, Ronnie. Former MK politician and military commander, Minister for Intelligence Services, ANC NEC member, and Central Committee member of the SACP. (Email to Mandla Radebe: 30 October 2020.)

Khumalo, Bongani. Activist and businessman. (Interview with Mandla Radebe: 22 April 2020.)

Martins, Ben. Former Minister of Energy and other posts in the Cabinet of South Africa, MP and SACP Central Committee Member. (Email to Mandla Radebe: 19 February 2021.)

Mavimbela, Vusi. Ambassador and former Political and Advisor to Deputy President Thabo Mbeki, Director-General of the National Intelligence Agency, Director-General in the Office of President Jacob Zuma, MK soldier. (Telephonic interview with Mandla Radebe: 19 April 2020.)

Mellet, Patric Tariq. Former Unionist, underground ANC, SACP, MK, ANC printer. (Email to Mandla Radebe: 3 October 2020.)

Mgabadeli, Hlengiwe. ANC Member of Parliament and high-school friend of Mzala. (Telephonic interview with Mandla Radebe: 17 September 2020.)

Mokhoanatse, Tshidiso (Alex Mashinini). Former underground ANC and MK soldier. (Email to Mandla Radebe: 3 March 2021).

Mosia, Lebona. Former MK soldier. (Email sent to Mandla Radebe: 7 October 2020.)

Motlanthe, Kgalema. Former South African president, unionist, underground ANC and MK. (MS Teams interview: 24 June 2021.)

Mtshaulana, Patric. Senior Council and founding member of the Duma Nokwe Group, and former MK soldier. (Email to Mandla Radebe: 16 February 2021.)

Naidoo, Celeste. Former ANC operative in London. (Telephonic interview with Mandla Radebe: 16 September 2020.)

Nduli, Dumisani. Former ANC and MK operative. (Email to Mandla Radebe: 26 November 2020.)

Nxumalo, Mpho and Balindelwe. Wife and daughter of Mzala Nxumalo. (MS Teams interview: 22 August 2020.)

Nxumalo, Mpho. Wife of Mzala Nxumalo. (MS Teams interview: 15 April 2020.)

Nzimande, Blade. General Secretary of the SACP and friend to Mzala Nxumalo. (Zoom interview: 30 November 2020.)

Nzimande, Phumelele and Blade. Activists and friends of Mzala Nxumalo. (Zoom interview: 12 October 2020.)

Pahad, Essop. Former Minister in the Presidency, ANC NEC member and Central Committee member of the SACP. (Zoom interview: 18 September 2020.)

Pampallis, John. Former special advisor to the Minister of Higher Education and Deputy Vice-Principal of the Solomon Mahlangu Freedom College (SOMAFCO). (MS Teams interview: 11 September 2020.)

Pepani, Lungile. Retired SANDF Major General and MK operative. (Interview with Mandla Radebe: 22 September 2020.)

Rabkin, Sue. Former Special Advisor to the Minister at Ministry of Defence and MK operative. (MS Teams interview: 28 August 2020.)

Russon, Raynauld. Former ANC underground operative. (Email to Mandla Radebe: 24 January 2021.)

Shabalala, Vuso. Former Special Adviser to President Jacob Zuma, ANC and MK operative. (Telephonic interview: 30 August 2020.)

Singh, Sunny. Former Chairman of Military Committee in Maputo, Robben Island prisoner, exiled member of MK, ANC Representative in Holland. (Telephonic interview: 29 August 2020.)

Index

A
AbaQulisi
   area, 22
   local municipality, 16
   region, 16
African National Congress (ANC), 2, 77, 111, 127, 143, 191, 195, 206, 259
Ake, Claude, 273
Alexander, Neville, 101, 156, 161, 272, 273
Alexandra Township, 55
Algeria, 263
al-Mahdi, Sadiq, 263
Amandla Cultural Ensemble, 6
ANC head office, 7
Anderson, James, 237
Angamuthu, Wasantha, 3
Angola, 5, 43, 44, 58, 59, 61, 62, 63, 64, 66, 68, 77, 78, 80, 81, 85, 86, 87, 88, 95, 97, 98, 103, 106, 107, 111, 112, 117, 124, 129, 133, 149, 150, 152, 232, 250, 252, 263, 265, 281, 297, 310, 321, 326, 358
Angolan camps, 87
Arenstein, Rowley, 205
Asmal, Kader, 151
AVBOB funeral services, 10
Azad, Ahmed, 231

B
Balfour, 9
Balindelwe, 1
Balindile, 2, 15, 18, 19, 20, 21, 22, 23, 57, 229
Barney, 120
Basson, Wouter, 228
Benguela, 63
Benin, 263

Berlin Wall, 257, 291
Bernstein, Lionel 'Rusty', 136
Bethel College, 24, 25, 28, 32, 38, 39, 40, 41, 70, 86, 90
Bethel, 24, 25, 26, 27, 29
Bhekuzulu township, 27
Bhengu, Dr Sibusiso, 30, 36, 311
Biko, Steve, 19, 44, 75, 175
Black, Marks
Bloemfontein, 17
Bloom, Tony, 288
Boesak, Allan, 145
Boksburg, 321
Bolshevik, 85
Bonner, Phil, 295
Botha, PW (Roelof 'Pik'), 120, 156, 176, 287
Botha, Thozamile, 238
Botswana, 29, 96, 97, 163
Brewer, John, 211
Britain, 254
British army, 86
British Library, 236
Brown, Manny, 172
Buchner, Jac, 95
Bulunga, Bhabhalazi, 13, 112, 113, 128, 129, 318
Bunting, Brian, 19, 151, 171, 219, 221, 222, 267, 307, 311
Bunting, Sonia, 171
Burns, John F, 55
Buthelezi, Mangosuthu Gatsha, 3, 4, 24, 31, 42, 45, 46, 50, 74, 75, 81, 116, 117, 154, 164, 170, 171, 186, 187, 188, 189, 190, 191, 192, 193, 194, 195, 196, 197, 198, 199, 200, 201, 202, 203, 204, 205,

206, 207, 208, 209, 210, 211, 212, 213, 214, 215, 216, 217, 219, 242, 253, 258, 259, 273, 289, 290, 302
Buthelezi, Mceleli (son of Chief Mathole), 188
Buthelezi, Sifiso, 10, 81, 118, 119, 122, 123, 124, 310
Butterworth, 24

C

Cabelly, Robert, 176
Cabesa, Quadro *see also* Mokhoanatse, Tshidiso, 78
Caculama camp, 66
Caesar, Julius, 31, 34
Callinicos, Alex, 262
Carter, Gwendolen, 273
Castro, Fidel, 230
Cato Manor (uMkhumbane), 98
Cele, Shakes, 13, 313
Cele, Sipho, 13, 313
Chabane, Collins, 104
Charlotte Maxeke Children's Centre, 154
Charlottesville, 298
Chicago, 299
Chief Albert Luthuli, 21, 46, 116
Chief Khambi, 16
Chief Mathole, 188
Chief Mnyamana, 190
Chief Mnyamana., 190, 191
Chief Ngolotjeni Nxumalo, 18
Chief Ntunja Mngomezulu, 122
Chikane, Frank, 145
City College, 298
Cleaver, Eldridge, 33
Clermont, 18
Cobbett, William, 262
Cohen, Robin, 262
Columbia University, 272, 273
Comrade Jabulani Nobleman "Mzala" Nxumalo, 307
Comrade Mzala, *see also* Comrade Jabulani Nobleman "Mzala" Nxumalo, 2, 3, 19, 25, 29, 30, 35, 47, 48, 51, 52, 53, 58, 78, 115, 146, 150, 161, 194, 203, 206, 251, 273, 307, 308, 318, 348
Conco, Zami, 189
Congress of South African Trade Unions (COSATU), 11, 13, 84, 117, 192, 298, 313, 318
Connor, Walker, 303

Cooper, Saths, 39
Coronation, 18
Cronin, Jeremy, 94, 170, 238, 315
Cuba, 77, 79, 91, 137, 149
Cuito Cuanavale, 44, 232

D

Dadoo, Dr Yusuf, 94, 95
Dakar, 181, 248, 340, 344, 357, 361
Dakawa Development Centre, 135
Dakawa, 135, 136, 137, 139, 141
Dangor, Achmat, 259
Daniel, John, 19, 80, 113, 170, 197, 238, 240, 272, 274, 275, 276, 302, 303, 311, 312, 313
Dar es Salaam, 138, 140, 165
De Klerk, FW, 254, 255, 256, 287, 309
Dhlomo, Oscar, 197
Diouf, Abdou, 231
Dlamini, Edwin, 84
Dlamini, Jabu, *see also* Dlamini, Jabulani, 115
Dlamini, Jabulani, 78, 113
Dlamini, Nkosazana, 39
Dlangezwa High School, 13, 29, 30, 31, 35, 37, 45, 48, 51, 70
Dlangezwa, 13, 29, 30, 31, 33, 34, 35, 37, 38, 45, 47, 48, 51, 56, 57, 139, 311
Dlomo, Albert, 109
Doe, President Samuel K, 265
Dos Santos, President José Eduardo, 265, 266
Double Agenda Author Mzala Dies, 3
Du Bois, 231
Duma, Bafana, 41, 116, 138, 139, 140
Duma, Sipho (Richard Sibengile), 138
Dundee Coal Company Ltd, 16
Dundee, 16, 17, 19, 41
Durban, 11, 18, 19, 24, 25, 38, 39, 52, 53, 56, 60, 69, 98, 99, 116, 134, 193, 199, 255, 289

E

East Germany, 111, 227, 243, 244
East Rand machinery, 2
East Rand, 54, 55
Eastern bloc, 243
Eastern Cape, 23, 24, 26, 29, 39, 41, 213
Eastern Europe, 296
Eastern Transvaal, 123
Ebrahim, Ebrahim, 130, 131

Edgar, Robert, 238, 267, 274, 297, 298
Edinburgh, 240
Edinburgh University, 240
Eduardo Mondlane University, 96
Egypt, 33, 138, 143, 146, 148, 281
Ellis, Stephen, 171
Empangeni, 55
Engineering camp, 63
Ernst College, 175
Esau, Cecyl, 13, 14
Essex University, 175, 237
Estcourt, 41
Etherington, Norman, 211
Ethiopia, 294
Ethiopians, 33

F

Fanon, Frantz, 76, 326
Fazenda camp, 60, 83, 106
First, Ruth (wife of Slovo, Joe), 4, 71, 90, 96, 101, 102, 127, 159, 192, 292, 294, 295
Fischer, Bram, 50
Fort Hare University, *see also* University of Fort Hare, 191, 289, 292
Fraser-Moleketi, Geraldine, 7, 13, 14, 313
Frederikse, Julie, 22, 33, 38, 49, 77, 322
Funda camp, 60, 64, 65, 67

G

Gabella, 59
Gaborone, 96
Gambalu, 59
Garang, John, 263
Garvey, Marcus, 34
Gauteng, 11, 2, 54, 144, 183, 321
GDR *see* German Democratic Republic,
Geneva, 30
George, Dumisani, 20, 21, 26, 27, 40, 57, 69, 163, 230, 306, 307
Gerhart, Gail, 23, 203, 223, 252, 272, 273, 274, 275, 276, 277, 278, 283, 284, 285, 286, 287, 291, 296, 298, 301, 303, 304, 305, 308, 311, 324
German Democratic Republic (GDR), 5, 62, 70, 74, 89, 90, 91, 92, 93, 98, 101, 137, 175, 234, 244
Giliomee, Hermann, 260, 261
Gindi, Andre *see also* Rathebe, Joy, 62
Ginwala, Frene, 97
Glencoe, 18

Goitsemang, Paul, see also Shabalala, Vuso, 99, 123, 131, 132
Goldberg, Denis, 50
Golela, 69
Gomas, John, 241
Gool, Cissie, 241
Gorbachev, Mikhail, 233, 243
Gqabi, Joe, 93, 292
Gqubule, Thandeka, 23, 257, 258, 268, 273, 274, 275, 276, 278, 283, 284, 288, 291, 316, 319
Gramsci, Antonio, 158
Groote Schuur, 282
Groutville, 117
Guevara, Che, 121
Guma, Professor SM, 115
Gumede, Archie, 192
Gwala, Harry, 8, 13, 49, 80, 241, 242, 243, 244, 258, 267, 289
Gwala, Mafika Pascal, 49
Gwangwa, Jonas, 6, 19, 23, 6, 137, 153, 175, 275
Gwangwa, Violet, 275
Gwangwa-Nxumalo, Mpho (wife of Mzala), 2, 4, 6, 7, 9, 10, 12, 14, 80, 137, 138, 139, 140, 150, 153, 154, 162, 163, 164, 175, 220, 221, 229, 230, 231, 235, 258, 278, 305, 306, 307, 310, 311, 312, 318, 322

H

Hammanskraal, 157
Hammersdale township, 51
Hammersdale, 112
Hani, Chris, 7, 9, 60, 90, 124, 147, 150, 172, 173, 246, 247, 258, 273, 275, 317, 318
Harber, Anton, 273
Heidelberg, 9
Hlobane, 16, 18, 20
Hluhluwe, 112
Hoffman, John, 237, 324
Howard University, 238

I

Inanda Seminary, 18, 19
Inanda township, 18
Ingwavuma, 116, 119, 121, 122, 123, 124, 125, 126, 132, 133, 324
Ismail, Aboobaker, *see also* Rashid, 65

J

Jan Smuts Airport, 1, 7, 9
Japan, 153
Jele, Josiah, 296
Jenkin, Tim, 100, 101
Jesus College, 308
Johannesburg, 1, 2, 7, 12, 13, 14, 55, 99, 184, 286, 308, 321
Johnson, RW, 88
Johnson, Shaun, 273
Jordan, Pallo, 4, 66, 72, 73, 85, 91, 151, 175, 197, 210, 221, 228, 273, 279, 280, 310, 319
Jozini, 124

K

Kabwe Conference, 58, 79, 133, 150, 156, 209, 279, 280, 282, 287, 292, 321
Kabwe, 58, 79, 80, 107, 133, 134, 150, 151, 156, 209, 281, 283, 290, 308, 321
kaCetshwayo, Dinuzulu *see also* King Dinuzulu, 16
kaMaphitha, Zibhebhu, 16
KaNgwane, 123
Kaplan, Norman, 172
Karis, Tom, 23, 272, 273, 274, 275, 276, 296, 298, 299, 301, 302, 303, 304, 305, 308, 311
Karl Marx Stadt, 175
kaSolomon, Cyprian Bhekuzulu, 118
Kasrils, Ronnie, 5, 13, 23, 66, 67, 68, 70, 71, 72, 74, 75, 78, 79, 81, 84, 86, 89, 97, 98, 101, 110, 113, 115, 120, 122, 123, 124, 129, 172, 221, 246, 247, 248, 249, 309, 315, 316, 319
Kaunda, Kenneth, 59, 288
Kaunda, Lakela, 3, 196
Kemp, Stephanie, 172
Kente, Gibson, 25, 41, 86
Kenya, 252, 266
Kérékou, President Mathieu, 263
Khambule mission, 22
Khumalo house, 27
Khumalo, Bongani, 23, 22, 27, 40, 41, 42, 56, 74, 78, 79, 80, 81, 87, 103, 120, 147, 205, 317
Khumalo, Jabulani, 78
Khuzwayo, Judson, 112
Khuzwayo, Wiseman, 51
King Cetshwayo kaMpande, 86, 190, 203,

King Cyprian Bhekuzulu kaSolomon, 204
King Dingane, 190
King Dinuzulu, 190, 206
King George V Hospital, 18
King George V, 311
King Goodwill Zwelithini kaBhekuzulu, 118, 204
King Jr, Martin Luther, Reverend, 21, 32, 34
King Moshoeshoe I, 207
King Moshoeshoe II, 207
King Mpande, 190
King Mswati, 109
King Shaka, 18, 189, 190, 191, 203
King Sobhuza II, 17, 109, 110, 118, 120, 207, 264
King Solomon, 203, 205
King Zwelithini, 3, 118, 119, 191, 195, 204
Kingdom of eSwatini, 109
Kingsley, 22
Kliptown, 19, 157
Kodesh, Wolfie, 71
Korchagin, Pavel 'Pavka', 320
Kotane, Moses, 241
Kruger, Jimmy, 55
Kubheka, Themba, 39
kwaDlangezwa, 34
KwaGadlaza cemetery, 11, 13
KwaMashu township, 25
Kwanza Sul, 59
KwaZulu-Natal, 7, 8, 15, 16, 18, 46, 47, 121, 124, 183, 197, 244, 258, 267

L

La Guma, Alex, 165
La Guma, James, 165, 241
Ladysmith, 41
Lagu, Lennox, 58
Lamola, John, 240
Langa, Mandla, 39
Latin America, 32, 240
Lebombo mountains, 123
Lee, Stephen, 100, 101
Leeuwspoor, 125
Leicester University, 237
Lekhanya, General Justin Metsing, 263
Lekota, Mosiuoa 'Terror' *see also* Lekota, Terror, 290
Leleki, Kenny, 66
Lemba people, 33
Lembede, Anton, 184, 274, 302, 312, 313

Index

Lenin School, 175
Lenin, Vladimir, 8, 169
Lesotho, 60, 97, 207, 208, 263
Levin, Jonathan, 113
Levin, Nonceba, 113
Levy, Norman, 172
Liberia, 264, 265
Libya, 129, 239
Liliesleaf Farm, 50
Líster, General Enrique, 145
LomawaNdwandwe, Inkhosikati, 18
London College of Printing, 173
London, 1, 3, 5, 6, 7, 14, 30, 75, 78, 94, 97, 110, 133, 148, 154, 164, 169, 170, 171, 172, 173, 174, 175, 187, 195, 196, 197, 202, 203, 216, 219, 221, 223, 227, 229, 230, 236, 237, 238, 239, 240, 241, 242, 244, 249, 259, 268, 269, 270, 278, 282, 289, 297, 298, 301, 304, 305, 306, 307, 308, 309, 310, 311, 312, 313
Lourenço Marques, 97
Lourenço, President João, 266
Louw, Dawid, 16
Louw's Mountain, 16
Louwsburg Combined Primary, 23
Louwsburg Rural Magistrate's Court, 10
Louwsburg, 7, 10, 15, 16, 17, 40
Luanda, 4, 59, 62, 65, 66, 67, 69, 83, 86, 310
Lusaka, 1, 58, 67, 94, 96, 110, 117, 149, 164, 170, 171, 175, 193, 248, 277, 283, 289, 293
Luthuli House, 309
Luthuli, Albert, *see also* Chief Albert Luthuli, 28, 41, 78, 116, 122, 191, 201, 205, 207, 208, 209, 213, 214, 318
Luthuli, Nokukhanya, 116
Luthuli, Wordsworth, 209

M

Mabandla, Oyama, 171
Mabhida, Moses, 84, 93, 289, 292, 293
Mabitsela, Edwin, 68
Mabizela, Stanley, 115
Machinini, Theresa, 248
Madikizela-Mandela, Winnie, 209
Maduna, Penuell, 51
Magubane, Bernard, 73
Mahabane, Rev. ZR 185
Mahamba border, 118
Maharaj, Mac, 94, 95

Mahlangu, George *see also* Mazibuko, George, 66
Mahlangu, Solomon, 58, 61, 66
Majola, Sisa, 128, 162, 183
Make, Cassius (Job Tabane), 59, 290
Makgothi, Henry, 285
Makhathini, Johnny, 171, 192, 287, 289
Makhubu, Mbuyisa, 54
Malan, DF, 15
Malanje, 66
Malcolm X, 32, 33, 34
Maloka, Eddy, 66, 79, 113, 119, 130, 133
Mandela, Nelson, 2, 10, 30, 41, 94, 105, 191, 208, 209, 211, 216, 217, 245, 250, 253, 256, 262, 271, 279, 284, 289, 290, 292, 293, 294, 312
Mandela, Winnie, *see also* Madikizela-Mandela, Winnie, 258, 283
Manghezi, Alpheus, 136
Mangope, Lucas, 160, 256
Manong, Stanley, 63, 66, 80, 149, 151, 152
Manzini, Mandala, 121, 280
Maphumulo, Shadrack, 99, 110, 124, 134
Maputo, 58, 93, 94, 95, 96, 97, 98, 99, 100, 101, 102, 105, 107, 110, 111, 112, 116, 120, 123, 131, 134, 286, 292, 294, 309
Marcus, Gill, 34, 173, 175
Mare, John, 55
Mariannhill Teachers' Training College, 19
Marks, JB, 60, 292
Marks, Shula, 211, 237
Martins, Ben, 8, 9
Marx, Karl, 169, 323
Maseko, Florence, 98
Masetlha, Billy, 13, 313
Mashamba, Steven, 95
Mashinini, Alex, *see also* Mokhoanatse, Tshidiso, 78, 79, 80, 98, 146, 147, 248, 249
Mashinini, Rocks, 98
MaSimelane, Alzina Ndwandwe, 6
Masondo, Andrew, 5
Masuku, Thomas, 61
Matanzima, Kaiser, 50, 104, 160
Mathiane, Nomavenda, 23, 193, 194, 195
Mathole, Inkosi, 205
Matlhako, Chris, 125, 313, 314, 319
Matola, Florence, 61, 95, 96, 117
Matsapha, 112, 121
Matshana, 17

Mavimbela, Vusi, 9, 13, 20, 21, 23, 13, 22,
    30, 31, 32, 33, 34, 35, 36, 37, 38, 39, 43,
    45, 47, 48, 50, 51, 52, 53, 56, 58, 61, 67,
    149, 150, 239, 314
Mavuyo, Thabo, 64
Mayekiso, Moses, 297
Mayibuye, Peter, *see also* Netshitenzhe,
    Joel, 291
Mazibuko, George, *see also* Mahlungu,
    George, 66
Mazimbu, 135, 136, 138
Mbeki, Govan, 10, 96, 109, 148, 210, 213,
    214, 215, 216, 217, 241, 250, 285, 286,
    287, 294
Mbeki, Thabo, 93, 96, 109, 148, 250, 280, 287
Mbembe, Achille, 273
Mbokazi, 57
Mceleli, 188, 194, 204, 205, 206, 214
McFadden, Gavin, 113, 120
Meijer, Lucas, 16
Meintjies, Frank, 13
Meli, Francis, 72, 154, 156, 172, 233, 240,
    280, 298, 315
Mellet, Patric Tariq 'de Goede', 7, 23, 172,
    173, 174, 187, 229, 235, 236, 240, 241,
    242, 245, 247, 256, 257, 267, 268, 314,
    317, 318, 319
Menzi High, 69
Meriam, Mengistu Haile, 294
Merrett, Christopher, 188, 199, 211, 212
Mfeka, Xolo, 23, 25, 26, 29
Mgabadeli, Hlengiwe, 12, 23, 30, 32, 34,
    35, 36
Mgijima, Ralph, 39
Mhlongo, Elfas 'Qhofa', 10
Mhlongo, Enoch Reginald, 96
Migwe, Khumalo, 78, 79, 80, 88, 103, 126,
    146, 147
Mji, Diliza, 52
Mkhatshwa, Jabulani, 78, 172, 231
Mkhize, Dr Zweli, 206
Mkhize, Khaba, 197
Mkhonza, 54
Mkhwanazi, Riot, 99, 123
Mkwayi, Wilton, 264, 265
Mnandi, Nana, 13, 313
Mngomezulu, Jameson Nongolozi, 121,
    122, 123, 125, 126, 134
Mngomezulu, Mbalekelwa, 122

Mngomezulu, Ntunja, 122
Mngomezulu, Nyawo, 126
Mnxayibane village, 17
Moabi, Max, 59
Modise, Joe, 93, 149, 296
Moeti, Sello (Michael Lebese), 172, 237, 310
Moi, President Daniel arap, 266
Mokgabundi, Motso, 96
Mokhoanatse, Tshidiso, *see also* Mashinini,
    Alex, 78, 146, 248
Mokoena, Timothy, 87
Molale, Solly, 104
Molefe, Popo, 145
Molokoane, Richard, *see also* Barney, 119
Moloto, Grant, 104, 196
Moloto, Pitso (Ryder), 104
Mondlo mountain, 22
Moodley, Strini, 39
Mooiplaats farm, 16
Moolman, 125
Morogoro, 60
Morris, Mike, 291
Moscow, 62, 63, 175, 294, 295, 296, 310
Mosia, Lebona, 5, 23, 71, 73, 89, 90
Motlanthe, Kgalema, 208, 316
Motlaung, Mandy, 66
Moumbaris, Alex, 100, 101
Mount Majuba, 9
Mozambican border, 57
Mozambique, 43, 44, 53, 57, 58, 61, 62, 88,
    93, 95, 96, 97, 99, 101, 102, 103, 109, 110,
    117, 120, 121, 122, 130, 133, 134, 135,
    144, 209, 231, 232, 252, 286, 297, 326
Mphemba, 36, 37
Mphephu, Patrick, 36, 37, 160
Mpumalanga township, 112
Mqwebu, 36, 37
Msimang, Mendi, 310
Msomi, Patrick *see also* Swanepoel, Moses,
    23, 62, 67, 164, 310, 318
Mthethwa, Mfaniseni, 10, 20, 23, 21, 22,
    24, 27, 57, 190
Mthiyane, 31, 35, 36, 37
Mtolo, Bruno, 27
Mtshaulana, Patric, 23, 62, 67, 70, 71, 75,
    83, 84, 89, 90, 91, 134, 137, 138, 309
Mugabe, Robert, 125, 287, 288
Mwandla, Balindile Elsie, 18
Mwandla, Kenneth Khulekani, 56

Index

Mwandla, Leonard Funizwe, 18
Mzi, 187, 242, 318

N
Naidoo, Celeste, 7, 12, 13, 23, 12, 14, 98, 99, 173, 174, 187, 216, 221, 255, 267, 268, 269, 309
Naidoo, Indres, 96, 97
Namibia, 74, 232, 233, 250, 264, 326
Nandi (mother of King Shaka), 190
Natal Colony, 17
Natal Midlands Alliance, 12
Natal Midlands, 7, 8, 9, 10, 13, 61
Natal Province, 55
Natal, 8, 11, 23, 3, 7, 8, 9, 10, 12, 13, 17, 18, 24, 39, 41, 46, 49, 55, 61, 81, 83, 84, 99, 110, 111, 112, 115, 116, 117, 121, 122, 123, 125, 131, 132, 191, 192, 198, 199, 200, 210, 211, 216, 255, 263, 266, 267, 271, 273, 283, 286, 288, 289, 295, 313
Ncome (Blood River), 9
Ndaleni Teachers' Training College, 18
Nduli, Dumisani, 9, 21, 23, 112, 113, 116, 117, 118, 119, 121, 170, 172, 175, 197, 202, 203, 281
Ndulinde, 18
Ndwandwe, Bamba, 27
Ndwandwes, 18
Neethling, Lothar, 228
Netherlands, The, 6
Netshitenzhe, Joel, 5, 23, 67, 71, 79, 80, 81, 170, 196, 197, 315, 316, 319, 327
New York, 274, 298
Newcastle, 16, 41
Ngalitshe, 120
Ngculu, James, 63, 65, 83, 84, 86
Ngesi, Themba, 96
Ngidi, Nhlanhla, 51
Ngoje Division, 16
Ngoje, 7, 9, 10, 11, 14, 15, 16, 17, 18, 19, 20, 23, 27, 41, 313
Ngomane, 190
Ngoye University, 196, 281
Ngoye, 40, 43, 45, 46, 47, 48, 49, 51, 52, 54, 55, 56, 58, 188, 249, 268
Nhlapo, Welile (Welile Mkhize), 280
Nimni, Ephraim, 237
Nkabinde, Professor AC, 25
Nkabinde, Sifiso, 10
Nkadimeng, John, 290

Nkomo, Aubrey, 274
Nkomo, Barbara, 274
Nkomo, Joshua, 277
Nkomo, Mokubung, 211
Nkosi, Kwetshi, 10
Nkosi, Stephen, 61
Nkosi, Zakes, 10, 21
Nokwe, Duma, 41
Nonceba, 23, 113, 115, 117, 129
Nongoma, 17, 123
North Africa, 122
Northern Transvaal, 55
Northern Zululand, 123
Novo Catengue, 60, 63, 64, 68, 70, 95
NP government, 19
Nsibande, 208
Nsibande, Cleopas, 208
Ntshangase, Vuyani, 23, 28, 29, 190
Ntuli, Professor DBZ, 25
Nxumalo
   family, 18
   homestead, 11
Nxumalo- Zitha, Phasha, 10
Nxumalo, Balindile Elsie, 2, 15
Nxumalo, Justice Seth Benjamin, 2, 15
Nxumalo, Professor Otty, 21
Nxumalo, Titi, 67, 119
Nxumalo-Zitha, Phasha 10, 118, 128,
Nyawo, Nokuhamba, 121
Nyawuza, 146
Nyembezi, Aubrey, 38
Nyembezi, Manqoba, 37
Nyerere, Julius, 59
Nzima, Sam, 54
Nzimande, Blade, 5, 6, 8, 10, 12, 13, 15, 23, 48, 54, 55, 56, 236, 238, 242, 243, 244, 246, 267, 268, 269, 270, 278, 308, 309, 322
Nzo, Alfred, 68, 149, 283

O
o KaManekwana, Nozigqoko Zulu, 204
O'Gara, Che, 68
Ohlange High School, 134
Ongoye, 51
Open University, 3, 156, 237, 238, 239
Orlando Stadium, 53
Ostrovsky, Nikolai, 320
Owen (son of Matshana), 17
Oxford, 6

P

Pahad, Essop, 4, 9, 19, 23, 4, 171, 172, 219, 220, 221, 222, 231, 242, 243, 244, 315, 316
Pampallis, John, 12, 23, 138, 173, 197, 238, 309
Pan Africanist Congress, 272
Paris, 273
Paton, Alan, 266
Pepani, Lungile Chris, *see also* S'bali, 23, 67, 68, 70, 86, 90, 92, 93, 113, 234
Phakathi, Samson Velefini 'Mkhende', 23
Phasha, Essential, 2, 10, 11, 19, 20, 21, 23, 24, 26, 27, 34, 36, 38, 57, 129, 163, 307, 310, 311
Phinda, Samuel, 96
Phongolo, 116
Phumelele, 5, 10, 12
Phungula, Johannes 'Pass Four', 122
Piet Retief, 125
Pietermaritzburg, 11, 22, 170, 189, 193, 358, 360
Pieterson, Hector, 54
Piliso, Mzwandile 'Mzwai', 63, 72, 84
Pityana, Sipho, 255
Plaatje, Sol, 15
Pollsmoor Prison, 292
Poloko, 173
Porto Amboim, 59
Portuguese, 43
Prague, 4, 219, 220, 221, 223, 243
Pretoria Central Prison, 100
Pretoria, 2, 9, 44, 88, 100, 101, 111, 119, 120, 155, 156, 158, 181, 192, 210, 250, 264
Prince John, 311
Prince Mcwayizeni kaDinizulu, 118
Princess Constance Magogo Mantithi Thombisile Ngangezinye, 206
Princess Magogo, 205
Princess Phikisile Harriet, 190, 206
Pupuma, Lesley, 120

Q

Queen Mary, 311
Queen Thomozile Jezangani kaNdwandwe, 118
Quibaxe, 60

R

Rabkin, David, 23, 94, 309, 314
Rabkin, Sue, 94, 95, 96, 97, 98, 99, 100, 101, 102, 103, 104, 105, 109, 133, 197, 309, 314
Radio Freedom, 5
Ramone, George, 264
Ramos, José, 96
Rashid, *see also* Ismail, Aboobaker 65
Rathebe, Joy, *see also* Gindi, Andre, 62
Reagan, Ronald, 176, 207
Rhodesia, 59
Richards Bay, 18
Richmond, 18
Riding, Alan, 77
Riot, 99, 104
Rivonia, 7, 45, 50, 105, 137, 208, 213, 265, 282, 286, 289
Robben Island Prison, 292
Robben Island, 14, 45, 51, 94, 97, 99, 104, 209, 243, 283
Royal House, 118
Russon Senior, Joseph 'Jabavu', 115, 116, 120, 121
Russon, Raynauld, 114, 115, 118, 119, 120, 310, 318
Ruth First Student Orientation Centre, 135

S

S'bali *see also* Pepani, Lungile Chris, 67, 68, 86
Sachs, Albie, 96
Saloojee, Cassim, 145
SASO *see* South African Students' Organisation
Savimbi, Jonas, 43, 263
Scheppers farm, 16
Sebe, Lennox, 256
Sechaba, 3
Seme, Dr Pixley ka Isaka, 190, 206
Senegal, 181, 231, 248, 340, 346, 358, 361
Seth (Sethi), *see also* Nxumalo, Justice Seth Benjamin, 17
Sethi, 17, 18, 19, 20, 21, 22, 23, 24, 26, 29, 57, 311, *see also* Nxumalo, Justice Seth Benjamin
Sethunya, Richard *see also* Mtshaulana, Patric Mzolisi, 62
Sexwale, Johnny, 65
Shabalala, Vuso, 23, 34, 35, 36, 37, 47, 48, 54, 55, 56, 58, 60, 61, 93, 98, 99, 105, 106, 107, 110, 111, 122, 123, 124, 125, 131, 132, 133, 202, 203
Shaw, Danny, 326

Index

Shell House, 7, 12
Shiselweni area, 18
Shope, Mark, 68, 70, 71, 72, 76, 171
Shula, 302
Sigxashe, Sizakele, 280
Sihlengeni, 27
Simelane, Alzina, 17
Simelane, Goodwill, 129
Simelane, James, 113
Simelane, Jerry, 115
Simons, Jack, 64, 68, 70, 71, 72, 90, 101, 151, 154, 155, 171
Singaye, Benjamin, 133
Singh, Sunny (Bobby), 23, 97, 98, 99
Sisulu, Albertina, 145, 208, 241, 254, 282, 283, 292
Sisulu, Walter, 41, 97, 184, 208
Sithole, Mandla 'Stokes', 112
Sitsubi, Charles, 63, 64
Sizwe (son of Mpho), 1 ,137, 162, 163, 221, 229, 306
Skweyiya, Zola, 151, 152
Slovo, Joe, 9, 60, 71, 73, 93, 96, 100, 101, 104, 131, 132, 149, 150, 230, 251, 256, 272, 286, 291, 292, 293, 294, 295, 296, 297
Smith, Jack Shepherd, 193
Sobukwe, Robert, 75, 117
Solomon Mahlangu Freedom College (SOMAFCO), 135, 137, 138, 139, 146, 154, 273
SOMAFCO, 135, 285, *See* Solomon Mahlangu Freedom College
Somhlolo, 18
Sompisi, Ndlela ka, 190
South African Airways, 1
South African Communist Party (SACP), 3
South African National Civic Organisation (SANCO), 11
South African Students' Organisation (SASO), 29, 32, 33, 35, 39, 41, 44, 46, 47, 49, 51, 52, 53, 54, 73, 101, 215, 280, 290, 322
Southeast Asia, 240
Soviet Union, 44, 63, 70, 71, 74, 77, 85, 89, 91, 98, 99, 101, 111, 153, 175, 219, 221, 222, 233, 243, 244, 249
Soweto, 7, 19, 53, 55, 56, 59, 61, 68, 74, 75, 88, 94, 98, 106, 110, 121, 137, 138, 145, 171, 186, 193, 238, 280, 293
Sparks, Allister, 2

St Francis High School, 112
Stalker, Brenda, 248, 249, 347, 361
Standerton, 9
Steijn, Callie, 95
Stewart, Peter, 66
Stofile, Mongezi, 290
Suckling, John, 262
Suttner, Raymond, 50
Swanepoel, Moses, *see also* Msomi, Patrick, 62
Swazi Kingdom, 133
Swaziland, 5, 17, 18, 19, 52, 53, 58, 61, 69, 96, 97, 98, 99, 109, 110, 111, 112, 113, 116, 119, 120, 121, 122, 123, 124, 125, 126, 128, 129, 131, 133, 134, 135, 143, 149, 170, 202, 204, 207, 263, 264, 272, 286, 309, 310, 319

T
Tabane, Job (Cassius Make), 120
Tambo, Adelaide, 2, 277, 310
Tambo, Dali, 278
Tambo, Oliver (OR), 2, 3, 4, 9, 13, 15, 19, 45, 60, 65, 72, 75, 77, 80, 93, 136, 154, 170, 171, 173, 183, 184, 185, 186, 201, 208, 209, 216, 242, 246, 247, 253, 271, 277, 278, 279, 280, 284, 287, 290, 292, 293, 294, 302, 303, 304, 305, 306, 307, 311, 312, 357
Tanzania, 1, 27, 59, 60, 61, 62, 67, 130, 134, 135, 136, 137, 149, 150, 201, 207, 225, 254, 273
Taylor, Charles, 265
Temkin, Ben, 189
Temko, Ned, 111
Thaba Bosiu Mountain, 207
Thatcher, Margaret, 255
The Hague, 265
Themba, 39, 96, 104, 222
Thobejane, Senti, 273, 299, 301
Thompson, Leonard, 302, 303, 304
Tiro, Abram, 29, 32, 51
Titi, *see also* Nxumalo, Titi, 2, 6, 7, 12, 20, 21, 23, 26, 27, 28, 38, 40, 57, 61, 64, 67, 69, 70, 80, 81, 118, 128, 163, 164, 229, 306, 307, 317
Tolbert Jr, President William R, 265
Tongagara, Josiah, 317
Transvaal, 10, 17, 45, 47, 98, 144, 184, 194
Trotsky, 222, 223, 279
Tshabalala, Manto, 140

Turfloop (University of the North), 103
Turfloop, 51, 55
Turok, Ben, 299
Tyrone, Terence 'Trixie', 39, 49

U

UBLS, *see* University of Botswana, Lesotho and Swaziland
UDF *see* United Democratic Front
Ulundi, 117
Umlazi, Durban, 69
Umtata, 259
Umzinyathi District, 18
Union of Soviet Socialist Republics (USSR), 62
United Democratic Front (UDF), 8, 12, 44, 46, 84, 117, 119, 145, 157, 158, 160, 192, 210, 215, 259, 283, 285, 313, 318
United Kingdom (UK), 175, 306
United States of America (USA), 6, 43, 80, 88, 111, 171, 176, 177, 179, 180, 225, 226, 227, 245, 249, 253, 267, 271, 272, 275, 297, 301, 302, 305, 308
University of Botswana, Lesotho and Swaziland (UBLS), 115
University of Fort Hare, 39, 76, 184, 205
University of London, 305
University of Natal, 197, 309, 322
University of South Africa (Unisa), 40
University of Swaziland, 112, 115
University of the North, 49, 55
University of the South, see also Novo Categue camp, 70
University of the Witwatersrand, 292, 294
University of Virginia, 274, 297
University of Zululand, 40, 41, 43, 46, 55, 62, 70, 188, 239
Unterhalter, Elaine, 23, 169, 228, 239
US, see United States of America, 43, 44, 66, 136, 176, 178, 179, 180, 182, 227, 228, 265, 272, 273, 276, 278, 285, 298, 301, 302, 324
Utrecht, 9, 16

V

Vaal (PWV) region, 2
Vaal Triangle, 144, 145
van Diepen, Maria, 234, 237
van Zyl, Gideon Brand, 205
Viljoen, Dr Gerrit, 261
Violet (mother of Mpho), 67, 154
Volksrust, 9
Vorster, BJ, 116
Vos, Suzanne, 194
Vryheid High, 69, 70
Vryheid, 12, 18, 21, 23, 9, 10, 21, 22, 24, 27, 40, 41, 123, 313

W

Walvis Bay, 264
Waschbank, 17
Washington, 292
Wembezi, 41
West African coast, 264
West Rand, 55
Western Cape, 56
Williams, Martin, 196
Williams, Phumla *see also* Maseko, Florence, 98
Witwatersrand, 2
Wolpe, Harold, 175, 237, 238, 239, 285
Woods, Donald, 175
World Marxist Review, 4
World Trade Centre, 9
Wyley, Chantelle, 188, 211, 212

X

Xipamanine, 96
Xuma, Dr AB, 184

Y

Yale University, 3, 272
Yengwa, MB, 192

Z

Zambia, 6, 7, 59, 60, 68, 96, 107, 153, 154, 162, 163, 207, 225, 254, 308
Zembe, Zola, 173
Zimbabwe, 10, 74, 96, 97, 130, 163, 317, 326
Zitha, Tom, 129
Zulu royal family, 189, 190, 202
Zulu Royal Family, 4, 118
Zulu Royal House, 16
Zulu royals, 210
Zulu, Joshua, 209
Zululand, 7, 8, 9, 11, 12, 16, 24, 30, 39, 45, 54, 56, 203
Zuma, Jacob, 58, 61, 96, 97, 99, 109, 121, 126, 131, 133, 250, 267, 318, 319
Zuma, Thando, 248
Zwide ka Langa, 195
Zwide, 1, 154, 162, 163, 203, 221, 229